A Drip in the Creek
a memoir

Acclaim for

A DRIP IN THE CREEK

a memoir

"*A Drip in the Creek* is a clear-eyed account of the end of a life; of grief bathed in the waters of love and humor one drop at a time. An important read for anyone facing one of life's most monumental truths."

Dana J. Kennedy, Communicator

"Melanie's poignant story of her husband's courageious battle with pancreatic cancer will touch your heart, as you read about her expereineces of great love and loss. Her ability to find humor and solace in the face of overwhelming odds will make you laugh and cry. Melanie's story is a must-read for anyone who has loved and lost or battled serious illness."

Nancy J. Kincaid, MA, APR Press Secretary

A Drip in the Creek
a memior

by

Melanie Reagan

Melanie Reagan
September 6, 2014

Printed in the United States of America

First Printing, 2014

ISBN 0-978-1-62620-213-9

Creative Impressions Press
1271 Washington Avenue #228

San Leandro, CA 94577

www.adripinthecreek.com

Dedication

This book is dedicated to
my husband Bart Reagan
and to my dad Dr. Mike Polka,
two of the strongest men
I have ever known.

Contents

Foreword

I first met Melanie Reagan nearly a decade ago. She would pop into my office on occasion and bring with her, an effervescent, warm and genuine spirit. Her ability to see tremendous possibility in everyone is one of her prominent gifts. Melanie believed in me at a time when I needed it most and I will always be grateful.

Upon Bart's diagnosis it was evident that Melanie would not be entertaining any thoughts of negativity. This was only a disease and Melanie would fight it with Bart. Melanie was Bart's warrior, advocate, cheerleader, comedian and wife. She stayed strong for us all.

As you read this memoir you will feel privileged that she brought you along on her journey with Bart. You will fall in love with their friends and family, understand real strength and enjoy their humor. Through this book you will experience real life conveyed moment to moment like drips in a creek.

Cindy

Preface

Suddenly learning that my husband had terminal cancer was life-altering and overwhelming. Family, friends and colleagues all wanted to know how Bart was doing and soon enough we were deluged with hundreds of well-meaning inquiries. My sister Sandi suggested posting updates on a website called Caring Bridge which is designed to address this very issue and which allowed us to easily share information to interested parties en masse and on a regular basis.

The Caring Bridge blog began as a way to keep others informed but transformed into something much more.

Sharing daily moments of life, like drops of water, little anecdotes began to collect and soon it was like a pooling spring from which all drank.

I hope that in some small way these stories help smooth the path for others navigating such a journey.

Melanie Reagan, Cameron Park, California

Acknowledgements

I thank the many dedicated nurses and caregivers who selflessly care for terminally ill patients. Often despite their own grief they continue day after day.

I must also thank my family, friends, and neighbors. And to all the guest book signers and readers who encouraged this project. We got a good drenching of love, generosity and kindness that touched our hearts and extended Bart's life beyond all expectations.

My heartfelt appreciation also extends to dear friends, Caryn of Eikon Photography, Jeanne, and Cindy without whom I could not have completed this book.

Countless others contributed in deed and spirit notably Stephanie, Nicole and Emily.

Prologue

January - I was trying to do the impossible: figure out how to organize my day. Then the phone rang. My ninety-six year old dad had had a stroke and was in the hospital. Surely this was it, I thought. No one that age gets released from the hospital; but evidently they do. To make a long story short, Dad (aka Dr. Mike) got the all-clear and was home before we could even organize travel plans. They don't make humans like that anymore. Still, the family was on notice. That was January and it would prove to be a challenging and life-altering year.

By April, Dad's condition took a turn for the worse, and family from all over the country had arranged travel to be by his side. It was Destination: Weaverville, my home town in California.

I drove across the ratty old wooden bridge situated just before my parent's house, its familiar rumble signifying the end of a long journey and arrival at the old homestead. As in most trips here, I took a mini-walkabout on Mom and Dad's property upon my arrival. The smell of mountain pines and fresh air was like an elixir. I made a quick trek to the creek just to look around and get re-acquainted with my childhood stomping grounds, and reflected that all of the early adventures I can remember seem to center around running water.

Looking down at Garden Gulch Creek, I recalled how it flowed with each season. Often just a trickle, but other times foaming white water would roar angrily over the top of the little dam my Uncle Johnny had built. In the summer, the creek was just a dry rocky bed with tiny pools of algae and frog eggs. The dam (complete with all of our handprints) was erected so Dad could provide water to the horses and irrigate the tree farm and random landscaping.

The dam never really held back any water, but eventually a deep hole developed on the downside that was enough to submerge a pump. If the water level in the hole got too low, the pump sucked air and that was bad. A thousand times my internal parent tape had replayed Dad's stern warning, "never ever turn the pump on unless you have checked the water level first." I wasn't sure what damage would actually occur, but certainly I would endure a miserable life without parole if that pump ever sucked air. Down there at the "crick" many a memory came to mind as I stared at that old pump submerged safely underwater, just as it should be.

One of the "memory logs" that I treasure is of my neighbor, Christi, as she and I frequently walked home together from school along the path of Garden Gulch Creek. We were six years old and had rather profound discussions for first graders. It took us a long while to walk a short distance because we stopped at every towering Digger pine tree along the way, knowing that those ugly cones released a handful of pine nuts when thrown hard on the pavement. If you didn't smash them to a paste with your rock, they were delicious; but harvesting enough for a sufficient snack took time, especially if we had to climb the tree to shake them loose.

We asked each other worldly questions just for fun. How do jellied frog eggs get to be frogs anyway? What's talent, and do we have any? If so, could we do a talent show? What do you want to be when you grow up? And…what's our one biggest wish right now? I remember my answer to that one; I wished my parents would live forever. Not having parents was unimaginably scary to me. I later told my dad about that wish and his response was, "So far, so good".

These reminiscences were delightful and warm, and even though that week had been a dreary wet one, April 15th saw a rebirth of the sun. The rain stopped and sunshine reigned as Dad slipped quietly away that afternoon in the very place his career began, Trinity General Hospital. Dad was the town doctor with hospital privileges, so we kids spent plenty of time around there, riding our bikes outside the ER on hospital walkways, helping nurses fold and patch sheets, and even getting occasional gurney rides. This day we had to let Dad go, and we cried. Mom and I were the last in his room.

Mom finally murmured "What do we do now"? The way she looked at me so tentatively and asked that question floored me and my answer was simply, "I don't know Mom, I've never done this before". Mom cracked a smile that soon ignited full blown laughter. Neither one of us had a clue what to do. The moment struck a chord, but instead of crying we just laughed until it hurt - but that's our way. My family always sees humor in the most bizarre of circumstances, and this most intense life moment was no different.

Outside, it was a bright beautiful day so we walked home in the glory of Dad's life well-lived.

My husband, Bart, was very close to Dad. Both had hailed from McKeesport, Pennsylvania, they were graduates of the same high school, stalwart Steeler fans, and passionate, proud and patriotic fiscal conservatives.

Like Dad, Bart never complained, so it surprised and alarmed me that he still had this chronic back pain complaint well after we returned from Weaverville after Dad's service. Bart had already been to the doctor about this pain before Christmas. I was beginning to get worried.

Do not seek for all to come about as you wish but wish for everything to come about exactly as it does for it is not an event that troubles, but the meaning given to it. Make the best use of what is in your power and take the rest as it happens. Only then will you be calm and on a journey of happiness.

Be free for God entrusts you with yourself, never to say you are alone for you are not alone, God and genius lie within.

Epictetus – Greek Stoic Philosopher (55 – 135 C.E.)

Chapter One

Sun Shines Through

August 17 we got our solar panels activated and Bart texted me at work to express his excitement about the solar finally going online. I knew he was happy because he never abused punctuation, and this day I got three exclamation points in his text.

That same day, we met at an oncologist's office to get the results of Bart's test to see what was going on with his back pain. After the obligatory long waiting period, the oncologist delivered news worse than we'd expected: stage four pancreatic cancer. It had spread to Bart's liver and was therefore inoperable. The oncologist left the room. I turned and stared at Bart's face; he looked back at me and said "I'm sure glad I got that solar installed". We both started laughing and were still chuckling when the doctor returned.

We know he found the Reagan sense of humor quite perplexing but what were we to do? Bad news is bad news.

Driving home we decided we would go out for dinner. If we couldn't celebrate good news, then we would celebrate bad. We couldn't fathom cooking anyway, and Bart wanted a beer.

The cordial restaurant owner greeted and seated us like always, but when she asked how we were, there was a pause. Bart looked at me and I expressed out loud what we were both thinking. "We can't lie to her", I said, so Bart replied, "I just found out I have cancer so we thought we'd go out to dinner".

As much as I don't like to make people feel uncomfortable it's less distasteful than lying to them. Truth is so much more respectful.

In that vein, the chapters that follow are excerpts from our online Caring Bridge postings and chronicle moments from day to day as we commenced paddling upstream without our respective paddles.

A Port in the Storm

August 27

A power port is a device that facilitates injection of chemotherapy. The implantation of Bart's power port at Mercy Hospital went without incident. Bart was up and about in no time, but had significant discomfort and pain in his stomach and back. One more blood test and a course of antibiotics, then Bart would be ready for chemotherapy.

We were set to go to Sierra Oncology Center on Creekside Drive August 30. Here's to killing cancer cells.

A day with football on TV and no doctor visits, that's a good day. Bart's managing fairly well. Our neighbor came over thankfully providing counter commentary for Bart. He loves to talk football, and I'm not knowledgeable enough to be interesting.

Besides, I'm busy double-cleaning the hardwood floor. I accidentally polished the whole kitchen with pesticide spray. I wondered why it smelled so bad, and then I remembered the empty floor cleaner spray bottle was used on those nasty beetles…it's no wonder the surface wasn't as shiny as usual. The spray bottle is labeled now. I hate to admit it, but it was me, and I know better than to commit the sin of not labeling pesticides.

August 29

Bart had a bit of a rough start to the day but settled in with a heating pad on the couch and watched televised golf. He gets hot and cold and has his fair share of intestinal distress. Still, he manages to share aggravating political news and of course top sports. As long as he gets fired up about politics and watches football, it can't be all bad.

August 30

Today was the first tumor-kicking chemo session and it was a long one (7 hours). The good news: Bart was equipped with a pump. The pump will dispense the next phase of his chemo treatment while resting in the comfort of our home. His little pump buddy will dole out the goods from now until next week. For you medical junkies: today's meds included Zofran & Decadron (anti-nausea), calcium/magnesium, oxaliplatin, CPT-11, Leucovorin and 5FU (I know, FU seems appropriate here doesn't it?).

Bart's looking a little pale and tired, resting with the heating pad. It's a two-pain-patch evening and so the fight begins.

August 31

A Note from the man himself, Bart Reagan:

Here I am the day after my first chemo and things aren't too bad. Yesterday was 7+ hours of great joy. I felt like saying "Please sir may I have another?" when it was over. Instead I told them I would stop by the front desk and tell them where to mail my paycheck.

After that they inserted a pump so I could get the drugs 24/7 (so I don't have to spend another 7 or more hours there again).

This reminds me of the scam they played on me when I had my tonsils out. Told me I could have all the ice cream I wanted, I just didn't want any damn ice cream.

I can have all the beer I want; I just don't want any damn beer.

On a bright note I am feeling better today than I have all week. Could be all in my head but many folks say there is nothing in my head.

Bart

September 1

Not a good night for Bart. Nausea meds couldn't quite get the job done and he was up several times during the night. The next morning was not much better and Bart couldn't keep the meds down.

His condition forced a trip to the chemo lounge, intravenous fluids and nausea drugs dripping into his system for several hours.

The next heavy duty chemo is scheduled next week.

Another Day, Another Drip In the Creek

Bart's not feeling much like tying one on for sure. I drove him back to the lab for pain meds and hydration. It was only a two hour tour today, so I took a nap in the car.

Back home, Bart got himself situated at command central on the couch to rest. Fighting for your life isn't for wimps and Bart never complains.

Except about food. He's got to eat, so cravings are a blessing in disguise and Bart seems to get them daily. Naturally nothing he craves is ever in our kitchen, freezer, or pantry. His craving du jour was a Subway sandwich comprised of turkey, mayo and provolone cheese on sour dough, with none of the veggie-type fixings. I thought that was the only reason one went to Subway was to get all that other stuff piled on. Bread and cheese I can do at home, but no, a craving is a craving. I fetched it, he ate it, and that's the good news.

September 2

Our family got a huge and wonderful surprise. The door swung open and there was our Army Officer son Matthew! He flew all the way from Fort Benning, GA to spend a few days at home. It's just what the doctor ordered.

September 3

It's a good day. Bart is on the computer. We all enjoyed delicious quiche prepared by dear friends. Matty and Bart are watching a funny movie. Life seems normal and that's a comfort.

We can't have too much of a good thing apparently. Bart was feeling pretty good until late afternoon, cramping, pain and general discomfort. The doctor didn't have any new ideas other than we continue to do what Bart's already doing. Tough to see someone you love so much in so much pain. He's an amazing guy, though, and messages of support and humor from friends give him a smile.

September 4

Bart likes seeing the bros (Matty and Dallas) together again. He sat outside on the deck to dine on the breakfast of champions: cheerios, banana, apple sauce and a cup of Italian roast coffee. The light breeze was nice, a welcome change of weather.

Bart had been feeling dizzy and a bit out of it so he changed up on the heavy duty pain meds. He's sporting double pain patches supplemented with Advil which allows him to feel more "with it" and able to stay awake for longer intervals. (It helps to be wide awake when "constructively criticizing" a teenager.)

Today's craving? Chicken pot pie. Bart can eat anything he wants, although he does not recommend this chemo diet, too many side effects.

Sunday is a day of rest. He rested and spoke only a few words. By late afternoon Bart had severe cramping, bloating and hip pain. The doctor says it is likely a side effect of one of the chemo drugs and suggested he drink Gatorade. Bart's got to recover enough to continue with this chemo adventure again.

In the meantime, Dallas had a great day on the Lake with his big brother which is exactly what he needed. Life is tough enough when you're 16.

September 6

A trip to Urgent Care ended at the Hospital Emergency Room. Medical emergencies always seem to occur on holidays or weekends. Bart reported severe cramping and diarrhea. He was weak and barely able to walk. No matter how much he drank he appeared dehydrated, sometimes dizzy.

It was dehydration and a high sugar level (319, and it's supposed to be less than 100). Bart's blood pressure dropped significantly when he stood up. For almost 9 hours Bart got intravenous fluids since due to the stomach pain there was no way he could drink enough to catch up on the lost fluids. By 11:30 he was admitted to the hospital.

Chemotherapy was cancelled.

Bart wore his Air Force Academy hat all day and night in the ER, never took it off, and sported his West Point grad T-shirt with Matty's name on it. You can't ever take "proud" out of a dad.

September 7

Hospitals aren't particularly conducive to a restful night's sleep, but it was a blessing for Bart to be there. He took 5 liters of IV fluid infusions before his tissues began to hydrate. Nurses woke him up every hour or so for blood draws, meds, and IV. Doctors say his condition creates a higher risk for blood clots, so a blood thinner was added to the medication regimen.

Pain management is an ongoing experiment. What delivers maximum relief with minimal negative effects? We learned today that cancer messes with one's pain tolerance level, reducing it substantially.

By noon, Bart was sitting up and talking, enthusiastically sharing information about our solar energy system! (Tell Solar City the Reagans sent you, we could get a toaster.)

What a difference a day makes, but he will need to spend another night in the hospital. It's a delicate transition from IV to solid food, even apple juice produced wrenching cramps. Bart's system has been traumatized.

We do not know when he might be well enough to undertake the second course of chemo but that's our goal. If those tumors shrink then the pain subsides proportionately.

I teased Bart that this is probably the only circumstance where a man would actually wish for shrinkage, to which he heartily agreed.

We got home from Mercy Hospital, and Bart settled onto his leather couch. I ventured off to procure the latest greatest meds prescribed by the ER docs. I was off to the primary care doctor, then back to our favorite pharmacist in Cameron Park.

We recognize that until some tumor-kicking chemo takes effect, he will feel a level of discomfort that most of us cannot imagine. I mused about how odd it was that I became so elated just to enjoy comforts of "normal" with Bart, lap blankets and a movie. That's all it takes right now to be happy, semi-normal routine.

Bart had a restless night. Maybe he was conditioned to wake up regularly from the hospital stay. He says if only he can get his stomach to quit cramping and his back pain to ease, then life would be easier. He consumed almost a full cup of my smoothie concoction. He's also trying out a new anti-nausea bio band. Every bit helps.

September 9

Continued stomach pain and my blender drink wasn't the panacea I had hoped. Bart is weak so we just talked about walking; maybe we will tackle the driveway tomorrow if he's feeling up to it. I try to get him to eat, and Bart swears I was a Jewish mother in a former life.

When I asked him if I could get him anything this evening he said, "yes, you can get away from me" which made us both chuckle. So I did. I went to Taekwondo while Bart and a neighbor watched football.

New Routines: Drop Dallas at school 6:25 am; blood test appointment at Oncology Center 9 am, then to primary care doc; pharmacy, grocery store and then home. With meals and driving that's almost a whole day in errands.

New Normal: Bart had a good day! When he feels comfortable, alert and eats, I feel great. His cramping subsided and he appeared more active. Whenever Bart yells at the TV it's a wonderful sign. We had watched the movie "We Are Marshall" and then Marshall (same school portrayed in the movie) was playing football on TV. Bart also enjoyed watching West Point vs. Hawaii where Army almost pulled it off. He and our son Matthew were cross-country texting the game highlights.

This afternoon, much to Bart's annoyance, a nice couple showed up to purchase our guest bed, since our guests evidently don't dig flotation-style mattresses anymore. My technical ineptitude required that Bart assist me in the flotation mattress draining adventure. He had to see for himself that the pliers weren't where he said they should be which entailed several trips to the garage, earning me the stink-eye roll a few times.

His annoyance turned to mild amusement when I turned up on the porch soaking wet, covered in red clay mud and looking like I'd been mud wrestling and lost.

We now have a new erosion fissure on the side yard. Oh well, I needed to dig steps on that hillside anyway.

A Note from Bart:

My blushing bride and others feel I need to post on Caring Bridge. So without further adieu here it comes straight from the horses a--, er I mean, mouth. This last week was a bit testy to say the least. All my Chemo had to be put on hold until I regain some semblance of strength. This is the least I have weighed in 30 years.

I am itching to get back to golf.

I truly am deeply humbled by the outpouring of love and affection from so many folks. Are you guys sure you have the right guy? :-D It's nice to have friends. Okay, enough mushy crap. Here's how it's going to go: (My words)

Tomorrow more blood work through the port. This unique device is under my skin (like some people who annoy me) and looks like a third nipple. It is a rubbery bump where doctors, nurses, radiological technicians, and anyone else sticks needles in to add or remove fluids willy-nilly.

There is a long tube that comes out of the back of the power port device, curls around a little and goes into my jugular vein. Not as bad as it sounds, but I did have to give up my MMA fighting career because of it. The device makes me black out easily. Come to think of it I don't think that was me. Disregard. I'd have to put on weight to go flyweight anyway.

The good news about the port is they don't have to dig around in my arms (or wherever they think is good) to remove blood. I'm on a quest to try out "all" the new high-tech (or low tech) devices.

I had a new taste experience today. Have you heard of this wonderful new product? It's called "beer". People tell me the stuff I had wasn't really beer, it was called Keystone Light, but it tasted like the nectar of the Gods to me. If all goes well I may have another tomorrow.

My hope is that the second chemo isn't seven freaking hours like the first one. I thought my butt was going to fall off. If you ever want to buy a Lazy-Boy, go to your local oncologist, have them tube you up, then put you next to a woman who thought she was in the Arctic. I was sweating profusely. They told me to dress warmly? Holy Crap! If I took any more clothes off I would have been arrested and taken to jail for indecent exposure (says who anyway? It looked pretty decent to me). :-D

Y'all take care.

P.S. Any lack of coherence I blame directly on the new "beer".

Love, Bart

September 13

Bart's in no shape for literary elegance tonight.

He was puking his guts out moments ago but did regain enough composure to comment on how mad our neighbor must be right now because San Diego is losing to Kansas City.

For some pretty good news: Bart's oncologist allowed him to go ahead with chemotherapy today but not the full chemical panel as expected, sort of "chemo light". After five hours in the chair, Bart was outfitted with his little friend the chemo pump again, which will dispense dosages for the next few days.

We are happy to resume the battle against the beast but the delay is an inconvenient reality. Bart has diabetes as a result of the pancreatic cancer. Instead of his usual diabetic medication by mouth, he must now add daily insulin injections to the routine.

If that isn't enough, our teenage son had his first heartbreak tonight. His girl broke up with him. We didn't even realize it was "official" enough for a breakup. Gee, stuff happens at warp speed nowadays. It must be technology. At least she didn't do it by text.

September 14

Bart was very sick. The moment he felt as though he could ride in a car without puking, we drove to the doctor for insulin "show and tell". It was a car ride he did not enjoy. Poor guy. He sipped and snacked until something stayed down.

As for the youngest kid, the "girl" called tonight and wanted to talk, so of course, he was on her door step in a nanosecond only to return home twenty minutes later.

We knew when he walked in. It must have been the, "we are just friends" speech. Alas.

Chapter Two

Et Tu Phaddeus

September 15

It was a good day. Hallelujah! We went into the chemo lab for a few hours of anti-nausea, pain meds and fluids through the port. Home by noon and lunch stayed down.

The doctor has said there will be six more weeks of chemotherapy and then judgment day, a CT scan to see if the chemical regimen is working.

At that time, we will travel to UCSF for an auxiliary consultation to determine the best chemo cocktail moving forward. Let's hope politicians can work as well together for a state budget!

This evening, a most glorious occurrence, Bart laughed out loud. He was watching comedian CK Louis. For God sakes don't let your kids in the room if this guy is on, but for adult laughs, he gets good marks. Never underestimate the power of silly laughter.

September 16

Today wasn't so good. Bart had cramping which led to intense nausea and vomiting throughout the day. Apparently it's just a delayed chemo reaction.

It seems the worst occurs two days after chemo. Bart had a late craving for tomato soup and grilled cheese. Of course, I'd already been to the store and pharmacy three times by then. Raiding the pantries of our

Sudbury neighbors didn't work either. Not a can of tomato soup between us. Bart's mood was down.

He perked right up though when daughter Megan showed up on our doorstep. Just like when Matty, her twin, visited, it was a buoy for Bart. Megan and Dallas happily went to the market for the tomato soup. They prepared dad's soup and grilled cheese which hit the spot.

Incredibly, the new bed also arrived. Bart strongly encouraged (understatement) us to get with it so Meg could sleep in a bed. Megan and I bravely accepted the "assembly required" challenge and successfully accomplished the deed. If only I had remembered to buy sheets.

September 17

No nausea! That's a red letter day, my friends. Our daughter, Dr. Meggie helped me go through all the medications and chemotherapy protocols, sorting and compiling materials in a binder. We're on our way to a med schedule that gives Bart more comfort and quality each day, and I feel more organized.

Meggie, Bart and I settled in to watch a movie. Dallas and the "former" girlfriend went to the Bruins football game. We don't know how that twist came about, but should hear more after the game. Isn't it emotionally illegal to date someone who gave you the "just friends" speech just twelve hours prior?

We don't get it.

Note From Bart:

Sept. 18th was a pretty good day. I watched a little college football.

My days have been boring: I eat, I sleep, I crap ... repeat. But at least I've eliminated, for the most part, cramping and puking. I'm looking to get back to the golf course just as soon as my friends can put up with the "hit ball, drag Bart" routine.

To my cousin Butch: I do remember the days when we were lucky to eat tomato soup and grilled cheese even if we weren't Catholic.

I want to get a dog as a companion. One would think that would be easy. But not when more than one person is involved. The decision process in this family became complicated.

I wanted a small-medium dog, no particular type, just not a puppy. Even without the cancer I don't have time to train a fresh dog. Mel doesn't really want a dog at all so we have worked on her to come around and offer input. She doesn't want a dog that sheds and it must be housebroken and fixed. Dallas just doesn't want an ugly dog.

So from the stringent requirements (when we get our act together), I think we are getting a small to medium hairless stick, that doesn't shed. I won't need to worry about it being housebroken ‘cuz it won't pee much. And I'm pretty dang sure it won't reproduce.

So while we save a lot of money on stick (dog) food, water, vet bills etc. I'm pretty sure the dog (stick) will be boring. Maybe we can get a whole branch :-).

I'm going to take a nap soon so I can rest up before bed time.

Bart

September 20

It was a busy full weekend. Bart sent the kids, Dr. Megan, Dallas, and Matty (via cell) to every animal shelter in three counties. Bart was bound and determined. Sunday Bart sent me with the kids, along with our neighbor Caryn for photographic documentation of a dog day afternoon.

Bart kept in touch via text every step of the journey. Almost every dog we sent pictures of, he responded, “yes looks good, get it!” We took our directives much more seriously. This had to be a strategic selection process.

Much to Bart's dismay, we came home sans canine after an all-out two day search.

I got nervous about letting Bart and the kids choose a dog so finally I said, I'll go alone since we all know I'm the one who will end up taking care of this pet.

I drove to the pound and quickly selected an overweight little mutt who seemed cheerful enough. The kids immediately dubbed him "Fatty". He didn't quite fit the "stick" criteria but pretty close. He's some kind of non-shedding, 6-year old short-legged mutt that doesn't bark much, plays fetch and loves everybody and other dogs. The folks at El Dorado County Animal Shelter weren't sure if he was part Poodle or what. Best result is that Bart is happy we even got a dog. The kids think he's weird but he'll do.

We believe the chemotherapy may be working.

For the first time since chemo began Bart has enjoyed a number of comfortable consecutive hours and delayed taking pain medication. He even helped a few friends with computer issues.

I think it was a boost to have daughter Meg accompany him to his oncology appointments. She asked questions and got answers. The oncologist seems to like her a lot better than me. She gets it.

Bart is resting up for Monday's chemo. The new little dog slept with him most of the day while I was at work. We agreed that dinnertime discussion tonight would center around naming the chubby little canine once and for all.

Everybody seems to like referring to him as "Fatty" but it's embarrassing. The dog groomer's reaction made me think a more diplomatic moniker would be best.

Names bandied about: Biff, Phaddy, Phaddeus-Thayer, Sparky, or Toby. As usual, the problem is getting everyone to agree. Megan herself had the name: "baby-girl" on her crib for a week after she was born. Indecision comes naturally to this clan.

September 22

A Note from Bart:
Dear friends:

I feel compelled to share my thoughts today on food. I never expected food to be an ever-changing topic of conversation beyond the idea that "I like to eat it".

You have all been most magnanimous, generous and giving. Friends, family and neighbors have prepared delicious foods beyond our wildest expectations both in quantity and quality. Please don't ever be offended if the one person the food is intended for (me) doesn't partake as much as I would like.

Here's the lowdown... I don't have much of an appetite any longer. I wake up feeling like I could eat anything and everything, until actual food is in front of me. Then, a combination of factors prevents me from enjoying a meal.

I see food and it looks great. I sniff it and it smells wonderful. When I try to eat, my taste buds do not work. They have been altered somehow through chemotherapy. Food tastes like nothing I have ever put in my mouth before (and believe me when I say, that's quite the statement). I have shoved some pretty indescribable food items in my pie hole over the years, some best left alone. So while I do my best to gag back whatever foods I can throughout the day, it's harder than I ever imagined. I mean come on, even BEER, my lifeblood, has no taste. That is just wrong.

I barely suck back a few tablespoons of soup or a few bites of Jell-O or some protein bar in the end. I'm working on eating and keeping it down. One of these days, I hope to taste all of the beautiful culinary creations you have so lovingly prepared.

Overall, this weekend has been less pain, not as much nausea and reduced cramping too. Now it's just a matter of getting my golf swing back. I also hope to take little walks with our new dog Phaddy/Biff/Sparky/Tubular or whatever we settle on calling him.

One cool thing about being in this weakened condition is that no one asks you to do stuff like clean the solar panels, take out trash or do the dishes or anything. I get to hang with my dog, my peeps and relax. I suspect there will be payback on the back end.

Bart

September 23

Red letter day! I went to work and Bart went for a walk with the little spark plug dog. I hated to miss this premiere excursion. Bart was winded, but so was the dog. Did we mention the dog is on the chubby side? He grunts like a pig, honking and snorting and sometimes wheezing but trots along quite happily and easily on the leash. I think the extra poundage and pig noises add character. They're quite a pair, Bart needing to gain weight and fat little dog just lapping up the moment. There's a lesson there somewhere.

Be more like dogs. Enjoy each moment no matter who's wheezing.

By early evening our extended family from next door (3 young kids) came by to hug Uncle 'Bark'. They asked if Uncle Bark got a haircut. Bart's "chemo cut" is most noticeable. We think it's just one less personal grooming task to have to worry about. Hair is NOT a necessity.

A Note from Bart:

I hope my chemo is easy so I can have an interactive visit with relatives next week. If not, they will get to stare at sleeping Bart with my mouth hanging open and maybe a grunt now and then.

I remember the immortal words of George Burns or somebody "If I had known I was going to live this long I would have taken better care of myself".

Love, Bart

September 24

Walking with Sparky dog the day before wore Bart out. We're thinking the name Sparky suits this guy. "Obesey" though was a close second. By late afternoon Bart was sitting up and moved to the back deck for a little sunshine.

He put his feet up and read a little book about faith in God. He even asked for a tiny sip of chilled white wine. In healthier times he and I would sit outside after work chatting with a glass of wine. Bart retired back to the couch as it got too hot quickly. Sparky assumed his position on Bart's lap and they napped.

Bart says he has to rest up for bedtime.

Fat Sparky kept Bart company which reminded him that human visitors should not wait until he feels better because that's all relative now.

September 27

Bart's buddy Bill, Marty and Matt made up the team for Sunday football. A few sips of holy barley & hops Nectar of the Gods a.k.a. Bud Light even touched his lips but all that TV football wore him out. He was ready to rest up for bed.

Dallas' buddies seemed to enjoy "sport eating" all day and night. Bart used to call number one son, "Matt the Inhaler" for eating cereal out of a mixing bowl among other things but Dallas appears to be the next evolution of an "inhalation machine".

Setbacks Happen

We are pros at the routine now: co-pay, sit in the waiting area to be beckoned, weigh in, a nurse draws blood, choose a recliner and then the main meal, IV bags-o-goods for the next 6-7 hours. I was at work only a short time when I got a call to get back to the chemo lab right away.

There was a serious problem with Bart's port. His chest above the right collar bone was swelling up badly and he felt a burning sensation. Somehow the port needle had shifted or dislodged. Chemo drugs were being delivered into subcutaneous tissue instead of his jugular vein. We were told to immediately transport him to a facility for emergency repair. It was too late to resume chemotherapy that day.

September 28

We had hoped vicious side effects (horrific gut-wrenching nausea and utter exhaustion) would be lessened this time. Nice thought but no rest for the wicked. Bart was up so many times during the night and didn't exactly start off the next day with a breakfast of champions either. Clutching the brass bucket so early is not a good sign. I brought that bucket home from a garage sale a few years ago. Bart rolled his eyes way back then, but it has become the vomitorium of choice since this ordeal began. No other vessel will do.

He looked at me with a desperate expression that said "can you see how much freaking fun I'm NOT having"?

He had little energy but managed to walk to the couch to rest. We both napped and woke up too late to be on time. We were more than fashionably late to chemotherapy which didn't even seem to rise to any level of importance to the nurses. I think they're used to it. Still, no matter how early or late, you still wait in the waiting room. I guess that's why it's called the waiting room. I've never known it to be the "hey, you're on time, we'll see you immediately" room.

Strapped into a chemo recliner with his sack of snacks and bottle of Gatorade, Bart shooed me away. No space to loiter, he said.

Four hours later Bart called me. As I drove up he was seated on a cement bench outside, wiped out. He lamented that other cancer patients come and walk on their own yet he needed extra time and support to make it out of the building.

Bart was too weak to talk. Once in the door, he grabbed the brass bucket and commenced regurgitating the meager snacks consumed throughout the day. Will somebody just tell me what to do to ease this man's suffering?

Sleep was the only thing to calm his retching discomfort. The friendly little chemo pump churned away.

Dallas busily worked on his chemistry project. I tried to help fix his homework lamp but in the process blew the fuse (okay, so I guess it's called a circuit breaker nowadays). The teen lair section of the house went dark. Flashlight in hand, I went out to the fuse box, uh, circuit breaker.

The most difficult aspect of this task was figuring out how to open the damn thing, to remove the metal cover! Latches used to be simple, now they're just fancy enough to make you feel stupid. Reset the fuse, excuse me, I'm dating myself again, circuit breaker. Whatever! Bart was barely able to feign interest but did inquire if I had fixed it. Yes, the lights are back on but the lamp has been murdered.

September 29

Bart has not eaten for almost two days. The chemo nurse assured me he had been given enough IV fluids to take the edge off.

He sipped a little and threw up a lot.

Popsicles turned out to be a bad idea because chemo causes cold sensitivity like pins and needles in Bart's mouth. He said he felt "touchy queasy".

He petted the Phaddy Sparky dog and decreed that golf balls are not good Phaddy dog toys. They fit perfectly under the coffee table and ottoman then he barks until someone gets them out. (The name, Sparky, was drip by drip evolving into Phaddy, which was a more polite form of the original handle, Fatty.)

This fat little dog seems to add a new dimension of playfulness to the household. We enjoy the little guy's antics except when he jumps on Bart's lap a little too close to the jewels.

A Note from Bart:

This week was a roller coaster ride. Went in for my Chemo on Monday feeling pretty good then about 1/3 of the way through treatment things started to go awry!

A large lump, or swelling, started to form just under where the needle entered my jugular vein. It appears that some type of sheath had formed which allowed nothing in or out.

I needed to go to Roseville, evidently the only facility that can perform the repair procedure. They had me undergo a port dye test to see where the dye was going. Evidently, not where it was supposed to go. Now the fun stuff...when the test failed, as everyone assumed, the next step was replacement of the needle. It was 4 PM and I had eaten a banana and granola bar at noon which meant I could only have the procedure done if I did it under local anesthesia, not a general. I was awake the whole time. The procedure involved sliding the old needle out while sliding the new needle in, then repositioning it. All in all the pain was bearable, except for the part when my pain meds wore off. I got only 1/3 of a chemo session today.

The Fight Resumes

A Note from Bart:

After a 6-7 hour day of more chemo I was wrecked. They connected a pump. Came home slept, threw up and drank fluids.

I woke up feeling much better, except for all the crap Melanie had to clean up. I'm looking Maar-vo-lous. And we all know "It's always better to look good than to feel good". I pounded back an In-n-Out burger, a large plate of watermelon and some Apple Hill apple pie ala mode. I haven't eaten so much in one sitting since, I can't remember.

Take care and love, Bart

A Note from Bart:

I wanted to follow up regarding the movement of the needle in my jugular without general anesthesia. The pain is interesting because it was unique. Ever have babies 12-18 months or so old try to pick the hair off your arms or legs? Remember how that felt? Not good but not that painful. That's how it felt when the surgeon made the incision to move the needle.

It's Saturday and I am enjoying a fairly good day, watching a little Ryder Cup golf, wishing I were out on the course. I forced my wife to ride in the car with our 16 year old driver to go get pastries at Heavenly Donuts. Here I am sipping tea with a blueberry doughnut.

Go Steelers! Bart

Operation Supermarket

We had a big grocery list. Bart was feeling pretty good, albeit tired due to a lack of sleep but his pain level was down. I convinced him to accompany me to the store. I could see he was a little winded just walking from the parking lot so I suggested Bart use one of those electric grocery carts. He looked at me, rolled his eyes and reluctantly agreed.

I couldn't help it. As he assumed the drivers' seat I got a big smile on my face. Bart was in no mood though. He read the instructions out loud and I really couldn't help it. I started to chuckle, okay, laugh out loud. He stared me down and said "it's not funny". But it really WAS a little funny. Here he is in this contraption with a giant orange flag pole on the rear end. He insists that the forward and back labels had been switched because when he pulled the forward lever he shot backwards and hit some

Halloween display, then he jerked forward with what he said was the reverse lever.

Now I was full blown, doubled over, knee slapping, laughing and I really couldn't help it, really! Our first motorized cart trial and we were mowing down end aisle displays! The scene was just hilarious to me. I was trying not to snort or cry from laughing so hard. Bart sternly faced me and said "if you don't stop laughing I'm going to drive this thing right out of here". He was so serious that I earnestly tried to pull myself together.

Then he hollered at me to stay up with him so he didn't have to turn around. I was trying, but the way Bart was weaving through the aisles just made me laugh all the more and I couldn't keep up with him. I felt mildly guilty for finding this whole scene so funny and if you knew Bart, it'd just be the last thing you'd expect. And that flag!! It was like bumper cars. I was picking up soup cans and cracker boxes in his wake.

I just had to share this with someone who could appreciate it so I called my daughter Megan who made me feel so much better because she was laughing as hard as I was when I told her what was happening at the Cameron Park Bel Air that morning. We even ran into her classmate, Cody (almost literally) who works there. At one point I lost Bart altogether. He was apparently trying to make a U turn but he didn't remember to do the hand signal.

Cody was on the case though and threatened to announce Bart's disappearance on the intercom. Bart obviously got the hang of maneuvering the machine at top speed, but navigating the store was pretty random and haphazard. I found myself jogging around just to find him. Just like a kid, he was putting stuff in the cart that wasn't on the list.

Outside, on our way to the car, Bart even high-centered the cart on a speed bump in the parking lot! As he was balancing like a teeter totter he threatened to leave the cart right there and walk to the car. The courtesy clerk was most helpful in lifting Bart off the bump. I've never had such a time at the grocery store in my life, even with the twins when they were little.

I only wish Bart had been in a better mood to enjoy it as much as I did. He seemed so annoyed by my amusement last night. Today however, he chuckled a little himself.

What a difference a day makes.

Chapter Three

Full House

October 6

I had a nice visit with my sister-in-law Joanne (Pittsburgh, PA), and her son, our nephew Michael Reagan (Phoenix, AZ).

They flew in from Phoenix. Michael's lovely wife had to stay home with their 3-year old twin girls who were ill. Bart avoids public gatherings because his immune system is so low and a common cold would present untold complications.

Their visit was all too short. The excitement and extra attention seemed to make the Phaddy dog delirious and confused. He had a few uncharacteristic indiscretions in my dining room! It was going so well the week prior, then bang! He decides the dining room is remote enough. No one goes in there so it must be like the outback or something and available for his pooping pleasure. It is not pleasant for me, that's for sure.

We doubled up on the "walkies" and neighbors commented that Phaddy Sparky dog may be losing some of his bulk. We hope he loses his fondness for evacuating his bowels on the dining room carpet too.

In other news ... we have added a new driver to the family. Dallas passed his driver's test with flying colors. The only deduction was in the parking lot at the Weaverville DMV. The lot is shared with the CHP and you're supposed to drive around the DMV side to exit. I probably made the same mistake myself.

This morning Dallas drove himself to school and to his drum lessons in the afternoon. What a strange new world. The youngest reaches a milestone. Remember those second and third daily trips to the market?

Well there's a new personal shopper on the payroll now. And he doesn't poop in the dining room! What a bonus.

October 9

Bart has been a little down but not complaining. He's trying to negotiate a balance with over the counter meds on top of his prescriptions in order to manage a decent status quo. If only he could feel just plain normal for a change; that would make him happy. Sore throat, cough and general cold symptoms just add insult to injury.

Matty was flying in from Fort Benning, GA for the holiday weekend but that was only half the fun. On my drive home from work I received a call from Megan. Megan usually calls me on the home commute so it wasn't unusual. What was unusual was being on the phone with her (thinking she was in Tucson, AZ) and then seeing her emerge from the back deck while we were chatting! Bart and I were sufficiently surprised and happy to have the kids home together again for the holiday.

Megan accompanied Bart to his doctor appointments. It helped greatly having someone who spoke doctor. Bart had restless nights and tiresome days. Having the kids at home helped and I could see he was trying, but sometimes just engaging in conversation was too much of an effort.

When asked if Bart had any particular cravings he responded with "Yes, I crave feeling normal again". I prayed I could extract the pain he's feeling onto myself. It's so hard to watch someone you love in this much agony. Amazingly Bart endures. The fun and laughter of the kids is a "normal" and welcome distraction from the constant discomfort. Near bedtime he felt mildly better and hopes the trend will continue.

The kids decided that fat Sparky dog should be called “Phaddy”, it’s a trendier spelling. We shall see what sticks. Bart says "what will be, will be". I think sometimes Bart believes our family is just another episode of "The Office".

October 10

Sunday is a day of rest, unless you're at the Reagan house when all three kids are together at home. Bart did manage to rest up a little while most of us were out running around. Matt took the opportunity to teach Dallas a few new fitness routines so we followed up today with a trip to the gym.

Meg went to church and we made a plan to meet at home to discuss what would be on the Sunday fun menu. None of us wanted to miss out on each other's company.

The 3 kids decided to go to the batting cages then mini-golfing while Bart and I played with the dog and watched a little football. Bart got a craving for mac-n-cheese with hot dogs so I ran around the house getting ready to leave for the market. Bart kindly reminded me that his cravings only last so long. Sometimes there are just so many things to do just to get ready to leave the house!

The mac & cheese was a hit and he had a second helping!

Bart said he loves having the kids together again and I know he wished he could participate with a bit more animation. Nonetheless their antics were certainly entertaining even to the casual observer. Sadly, Matty leaves tomorrow but Megan has arranged to stay longer.

As for Bart's medical status, he got a green light from the oncologist to resume chemo. Tomorrow begins the fourth week of chemotherapy. Megan was very helpful in determining which of the chemo meds had caused the most adverse or toxic reactions for Bart in the past and they were able to adjust accordingly.

The doctor did order Bart in for daily hydration via IV however. He just cannot eat or drink enough to sustain himself adequately on a daily basis without it. Bart is a bit pale and too thin but he can still roll his eyes and get annoyed with us at times which is oddly comforting. I think he's most impatient that I'm not more computer savvy by now. I still say that an old paper address book is way more reliable than any computer. No paper address book has ever crashed and erased all its contents.

But I digress. Dr. Megan will take Bart to chemo tomorrow morning and deliver Matty to the airport. Dallas will drive himself to school and I will walk to the dentist's office.

It's quite remarkable to me that Bart isn't crabby; that he doesn't fret or express apprehension. He takes each day as it comes. My dad would say it is equanimity. We should all strive for it.

October 11

Bart's chemo went smoothly today. Our medical student (daughter Megan) made sure he was comfortable with plenty of snacks for the day. Then Bart sent her on a few errands. Megan drove Matthew to the airport then home to pick me up from the dentist. We got the car cleaned, shopped for a new dog leash, new alarm clock for Dallas, and the usual grocery items.

Bart completed his regimen early and we were home by 4pm. Megan set up a computer program for us to track and monitor Bart's schedule of medications. It will really help us make sure he doesn't get behind the pain train. Although he's exhausted tonight he did eat mac-n-cheese and kept it down. :)

Bart's little chemo pump buddy chatters away like paparazzi. We are all used to it now. Chemo does knock the wind out of Bart's sails but tonight NO nausea. Thank heaven for small favors.

Bart likes the new surround sound system he procured Friday with our credit points. It's definitely a new "boy toy". I'll be hard pressed to understand which remote to use to control what without the boys involved, so I won't be watching much TV without them.

As a post script the "Phaddy" dog is adjusting and has not had an accident in days. This is progress. He gets a couple walks a day. The dog is okay but Dallas is worse for wear. Apparently Matt's workout routines are a bit advanced for his liking.

"Phaddy" evidently escaped from the back yard but a neighborhood guardian returned the wayward pooch. As for the dog's official name ... the kids cannot resist calling him "Phaddy" with the cool spelling. It doesn't matter that Bart and I have been calling him Sparky all this time as it seems to us somehow more dignified. The kids think "Phaddy" is it. Never mind that he's losing weight and won't necessarily be "fat" for long.

'Twas a good chemo day, all considered. Bart is still hanging in there and it's past 10! He's had several cat naps but this is a good day indeed. Bart's testing the fine surround sound system he and Matty configured. One must give full credit to the technical genius of "volume" I guess. Hallelujah.

We're officially on our way to becoming hearing-impaired.

October 12

Bart's chemo intake yesterday was fairly smooth but boy the outcome sure isn't. About 5 AM Bart got really sick, continuous vomiting. He couldn't even keep the nausea meds down. His system just wasn't settling down at all. The pump was administering doses every few minutes which had to be adding to his discomfort. Because Bart felt no relief by morning it was back to the chemo lab for IV anti-nausea juice and fluids.

We got very interesting results from Bart's genetic testing thanks to our daughter Megan who can interpret that stuff. Bart has a genetic anomaly that makes some of the chemo drugs toxic to him, causing the most severe side effects.

Of course, we discover that little genetic gem after Bart has endured several rounds of this toxic torture. That pesky little gene was likely responsible for landing Bart in the hospital a couple times and for the gut wrenching this morning.

We were both wondering what was up because so many other chemo patients looked somewhat lively. We even asked the chemo nurses why those patients could walk right out of there and even drive themselves to and from when Bart could barely ambulate to the elevator without resting on walls?

They were most diplomatic with their answers, everybody's different, blah blah blah but we could see clearly that chemo was kicking Bart's ass a lot harder than most.

After a few IV bags of vomit killer (Zofran), Bart was feeling a bit better. At home he embraced a serving of chicken and stars soup. Later he craved cantaloupe and that stayed down too. He alternates between sleep and rest. I for one can appreciate the discernible difference between these two activities.

Next up on the fun menu is room temperature Jell-O. Food can't be too hot or too cold. It would feel like his fingers and toes were being electrocuted. Definitely a hair-rising side effect there. I hope the insulin we keep in the refrigerator won't light him up.

Bart's re-imaging scan is in 10 days. At that time, we plan to consult with pancreatic cancer experts at University of San Francisco where doctors can evaluate the effectiveness of the chemo protocols thus far and discuss what's best going forward.

As of now, all is quiet on the up-chuck front so life is good tonight.

School of Hard Rocks

Just when you think all is well, you're struck with inconvenient events that must be par for the course when parenting teenagers.

You can sincerely tell a teenager something 700 times and of course, they know it already. Then once you let them loose, they make the very mistake you've warned them about hundreds of times before.

After only driving a few weeks, Dallas hits a rock and damages the car enough to put it off the road. The good news is that neither Dallas nor the rock got hurt. The silver lining may be, just maybe, that this was a good lesson in the school of hard "rocks".

Bart patiently carried his little chemo pump and a flashlight and walked up to the street to peruse the damage himself. He was so calm and collected. On the other hand, I was not. This was just so inconvenient to say the least. It meant more stress and frustration at an already stressful time.

Cautioning the kid constantly did nothing! I was not having a good evening. Dallas had tugged at my last nerve. In the light of day, things might appear less dire. We had to sleep on it.

The neighbors sent their very talented son over to look at the car. Turns out they are familiar with "rock" damage of this caliber.

The boys generously offered to take on the repair job themselves. In addition, they would teach Dallas something about auto mechanics. Translation: they'll enslave Dallas to do all the heavy lifting. I made them promise me that. They also assured us that Dallas would hear their lessons of vehicular mishaps. Dallas will pay for the experience, literally.

Bart says other than this teenage strife, he is doing marginally better.

October 16

Bart's constellation of issues just weren't aligning so that he could sleep soundly. Megan took him on his daily sojourn to the "Creekside Lounge" (Oncology Chemo lab). After an initial problem with a clot in Bart's port; the nurses were able to hook him up for about 4 hours of IV juice.

Lab results showed a low hemoglobin reading. He was anemic. Bart also developed mouth sores, another unfortunate side effect so he was invited back to Creekside on Monday for more IV goodness.

My sister Sandi dropped by with her Beagle buddy so "Phaddy the sparky dog'" got to play with someone his own size for a short time. Bart was back home from Creekside after noon and then took a 3 hour nap. Megan and I went on a spree to buy over the counter treatments for mouth sores. It would be comfort soup in a can for dinner.

After collecting Dallas from a football game wherein his school's team lost horribly and humiliatingly to its rival, we (Bart, Dallas, and I) watched some TV.

We got a thrill seeing our neighbor Matt on the television news receiving an honor for bravery. Officer Matt had courageously entered a burning car to save a young man's life. What a guy, our neighbor, and a high note before hitting the hay. Dallas has an early PSAT test.

October 18

Bart was the first one up. He was in the mood for an old fashioned blueberry donut. After waking the kids they didn't waste time traipsing off to procure bakery delights before attending church.

Still suffering from painful inflammation and sores in his mouth, Bart dealt with the donut fairly well, all things considered. Sometimes a donut can be a delightful experience as long as you can stop at just one. Bart had no problem but some of us kept cutting pieces thinking those fractions didn't add up to two whole pastries.

Bart dutifully swirled and spit his morning concoction of mouth meds. Megan earlier prepared the blend of 3 elements containing cherry and mint flavors, not at all appealing to the patient. He indicated that it was somewhat painful to speak. Even napping dried him out because his mouth was usually open. I think we all nap open-mouthed if truth be told.

We scoured the town Sunday afternoon for Bart's craving: candy jellied watermelon slices but with no success. It's hard to find just the right snack to go with Chloraseptic, antacid and lidocane. Bart tried to be pleasant and not too crabby but the "conditions what prevail", as my dad would say, were less than ideal. I understood.

Tomorrow Megan will take Bart to his morning appointment at Creekside Lounge for hemoglobin and other goodness. He loves having her watchful and educated eye looking after him. He doesn't give her as much lip as he gives me either. She's going to be a terrific doctor. Even the oncologist thinks so.

We all hope this latest oral nuisance can be treated expeditiously and his blood regains the appropriate ratio of red to white cells. Arrangements are set for his scan October 22, and a consult with doctors at UCSF October 28th. Those results will help set the course for the next round of treatments.

I hear the dog snoring so it must be past my bedtime.

October 19

Bart had been feeling marginal for too long. It was beginning to cause me extra worry. Meg drove him to where the magic happens (Creekside Lounge). Four hours of treatment ensued. We were grateful for Megan who requested steroid treatment for Bart's mouth condition which was not part of the original Monday treatment plan. They agreed. It was a very good idea. Bart's post treatment blood work showed improvement and the mouth swelling went down.

After work I knew Bart was feeling a bit better when he protested my selection of oil change services. I was trying to be efficient by getting the tires rotated and oil changed at the same place. Nonetheless, he sent "words" via text "If you're not going to do what I say then quit asking me questions". And I thought I was doing so well with these automotive chores.

Bart ate a whole Marie Callender's chicken pot pie for dinner then peeled the lid off a full pint of Cherry Garcia ice cream and topped it with chocolate syrup. Bart said he's feeling better overall although his lips still hurt like a son-of-a-@#*. It was a good day; yes a good day after all. Bart had his special mixture of "swill" and a newly prescribed sleep aid to help him get through the night.

It'll be an early day tomorrow since I have to drive the new driver to school. Car repair class (aka the school of hard rocks) continues for Dallas. It's definitely keeping him busy (and broke).

October 20

A Note from Bart:

'Tis I, the sickly one. I thought while I had some semblance of strength left in me I would try to write. Most days I barely have the strength to get out of bed and lie on the couch. We are trying to get the doc to give me a hormone shot to increase my white blood cell count, which is very low. As for eating, food tastes like crap.

The second CT scan is on Friday to see if this course of treatment is working. My weight is as low as it was in high school and that's skinny. Depending on results of my scan, I may go to UCSF (Univ. California *San Fransicko*) never mind that it's a 3-4 hour ride and I can barely ride 30 minutes to the doc. It should be a huge blast!

Go Steelers!

Bart

Chapter Four

Assume the Throne

October 21

The patient is tucked away and sleeping. The insurance company (insert swear word here) finally approved a prescription to help Bart sleep. Insurance approval surely must come from doctors? I won't go there. The state of medicine is an issue upon which I could opine for hours. Consistent contact via email is a powerful tonic, good enough that you'd think the insurance company would have to authorize a prescription for it. Interest in his well-being keeps Bart buoyed and in better spirits. Some notes are as sardonic as Bart!

Meantime back at the homestead, Bart suggested we have a garage sale party and invite all of you to a "sale soiree" complete with adult beverages and bargain prices.

We're on a mission to sell or give away anything and everything that isn't essential. Bart and I agreed to purge (stuff not guts). We'd rather have the purchasing power for more "co-pays" than to have things. It was very cathartic. Not quite as good as a trip to the Weaverville dump, but satisfying nonetheless.

Bart's daily grind of pain management amidst other systemic bodily function challenges make it a tough go physically and mentally. All married couples should acknowledge that familiarly sometimes breeds contempt and that means spouses often feel they can snap at you with immunity. I've granted a Presidential pardon as far as immunity is concerned. But even still, a little break is therapeutic.

Since Dr. Daughter is in charge, I will travel to Weaverville, CA for the weekend. There is a high school football field dedication to my dad, which is a huge honor. Mom is also bequeathing my dad's leather recliner. Bart originally took Dad shopping to buy that chair. Dad and Bart both loved it. My mom, however, hated the thing. She's happy to see Bart get some comfort from a chair to share.

The chair affair began a few years ago when Dad said he didn't know how many days he had left but wanted to enjoy them in a comfortable chair. That very day Bart said "Mike, get in the truck". They drove the 50 miles to Redding and bought a brown leather recliner. The boys were overjoyed. Mom rather mockingly was glad "they" liked it, (read between the lines). Mom subsequently ordered a chair all her own. Hopefully you have a comfy chair or a whole damn couch that's of comfort for a "chair affair" all your own.

October 22

Bart got his Procrit hormone shot at Creekside Lounge. Let the red blood cells begin. Hesitation over administering the shot was because encouraging red blood cells also encourages tumors. Catch 22 that your body needs those cells to function but so does cancer.

Bart watched some television, played on his computer and awaited delivery of a much anticipated Fed Ex package. He was craving pierogies (Polish pasta pillows stuffed with cheese and mashed potatoes served with gravy). We prepared the frozen variety but thoughts of homemade pierogies danced in his head.

Late that afternoon the Fed Ex truck pulled up and pierogi paradise. Irish Joanne Reagan and her little granddaughters make some pretty darn great Polish food.

Scan tomorrow morning. Let's hope the power of the pierogi fuels him well.

October 24

The long-awaited Dr. Mike recliner arrived! It was a five hour drive with cargo piled high like Beverly Hillbillies. Torrential rains pelted the load all the way but thanks to the expert wrapping and packing by kindergarten buddies Peter and Jim, the load was perfectly secure and stayed completely dry. Sideways winds and rain persisted during the unloading process but Bart couldn't wait a moment longer.

Adding to the inconvenience of the weather, our gutter was gushing right over the garage like a waterfall. So getting the chair out of the truck seemed nearly impossible. Trying to out wait the downpour was fruitless. Bart summoned neighbors to come to the rescue.

I braved the driving rain, climbed a ladder and proceeded to unclog the debris that created the waterfall that perfectly curtained the tailgate. With my gloved hand I scooped out a double heavy handful of gunk. Suddenly it released free-flowing backwash that swashed over me like a barrel of Gatorade over a coach. Dirty leaves, branches and gallons of shockingly cold liquid drenched me so that I momentarily questioned my balance on the ladder. My neighbor valiantly held an umbrella, all the while chuckling.

There was no deflecting this downpour. Even after the attempted gutter clearing, water streamed off the roof in the same spot. Undeterred, Matt and Dallas lifted the unwrapped chair off the tailgate, maneuvered it through the front door and placed it in the anointed holy spot. Bart settled in with a satisfied look of comfort on his face and announced "I think I'll spend the rest of my life in this chair". We all smiled. He grabbed his blankie and took over as master of his domain. Grandma was thrilled to get the call that a new king had ascended to the throne.

A Note from Bart:

Report Card

There was good and not-so-good news. The main tumor in the pancreas shrunk some. Three others in the liver grew. This means taking a trip to UCSF. There could be different types of tumors that react differently to the drugs.

We'll make it a family overnight vacation.

I've lost more weight. If I keep this up Mel's going to outweigh me. No golf, no work, no jogging, no house or yard work. (That's the good news). I watch a lot of TV, surf the net, check emails and sleep. I feel like the e-trade baby.

Love, Bart

October 27

We called our trek to Bart's UCSF consultation in San Francisco a "family outing" since we hadn't had one in a very long time (minus Matty who's in Georgia). Bart, Megan and Dallas picked me up after work.

I drove. Bart was in the passenger seat grumbling about the drive, not so much about my driving, thankfully. Bart thought traffic would be a nightmare due to the impending Giants game but we sailed into the Bay Area via the carpool lane.

Crossing the bay, Bart said he was cold so we cranked up the heat. By the time we reached the eccentric little Japanese hotel, Tomo, Bart's teeth were chattering and he couldn't get warm.

We piled on comforters and Dallas' beanie. Even in Bart's weakened state he slapped it away, saying "I'm not wearing that thing, it stinks!" never mind that he has a life-threatening illness, for God's sake he can't wear an ugly stocking cap. His Army ball cap will have to do to keep in the heat.

We let him rest for a few hours but then he got too hot. Bart went to the bathroom and when he emerged, sweat was dripping from his head; he was weak and his breathing shallow. He was in shock. Meg told me to call for an ambulance.

We had barely checked in to the hotel and the paramedics were checking him out. En route to the UCSF Emergency Room dispatch diverted us to Central Pacific Medical Center.

Bart was admitted to the hospital in septic shock as Megan had suspected. She followed every procedure, read every scan, every lab result and kindly offered suggestions which really impressed Bart's ER caregivers. She was focused on his care and didn't want to miss a thing.

Bart got a blood transfusion. It was lucky we got to the emergency when we did or sepsis could have fatally damaged his organs. He was a very, very sick man.

Intensive Care

Our consultation with UCSF was in a few hours but because UCSF did not have privileges (whatever that means) at CPMC the consultation had to be cancelled.

Tests confirmed an infection in Bart's blood but the source was unknown and so begins a process of elimination. Megan suspected the port. Bart endured continued tests. Doctors eventually eliminated gall bladder, colon and heart as sources of infection. Lab work was done every few hours.

Megan coordinated communication between CPMC doctors and Bart's oncologist. It was reassuring to have a team of physicians agree on treatment. We expected that this trip would be one night only, but an extended stay meant we had to get Dallas home for school. I put him on a train and a few hours later my friend collected him at the Railroad Museum in Sacramento.

Meanwhile back at CPMC, Bart was looking forward to eating again but only ice chips, apple juice and broth.

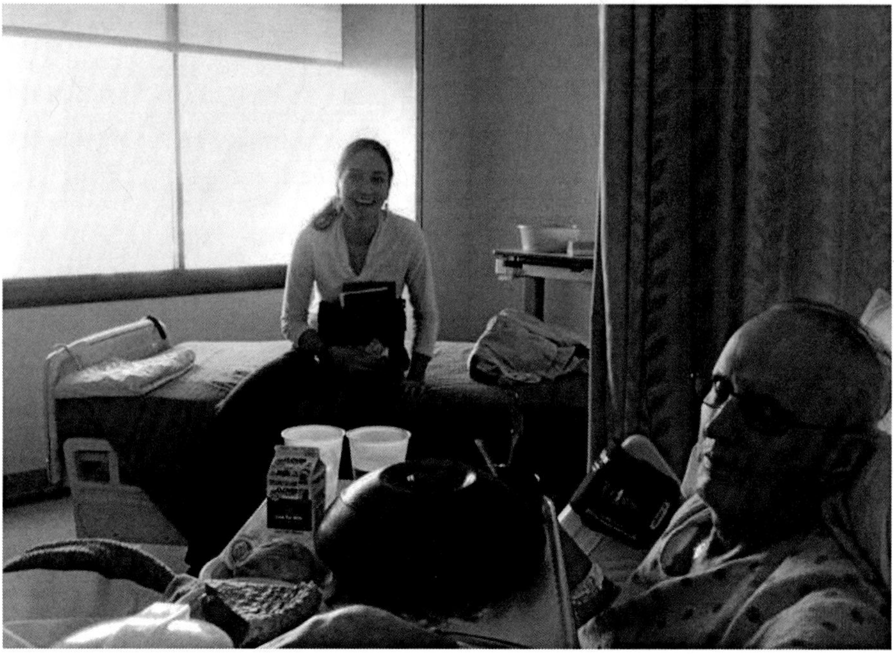

October 29

Megan dutifully jumped out of bed early, brushed her teeth, grabbed Bart's toys (charged phone and iPad) and trekked up the hill to the hospital. The source of his blood infection was indeed the PORT (access device in his chest, NOT bad dessert wine).

First the lab had to identify exactly what staph germ they were dealing with in order to know how best to kill it.

An infections specialist was called in and the bug identified. The port-catheter was removed because of the nasty critter, staphylococcus bacterium.

This guy leaves a gluey slime which sticks to things (like a plastic port) which meant infection could reoccur if the device is left in the body. For that surgery Bart's system had to be working properly and it wasn't.

Bart got pumped full of fluids to flush out the infection and bring up his very low blood pressure. As often happens, too much of a good thing isn't good and his lungs filled with fluid making it hard to breathe. Liver tumors also put pressure on his lungs.

Drainage takes time.

The ICU is not a very quiet or a private space. There is always chaotic activity, loud alarms, bright lights, buzzing, dinging, beeping, moaning and a lot of loud talking. Bart developed quite the affable relationship with one ICU RN. Sean believed that Bart was really John Tuturro in disguise (from the Transformers movie) because Bart mimicked the actor's voice. They bantered. Sean rolled a television set into Bart's curtained area of ICU. He chuckled every time Bart commented on the World Series.

One evening another ICU patient across from Bart was hollering nonstop about getting a TV. He desperately wanted to see the Giants play.

Bart told Sean he didn't really care about watching the series at all.

While we were there, I heard the guy yell "where the hell is my TV" and frankly I was a bit embarrassed for him.

Meg and I left for dinner and when we returned Bart had the TV parked directly in front of HIS bed! And it was turned OFF! The other patient was still screaming about why he couldn't get a TV. I was horrified. I told Bart "that guy can clearly see that you have the only TV and you are not even using it"! Bart said "He's not getting the TV either, you don't give a whining dog a reward for bad behavior do you"? I heard the "TV man" call for a nurse, so I discretely pulled the curtain across to conceal the television and Bart said "leave it open".

I said "but you're not even watching it and he really would enjoy the game so why don't you just be kind and generous and give it to him, you'd make his day - after all he's sick too".

Bart wasn't having it. "If the guy weren't such a jerk to the staff then I might, but he is and I'm not". (I do think that if a nurse HAD asked Bart, he would have given it up for the nurse, but I suspected a conspiracy here).

Bart was completely exhausted. His breathing was better and his blood pressure was good but he felt weak, barely able to speak, except in a whisper, and not often. We sat with him most of the day and evening. He slept continuously until about 3 PM when he woke and raised his arms questioningly as if to ask, "when are they taking this damn thing out, anyway"?

The surgeon squeezed Bart in as the very last surgery so we waited to get the call that he was in recovery. Once the offending device is out, he'll be treated with antibiotics for another two days, have his blood tested again and a "pick line" inserted. The PIC line is a far less invasive intravenous device through which blood can be drawn and chemotherapy can be administered should it be determined that Bart is strong enough to have another chemo treatment.

Tomorrow we inquire as to whether or not we can consult with a CPMC oncologist. Bart is at the point where he doesn't care if he gets a second opinion or not. Megan has kept the oncologist informed (our oncologist) and even contacted UCSF for some information. She really is brilliant with her medical knowledge and insight.

Bart has been moved from ICU to a regular hospital room tonight so he might get a little more sleep. Doctors say Bart won't be released now until next week. Our Japanese hotel is nice, but you wouldn't want to live there.

October 30

Today was a marginally good day for Bart so it was a great day for me. He was so alive compared to yesterday and the past few days. Last night I'll admit that worry washed over me, but this morning he was awake and fairly communicative. What a difference! A little fluid still in the right lung but his blood pressure was stellar, he had no fever and he was eating (a little) and walking around a bit. Though we shared some stilted verbal communications, I seriously have my suspicions that even when you're in the same room with Bart, he might still prefer email or text messaging! And he definitely hates to answer questions unless you're a doctor.

Last night, Bart moved from ICU to a patient room on the sixth floor. Mind you, we'd just left some mighty interesting roommates like Obnoxious TV Guy, Odorous Bedsore Man and John Doe who didn't have a clue as to whom he was. Room 658A was luxurious compared to the cramped space in ICU.

That's not to denigrate the magnificent ICU staff. All of the CPMC personnel have been great. It's just unfortunate they all rotate like they're on a merry-go-round so that you can't keep track. There are also so many titles. There are doctors, surgeons, interns, residents, specialists, RN's, social workers, personal care assistants, dieticians, physical therapists, transport staff, lab technicians, clergy etc. When I grew up nurses did all those things, but I digress.

Room 658A was a great room. That is, until we heard from the man behind the curtain, also known as 658B. Now I can't presume to know what kind of respiratory problem this guy had but I was pretty darn sure he horked up a piece of lung or something.

Megan lasted a bit longer but eventually she exited too. I think she might have been afraid something could shoot over on her. That curtain just wasn't cutting it. Bart didn't like it much either but he was thankfully drowsy from heavy-duty pain medication. We didn't say anything but the nurses must have, because this morning 658B had moved away. Nurse Emily said they wanted to see that Mr. Reagan got some restful sleep and 658B probably needed to sleep in some sort of tent anyway.

Now Bart has a gorgeous room with a beautiful view of the Golden Gate Bridge. Monday, he will get a pic line (peripheral intravenous catheter), which will serve a similar function to the port-catheter, hopefully without a high threat of infection. Bart must get IV antibiotics twice a day for the next few weeks. Doctors will arrange for a visiting nurse to administer the daily doses at home.

We really like our Tomo Hotel desk staff and have met them all. The elevators were often out of order but that didn't bother us. It definitely bothered the desk staff though when a guest who was stuck in the elevator called 911. This would be the second time in two days (Bart being the first) that ambulance and fire trucks arrived in front of Hotel Tomo.

The place is painted in loud colors like Japanese animated cartoons and it's loud otherwise too. I thought there was a Boeing 757 set for takeoff on the 3rd floor but turned out it was just the ice machine! Then at night some garbage truck (at least that's what it sounded like) kept clanking, revving its engine and banging over and over again during the night like it was stuck on a "bang-that-dumpster" setting. We had to cover our ears. What on earth could they have been doing at 3 AM for so long?

And yet, we have come to like the place even though we never got to have Shabu-Shabu in the hotel restaurant (Japanese version of fondue where you cook meat and vegetables in a boiling cauldron). Meg and I will drive to Sacramento tomorrow so she can catch her flight back to Tucson. I will return with sis Sandi to colorful Hotel Tomo for hopefully one last loud night with the ice machine. It's so much better than a horking roommate for sure.

October 31

Today was another marginally good day for Bart so it was a great day for me. Still there was fluid in the right lung but no fever.

Chapter Five

Lifeblood by the Bay & Baseball

November 1

The "infections" doctor teased Bart that he was probably feeling better because the Rangers won a game. I was concerned this whole week that it might be dangerous for Bart to be so vocal about rooting against the Giants. When in Rome, etc, and this is San Francisco after all. I think the staff was pretty good-natured about this cantankerous Texas fan.

Back at our home away from home...Meg and I were stepping out for a bit and felt awkward about causing the poor Tomo Hotel staff more grief due to the once again out-of-order elevator that morning, so we followed exit signs to the west stairs and doubled-timed it to the ground floor only to find that door alarmed: Emergency Exit Only! We trotted back up the three flights but that door was locked, no entry! Trapped, we looked at each and knew what we had to do. We ran back down the steps, I hit the crash bar and bolted through with a "Don't look back" attitude as an ear-deafening loud piercing shriek erupted.

We agreed on the run there would be no admission of guilt to the desk people that we caused the third alarm in so many days.

Sunday we drove back to Cameron Park and dear Dr. Meg had to be delivered to the airport. Sandi and I drove back to San Francisco the next day.

At the hospital, Bart was getting bored with medical incarceration. Blood tests still showed traces of bacteria plus a mild fever. Secondary infection was a big concern. The infection doc chose to stay the course: Cefazolen IV antibiotic.

He was right. Bart's blood tested clean 24 hours later. I brought him Woodhouse Fish Company clam chowder which he ate readily. At 10 PM he was watching election results. It pleased me to hear him express his old conservative self, even in an uncharacteristically mild voice.

The next day I got trained on giving IV drugs through the PPIC line (peripherally inserted central catheter). Next on the agenda is the mountain of paperwork for out-processing. That could take a day in itself.

Bart's release was timed perfectly coinciding with the Giants parade. The streets will be closed.

I must say that it was fun to walk past pubs and cafés hearing hoards of fans cheer and holler. San Franciscans were celebrating in the streets. What a fun atmosphere.

Bart dozed on schedule and kicked me out of his room. He isn't keen on visitors staring at him when he sleeps.

November 2

Giants fans continued to fill the streets far and wide. Estimates were four to five hundred thousand people, according to television news.

Bart and I took a final stroll around the sixth floor absorbing spectacular views of the bay and the Golden Gate Bridge.

Big fun for me had been anticipating the arrival of the famed hospital "courtesy cart" (food cart) because you never knew when it would come around. Nurses sang its praises and emphasized family could partake. Bart tried to shoo Mrs. Courtesy away while I was in the loo (water closet). (For some reason he didn't like the concept of me and free food). I tracked that sucker down though while Bart just shook his head.

I enjoyed my institutional snacks as Bart dozed off. Sandi meanwhile kept sending pictures of crab and culinary delights from Union Street. Sandi and I met up later to celebrate what could be our last evening in SF together.

November 3

Bart was 190 pounds when this ordeal began. This morning he was 155. Two decades ago he would tease me that my calves were always bigger than his, now he says my biceps are winning that competition too. While we talked about food, Bart felt his stomach cramp up after his meal. Sandi and I are the ones who should have had cramps. Our dinner was uncomfortably pricey, albeit nouveau chic. Just to add insult to injury Bart was watching the food channel. He would say you never know when food inspiration may strike.

Young CPMC resident Dr. H stopped by to say if all tests agree and there are no issues with Bart's PICC then release paperwork would be drafted.

I reflected on all the many shifts and rotations we witnessed. Familiar faces doing their jobs day to day, night after night. We experienced human beings who loved their work. We grew fond of the young residents who worked 80 hours a week. Bart told nurse supervisors and doctors that their charges did them proud. It struck me how Bart could be so direct and assertive with his own care, often demanding, but also communicating sincere praise. With his check-out imminent I felt an emotional sense of gratitude. It filled my head to the degree that tears formed. All these strangers saved Bart's life.

November 4

The sun was out and the air crisp in San Francisco as I powered up Buchanan Street for the last time. I thought it amusing that Bart ordered chicken fried rice for breakfast. It sounded good yesterday he said. He didn't eat it so I did.

The PICC line went into a large vein in his arm and threaded its way to a big vein leading into his heart. An X-Ray confirmed proper placement.

The case worker supervisor stopped by and said she thought another night was likely. That news sent me flying downhill to the hotel because we had to find another hotel. Tomo was booked solid. The Kabuki Hotel squeezed us into their remaining vacancy.

We zoomed back up the hill to the hospital in time to hear the lead doc say "yes" indeed Bart would be released that afternoon. Ah but wait, to discharge or not to discharge, that was the question.

Medical Discharge Paperwork

Bart could not leave until further treatment was coordinated between CPMC and Mercy Hospital in Folsom so it could take more night hours after all for all the transfer paperwork to be completed.

This is another lesson for our doctor daughter. Communication is always the key. The confusion over Bart's release was a result of problems between case management and attending physicians. Doctors may leave orders in the computer they assume will be filled. If not, doctors aren't necessarily notified in a timely manner. Sometimes it's not the case worker's fault but clearly there's a glitch in the hospital feedback loop.

A few hours later a face-to-face meeting was required to work out release papers for today and you would think he was getting released from prison with all the paperwork and forms being required.

We finally poured Bart into the front seat of the car and drove away right on time for rush hour. Our one night stay had lasted almost two weeks and the traffic was threatening to make it even longer. Bart couldn't make it out of San Francisco without using the term "ass clown" and no it wasn't a political reference, just about the challenging traffic. He said in his post-chemo scratchy voice "consultation be damned, I'm not coming back."

There's no place like home

Bart settled into his comfy brown leather throne! At last.

Antibiotics and equipment were delivered. Then there were errands and laundry to do before the nurse arrived to teach me how to administer Bart's antibiotics through the PICC line.

We had joyful moments when the neighbor kids came up to welcome Uncle "Bark" back home.

The kids got to collect all the Halloween decorations and then I rolled out a sheet of bubble wrap on the driveway for the jump up and down dance of joy. Poor Phaddy thought he heard gun shots though and ran inside while kids and their moms had fun jump popping like idiots. Bart made some comment about lunatics making unnecessary neighborhood noise which only served to spur us on.

Dallas gave his dad a big hug then bee-lined for the game room. Nurse man Jon taught me everything I needed to know, ever confident in my mission. Bart had a craving for Tilapia prepared with garlic, white wine, chicken broth, olive oil, lemon and capers paired with orzo, lima beans and fruit. Bart almost loved it. He used to double the garlic on every recipe but chemo has changed all that.

Bart said his stomach hurt but compared to the near death experience of the weeks prior a relatively happy evening was had by all.

I awoke about 4 am listening to Bart's barely audible snoring and laid awake for an hour or so. I felt comforted by that sound and wished I could trade my sleep time for more of his. How much more can this poor man take?

I got up at 5 AM to check on Dallas and Gus who chose to camp out on the back deck. It was so nice and cool outside at that hour. Bart used to be hot all the time, boy has that switched.

I prepared the Reagan boys' favorite breakfast of biscuits and gravy. Bart's taste buds have become acutely sensitive. He thought it was spicy! Par for the "post chemo taste bud" course I suppose. I don't even season anything anymore. I don't care for such a pile of carbohydrates myself but the three boys had no complaints.

Small Joys

Bart didn't have the energy for walking outside today but we vicariously enjoyed watching cadets exert themselves in Army vs. Air Force football. Air Force won and since they beat Navy, they took the Commander in Chief's trophy for the first time since 2002. We have a spirited rivalry with a dear friend. Her son is a Naval Academy Cadet.

I squeezed in a quick run before my nursing premiere. While running I thought about TKD and how I've struggled with fifth degree black belt training injuries and yet Bart's struggle is light years more difficult, intense and relentless. I am so humbled by his fortitude and yet a little scared myself.

I made it back in my usual 44 minutes, in time to clean up for Bart's IV antibiotic treatment. Since the port infection, call me paranoid. Bart says "enough sterilization already" but he had to humor me. I don't want a repeat of the infection hell we went through before.

Post IV dinner: au gratin potatoes, meatloaf and vegetables which almost appealed to Bart. It was most assuredly a hit to the likes of Dallas and his pal Xander.

I baked chocolate chip cookies for dessert which didn't quite make Bart's cut either, too crispy. I never seem to take them out of the oven soon enough. The boys still took them off my hands.

Bart tried to find inspiration again from the food channel: Diners, Drive-Ins & Dives.

November 7

A Note from Bart:

I had a week or so of my life stolen and no idea what happened during most of that time, except for lots of blood and needles.

During one moment I thought I was hallucinating but Mel assures me I was not. Twice they offered me a harp player. I was aware enough to refuse that sort of crap. Why the heck would I want a harp player? Were they trying to tell me something

And then they said a "visualization" expert would visit me and that I had scheduled it. Now I may have been out of it but do any of you seriously think it's me? Would I ever invite a stranger into my room to take me to my happy place?

No harp player or visualization experts. Instead I saw lots of doctors, nurses, needles, shots and sleep. Still I felt like I never actually slept. I think that's part of their plan.

I'm feeling waaaaay better. Pain comes and goes but its improving.

Bart

Post Script on the Harp and Visualization Thing

Chaplains visited Bart regularly at CA Pacific Med Center Hospital in SF. I happened to be with Bart the day Chaplain 1 came to our curtained cube. She actually said "I have a brilliant idea" and the moment I heard the word "harpist" I did a full spit take (almost choked) but suddenly realized how rude that reaction would be to this most sincere chaplain. I quickly recovered by pretending I had a little cough, trying all the while not to smirk, even a little. The image in my mind's eye of some huge harp in this crowded ICU serenading my husband Bart was just too much. I looked at Bart and his eyes said it all. To throw a tiny bit of fuel on the fire, I composed myself enough to say "Oh, that's interesting, what do you think, dear?"

I was curious about how Bart would get out of this situation because she was so very excited about arranging this performance for him. Bart said "not this time" or something to that effect. I was laughing on the inside and exchanging knowing looks with Megan.

I patted him on the back because he evaded obvious embarrassment. There was just no room for angel music here. It most certainly would have been a misplaced source of comedy. I could just hear Nurse Sean commenting about John Turturro and harps. It would have been a complete culture clash.

Now for the visualization specialist. Bart was ensconced in the lovely 658A. This room was visualization-rich already, an inspiring view of the Golden Gate. Nurse Cate sat on the end of Bart's bed and informed us that the visualization therapist would be arriving for Bart's appointment in 10 minutes. At this announcement, my head whipped around to Bart with the question, "who are you and what have you done with my husband?" burning in my eyes. Cate said the appointment had been ordered on Bart's behalf! I was taken aback.

Was Bart getting soft? Was he suddenly getting in touch with some sensitive side I had not yet witnessed in almost three decades? I never expected Bart himself to partake in what he would characterize as some touchy feely, warm fuzzy exercise.

At that moment I thought it would be more entertaining to have an open mind, so I said, "Bart, it couldn't hurt to try something new? I've heard it can be quite effective for many people." He looked at me as though I'd lost my mind. Visualization ETA was now 5 minutes and counting so Bart did not hesitate. He told Cate in no uncertain terms, "cancel that, it's not me." To her credit Nurse Cate made sure Bart was serious before acting. We wondered who in the world ordered this and I joked with Bart for a few minutes chiding him that I truly would have liked to see him follow along with the program. Of course, he gave me the stink-eye.

Another Day Another Donut

Bart awoke with a stomach ache. He had no fever though. Later some nausea but squelched it with appropriate meds. He finished a donut but couldn't handle anything else so he slept until late afternoon. I tried to coax him awake with aromas of soup and toasted banana cranberry bread.

Bart said he hates to take so much pain medication because it makes him sleepy all day. I do miss his company when he sleeps so much. It's the hardest when I see Bart in pain and I cannot extract any of it from him. I welcomed his complaints, questions, even anger but Bart is the model of acceptance, endurance, courage and strength. However, his ebullient humor gets buried by pain and discomfort. I know when I can and cannot engage him in conversation. Even daily email jokes and such do not evoke a response. Maybe a cup of soup or Ben & Jerry's Cherry Garcia with chocolate sauce might evoke something.

November 9

Monday Bart slept in until almost 10 AM.

Sparky/Phaddy dog was completely content to sleep as long as anyone stayed in bed. He's good like that.

Bart's stomach hurt but he ate Honey Nut Cheerios and a slice of Tracey's toasted cranberry banana bread. Bart worried that taking the nausea meds would make him too sleepy. Medication balance is clearly a sentient dance.

The oncologist discussed timing for the next chemo regimen. Bart must stay adequately hydrated with a complete course of antibiotics in order to be strong enough to contend with the chemo. That means he must take in IV fluids and supplemental pancreatic enzymes for the next ten days. He simply cannot eat or drink enough to keep up with fluid and nutrition requirements without this help.

Our appointment was at 2:30. We waited an hour. The doctor reviewed events of the past month (less than two minutes) then suggested chemo start next week. When I relayed how severely fatigued Bart has been he changed his mind. We would embark on an 11-day course of antibiotics before resuming the next regimen.

The new world order is daily fluid/nutrition IV appointments at the Creekside Lounge. The oncologist was in concurrence with our daughter Megan that Gemzar and Xeloda would be the best chemo combo to proceed with. I was reassured to hear our daughter had called UCSF specialists herself just to get another opinion. So many offer sincere advice relating their experiences with cancer that it often gets confusing. We want to do the right thing to have the best results. It's not an exact science.

Bart said he felt slightly better as we were driving home late from the chemo lounge that evening. Sandi hung with Dallas until we returned. She brought pot pies and Gas-X for Bart. We settled in and watched *Boon Dock Saints,* a good movie by our standards, just don't let your children watch it.

Tomorrow another round of nutrition and fluids. I am assessing whether Bart might be able to ride in a cart one day to watch his buddies play golf. I know he would enjoy it, especially if we don't run over Bill! That's another story.

November 10

A Note from Bart:

During all my ranting and raving about me, it occurred to me that I have neglected to mention the one person that means the most to me and without whose help and support I wouldn't have made it this far. It's, of course, my blushing bride, Mel. She is my rock. She cooks all my food, cleans, checks up on my meds and much much more, including driving me to and from these insane numerous doctor's appointments. My dear I love you with all my heart and you keep me going. Thanks much for all you do and nary a complaint.

Love, B

Chapter Six

PICC, Pierogies & Pancakes

November 11

Ok, so I must confess. Wednesday I awoke with a start. Did I post on Caring Bridge? I was afraid to read what I had written Tuesday night. You see when Lori came over I gladly opened a bottle of red wine. I haven't been drinking wine lately because my dear drinking buddy Bart lost his taste for it, never mind that it doesn't go well with chemo. We enjoyed a bottle (possibly two) while conversing and sitting with Bart.

As commonly happens when I'm a bit "happy" I repeat myself. So there you have it, one reason for abundant redundancy on Tuesday night's post. Lesson learned; Never think you make complete sense when you're half in the bag.

Right now Bart is having a terrific evening. He received the usual cocktail of anti-nausea, steroids and fluids at Creekside Lounge on Veteran's Day plus a Happy Veterans Day cake and Apple Hill donuts surely contributed to his elevated spirits.

He was talking to me and listening to country music. It's so nice to feel like life is normal. Our friend Gayle came to visit too. She and Bart recounted fun Weaverville memories like when her husband Tom and I set off cherry bombs my dad dug out of his basement shop while we were there visiting one summer.

It was Fourth of July. Cherry bombing was an activity that Bart and Gayle strongly opposed and they voiced their concerns sternly. Undaunted, Tom and I set up the blast site. We just had to light these things off no matter what. So, Gayle, Bart, my mom, and dad and kids sat on the front porch benches watching. Naturally, as we should have expected, Bart and Gayle (Mr. and Mrs. Safety & Security) were right. The first bomb was good, the second one caused a minor dust up. Dallas noticed Grandma's forehead was bleeding. Cherry bomb #2 evidently blasted a driveway pebble straight at her and hit her right between the eyes! Dad said it was just a flesh wound. But it was enough to put a very large damper on our exploding fun.

Bart also enjoyed brief visits from Sandi, and a few friends and neighbors. Bart was wide awake until nearly 11 PM. A stellar day to see Bart feel like himself again. I felt very happy reveling in how much I appreciate every little tiny aspect of a normal day when Bart is engaged in it.

Tomorrow the nurse arrives early to change his PICC dressing then it's back to Creekside Lounge for the last time this week. I'm hoping and praying that Bart will be feeling this good or better over the weekend. If so, it could mean a ticket to ride in a golf cart. Although after the grocery store experience we had in October, I don't think I'll let him drive.

November 12

For Bart a breakfast of champions, Cheerios and banana with just the right amount of milk was on the menu. (I'm learning these delicate nuances of preparing his cereal in just the right way.)

Nurse Jon showed up on time to change Bart's PICC dressing. I delivered Bart to the "lounge" with his phone and iPad for the final 3 hour session of the week.

Back home, my girlfriend Gayle helped with some long neglected chores. What a glorious gift, friends who bravely tackle someone else's dirt!

That afternoon Bart had a hankering for an ultimate cheeseburger. We found just what the doctor ordered at Jack-in-the Box. Bart ate as much of it as he could. I was rooting for him to consume all those calories.

Bart had some disconcerting stomach discomfort even before the burger. It continued throughout the day and into the evening which was disappointing because we'd had such a terrific day yesterday.

The bright spot was when a package arrived at dusk. Bart's sister Joanne shipped another big box of homemade pierogies. Those fun little Polish pillows of pasta and potato are certainly at the top of Bart's comfort food list. He almost felt good enough to go online tonight but instead his focus and energy was steered toward over the counter meds to help his stomach.

Only two more days administering IV antibiotics through the PICC. Monday morning it's back to Creekside Lounge for the next regimen of chemotherapy, Gemzar and Xeloda. The chemo nurses assure us that this round should prove to be a lot less brutal than the first four weeks.

Time will tell.

Before bed, Bart said he's visualizing oatmeal, raisins and brown sugar for tomorrow. We all thought he wasn't into that visualization thing? He's visualizing sleep right about now.

November 13

It's Saturday and lots to do. Bart had a decent night's sleep. He said he only got up once. Both Bart and the dog had oatmeal for breakfast, only the dog didn't get raisins with his Kibble.

Dallas and his friend Timmy wanted heart-shaped waffles. Dallas picked up a heart waffle maker he found along the road a few months ago while walking home from school! It was out on the street for the trash collector, but Dallas was excited, thinking he picked up a veritable treasure. Dallas, Megan and Matthew cleaned it thoroughly and wrapped the cord with electrical tape. I hate the concept of fixing up somebody's obvious trash for food preparation. It also ruffles me that I even have to allow cupboard space for this faulty appliance. But, the waffles were apparently tempting enough that Bart even had one with peanut butter. Nonetheless, all three boys (Bart, Dallas and Tim) ate heart-shaped waffles until the batter was gone.

I had a list of errands to complete today: laundry, pick up prescriptions, grocery shopping, bank, dry cleaning, UPS mail, several deliveries, prepare lunch, walk the dog, go to the gym (time permitting), and check to see if Dallas had completed his assigned tasks and if not, apply consequences - which would probably be the case.

Bart had chicken and stars soup followed by pudding. Even though it was a nice day, Bart was not feeling the love for the outdoors. It was way too cold for him. I understood. The hellacious San Francisco septic shock experience and extended antibiotic treatment took its toll. Bart had been through something none of us can fully comprehend and/or appreciate. He just accepted it and persevered, albeit weaker from the experience.

I was so grateful Bart was even awake, responsive and decisive. It was shaping up to be a good day considering. Bart said he was master of the remote controls and was quite calorically-satisfied, so he insisted on pushing me out the door.

All the while running errands I was thinking of my colleagues competing in the Pacific Five Star Taekwondo championships. I had twinges of wanting to be there competing myself but delighted to root for my black belt buddy, Lisa.

I couldn't wait to hear. We know patience and hands win fights. For us older broads, wisdom can beat a younger, faster opponent and Lisa proved it today. She won.

Bart uttered something about knowing all along she could do it, but it was so sweet to hear firsthand she had triumphed.

Bart had to have Joanne's pierogies even though they were still frozen. When Dallas heard the pierogies had arrived he absolutely agreed.

The pierogies were delicious and fun. When a food arrives from 3,000 miles away, prepared by your sister, it is special. Pierogies are labor intensive, then to freeze, pack and ship, is real love. We are certainly appreciative recipients.

Sandi called to report that Jasper (the family Beagle) might have had fleas when he visited our house. I was sentenced to a furious vacuuming session and extended laundry experience. Our dog seemed fine but I felt exasperated at any sign of scratching. Bart didn't seem concerned so I decided not to worry about it either.

I wrapped Bart's PICC arm with plastic wrap and tape so he could splash about freely or quietly soak in a soothing warm bath. His dry skin drank up soothing elements in the water. Feeling mildly better, he got appropriately outfitted with clean cozy jammies.

We settled into our chairs for a little Iron Chef before bed. The dryer let me know it was time to collect the linens. Bart finds his leather reclining "throne" comfortable enough for sleep. It's good to have a good fitting chair especially when the bed isn't made.

November 15

Like the harpist and visualization thing, Bart thought bath time needed some explanation. I was to assure his good buddies that he's not getting all bubbly and soft or anything. The "bath" idea came about because his left arm can't get wet. That's the one with the PICC line. Even with plastic wrap and tape, the shower seemed too dangerous. I was more than paranoid about infection so we thought it best to bathe with his wrapped arm on the side of the tub.

Bart slept better than I last night. I had waves of volcanic heat wash over me several times and didn't want Bart to freeze by turning up the fan. I got him an extra blanket and cracked the window a bit. These annoying fits of fire surely must fizzle out at some point but when?

The dog also woke me a time or two with "snorty" pig noises. In the beginning, we brought his bed to our room each night and he'd sleep on the floor. The problem was that I couldn't be sure he'd stay in his bed. I was afraid he'd skulk off quietly and leave me a surprise in the morning. I didn't know this dog well enough yet to trust him.

We did discover however, that our bed was high enough to make him very hesitant to jump off. I don't think those short little legs could tolerate the impact 25 pounds of girth would have hitting the floor from such a height. He could break a leg or two.

We decided to put him up on our bed at night. It's been working out really well too because no matter how long one of us stays in bed he stays there too. Aside from the funky little pig noises and occasional snoring, the little dog was quite content with these sleeping arrangements and so were we.

This morning Phaddy/Sparky was sacked out (sleeping in). I picked him up as usual to put him outside. Apparently the snort that woke me during the night wasn't connected to snoring at all.

He was horking up his dinner on my bed spread. He rolled over on it and his big belly was covering it up. Talk about a rude awakening, this was not the kind of thing I wanted to contend with first thing on a Monday morning. But at least I could wash the bedding….. again.

Off to Creekside Lounge for the first day of a new and hopefully improved chemo regimen. We met with the oncologist first. He determined that the full Gemzar/Xeloda dosage might be too hard on Bart in his fatigued state.

He ordered 20 percent reduction or "chemo light" until Bart was stronger. The doctor had hoped Bart would be more active, able to get out and about but since the trauma of San Francisco, Bart's been wiped out. As much as he tries to eat he continues to lose weight.

We reported that the antibiotic course was complete but we got a perplexing call about delivery of 20 more syringes. Miscommunications happen and we were able to intervene before delivery. The pharmacy insisted that the oncologist ordered the continued treatments but he knew nothing about it. Some wire got crossed when Bart was discharged in San Francisco. Perhaps the CPMC Outcomes Manager checked an extra box. That's why I now carry around this giant binder filled with all Bart's medical information, directives, prescription/medications lists, doctor notes, schedule, insurance papers, receipts and resources. You never know when you're going to need it. I've learned that you cannot expect doctors to have all the answers or all the necessary information at their fingertips.

We asked about getting home health hydration. Our nurse Jon said it was simple enough. The oncologist wasn't as keen on the concept. Instead he ordered Bart to come in daily for fluids and told us to step up the monitoring of Bart's diabetes. That could be making him more fatigued. He said our primary care doctor should adjust Bart's insulin accordingly. Frankly, it would be so much more convenient if we didn't have to go to a different doctor for every little thing. I worry that the right hand won't know what the left hand is doing. It just seems safer and more pragmatic for one caregiver to direct the whole show at this point.

It was a busy day in the "lounge". Bart had to wait quite a while for a chemo recliner. He eventually got his preferred chair in the corner. Five hours later we headed for home. We had Bart's weekly schedule, directions for taking the chemo drug Xeloda in pill form and a book of recipes for cancer patients.

I was anxious because Bart hadn't eaten all day. Yet all he could manage was a little noodle soup, apple sauce, and later a non-dairy protein shake. This new chemo regimen has more dietary restrictions and challenges.

When we got home, Bart requested I sit with him to watch a few of his favorite TV shows while Dallas did the chemo diary. When Bart dozed off I did the laundry transfers.

I felt a bit sad today. Bart and I had both hoped he would be strong enough to undergo the full shot at slamming this beastly disease. But we were glad to get started on this new regimen nonetheless.

I hate to see him so exhausted and weak. That's the worst. I want him to be strong enough to enjoy his life without pain and distress. We understand it may have to get worse sometimes before it gets better so we grip hope tightly and pray for a miracle.

Now excuse us, but we've got a television show to watch.

November 16

Bart was eager to get to the lounge. He had a fairly good night but did get up 4-5 times with some nausea but no vomiting. The usual morning cramps were present but Bart chose oatmeal sans raisins to help settle his system. Sandi took Bart to and from his appointment so I could get work done.

The little dog was with me on the driveway as they drove off. He suddenly saw a jogger and her yellow lab on the upper road (I don't think he likes blondes) and took off running in her direction on the lower road.

I yelled! Phaddy stopped but when I got to him I could tell he was sporting some tough attitude, a fight or flight sort of mode. I tried to scoot him back home but he stood fast like a mule. That's when I tried to pick him up and he bit me.

Well, I am not having any of that action! To be crystal clear, I am the alpha dog here. I pinned him down like a wrestler. He still tried to bite me again when I picked him up so I pinned him again then drug him home.

On the porch he was so sweet and sorry. The blondes were long gone. I just don't understand this dog sometimes. Maybe I need a canine shrink.

I went into the house, washed my sore hand then ate a whole pint of Ben & Jerry's Cherry Garcia ice cream to make myself feel better, 960 calories in one sitting.

I think a confluence of sadness occurred when I was alone with the ice cream. The dog bit me, puked on my good bedspread and our oncologist had to use the words "there is no cure" out loud on Monday. He seemed to want to remind us that our goal is to slow down the cancer but not eliminate it. Maybe he was telling us not to put all our eggs in this chemotherapy basket.

But we feel very much in the fight and very hopeful. Bart doesn't even entertain any alternative. Miracles happen every day. I had much to do before Bart got home and getting my head together was on the list.

I felt scattered all day but did get to the market with my little Betty Crocker cancer cookbook. Bart marked all the recipes that sounded good. It was comforting to have a meal plan and all the ingredients at the ready. Bart wanted shepherd's pie again. I was happy to oblige but hit myself in the head with the pan as I was pulling it down from the hanging rack, awkward. Cooking was never my strong suit. I'm getting better I think.

Bart ate well and snacked today. He even had a second helping of shepherd's pie. He complained of heartburn and mild nausea but corrective meds finally kicked in after dinner. He then took his chemo pills.

What a blessing when friends came to call on Phaddy dog. Dallas had a lot of homework and drum practice so he successfully avoided the task of walking Phaddy.

Bart's checking email and reports feeling better. He even walked from kitchen to table to throne. He's much more active than the last chemo adventure.

Bart says he feels fine right now. Fine could be a relative term, but he looks good and is wide-awake dabbling on his computer. At one point, he asked me to retrieve some power cords and connectors, which was quite the task for someone as technically challenged as I am. It was difficult for Bart not to be annoyed by my lack of rudimentary knowledge. Part of his frustration was because he just did not feel up to going down the stairs. I must have made five trips up and down to find the right power cords to fit the job.

I often ask Bart what he's thinking about. Makes me chuckle because he usually says "nothing". He tells me that when a guy says "nothing is on his mind", he really means it. There are no deep thoughts like Jack Handy going on there. Nothing means nothing. I have learned to accept that over the years.

I'm thinking nothing is probably good. Everything (like a miracle) could come from nothing so anything is possible. We believe prayer is all powerful and we have powerful numbers praying for us.

November 17

A Note from Bart:

Well all after 1/2 week on the new chemo I give it two big thumbs up. So far the nausea is mild, no vomiting and I feel pretty good most of the day (not tired all the time). I attribute some to the daily hydration (1000 cc's of saline) and some to the new cocktail. I'm also trying to keep my blood sugar stable.

I'll keep you up to date if anything changes. My appetite is getting better but my taste buds are still not back.

All in all I was able to traverse the stairs two times today. Feel a little stronger each day. Not sure if I'm gaining weight but I'm trying to stop losing.

Today was a crap weekend sports-wise, all my favorite teams lost. Next week will be better. You guys keep writing your witty comments online I love reading them. Maybe that is what's keeping me going, that and God. Right now I am open to any and all avenues for help.

Bart

November 19

Bart feels good today by comparison. Sometimes he's bloated and mildly short-tempered but it's definitely an improvement over how he felt weeks ago. He ordered pancakes for breakfast. It's one of my specialties. I made pancakes for all the kids whenever friends slept over. I sometimes added secret treasures to the pancakes and the kids would win prizes or extra helpings if they discovered miner's gold or some other treasure in a hot cake. It was fun. I didn't bury anything obscure in Bart's breakfast. He's not in any mood for surprises.

If I may digress a moment and provide background on yesterday's happenings:

I drove home from work and passed a tree removal service van on the road above our house. They were cutting down some extremely large Digger pine trees in the county-owned median. Those huge trees shaded our home and provided a cozy woodsy ambiance for the lower street. They did however block views for some homes on the upper side.

To my shock and dismay, eight giant Digger Pine trees went down. Bart agreed that it was a travesty to lose so many grand trees. I called the removal service and the county to no avail. What's done is done.

The whole neighborhood has changed now. It is stark, bare and different. Four or five gray squirrels ran around aimlessly, back & forth across the road wondering what hit them, looking for new homes.

I felt very upset. The neighbor who employed the tree service came to my door and apologized. He said the county didn't care what he did in the median as long as he paid for it. The price tag was close to $3000 for the multiple large tree removal. They thought it was well worth it to restore their panoramic view.

I was sad to see such majestic trees annihilated, and I was sympathetic to the poor homeless squirrels. No doubt feeling my sympathy for his plight, one of the squirrels decided to squat at our house, taking up residence in our eaves.

To the squirrel it may have been a good place to nest, but it was a bad place if I was to maintain sympathy for small rodents.

I soon noticed that all our American flags were missing from the porch. I thought maybe Dallas took them for some crazy thing. Then I was hearing things. I ran outside and caught that little gray bugger dropping acorns down a vent pipe on our roof. I grabbed a ladder and climbed up there. I discovered all my little American flags! They were part of his mass nesting material. He had also chewed a large crescent hole into the fascia board under the gutter. This is war.

Bart told me to put chicken wire over the hole to block the squirrel as pest control experts had advised. Where am I going to get a tiny piece of chicken wire anyway, and do I really want a skid-row-chicken-farm-thing going on in front of our home?

No worries because we had a new secret weapon, Phaddy the sparkplug dog. He would certainly earn his keep. For the first time in 5 years we had a dog, an instinctive protector.

The squirrel would get scared and move. I was sure of it.

While Phaddy dog was serving a time-out on the porch for having run away from me yesterday, I was working in the kitchen and a gray squirrel caught my eye through the window. That brazen squirrel was in close proximity to Phaddy dog. WT??? I watched in disbelief. Surely he would go crazy with this squirrel's encroachment in his territory no matter the hour.

That rodent was boldly sitting up on the driveway right in front of this dog! "Squirrel jerk" was just taunting Phaddy. He even had a nut in his paws, nibbling away with arrogance. Our tubby canine still slept! I was frustrated. I've squirted this damn squirrel with the hose, destroyed his nest, and done everything short of smoking him out.

I thought Phaddy dog would certainly work for us. He could intimidate the creature somehow, bark, chase, growl, bite whatever.

At least he could scare it away.

What happened next just sent me flying. That friggin' squirrel was getting aggressive. He charged the poor dog. I bolted out there yelling and running for the hose. How discouraging to think you have to protect your own watchdog from a stupid squirrel.

I had better things to do.

It was shaping up to be an insanely busy day. Why so hectic is the phenomenon of being human I suppose? Or was it just me?

A friend thankfully drove Bart to his appointment. I worked from home then embarked on a huge errand list. Little did I know that simple things would take three times as long?

I even split the list of tasks with my sister. I collected Bart from Creekside Lounge and delivered him to his throne, then took off to complete the errand list for the day.

Bart sent me a text questioning my order of priorities. He was right in doing so. I do the tasks but not always in any particular order; I just work the list. He's trying so hard to train me. I wish my brain worked like his, I really do, but it doesn't.

Sugar Be Damned

There's a lot to learn about diabetes and the related accessories you have to acquire knowledge of and how to use. Again, I could use the phrase, "school of hard knocks". I successfully ordered and received the insulin prescription and assumed the injection needles would be provided, but no. I needed a script for those too and wow are they expensive.

I called the doctor and he said he faxed it a month ago as I had requested, but when I called about the order, the mail order pharmacy had never heard of it. I was feeling frustrated. I called the doctor again. They verified that the fax went through and said it wasn't their fault if the mail pharmacy didn't get it. Okay, but how does that help me now? I was beginning to fume at this point. Don't care who's to blame; just get me the needles please, now.

Bart told me today he also needed a refill of the strips and pins used to draw blood and check his sugar levels. I had a coupon for those so I assumed I could buy them over the counter. No. No one told me you had to have a prescription for that stuff too. But I had a coupon! Naturally, when we called the doctor's office they were closed until Monday. As Rosanne-Rosanna-Danna would say "if it's not one thing, it's another." Never mind.

November 19

I'm loving this new chemo regimen. Bart says he's not loving it for obvious reasons, but from my point of view it's definitely better than the last one. He's not puking and is often up and about. Perhaps the daily sojourns to the Creekside Lounge have supplemented Bart's systemic ability to process the drugs and maintain a semi-normal routine. Whatever, it's infinitely better.

A friend came to transport Bart to Creekside. They barely got out the driveway and I was getting texts from Bart. "The squirrel is on the roof. Get the BB gun." I ran out there but the squirrel was gone. I did see that the blasted rodent had badly chewed the chimney pipe. My burning hatred for this creature was cresting. Online there are friends who post possible solutions. Clearly we need a moat.

Bart's latest weigh in at Creekside was 146 pounds. This chemo diet is out of control. I told Bart if he dares to approach weighing less than me we're going to fight. We have always joked about his skinny wrists and ankles that are no match for the big boned Polka genes of my ancestry. Dallas gets teased for having tree trunk legs. He looks just like Bart except for the giant appendages. Blame the Polkas for that.

On our drive home from Creekside Monday, Bart and I had a brief discussion about calorie consumption. I had to laugh when Bart said "when we get home I'll take one of those Glucerna diabetic drinks then you can make me one of your f@!&*ing fruity smoothies."

I took it as a compliment because it was tacitly implied that he would drink it if I made it.

November 20

Our friend Jeanne arrived today. Despite the rain, wind and cold it was a wonderful, happy day here in California. Bart must have been feeling pretty good because he was up early politely demanding blueberry donuts so I got up (before I was ready and still in my jammies) and drove off to the bakery.

When I returned, Jeanne was up and already cleaning the kitchen. How exciting.

Bart was alert and eagerly awaiting the heavenly donut. What a delightful taste experience, the donut. Can you make a glazed donut without the glaze? It would still be an exquisite delight for diabetics without all that sugar. Bart ate both blueberry and glazed. We also tried a new one, the splendid French twist. There was some discussion about buttermilk, old fashioned, maple bars, cake, fritters and sugar donuts. We were all struck by how much fun donut knowledge is to exchange and enjoy.

I cooked some fun recipes from the cancer cookbook, turkey chili, minestrone soup, then tonight Bart wanted spaghetti and meatballs. He's lost his affinity for garlic and spices unfortunately but he ate pretty well starting with the donut breakfast, chicken Kiev lunch and spaghetti for dinner.

On today's schedule is the ultimate chemo haircut. It went beautifully, Jeanne doing the barbering, me doing the photo documentation, hot towel application and scalp massage. Bart said he enjoyed it. (that's miraculous in and of itself) Who wouldn't enjoy two women pawing over you? It was actually quite fun for all three of us.

Though it was a good day for Bart, it wasn't so good as far as his sugar levels. His sugar counts were higher than they ever have been. His pancreas is not functional because of the cancer. We are trying to treat the malfunctions with traditional means adjusting the units of insulin. It's a challenge to figure out how much insulin to inject and when. His levels seem to increase as the evening progresses even though he takes his insulin injections daily on time.

It's been frustrating to coordinate between our primary care physician and our oncologist. We would really like to see one lead physician take control. Too many doctors calling the shots is confusing and *not* ideal for best patient care. Friday we asked if Bart's diabetes monitoring could be taken up by Creekside. Multiple visits to different doctors create a strain on Bart, delays treatment, and is extremely inconvenient, not to mention more expensive.

Bart had a wonderful day today according to my standards. Bart was so talkative and interested in conversation. It's helpful to have someone new to converse with. I experienced several moments of joy when Bart seemed like himself again. It was heartwarming and fulfilling.

Phaddy behaved himself too, staying close to Bart as the wind howled outside. He got to walk in the rain today. His little legs are so close to the ground though that he was completely soaked by the time we got home. At least he's had no accidents in the house now for a couple weeks. Success. But just in case I leave the duck fencing up so that he can't sneak off to a remote part of the house to leave a deposit.

We had to deliver Dallas to and from a friend's house among other things. It was a busy yet productive today. Bart did report that he had a really good day. His smooth chrome dome is part of it. He enjoyed the process and even better, his ball caps still fit well despite the loss of hair.

We're expecting inclement weather tonight so we should all sleep well. It's great to have the comforts of a family home, cozy bed, and good company when the winds and rain are beating at the windows.

Dallas informed us tonight that the girl he liked so much chose a different boyfriend. He said he was mildly bummed and didn't want to talk about it other than to say he knew he must have been too cool for her. Dallas seemed a lot happier than he was with the first breakup. Experience must have been a good teacher.

Dallas also told us how excited he was about a story he was composing for creative writing. This was a tremendous thrill for us to hear how much he was looking forward to this project.

Chapter Seven

Boys, Ball Cap and the Art of Insulin

November 21

I think Bart hopes his hair grows fast so he can have a repeat performance of the spa treatment. Despite the chrome dome, Bart still prefers to sport his ball caps even though Dallas did offer his stocking cap with the dingle balls. Bart was not amused.

Bart requested pancakes and eggs sunny side up this morning. I was unclear as to whether or not I had to ease the egg over with the spatula or just cover the egg with the pan lid and a few drops of water to steam it like my mom did. I nervously broke one egg trying these techniques before Jeanne told me it works best with room temperature eggs and low heat. Eggs-cellent! Bart got one steamed and one sunny side. He ate them both on a short stack of hotcakes. I learn something new each day.

High hopes that today would be another good one, although Bart was severely fatigued. His only activity besides watching football was walking from the throne to the bathroom and back again. Bart slept most of the day but he did eat well: chicken and stars soup, grapes and cookies. I thought he'd have more energy in the afternoon but he was just too tired to consider walking anywhere other than the bathroom.

Jeanne and I made good use of the day by organizing contents of the kitchen cabinets. Cooking and cleaning operations might be more efficient now. We woke Bart for dinner. The nap certainly didn't hurt his appetite. He ate every bit. It's funny how we revert to treating adults like toddlers when they're sick. I resisted the urge to praise him for cleaning his plate. When my sister, mom, and relatives arrived everybody chimed in with a few clean plate compliments of their own. Bart is good at ignoring us and our juvenile humor. He's too busy using every fiber of his being to keep this cancer at bay.

When family members left, we urged Bart to call up the movie menu and he was pleased to do so after a day of football. We three (Jeanne, Bart and I) cozied up in our respective places and Bart warned us that he'd likely be visualizing the inside of his eyelids soon. He did not disappoint. Shortly after the film began he was snoozing. The throne is ultra-comfortable.

I woke him for his evening dose of chemo, pain and nausea pills. We checked his sugar level as well and it was high...236. My concern is that Bart sticks to exactly what the former instructions were before his levels went haywire. I assumed Bart would do as the San Francisco nurses did, adjusting units as you go along. It was some guesswork, some trial and error. We took bets at CPMC as to what Bart's number would be at any given time. That's why I remember the process so well. Losers were supposed to buy coffee. The complimentary courtesy cart coffee was a loser's bargain bonus.

The point is that Bart won't consider altering even one unit of insulin until he checks in with the oncologist. I respect that, but at the same time we had 9 days of training on this subject in San Francisco and it worked. This could be why Bart was lethargic today. I absolutely needed him to be a bit more flexible in order to manage this situation and fast. He wasn't listening to me.

Bart was so weak and dizzy that I called the doctor. I explained the situation and then he asked me what I wanted to do. What I wanted to do? Really? Why did he think I was calling him? What a loaded question. Bart was having symptoms under the list labeled: call your doctor immediately. I wanted that doctor to help me assess whether or not I needed to take Bart to the ER tonight. Ultimately, it was Bart who helped me decide what to do, not the doctor.

Bart said calmly that he always crashes two days after his last course of IV fluids. He was drinking and snacking with no fever so we'd ride it out tonight. Bart sucked back 24 ounces of electrolyte drink in about 15 minutes and I had already filled that bottle 4 times, yet we still worried about dehydration. It's odd that one can drink so much all day long and remain dehydrated? Having your pancreas jacked up really throws off the whole bodily system.

We walked a somewhat disoriented Bart to bed around 11:30 PM. It was a slow trek. It was cold so I slipped a stocking cap over his smooth head and he was asleep 30 seconds after his head hit the pillow. I hope I can do the same.

November 22

It's Monday. Bart is scheduled for the next Gemzar chemo treatment at Creekside Lounge. The plan for this regimen is Gemzar every Monday for three weeks and Xeloda oral dosages in pill form twice daily for the three week cycle.

Our friend and escort du jour arrived to transport Bart to Creekside Lounge. I worked from home. Dallas awoke with a dry cough so it was off to the market for cough syrup and other essentials.

Clean Jeanne departed at noon. Parting is such sweet sorrow. Afterwards, I presented Dallas with his list of chores. Naturally, the pooper scooper duty was the one he protested the most. I generously offered to be the bag holder which was ever so mildly entertaining. I showed him how to do it and provided lots of plastic bags yet he still feigned bouts of dramatic heaving, but did the job and not a poop was left un-scooped.

Although I did carry the bag to the trash can for him, as Dallas insisted that he could not wait to wash his hands ASAP. He has such flair.

I made it to an overdue appointment to color the gray away. The salon transformation is a boost to the psyche.

All the while I was trying to reach Bart. What did the tests show and how was the chemo going? Bart's not one to call, but I wasn't getting any texts from him either.

After the new "do", mail pick up, pharmacy, bank and then home.

Bart was back and mildly hungry. I quickly prepared his food, did several loads of laundry, walked the dog, returned messages and filed the latest medical receipts and bills in the binder. Only after all that did I get the update from Bart.

He said the oncologist decreed all chemo treatments would be suspended until Bart gets stronger. He got an extended course of fluids instead of chemotherapy, same tomorrow.

It will give us time to figure out how to manage the insulin. Bart ate well but the sugar check was unacceptable, 327. It's supposed to be less than 100. He needs more insulin.

Based on Bart's numbers, we have an appointment tomorrow after the lounge to see our primary care doctor for more specific instructions on how to administer subcutaneous insulin.

Bart's doing better as the evening wears on. We are even attempting to watch a DVD. So far, he's awake, checking email and snacking on pretzels and grapes. Another sugar check was still too high. We hope to learn how and when to administer the proper doses of insulin to level him out better than this.

We made it through a whole movie and Bart's still awake. All in all a pretty good day despite the bad sugar scores, but we aim high I guess.

November 24

"If it's Tuesday it must be Belgium" or in our case, Creekside Lounge. I suppose most people younger than Bart and I wouldn't remember that movie.

Bart didn't seem to have nearly as much discomfort as usual. It was a cold day.

Bart wanted to leave early. He also said he was up for one of my protein smoothies. Still he ate cereal with banana while waiting for me to prepare the special blender concoction. While Bart got his "lounge stuff" together I put the Cuisinart through its paces. Presented him with the cold cup, but Bart said "No, it's too cold, can't drink it right now". No problem, the smoothie became freezer cubes to live again another day in the whir of the blender. Bart sat by the fire.

I put the dog out, made coffee, gathered the "sweet sheets" (Excel sugar level charts), the medical binder, my phone and list. Then I got dressed and took Phaddy dog to the boys downstairs.

Bart announced with clear irritation that it was already too late to leave early. Just so things feel normal around here I responded with my own "tone" that communicated similar annoyance at feeling hounded. I was hurrying to get everything together. Bart was already in the car and questioning whether I ever prioritized any of my actions.

As we backed out of the driveway he told me I was not a very pleasant morning person in so many words. I knew I should bite my tongue and I also knew he was probably right, but no, I just had to talk back because I was so mad at myself for forgetting the binder! It was surely because I was rushed.

We were both tweaked for a time yet this exchange was somehow comfortably normal.

Bart is of the military mentality (with which I agree but just cannot consistently comply) if you're not 15 minutes early then you're late. It's just that he's so rigid about it to the point of ridiculous (in my opinion). Perhaps this is why I unconsciously push the envelope in many instances, although that behavior sounds so premeditatedly passive-aggressive that I am humiliated to even acknowledge it.

Bart has always been the guy who declares family departure times.

"We are leaving by 9 AM" he would announce. I would remind him that it's a self-imposed deadline and we should not be so rigid as to get in a huge unnecessary family fight over failure to drive away at the bewitching hour. There was no steadfast reason why we had to undergo such stress to meet a deadline that he arbitrarily chose!

I thought my rationale was somewhat pragmatic on this point. Mom and Dad never cared whether we arrived at 1PM or 4 PM or even 8 PM for that matter. That argument, albeit reasonable to me, was not going over well. We were never going to agree on this issue. Bart could see that what I was doing in the moments prior to takeoff was not related to getting us on the road.

My thought processes were different. I didn't want any of my plants to die and upon returning home didn't want to see old dirty dishes in the sink representing chores I wouldn't want to do.

In retrospect, perhaps deadline pressures were nothing more than our clashing ideologies and Bart trying to deal with my ADD.

After dropping Bart at Creekside, I returned calls, picked up Dallas' prescription from his doctor, went home and made waffles (yes, the awful heart-shaped device Dallas scored on the street) for Dallas and his friends. Then there was laundry, lunch and work to catch up on.

I picked up Bart for a late afternoon appointment with our primary care doctor to discuss insulin options.

Here's the plan we came up with: Bart will still inject 6 units of Lantus (long acting insulin) as before, once a day. Beyond that, we must pre-calculate just how many carbs Bart will ingest in a meal and determine the units (of a different insulin) to inject before that meal.

Figure a half unit of this fast-acting insulin Homolog per 10 grams of carbohydrates. The aim is to keep Bart hovering around 150. His levels have been in excess of 300. That alone can make him feel mighty crappy.

November 25

It's Wednesday morning and Jon the home health nurse would be here any minute. Bart wasn't good, he had bloating in his stomach yet he didn't complain, just reported.

Jon arrived and drew blood but didn't have necessary supplies to change the PICC dressing so he indicated he would have to come back later. When we told him that Bart would be at Creekside Lounge Jon inquired, "what kind of joint is that"? We told him it's where cancer patients are served their cocktails in a lounge chair and Jon seemed relieved that Bart wasn't spending his afternoon at some smoke-filled honky-tonk.

Jon left and we began the routine scramble to get ready to go. We would be dropping Dallas off at his friend's house so Bart wanted to leave early.

I put my phone on the medical binder so I wouldn't forget it this time. As I was putting on my shoes, Bart told me to warm up the car first. He was freezing. Did that, then herded Dallas. For some reason, the moments prior to our family going anywhere always becomes chaotic. The boys were singing happily, but also dropping shoes and items of clothing en route to the car. I suggested a grocery bag for clothes, but no, they just threw them in the back seat. What's with that? Bart is hollering "hurry up" and showing signs of frustration while Phaddy dog waits to be put outside.

We dropped the boys off and saw that no one ever closed the trunk!

On the freeway, I asked Bart what he was thinking about and he said that he was thinking about how he had forgotten his lounge snacks. At that moment, I realized that I too had forgotten stuff, my phone and the medical binder.... again.

Bart walked weakly to the Creekside elevator and it struck me just how very strong he truly is. No matter what he faces each day he takes it as it comes. He's not happy about it, but he's determined not to give up and does whatever it takes.

October 2nd was the last time I got Bart to go grocery shopping. This time, he assumed the driver's seat of the bumper car. He raced off, testing the brakes right away almost running into a lady rounding the corner in the produce section. I smiled, thinking "here we go again."

While I was at the pharmacy counter getting instructions on the new insulin, Bart was off and away. I caught up with him at the conclusion of his shopping adventure. He assured me that he had not cut corners and left the end aisle displays still standing. He insisted on driving the cart to the car. I briefly recalled his high-centering the thing on a speed bump last time but he expertly avoided such obstacles today.

Next stop, UPS store for mail. Bart said he was expecting two bookmarks so I should check the box carefully. Let me explain. Checking UPS mail was never something I did before. Bart and Dallas took care of it.

Last year, we were all together in the car so Bart sent me in to get the mail. On the way home, he asked what was in the mail. I told him it had a magazine, junk and a nice laminated bookmark! Bart and Dallas looked at each other and smirked and Dallas said, "Mom, that's a notice you have a package, not a *bookmark*." From then on, we've called them bookmarks.

Indeed, two bookmarks and two big packages. As I carried them out we ran into our friend Viola and her youngest son from Sogno Winery. It's like a little drive-by surprise when you encounter friends on the street.

It's an exciting night because both Matthew and Megan arrive. It's going to be a good Thanksgiving.

November 27

A Note from Bart:

I am posting tonight because, even though there is nothing to report, Mel is insistent. So here it goes: there is nothing new to report. I feel fairly good and spent the day getting my blood sugar stabilized.

I think part of my earlier woes had to do with sugar levels out of whack. With daughter Megan, and my doctors, we are fixing insulin doses to hopefully control my up and down moods. If I'm in a good mood I might tell you about it.

Bart

November 28

The other night (late last week) Bart told me it would be very cold and likely end up being the first freeze.

That was like an electric alert. Last year I didn't pay enough attention to the weather and failed to protect our lemon tree from the big freeze. I lost dozens of beautiful Meyer lemons.

I was NOT going to lose my whole crop again this year so I flew out of my chair searching for sheets. I found a twin fitted flannel sheet I was willing to sacrifice, donned my hooded sweatshirt, and ventured out the back door, down the stairs, across the lawn to my beloved tree/bush. Dang! That brute had really grown this year. It was a whole lot bigger than I thought it was.

My twin fitted sheet was a mere handkerchief. It would cover maybe two branches at most. I had done such a hack job last season trimming off all the branches, which were heavy with rotten fruit, that new growth was shooting out limbs in all odd directions.

It was really dark out that night, we had no lighting in this area of the back yard and it was really cold too.

It was tough to maneuver the sheet over the almost ripe lemons. It kept popping off, so I had to manage my way through the carpet roses in order to pull it around to another location. The small barbs of the spreading carpet roses were bad enough, but lemon trees have these long needle-like spikes that easily draw blood if you're not careful.

That stupid sheet was futile.

I decided I had to try one last time, but as I attempted a graceful jump over the sprawling rose bush my sweat pants got stuck on a spiky lemon branch. It nearly pulled my sweats clean off. I slid on the river rock and went down. It made me laugh at myself, lying there on the cold rocky ground. The sheet was just hanging there and I was trying to gather up my pants.

Mother Nature and I were going to fight tonight.

I came in the back door and Bart just looked at me with the "what the hell have you been doing out there" look.

I told him that the job was a lot harder than I realized and I needed more supplies.

I donned heavier gloves, bungee cords, more sheets and two tarps. Bart just shook his head as I went back out the door.

I couldn't get those bungees to grab hold and got slapped in the face by a flinging branch.

I moved carefully around mother lemon because as I may have mentioned, our home is on a slope. It gets pretty steep on the west side too. Sure enough, I began to slide in the wet mud, slowly at first. I grabbed a branch, felt the stab of those spikes right through my gloves, the branch running through my hands as I went sliding quickly all the way down the hill on my stomach.

This time as I came through the door, Bart looked at me and asked "what the hell happened to you?" I was freezing. There were leaves in my hair, I was covered in mud, and looked a bit battered and beaten.

As much as it hurt I had to laugh at myself. "Lucy, you've got some 'splaining to do"!

I knew if Bart felt better he would be laughing out loud himself.

I told him I needed more bungee cords and he told me I was crazy.

I ended up using nearly every bungee cord we owned and finally got the tarp to stay put, which covered only about a third of the tree, so I just left the sheets to fend for themselves.

The next morning in the frosty light of day I went out to examine my work. Our neighbors must think a camp of homeless derelicts have squatted around our citrus tree.

We had a fun and filling Thanksgiving with the three amigos (siblings Matt, Meg & Dal) together again. These three can make even the simplest of things a game. For instance, since the kids have been here, Bart's sugar check rituals have been quite the team sport. We act like Bart's Boosters or a bunch of high school cheerleaders if the news is "sweet", pardon the pun, so whenever Bart checks his sugar and it's in the A range, (under 200) we all raucously cheer and hoot as though the Steelers scored a winning touchdown.

It occurred to me during all the hoopla that this outburst of approval was exactly the same kind of cheering that Bart and I did when the kids were potty training. Oooh, good job, you went in the toilet.

We are finally getting the hang of the "art of insulin".

The twins went home. I drove Dallas to school at 6:30 AM and Bart to Folsom. Bart waited patiently for an hour and a half to get a recliner at the very popular Creekside Lounge.

Although we prepared for a new round of chemotherapy, Bart said the nurses told him not today, only hydration and anti-nausea meds. There was no reason given, just a change in the schedule.

It was a pleasure to see a clean kitchen when I got home. And the boys (Bart and Dallas) had prepared dinner. They heated up some leftover turkey, smashed some potatoes and opened a can of vegetables. Joy.

Dallas did his duty. He harassed Bart until they logged figures into the nightly chemo diary, which was entertaining. Bart with his sharp answers laced with annoyance and Dallas assuming the parental role scolding his dad playfully for giving him "attitude".

Bart feels okay tonight. We realized it was a huge mistake not to bring insulin with him to Creekside. He was there all day and did not get insulin until 4 PM, too late to catch up. The reading was 346, way too high. That makes him feel crummy. 120 would be a perfect score. For Bart, staying under 200 is good and hovering around 150 is superb. Bart feels good enough to cancel Creekside for the rest of the week.

Dallas was unusually talkative with us tonight. When it rains it pours. Apparently the young lady that dumped him two weeks ago thinks she made a huge mistake.

Dallas said he'd already moved on but the call was a cause for confusion. The girl next door (actually about five houses down the street) is the current object of his affections but he said the phone call reminded him why he liked the other girl so much.

I could see he was tormented. I listened mostly and thankfully Dad didn't comment either. It's uncommon for Dallas to even discuss these matters so we didn't want to interrupt. It was touching when he hugged Dad and said "I love you, Dad, and forgive you for yelling at me during chemo diary even though you have an excuse."

In return, Dad apologized for his tone.

Bart announced "Bedtime for Bonzos". It's one of his favorite sayings; and for you young-uns, it is Ronald Reagan's famous monkey movie. (Rent it, it's likely really cheap).

Chapter Eight

Life is Good

December 1

We got home from work about 6, picked up prescriptions, Chinese food and UPS mail. Bart did fairly well today with insulin staying under 200 and this evening another good score, 178. But Bart has been uncomfortable for three days and warned me that we might have to call the doctor if he didn't get relief tonight.

Some fellas came by to purchase the twins' old skis, boots and poles I had posted for sale. The buyers saved me a trip to the ATM.

I drove off to the store. A last-ditch effort to find over the counter relief for Bart's intestinal pain. He had taken all four of the recommended remedies so you know it's got to be painful when one requests the "Fleet". Nobody volunteers for that.

Meanwhile Dallas informed me he decided which girl to ask out. It's not the girl next door, but the one who lives far away. He said he talked to "neighbor girl" about it and said he would know tomorrow how she handled the news. Dal said one factor was that neighbor girl's parents were not enamored with the Dal man. Dallas thought that it would be tough going if her parents weren't taken with his charm.

I found this quite interesting and maybe reassuring. I wasn't quite sure yet. Over the holiday weekend, brother Matty facilitated Dallas' move to his former upstairs bedroom. He had moved downstairs a while ago sleeping on the couch down there.

Bart and I thought it was too removed. It's ridiculous to have to call your son on his cell phone to come up for dinner. Dallas could shut himself off more or less and that wasn't working for us. Bart and I would have had to force the move yet amazingly Matty was able to get it done quickly.

We think it had everything to do with the fact that Dallas was motivated by the prospect of using Matt's HDTV for his video games.

Matty bought the $450 TV for $200 by sacrificing a big chunk of sleep. Black Friday was quite the shopping excursion for the kids. We programmed the new grind and brew coffee maker for 2:45 AM. Matty, Megan and Dallas then waited in line at stores to get extra special sale items. I think the kids finished all their Christmas shopping by 8:45 AM.

We're awaiting news of progress outside Bart's bathroom door. He emerged to relay tempered success. That was the good news.

The bad news was that I would need to employ the plunger. Bart said he hated to ask me and if he were strong enough he would have done it himself. I fashion myself somewhat of a plumbing apprentice now after employing channel lock pliers to the under sink elbow in order to clear clogged sinks. Bart was much relieved later on so I sat with him while he watched a TV show, Fringe which I can't follow. I tune out when I hear "parallel universe" in any title.

Based on the evening relief Bart enjoyed (post Fleet) I'd say it was a pretty good day.

A Note from Bart:

Hi all, Happy December. My day has been good. Normal BM's, not too tired and ate well. Blood sugars under control. We are changing medicine so I don't need to take four shots a day, only two. I have to make sure my blood sugar levels stay normal all day.

Being sick is friggin' boring. I sit around working on my laptop most of the day praying for an email that gives me something to do. But hey, it beats the alternative. I'm hanging in there. Send me emails, I'll try and answer them (probably more than you want). I've seen most of the movies on TV and Netflix. Need some new material. Maybe I'll join Blockbuster.

For you guys who keep writing on the "bridge" I love reading it. I start chemo again next week. Will let you all know how that goes down.

Love y'all, Bart

I have not been out to the tree since my late night lemon fiasco. After that bosky undertaking, I have not gotten home early enough to take a look before dark. Maybe I'm a little afraid to see the results. What if I failed to protect the object of my labor? Whatever the case, it has certainly been a valiant effort.

This evening Bart ventured downstairs and returned with a scolding, "Who's the genius who thought it was a good idea to put my company check paper in the copier?" Obviously that was I. It was late, dark, and I had little patience to find a single ream of paper in Bart's vast expanse of littered desktop confusion. Besides, I needed to print something fast. Bart had a few sententious words, shaking his head, mumbling "unbelievable" over and over, but then he added. "You must hate it when I feel better". Bart felt good enough to voice his usual sarcasm with "attitude". I did appreciate seeing the old feisty Bart show up.

It was a really good day. I went to work, then transported Dallas to his drum and piano lessons.

Dallas had a lot of homework to catch up on so I took "Phaddeus Thayer Sparky Reagan" for a nice long walk.

What a blessing that Bart requested a simple hot dog, beans and leftover Chinese for dinner for it required but one skilled microwave operator (me). As I set to preparing this epicurean delight, Bart and I discussed having Dallas cook one meal a week. Dallas agreed so we shall see if he makes a culinary debut at all.

As for the unwelcome squirrel varmint, he's still up there but disappears for long periods of time. I chose to believe he had moved on, but no such luck. He's gotten really cagey. Whenever I hear his squirrelly noises I run outside but he always finds a way to escape unscathed. And to think I was so sympathetic to the plight of homeless squirrels until that one decided we had a vacancy in our home. Habitat for Rodents we are not.

It's been a wonderful day for me because Bart has been talkative, alert, sometimes even annoyed. He laughed a few times tonight. It's been lovely for me and a bit calming too.

Bart submitted his chart of sugar readings, and the doctor indicated the current insulin injections needed replacing with a new and different insulin that is both medium- and short-term acting.

Right now Bart is combining short-term and long-term insulin so it's four or more injections a day which is certainly not optimum. The doctor wants Bart to switch to moderately fast-acting insulin with some long-term elements so he will only have to do two injections daily. We'll try anything.

Holy mother? I just got a notice that there's a new journal posting on CB? Bart is winking at me, smirking really. I think he knew I was writing too. I believe the word is Schadenfreude. Look it up, although I'm not positive that's how to spell it.

Bart went to bed. He turned and gave me that "gotcha" gaze.

I think I will need to find the Neosporin before bedtime as I have paper cuts on my lips and fingers due to such a large volume of bills from our soiree in San Francisco.

It might be worthy to note that it's $1,600 for an ambulance to transport a patient five blocks in San Francisco. Don't let that happen to you.

December 3

I hope everyone was able to enjoy the pictures posted of our lemon tree homeless camp. It rained today. I was bummed that a perfectly good moving box got soaked in servitude to the almighty lemon.

You probably weren't able to discern my dad's old tee shirts in the photos. I used several and they fit well over some of the bigger citrus bunches. And to think, one or two in my family chastised me for taking those. Dad would be proud that his tees were integral in crop rescue.

Our friend and neighbor came over with his gutter-clearing tools.

I've tried to unfold our new-fangled ladder for about a year now yet Scott was able to decipher cryptic instructions and reconfigure in minutes, giving him a platform to forge through gutter gunk.

It's a glorious afternoon. Bart must have been inspired by clean gutters, he was ready to walk his dog. We walked all the way up to Scott & Heidi's and back again. Bart wanted to finish the loop but since it was the first outing in more than a month, I vetoed the idea.

A man and his dog: it was moving, fun and uplifting such a simple thing. He was mildly winded afterward but movement is worth it.

Life is good. It's a wonderful day for Bart so it was a superb day for me. Plus our gutters are ready for rain.

December 4

Bart got up about 7 AM and so did the dog. But when Bart wasn't forthcoming with the little guy's breakfast, Phaddy went back to bed and waited for me.

I prepared biscuits and gravy for Dallas and Bart. We were looking forward to seeing friends this day. Upon their arrival I was folding up the homeless camp surrounding my pregnant lemon tree and they assisted.

I had a list of about a dozen simple things to do. Nothing too taxing, change bedding, buying wrapping paper, put up Christmas decorations, gym, store and stuff like that.

One task got done. Even enlisting Bart and Dallas' help I checked off only one task. I like completing task lists but not today. #1 the tree was up, decorated and blinking away. Tomorrow we hope to take on item #2, outdoor lights.

The day was low key and relaxing. I always have a great day when Bart feels good. No walking adventure but Bart did plenty of surfing on his computer. He had pain and cramps but by comparison to some days, this was a good one. Bart went off to bed while Phaddy dog snored like a pig. I'm sweating like one, damn hot flashes.

If I weren't so invested in this stupid two star Ninja Assassin movie I'd already be in bed too. I must watch this lone ninja take out a clan of killers first.

Good night warriors.

December 5

Sunday is a day of rest, much like Saturday. I would characterize Bart as mild today. Not quite as good as yesterday. He said his side still hurts and he felt queasy after breakfast. Who would have thought that anti-nausea drugs would be a maintenance medication?

The new insulin regimen may be working. We were skeptical at first because we didn't give the other stuff a good try, but pre-dosing just wasn't a good idea. It meant snacking was out. The old routine was too labor-intensive and not conducive to weight gain. This new stuff may work better than constant carbo calculations and multiple Humalog injections. On Humulin Bart must inject twice a day, once before breakfast and again in the late afternoon, which has reduced the number of times he needs to prick himself too. His fingers were feeling like pin cushions when he was having to draw blood 5-6 times a day and use almost as many needles.

So far, so good - both readings today under 200.

The outdoor lights are still not up. Six other tasks on the weekend list, however, were checked off. By the time I brought Dallas, the "twinkly light elf" home from his friend's house it was raining.

Dinner was elementary: fish sticks, vegetables, macaroni and cheese. Good for the boys. I ate the broccoli. We did have a family meeting though. The three of us discussed Dallas' driving contract, we defined what demonstrating responsibility meant, reviewed weekly meal planning and learned that the final car repair part was due to arrive any day.

It was decreed that Dallas would be responsible for a meal a week including clean-up on a pre-selected mom work day. Dad agreed to serve as Dallas' assistant. I like this plan.

Bart was anxious to get back to the Steelers/Ravens game so he radiated impatience. He accused me of repeating myself anyway. When dealing with teens you're never really sure they hear you the second time or any time. I so worry about that kid. He organized his backpack tonight though, and tidied up his room, so hope springs eternal.

Bart and I stayed up late watching football commentary until they reported on the Army, Navy and Air Force games. We heartily root for our military. Our hearts are in it. It was a really good football day for Bart, Pittsburgh Steelers won! May all your teams rise to the playoffs.

December 6

Bart got up with pain under his ribs again. I knew it must be bad because he mentioned it. He rarely brings up pain unless it's different and/or has persisted for a long while. Bart bristled at the suggestion to call the doctor. He didn't want to cancel chemo yet again. That unnerved me a little but I understood his rationale completely.

Monday is always a busy day at Creekside Lounge. Bart was sent back to the waiting room after seeing the doctor. He waited almost two hours for a chair to open up. Sad to say that treating cancer is a much too popular business. Chemo du jour, Gemzar and various other helpful IV medications. Another all-day affair. This regimen seems more user friendly though. No vomiting. That's how you judge a good session of chemotherapy.

It was a long and tiring day for Bart. Our friend picked him up around 3 PM. I got home by 6 PM. Bart was hurting. Stoic and strong as usual, not complaining, but he wasn't happy. He asked for peanut butter and jelly. We were out of jelly but we're lucky to have neighbors with stocked pantries. I made vegetable/bean soup with all the not-so-fresh veggies left in the crisper.

May I just say something about the so-called "crisper" while on the subject? Why in the hell isn't it just called "the rotter"? That's what's really going on in there and we all know it. I have never ever known that drawer to keep anything "crisp" ever. Has crisp really ever happened? No. That drawer is where vegetables and fruit go to die. I swear they'd have a better shot at extended life just sitting on a regular refrigerator shelf like the rest of the perishables. Someone is lying to the public about "crispers". We can sustain life in international space stations and yet keeping anything fresh in the crisper forever eludes us.

I digress.

Dallas wouldn't eat my soup of healthy goodness and instead chose leftover mac & cheese with fish sticks. I can only hope that subtle modeling of good eating will someday somehow influence this child. I swear Dallas would live on pizza alone.

Miraculously Dallas did take Phaddy for a walk and even cleaned the "poop deck" with only one gentle prompt. Dallas needed to type up an essay for English which he did thankfully. He also completed Bart's chemo diary before announcing that it was time to "pone" (kill) some zombies.

No one had retrieved the homestead mail tonight, only UPS mailbox stuff had been picked up. I do not like checking mail in the dark and I'll tell you why. I once saw this movie where the killer used different and random ways to murder his victims. One was to put a rattlesnake in the mailbox. Now I don't believe that is going to happen to me but it's certainly possible that a black widow spider or something else really unpleasant might reside in there when it's dark. Dallas had already lost all our mini-flashlights kept in the front door key rack so I was going in blind. There was mail in there, but thankfully no insects, rodents or reptiles.

Not Water Under the Bridge

I've known Bart for more than 28 years and he rarely gets emotional. Today was one of those rare days I saw a current of emotion. A simple email touched his heart.

The context: Bart requested to be put on Chip Masters Golf Club's alternate stand-by list just in case he might ever return to golf one day.

The Club president wrote this: "No need to be put on an alternate or standby list, Bart. On behalf of the club, I am happy to announce you have been bestowed an honorary membership for the entire Chip Masters golfing season. We want very much for you to remain a part of our club so let's get these treatments out of the way and get your butt back on the course."

Bart shared this email with me as tears were welling up. He was truly moved. I'd never heard him choke up like this except the time I shrunk his all-time favorite sweater. I could see how much the sentiment of that membership meant to him. Definitely closer to his heart than the precious sweater, although he was mighty upset at that little mishap. Acute shrinkage was no joke he said, but that email evoked a truly powerful, and never-before-seen emotion. At some level he may have known there might not be a return to the golf course, but I clung to his appreciation of the "expression of love" as catalyst for his teardrops tonight.

December 8

A Note from Bart:

Today has been a marginal day. I've been fighting stomach cramps and pain most of the day. I blame myself. I didn't take any of my meds yesterday because I felt so good. Just shows the value of preventive measures. I won't make that mistake again.

Bart

December 9

I hate that squirrel.

First thing yesterday morning I heard a faint rat-a-tat-tat noise. Bart said he didn't hear anything at all. Loathing tends to heighten your senses.

I bolted outside at the speed of sound; my only weapon was a half-cup of hot coffee I had no time to set down.

There he was up there on the roof strutting. I had no gun, no hose, only my coffee cup. So of course I yelled at him. He scurried around and sat up a few times. I think he was curious about the shrieking, raving lunatic standing on the driveway. He disappeared over the roof to the other side, entirely unfazed by my richly phrased insults about his parentage.

Very good suggestions have come from the guestbook: get a trap from Animal Control, put a pile of peanuts in the front yard, watch the blue jays fight him over the welfare spoils then shoot him, poison him or put up chicken wire.

All those solutions are solid and appreciated, but they require me to make some effort and frankly I just don't want to. I resent that stupid creature for creating yet another project for me which I do not want right now.

I also realize that I may be the one whose most annoyed by that furry fiend so it's up to me.

As though I don't have enough stuff on my never-ending list. Some may think I possess ill will toward rodents. Yes I do, this one, very much so.

I now have much more empathy for my friend who used to tell tales of rampant and destructive squirrel activity in her backyard. I clearly understand how one can evolve into a state of adversarial seething over the very inconvenience of it all. But, having vented a little aggravated squirrel steam, I can let it go for tonight.

Bart is doing okay today. He has stomach issues, which are not at all good for a cheerful demeanor. He has little energy for walking but is alert, eating well, and doing Christmas shopping on the Internet.

He had to order his own gift from me this year because he was afraid of what I might get for him.

We currently have a two-foot round marble table between our chairs, (Bart's throne and my chair). Ordinarily it would be ideal but not so much anymore. We started off with one narrow plastic basket for his pills, then two larger plastic pill baskets.

We eventually abandoned those and filled a couple breadbaskets. Today there's another insulin supply storage basket. As my friend Jeanne would say, there's also "man debris": wallet, keys, remotes, his "Bite Me" ceramic mug, water bottle, mail, hand sanitizer, eyeglass cleaner, notepads, magazines, chargers, and so much other odd stuff I am incapable of identifying it all.

Needless to say, it's cluttered but I dare not say a word. Bart does not easily tolerate even the most generous anti-clutter standard. He did come up with a potential solution: a longer end table cabinet to replace the marble round. We could store the drug baskets in the cabinet and have more room on top for the lamp.

It amazes me how Bart can find programs to do anything he wants. His little friend Price Blink found the perfect cabinet table at the best price. That amazes me.

I suspect however that this solution to our constant clutter problem might actually extend the magnitude of stuff because we will now have concealed clutter and surface area will be dangerously open for more.

Wasn't it George Carlin who said, "Crap expands to fit the space available"?

Made a killer tuna casserole that was always a favorite for Bart but not anymore. He didn't like it. The usual tastes unusual. This oral chemo is dramatically better but has unintended consequences. (Funny, that's a phrase commonly used in the State Legislature, too). Dallas said it was delicious, so I feel vindicated. And no, it was not the tuna that had been stored in Dad's shop for 30 years......

December 11

A Note from Bart:

Today was an okay day. I had a little nausea and cramping but nothing I couldn't handle. Unfortunately Army lost to Navy…again. I would love for those kids at West Point to experience a victory over Navy. I've kept myself busy adding entries to our family tree. I have some software and it posts to a Web site. Pretty easy if I can just get my family to provide me with birthdates, wedding dates and places, and in-laws' names, birthdates, etc. Then I can populate the database. I've come up with lots of information so far. I just need to prime the pump some more.

I think my stomach issues will improve when this round of chemo is over. At least I hope. If I felt strong enough and it would stop raining long enough I'd start taking little walks. Soon.

Keep up the input, I love reading stories and reminiscing.

Love, Bart

December 12

Borrowing a common phrase from Bart, "I've been busier than a one-armed paper hanger" which is why there have been fewer postings this week. Rest assured that no news is good news.

Bart had a pretty good week, relatively speaking. He had the usual morning cramping, back pain, and queasiness, not much energy, but no vomiting, and his appetite has been good.

Bart kept himself well hydrated so he didn't need much of a top-off at Creekside and his blood work looked decent.

Bart is feeling pretty good watching football with an alluring plate of cheese, grapes & crackers. Unbeknownst to me, he was feeling really good a few days ago and skipped his regular meds. If I had a clue that's what was going on I would have reminded him about the last time we dared to get behind the pain train.

Bart's internal constitution never ceases to amaze. Bart is NOT a complainer. He endures without anger, regret or accusation. He accepts the hand he has been dealt. I see a calm resiliency. We discussed how things haven't gone the way we anticipated, yet there's no looking back. Bart promised that I would be the first to know if his positive outlook ever changed.

It's been quite a day. What happened with our Christmas lights is too deflating to relay at this late hour but I'll share those lessons later. It was almost a four hour endeavor and to think I was trying to surprise Bart? Ha.

Bart plans to discuss his quest for restful sleep with his oncologist tomorrow. In the meantime, sleep well.

December 13

While getting chemo this afternoon at the lounge, Bart talked to the oncologist about persistent gut cramps, increased back pain, extreme fatigue, and sleep issues. The upshot: augment and increase pain meds adding Norco interspersed with Dilaudid, up his Fentanyl dose and a sleep aid. We await insurance permission for timed-release sleep meds.

Twilight Buzz

The other night Bart said, "Forget Christmas lights this year". Ouch, that didn't sit well. Lights add a joyful glow and we must have them.
The outdoor light extravaganza was always Bart's annual duty with Dallas as the trusty (albeit bored) ladder holder. A couple years ago Bart's ladder got unstable in the bushes and he tipped over grabbing the outdoor lamp affixed to the side of the house to break his fall (so much for ladder guy).

Bart tried to explain to me what happened. I urgently interrupted "Did you break the lamp?" He teased me from that day forward about caring more about light fixtures than his safety. It still hangs loose on the house to this day. Every year after that, I could only get Bart to put up lights if I plied him with brandy and eggnog (heavy on the brandy), and made Dallas climb the ladder.

If I wanted lights this year I would have to figure it out myself. I negotiated with a friend and she took the deal. We were going to surprise Bart with a brilliant display across the house and up the driveway. Neither cold nor damp could dim our enthusiasm.

I unpacked two huge boxes marked "Christmas lights" and went to work. That new ladder is one heavy sucker. We inched away stringing lights for hours all excited about the big bright payoff.

You know when you suddenly get a sinking feeling that something might be terribly wrong? Well, Kathy was standing there at the very end of the string of lights we had carefully wrapped, strung, hung, and draped, holding a female plug. Impossible. There was no way to plug in the lights. Apparently we had strung them up backwards. I had no idea lights were directional.

No friggin' way were we going to take it all down to turn it around and string it up the other way - there had to be another, faster way. Racing darkness we tried adding light cord after cord that had both female/male ends. Somehow we would come full circle and plug 'em in. Not.

There are no light standards.

You've got your fatter ground prong plugs that don't fit into the other kind and visa versa. Nothing is compatible.

We thought maybe some fancy plug conversion device from the hardware store might fit into the porch lamp fixture (same light Bart did his Tarzan thing from). Kathy got up on the ladder to check it out. I was to unscrew the bottom as directed.

Without notice the glass fixture flew out of the housing. Boom! It obliterated my blue & white keepsake ceramic chamber pot (filled with dog water) spewing shards & splinters all over the porch and driveway. We both froze with shock. Amazingly the water-filled chamber pot must have broken the lamp's fall. Not even a crack.

We replaced a broken bulb and gingerly put it back together, finally admitting that we <u>had</u> to consult the experienced one. He actually succeeded at this chore in the past. Begrudgingly I went in. Bart shook his head at the news; I think he mumbled "dumbasses" under his breath.

He reluctantly came outside and announced that we would have to take it all down and turn it around. I protested. There must be another way.

He inspected the job, rolled his eyes, and shook his head the whole time with that "I told you not to do this" look. Bart also mentioned that plastic gutter grabbers were designed so we could have used a broomstick and avoided ladder positioning problems altogether.

Nothing is ever easy.

Resigned, Kathy and I looked at each other and began to unravel. Bart examined the string with the male end and found it not far from the porch. He told us to connect an extension cord at that juncture. We did so and re-hung the 10 feet we just took down and switched on the power strip. Some lit up, most did not. Bart said you have to replace the burnt out ones or buy new lights. With that he retired to his throne.

Unplugging and plugging little teeny tiny bulbs that never fit hoping for light was tedious. Each and every one of those microscopic do-dads seems to have a different fitting. There are green wide ones, white skinny ones, long ones, short ones, some serial, some not. Our fingers were numb. We quit. It was "good enough for government work" as the saying goes.

There's some old adage that says you can tell a lot about a person by the way they handle tangled Christmas lights. I'm afraid to learn what that might mean about me. Bart says I'm like a rabid dog with a bone once I'm attached to some hair-brained idea. But look! There's a flawed but lovely glow on the house this season.

I feel a twinkle bit better.

December 14

A Note from Bart:

Well, folks, it appears that one can become used to or tolerant of certain pain meds to the point they lose their effectiveness. I switched back to Norco 10/325 and my pain went away. So I am to rotate with Dilaudid. Don't know if it's every 6 hours every other day or what but for now I'm doing Norco the rest of today after last night's success. I even got some decent sleep (for me).

In reference to your squirrel post Butch, great idea about the .22. I don't think I can discharge a weapon in the town limits especially since my neighbor is a police officer. Very nice, but I don't think he could look the other way on that one.

Got our new table/magazine rack and needless to say some assembly required. Other than cutting and staining boards I don't see what they did. Such is the state of the world we live in. All assembly required.

Keep prayers and well wishes coming, I feel them working. Just a short update from me as I'm sure my bride will have much more to say.

Love y'all Bart

Drive

Bart was mildly put off that I didn't recall exactly what age-old injury he sustained while putting up lights years ago.

He said "I can't believe that you didn't remember vividly my ring finger almost getting ripped off. I had one hand in an ice bag and a beer in the other while you grilled me about the condition of the light?"

When you've been married as long as we have you tend to hone in on costly dwelling damage first. He was having a beer after all and his finger was still attached. Fortunately so was the light (for the most part) so it was all good.

Bart is doing really well tonight. Change is good. He thinks the switch up in medication made the difference.

Before I left for work he said Mexican food sounded like a plan for dinner. On my drive home I was to stop and get it. Traffic was slow so I wouldn't get home until well after 6 PM.

Bart couldn't wait that long. He said Dallas would drive him. Dallas evidently told Dad he needed to study and when Dal emerged from the bathroom Dad was gone. This was a good day indeed. Bart drove for the first time in months and dinner was waiting like old times.

December 16

Bart says that the new pain management program, alternating his supplemental oral analgesics with Fentanyl patches, is working much better.

Tonight, however, Bart's really sleepy. He was thinking the antidote might be a nighttime shower versus morning one, but the thought quickly perished. Before "whaling away in the shower" we would have to wrap his PICC (left arm) with plastic wrap & tape. He contemplated that and it was just too much.

As far as his chemo is concerned the Gemzar and Xeloda combo seems to be the best cocktail yet. No hellacious after-effects either. We pray the next CT scan will show that this kinder, gentler treatment is more effective at reducing tumors.

Enter the Dragon

Dallas is driving again. It was solely due to the generosity of his father who forgave debt and gifted new tires for Christmas. Dallas was out of cash and began to run up a considerable IOU with us. I saw this as his problem to solve and was more than content maintaining "carless" status quo. Why impose more worry by letting him drive? In a few months he would be allowed to drive with passengers… more worry.

The car, a.k.a. "Red Dragon," (dubbed by brother Matty when it was his car) waited comfortably at our neighbors' house until Dal paid us off.

I liked the no-car routine. Dallas woke me at 6:25 AM for a ride to school. then I would go straight to the gym. With Dallas driving himself to school sleep wins out over gym.

Dallas told us today that he shortened the car's moniker to just "Dragon" so that when he does take on passengers he can say, "Enter the Dragon".

Hopefully Phaddy doesn't snore too loudly to wake any sleeping dragons tonight.

The Call of the Kitchen

Phaddy's a mighty myopic food-centric dog. One whiff of kitchen activity and he will risk broken bones by braving a dangerous dive off the bed. Always lured by the possibility of morning morsels he wastes no time. Phaddy does this ritualistic little short-legged bobbing jump maneuver where his ears flop and he bursts with ebullience. He should be embarrassed by such ridiculous deportment over a bit of green bean or sugar snap pea. We're not even talking meat here. He will even troll the neighborhood for anything remotely chewable rutting around like a truffle-hunting pig seeking particles of ancient foodstuffs from near and far.

One day he came home with a burger. I was shocked and amazed. I left that burger in a drain pipe den on upper Sudbury for some feline strays that had kittens. It was a half mile away yet Phaddy sniffed it out and brought it back to our porch before the cats had a fighting chance.

That might have been the night he horked on my clean bedspread. After the very first puke incident I thought it prudent to put an old blanket over the area. The dog obviously didn't want to soil *his* blanket. He let loose just at the edge but all on the damn bedspread. All Bart could manage to say was "when did he eat all the pistachio shells?"

December 17

It's a frosty morning and to think I had removed the protective homeless shelter from our monumental lemon tree. I didn't read about any frost warning, Bart is the one who notes weather forecasts. I'm oblivious. I had to get to the bus stop. Bart was still in bed and I hoped he would rest better with Dallas and I out of the house.

I texted Bart from work expecting he would be having a day much like yesterday mild and comfortable. I guess you can't get too much of a good thing. He said he felt rough, tight with intense cramping and had heavy pain, not feeling much like conversing, emailing or texting. That weighs me down.

I told him to think about what I could do or prepare to help and while riding home on the bus I got word that a friend made pierogies! Dinner impossible solved.

I still had to stop at the pharmacy for prescription refills, get Bart's mail, yada yada yada and I couldn't wait to get these boots off. Thankfully our pierogie friend was already there when I got home. Bart's end table cabinet Christmas present had arrived and a lot of assembly was required. She could help. I gave them a toolbox then left them for other chores.

While the pierogies were heating up, I threw in a load of wash, vacuumed dog messes and Styrofoam debris then we rearranged the chairs. Bart's newly assembled cabinet could be put to good use.

Bart says it's going to rain. After last month's laborious citrus preservation episode I found out all that wrapping using bungee cords, sheets and cardboard was for naught. Sandi the soil scientist said just put Christmas lights on it. That's warmth enough to prevent freezing altogether. Now they tell me.

Of course the lights I strung up wouldn't work. Those lazy lemons better not give up to a little frosty weather. Bart and I want to share the sour taste of a hard-fought battle.

Dallas turned in early, about 8:50, and even came out to tell us to keep the noise down. He couldn't possibly have been exhausted from studying too hard, of that I am fairly certain. Dallas warned us gingerly this evening that his grades might not be what he (or we) had been expecting. Ergo, he spoke of Junior College. Egad, might he be contemplating living at home after he turns 18? We had an explicit house rule that check-out time from our family hotel was 18 years of age. I think Bart even posted the check-out time and date on the twins' bedroom doors.

Tomorrow is the last day of high school for the year. We expect the older kids to start rolling in early next week. Meg's husband Ben is back from Afghanistan, so he's coming too. Matt has a brief respite before Army Ranger School.

Bart felt better tonight than he had during the day boosted by the news all the kids were coming home.

We got an unexpected package delivered and ripped it open post haste. How many of you have a dentist who would send you a real mini-Christmas fir tree fully decorated? Quite a lovely little tree and if potted in a much larger vessel it could do varsity duty by next Christmas. It's a nice addition in our front window and we decided to call it the "Chan-Tree" after our dentist.

It's late. Dallas has finals tomorrow and I have an appointment with the pectoral drill press (mammogram). Bart has lab work to be done so we all better rest up for our respective tests.

December 17

Bart was still sleeping when Dallas and I left the house. I wasn't in the best mood. I woke up with a dry throat and hoped it was the result of sleeping with my mouth open, but I knew better, so I downed vitamin C with a chaser of Airborne because I cannot afford to catch a cold.

I didn't have the heart to wake Bart when I left. His sleep is so precious.

I had to get my annual vice-grip-o-gram out of the way that day, which was a nuisance but necessary. You wait in the lobby then wait again in that half robe thing. And what's up with asking your birthday every 10 minutes? Then they gather up half the skin off my ribs to get enough mass to smash.

Afterwards, the radiology technician asks you to wait around to make sure the images are clear.

By this time Bart was at Creekside Lounge and he texted that he felt like crap.

I had been waiting a long time just to be given permission to leave the radiology lab. Women who had arrived after me were leaving before me. I had no patience to wait because I wanted to get across the street to see if Bart was okay.

He insisted he was fine, so I took off to take care of some Christmas shopping. Well, not being a mind reader, how was I to know Bart actually wanted me to take him home when instead I was too long Christmas shopping? It's a common snafu with us as to who's doing what, where and when.

Fortunately, Sandi was nearby so it all worked out. Still I felt disorganized, stressed and worried so I went to the gym. Some frustrations are best washed away with sweat.

Bart got better as the day wore on. He asked me to pick up a dog toy for Phaddy. The dog had so much fun with squealing pig ornaments and gobbling turkey toys. All such things shredded by bedtime. The entertainment value, however, was worth the pig/turkey sacrifice.

Bart wanted Phaddy to have an early Christmas present. Enter the tough stuff pet toy bright green octopus. You could see the dog's eyes widen. He was literally quivering with such anticipation that his little tiny tail was a-twitching.

While I prepared dinner, Bart assumed the role of Howard Cosell announcing the play by play demise of the bona fide tough toy. It was amusing to see Bart watching so intently giving me "there goes the first leg, now an eyeball, the other eyeball" and so on through all eight legs, body, guts and then the squeaker. We left the mess to take a picture but random chores took priority until Bart finally cleaned it up himself.

Bart is feeling human tonight. He doesn't hurt. Last night he said he was in pain at bedtime but not now. In fact he just told me that he ordered a selection of other potentially entertaining objects for dog destruction online.

Let's hope they last longer than the octopus did. Our evening entertainment depends on it.

December 18

Bart slept in so I did too. Dallas kept coming in with Phaddy asking if we were ever going to get up. Dallas went to sleep around 7 PM on Friday so he was up unnaturally early. When Bart did rise, he reported a decent night's sleep and that was great news.

It was a blustery day and because of the wind some of the Christmas lights needed help. Lights around the door fell off because I had used the old brittle plastic brackets that Bart put up years ago. Today Bart was telling me they all needed to be replaced. He also warned that it was a

@$*tch. He was right. I got them in all right but didn't have enough leverage to shove clamps into the brackets but enough to jab a few unwelcome divots in the door jam. I didn't tell Bart about that. He'd find out soon enough. Or not, because I shut the garage door on the tailgate of the truck Friday. He didn't notice that either. No damage, so no harm, no foul. My fingers were cold and sore despite garden gloves. I didn't want to do this anymore.

So I made Dallas do it. His giant stature would be good for something. It was easy for him. If only he'd put the tools away when a job is done. It must be genetic. I've said the same thing to Bart over the years.

Bart ate well with minimal stomach cramping. He was talking and in a pretty good mood.

Fed Ex delivered things he'd ordered online which pleased him and our youngest neighbors came over with a present for Phaddy, an Army-Strong camouflage tennis ball on a rope. They each threw the ball arguing over whose turn it was next. The eldest boy announced that the youngest would have the last toss then they had to go home. For a six- year-old he is more responsible than I am.

You can almost pick Phaddy up by his mouth with this toy. I'm afraid I could rip his teeth out due to his generous girth. It's one toy he can't tear apart.

Phaddy is forever trying to get Bart to play. Once in a while Bart tosses something but not often. I always play. I wish I could ignore those pleading eyes like Bart does. Phaddy puts the toy right next to my knee on the chair then backs away slowly and waits eagerly. How Bart resists I don't know.

This evening our man of the house is eating candy and watching action movies. "Transporters" with Jason Statham is on. I had Christmas cards to address. Note: If you ever get a card from us good for you, but don't ever count on it and it won't arrive before the New Year. That's how we roll. I don't know how people do this every single year.

Bart doesn't understand why I don't weigh 400 pounds? Nice talk. So what? It was only a few hours after dinner, but I finished off the homemade moussaka courtesy of my Greek friend. A treat while addressing the cards. I considered it a snack. He reminded me that yesterday I ate all the spanakopita too. What can I say? I love Greek food. Feed a cold, remember?

I didn't feel good and Bart said "Welcome to my world". I told him that if I could take on his pain to ease the burden, I would. He said he knew that.

I recall a pivotal moment watching Bart suffer with his head hanging between his knees and it hurt me so to see him that way. Some days he utters nary a word - his whole focus is on simple survival. One moment there in the room with him I realized that I had to let Bart handle this himself because if I continued to let it hurt me so deeply I wouldn't have the spirit or strength to care for him. I would essentially be denying him the best I could give. I gathered myself and got to it. He was alive and I intended to keep him that way.

Bill graciously assumed his VIP seat for football while I ran errands. It was good. Bart liked having Bill's company as we all do.

Our friend Jeanne arrived late afternoon with ingredients for our nightly recipe from the Cancer Cookbook. Bart actually said he liked it, angel hair pasta with garlic, avocados and tomato. It was simple but good.

Today Jeanne and I picked up Bart's prescription then went on to fulfill Bart's grocery wish list. While browsing the bulk food section of the grocery store, I laid the prescription bag down by the cashews and then proceeded to the hot soups and checked out. Only after we got home did I realize I left his prescription bag by the bulk foods. I called but no one had turned it in so Jeanne suggested we go back to the store sooner rather than later. As I checked in at the pharmacy counter Jeanne found the bag by the bulk foods; the receipt was there but the pills were missing.

Store security plans to review security tapes to see if they can identify the person who took the drugs. We shall see.

Bart wanted raviolis for dinner so we were happy to oblige.

We awaited the arrival of the kids who were due around 9 PM. I was excited for them to see all the Christmas lights lining the driveway. We told them they were to "follow the light".

After they drove in, we did the dance of joy and then the kids ate most everything in the fridge. That's when I made a maddening discovery. I was admiring the outdoor lights, but something was wrong. I went out there and saw that more than half of all the outdoor lights were dark! What the hell kind of timing is that? Bart thought oh no, it's 10 PM and no time to be engineering light repairs which he was afraid I might take on at this hour. Even though the outdoor cold would have felt quite good, since I am so volcanically hot most of the time, I threw my hands up in despair and decided it must be bedtime. We would have to investigate this debacle in the morning. I had no voice left and needed a decongestant badly.

Bart on the other hand had a very good day. He's still up in fact. I might actually be first to bed for once.

He and Matty are both working on their i-Pads. Jeanne, Ben, Megan and Dallas are all tucked away in their respective sleeping places. It's wonderful to have a full house even if the lights of joy are out.

December 21

At one point last evening Bart said "pass the real candy". He had checked his sugar level and it was, for the first time, too low at 91! Bring on the goodies. He ate a few pieces of candy and a cookie or two. This new stuff (Humalin) appears to be working. That's one Christmas gift we'll take.

As for the stolen prescription, it's going to cost $25 to replace. Security will take another 3-4 weeks to do their thing before reporting back to us and I suspect the conclusion will be "we were unable to identify the person or persons who took your husband's prescription but should any new information arise we will let you know" or something to that effect. I'm sure of it. My forgetfulness is starting to cost us. I'll blame it on the common cold.

Jeanne graciously dropped Bart at Creekside Lounge this morning on her way back to Chico. Matthew will pick him up this afternoon so I can finish these Christmas cards. Please know that if you don't get one, good for you. We must know you well enough that "Merry Christmas" is implied and not necessary to convey by USPS. Besides, Bart says he doesn't like cards with pictures anyway. You can see the same pictures on this site without the postage.

Megan, her husband Ben (who just got home from Crapghanistan, also known in other nomenclature as Afghanistan) and Dallas left for Weaverville this morning. They're collecting Grandma and returning with her tonight! That's more than 9 hours of driving. Just thinking about sitting that long makes my arthritis flare up.

It was odd for all of us to contemplate our first Christmas in Cameron Park and not Weaverville, but then it dawned on us: apparently we must have holidays wherever the chair is! That leather throne has always been the centerpiece of holiday festivities. Just the occupant has changed.

Bart is back from Creekside. He's feeling good. Bart loves hanging with oldest son Matty. They are watching the movie "Town". I was amused to see the ratings for movies on Bart's online system. It says stuff like, "This movie is rated 3.5 stars which is our best guess for Bart." The more he rates, the more it knows apparently. It's kind of spooky and space-aged. Oops, I'm not to use that term anymore. It's "high tech" now according to the kids. They laugh and say "we've pretty much been going to space our whole lives, Mom."

Squirrel update: Our marksman son Matt is game for target shooting but my neighbor Scott actually consulted a "squirrel specialist" who suggested ammonia soaked rags in the lair. I like the simplicity of that solution. I didn't like the thought of disposing of the body. Bart often tells a story of when we had to put our dog "Pignacious" to sleep. Long story, but my dad wanted a pet pig. Those were too costly but Bart didn't want to disappoint.

A puppy from a box in front of Tops Market was free and we could call her Pig. My mom however, went ballistic and informed us we would be taking that dog home with us. She wasn't a good dog, quite paranoid and she bit the kids without warning.

Bart dropped Pig off at the vet clinic that fateful day and started to walk out the door. The receptionist stopped him and said "Do you want the body"? Bart turned around and said "Lady, if I wanted the body, I would have killed her myself".

I'm off to the kitchen to prepare the nightly fare. Beef stew in the crock pot. Then we'll await the arrival of Mom, the matriarch of the family and we'll have Aunt Sandi over for the evening meal. May your holidays be sweet and your sugar levels low (but not below 100).

December 23

A Note from Bart:

Hi folks, I'd like to take some of the pressure off of my bride when I'm feeling well enough to post. Not much to report. I'm feeling pretty good and trying to stay that way. Poor Dallas has strep so he isn't allowed near me for 24 hours. Since my immune system is down, if I get it I may end up at the ER. Trying to make sure that doesn't happen.

We are enjoying a visit from Matthew, Megan and her husband Ben.

Next week I start chemo again, third set of three then I get another CT scan to see if it's working. Keep your fingers crossed and pray for me if you see your way.

Short post as I said, not much to report so back to the Steelers game.

Love y'all, Bart

December 24

A Note from Bart:

I had to add a couple things:

1. I'm not sure everyone knows this is a place to post messages but we cannot answer from here. If you want a reply send a private email.

2. Yesterday Dallas got very hungry and his mom was gone. He walked out of his room with his ear muff pulled over his mouth and when I said not to touch anything he said not to worry he had socks on his hands. I'm glad he was looking out for his dad and it really was funny to see.

December 27

A Note from Bart:

Hi all,

I started the third week of chemo today. I do three sessions of three weeks, two weeks on and one off. After two weeks I will have my CT scan. So far so good as far as the treatment goes. A little more stomach upset than I've had in the past but nothing I can't handle.

I get one day of IV chemo and two weeks of pills (Xeloda).

Everything else is winding down after the big Christmas festivities. I can't take big crowds and lot of noise anymore. Quiet is my thing. :-)

Meg and Ben go home tomorrow, Matt leaves Thursday and Mel is taking her mom back home tomorrow. It will be just in time for a big winter storm that's supposed to hit us starting tomorrow.

Stay in touch and I hope y'all have a safe, healthy and prosperous New Year.

Love, Bart

December 28

A Note from Bart:

All is quiet on the home front. We're almost back to normal. Mel took her mom home and now may be stuck in Weaverville due to snow, until Thursday or Friday. Matt leaves Thursday to get ready for Army Ranger training which begins January 2nd. So Thursday night will be either me, Mel and Dallas or just Dallas and me.

I'm feeling pretty good after the latest Chemo. We had a good Christmas and are looking forward to a great New Year.

We are enjoying a major rainstorm but not cold enough to snow. So I "have" to stay in and watch TV. Bummer! :-)

I'll report when there is more to say.

Love y'all Bart

Happy New Year is near.

There have been few uninterrupted moments to sit down, let alone write, because neither Bart or I wanted to miss out on any family fun.

Bart has been feeling relatively good this Christmas so it has been a wonderful week. The Gemzar/Xeloda chemo combo has been so much kinder and gentler on Bart's constitution.

Caring Bridge notes are several days old but since they were already composed, I'll add these holiday highlights.

After daughter Megan, son-in-law Ben and Dallas did their Tuesday 10-hour turnaround drive to and from Weaverville to pick up Grandma (and Dad's truck), life got revved up. Megan and Grandma pulled into the driveway after 6 PM. Ben and Dallas drove up a while later. The door shot open and Dallas with his head down made a beeline for the bedroom. He had a headache so bad that light and noise intensified the pain. We were trying to get dinner on the table at that moment. I went to his room with a cold washcloth, a couple Excedrin and some soothing motherly words, then back to the kitchen.

While pulling rolls out of the oven, I heard my cell phone ringing. It was Dallas calling from the bedroom!

Dallas said he felt really sick. I bolted for the wastebasket. Returned with the bathroom pail in less than 7 seconds but it was too late. He'd already heaved three times. This poor kid threw up the pain pills. Momentary quandary; no way Dallas wanted the light on. Meg said he needed to sleep. I had to get dinner on the table. It was really dark in there. Dallas wanted to be left alone. He seemed okay with it. I closed the door. Oh dear. Clean-up would have to wait for natural light.

Early Wednesday, 6 AM, the three big kids took off for the ski slopes. They didn't want to catch anything either.

Dallas awoke still feeling ill so Bart and I looked at each other knowingly. I sighed and drove him to Rapid Care for a strep test.

After waiting in that infernally hot vestibule, we were called into an equally steamy exam room.

Sure enough, strep, so Dal got a shot in the butt and would have to serve a 24-hour quarantine, but first we wait another 20 minutes (in case of adverse reaction). I plucked the first thing I saw, a couple rubber gloves to fan myself. It felt like Pennsylvania on a hot humid summer day in there.

Bart alerted his oncologist to the situation. Relatives were to bring Thursday dinner but "quarantine kid" thwarted those plans.

Dallas didn't seem bothered by the isolation sentence. He apparently had a lot of zombies to destroy and other important military missions via Xbox.

The rest of Wednesday and most of Thursday was spent sterilizing, cleaning, laundering and running around collecting prescriptions, shopping, delivering stuff and other such last minute busy work. Bart was busy shopping online.

Bart suddenly announced that our digital camera was failing and he would like a new one for Christmas. The family bolted into action in all directions. Matt apparently headed straight to Best Buy while Meg, Ben and I searched another store meanwhile Bart and his friendly online assistant "Price Blink" were narrowing down the best Internet deals. Moving too quickly to communicate or coordinate, our ADD family ended up procuring two! Fortunately, Bart was able to cancel his online order as Matty's purchase was the superior product. We still insisted that Bart unwrap the camera and feign surprise come Christmas Eve. It was his Christmas Eve bonus besides feeling good.

Christmas Eve was truly a blessed red-letter day. This was Bart's first pleasure outing in months, other than Creekside Lounge and the ill-fated venture to San Francisco. Dallas took one for the team and stayed home. He wasn't a big cioppino fan and said he didn't want to feel like a leper either.

Bart thoroughly enjoyed Mom's traditional Christmas Eve cioppino and the company of family at Sandi's house. We got home that night, opened the door to witness Dallas dancing about and talking on the phone. He wasn't too broken up about being left out.

In fact he said he enjoyed having the house to himself and the freedom from isolation for a few hours.

The family arrived Christmas morning to my proud puffy pancake breakfast and lime fizzes. The biggest thrill was seeing Dallas open a gift from his cousin. We watched the drummer boy's eyes light up at a pair of glowing blue drumsticks that brightened with each beat and a "Weapons of Mass Percussion" shirt, which he donned right away. To round out "the look" there was a fringed dingle ball Mohawk stocking cap. The Dal monster loved it.

Thanks to Matty and Bart, the Christmas lights of joy got fixed. Bart knew exactly what was wrong. I'd had quite enough bulb casualties, blown fuses and raw frozen fingers by that time. Only one of my terra cotta planters got run over this year. Last year my sister took out a big one as well as some of the solar lights. Garden sacrifices always good for a laugh.

Seeing Bart laugh and watching him enjoy the holiday was the best Christmas gift of all.

December 29

I was still in Weaverville when Bart contacted me at 3 PM to report that he was in the Emergency Room at Mercy Folsom. He felt pain and had swelling in his lower right leg this afternoon about 2:30 and had the smarts to know it could be a blood clot, very serious. He called 911 to be transported by ambulance. Bart did not want Dallas driving him in case something should happen. Dallas' job was to stay home and man the phones, so to speak. Sandi and Matthew were out signing important papers at a Title Company. They went straight to the hospital from there. Megan and Ben were halfway to Tucson. Being 250 miles away was frustrating. Bart had been doing so well.

ER doctors admitted Bart right away. He did indeed have a blood clot, no idea how large. The treatment is the same. Bart told me he could be in the hospital 2-5 days depending on the success of the treatment plan. He's still in decent spirits although very tired.

The doctors are doing all they can. Bart's on Coumadin, a blood thinner. He will also have to self-administer another shot besides insulin.

There has been snow and freezing temperatures over Buckhorn Mountain so I will leave Trinity County tomorrow morning.

December 30

Bart is home! His hospital doctor said if he's willing to give himself the shots, then there's no reason why he shouldn't be released. Bart's buddy, Gary, was pleased to bring him home this afternoon and Bart is happy to be back in the saddle again, the leather "throne" that is. Bart is in complete control of the remotes tonight. Notice, remotes is plural. If Bart isn't here then I would not even have the technical know-how to watch television at all. Perhaps it's better that way.

Bart may continue his oral chemo regimen as well. He missed only two days of Xeloda treatment. He's giving himself 4 shots a day now but we all agree, it's better than the alternative.

The drive from Trinity was relatively uneventful. There was a mudslide on Buckhorn but ultimately it was a beautiful day and an easy trip. I stopped in Yolo County to drop stuff off at my cousin's place. Got back on the freeway and a nice fellow in a pickup truck gestured to me that my tailgate was open. I had noticed whiffs of a suspicious scent anyway so was happy to exit at Garden Highway. Turned around in a gated condo, closed the tailgate and checked my shoes. Sure enough I'd stepped in it. Took the shoes off and left them right there on the grass at the curb. Used my handy antiseptic wipes and drove home in sock feet.

At this time the dishwasher is loaded, Bart is comfortable and fed. The dog has re-acclimated to the home environment. He's wearing his new reflective collar, courtesy of Matty.

It's time to relax. I wish a Happy New Year to everyone. May you have lots of champagne on ice.

Chapter Nine

Bart, Blood & Blockbusters

January 1

A Note from Bart:

Hi all. Happy New Year. I hope it brings you joy, happiness, health and prosperity. As you might imagine our New Year's "celebration" was very muted.

I don't drink anymore (it doesn't taste good) so we just watched a couple of comedy shows then watched poor Dick Clark ring in the new year. We had the pleasure of best friends Jeanne and company to help us celebrate. We couldn't ask for anything better.

As for me, my leg is still a little sore. I'm supposed to limit my use of it for the next couple of weeks. I take extra shots in order to prevent this clot growing and getting any new ones. So far (couple of days) it hasn't been a problem.

We are doing well this New Year and look forward to some further good news this year.

Happy New Year to all my friends

Love y'all Bart

January 3

A Note from Bart:

Hey everyone, a bit of good news today in advance of the CT scan next week.

There is blood marker they have that indicates the presence of cancer. As with most things lower numbers are better and I don't know what "normal" is but, this marker, CA 19-9, went from 61000 to 48500. They tell me that is a good sign. Next week we do the CT scan to confirm.

I'll keep y'all informed as I know. *love Bart*

January 6

A Note from Bart:

I hesitate to post when there is nothing to report. But here goes.

I'm doing well, waiting for my CT scan.

I feel pretty good overall, at least as well as can be expected under the circumstances. I have to take lots of pills every day to maintain but I'm not complaining. My leg has stopped hurting from the blood clot and I think it is going away.

I wish I had more news but when I do you guys will be among the first to know. My CT scan is next Tuesday.

Thanks to y'all love, Bart

January 7

It's not a very active day for the Bart man. He said his stomach was off, some bloating and general upset. It did not affect his appetite however. Dinner was chicken Kiev, Rice-a-Roni, applesauce, green beans and grapes. Bart decided to forego the green beans. Phaddy dog enjoyed a few French cut beans in his meal per the vet's suggestion. Being as food-centric as he is, the dog will eat most everything, making training easier. I actually taught him to sit with a carrot.

Bart does enjoy the amusing little fellow and beyond a few upchucks and an accident or four, he's a fun addition to the family.

Recently, I tried to toss a few of the eviscerated shells that were once toys but Bart wouldn't have it. Phaddy plays with all of them, he said. The quiet stuffed bat Grandma gave him remained perfectly intact. He only destroys the ones with squeakers.

It is fun to see Bart enjoy the dog's antics, fetching and shaking the shreds of material that once were toys. Phaddy is certainly a playful little guy for six! We have noticed gray hair in his beard. The aged wisdom must have taught Phaddy that WE are the alpha dogs in this domain because we've had no more nipping nonsense.

Bart and Dallas took Phaddy to the grooming salon the other day while I was at work. He looks like a whole new beast, all fluffy and trimmed. It almost made him appear thinner. Still the dog is no help whatsoever when it comes to the squirrel.

I fear the squirrel is getting smarter and more deceptive. This morning I woke with a start. I heard him. The noise came from a new direction though and I was suddenly afraid that he had moved to the solar side of the house. Pity the squirrel that messes with the Reagan's solar panels.

Bart was asleep. I ran to the garage, grabbed the BB gun and flew out front to the top of the road so I could see. I was pumping the gun all the while, scanning the roof, ready to aim and fire. At that moment no less than four or five vehicles drove by, some noticeably slowing as they passed. Suddenly horrified, I realized that here I was atop my driveway on the road with crazy bed hair, in old pajamas and brandishing a weapon!

I retreated quickly before somebody called the Sheriff.

Bart was up and in his chair when I came in. He was not a happy camper, admonishing me for even considering shooting a BB gun in a residential area.

I just wanted to scare him, said I. Bart rolled his eyes but did betray his thoughts that Squirrel would certainly have watched in wonder to assess what kind of predator this was. Squirrel 1, Reagans 0.

Dallas has two friends over tonight. They appear relentless and eager to kill zombies, apparently loving every minute of that action too. Bart was less than impressed. Bart instructed Dallas in no uncertain terms that his chores needed to be done before any group zombie massacre ensued. A reluctant but compliant Dallas completed his chores but with very little enthusiasm. Could he exert less effort? I rather doubt it.

I am very happy to report this evening that Bart's voice is back. He's not exactly yelling at us yet (totally normal situation), but a more Bart-like projected tone has returned. I wondered why I felt so positive the other day and realized it was because the tenor of Bart's voice sounded more like it used to, healthier, stronger. I believe it's a sure sign of healing.

The CT scan is set for Tuesday. We expect to receive a confirmation of our suspicion that Bart is kicking some major tumor ass this round.

It's time to watch Jeff Dunham comedy courtesy of my Trinity High buddy D. Kick. We discovered a certain shared twisted Trinity sense of humor.

It was a fairly good day for Bart. He got up at 8 AM, administered his Lovenox shot, then went back to bed and slept until 10 AM. His leg doesn't hurt anymore but he will continue with Lovenox shots for at least another 30 days.

Bart was alert and awake until about 3 PM when he began to get really tired despite several catnaps between games. It was a full day of football for Bart, Green Bay and Baltimore.

It always amazes me how much time it takes to do simple everyday things. Maybe it's just me. A relatively short list of Saturday errands still took half a day. I didn't get any housecleaning done. My scope has even narrowed to just the "public" areas. Cleanliness standards around here have diminished considerably. Bart and Dallas don't seem to notice nor do I think they care much.

Dallas gambles with "hamper roulette" lately, pulling out whatever looks clean enough. I resist washing his stuff because no matter what I'd select to fill out my load, it would always be the item containing headphones or some other expensive electronic bit. The sheer number of i-Pods and headphones I've killed embarrasses me.

Speaking of killing, Phaddy got a gift today. He received the fourth (in a Christmas five-pack) of squeaky dog bears. Bart wants to dole them out sparingly. Phaddy's become proficient at ripping the guts out through their bottoms and murdering the squeaker post haste. This time I beat him to it, salvaging the squeak before he ate it.

Bart threw out the only other squeak thing our son-in-law Ben grabbed out of the jaws of death.

It's such a useful tool. The dog is mystified by the noise. He will stay close if one of us just squeaks periodically. It's like a miracle trainer tool.

If only I could squeak out a cure for barfing on my duvet cover. I used an old sheet for maximum coverage until the last episode. Phaddy must have taken a moment to scratch the sheet over enough to upchuck directly on the spread. We think the cause was ingesting just a little bit of dog-bear polyester entrails. Suffice it to say I've written off this duvet cover. Its life will certainly be measured in "dog years".

We're having pierogies for dinner tonight which is always a hit with the boys. Even more exciting, my friend Viola indicated authentic Russian "piroshkies" from her friend's Ukrainian deli might be forthcoming. Now that's something to live for. The Reagan family hasn't met a pierogie they didn't like.

It's time to transfer my laundry. If Dallas doesn't get his act together soon it will be hamper surprise again tomorrow for back to school. Bart and I informed the kid that check out time from this hotel is still 18 years old and he'll be taking his dirty laundry with him. Our words land on deaf ears at the moment.

All this laundry and so little time. No question that time is veritably the most precious commodity of all. There will always be more money to be made, somehow, but there will never be more time.

Right now it's time for Bart to enjoy a delicious dark chocolate brownie made just for him by a dear friend.

Bart says there's another quarter left in the Kraft Fight Hunger bowl and football doesn't watch itself. Go Nevada.

January 11

Judgment day (CT scan) and what a day it was.

It started with Dallas' alarm clock. Bart made sure we bought Dallas the loudest clock known to man. It's like a smoke alarm. It could wake the dead but didn't arouse Dallas in the least.

It scared me awake, frankly. Dallas was impervious.

After 15 minutes, the alarm noise was piercing my brain.

Of all of us, Bart needs his sleep the most yet it amazes me how Bart still engages in some of the morning responsibility ritual. He sets his own alarm just to make sure we are on track. (I would let Dal suffer from a tardy slip myself.)

Bart woke up and said, "Somebody better check on Dallas."

I sat up. Somebody? I'm the only other one here, so I guess I'm somebody!

Dallas did get himself to school on time but he was upset with himself about no shower, no breakfast.

I went to work.

My premiere Taekwondo instructor and friend Mr. D drove Bart to and from Creekside radiology for Bart's big CT scan. The moment we had been waiting for. Bart texted late afternoon that he was really tired and may not get the scan results for a few days. What?

I caught the 4:30 El Dorado Transit bus and at 4:40 PM I got an unexpected call from Bart. He never calls me. Bart's strictly an email or text guy.

Bart said the doctor's office called instructing him to immediately get to the Emergency Room at Mercy Folsom Hospital. The CT scan showed a pulmonary embolism (blood clot) in Bart's left lung.

Dallas drove Bart because the doctor said ambulance transport was not necessary.

Sandi picked me up at the bus stop and we headed to Folsom Hospital at 5:30 PM.

Bart was awake and tired but in good spirits. Dallas said he had a chemistry test to study for so we sent him home.

Bart told us that as the oncologist was hanging up, he mentioned that besides the pulmonary embolism, the CT scan showed that his tumors were shrinking!

As he was hanging up, are you kidding me? Bart recalled that all he said was the tumors are smaller. No pulmonary embolism would dilute this good news.

We fully expected Bart to be admitted to the hospital but to our surprise, the ER doctor said he could be released tonight.

Sandi and I gathered him up and headed for home. Bart requested McDonald's cheeseburgers for dinner. His blood sugar was low (74) so he ate a burger before injecting his insulin. Bart got very tired this evening but glad to be in his throne.

Tomorrow PG&E has scheduled a power outage all day. Bart's plan is to crank up the heat at 6 AM before they shut it off so he'll be more or less comfortable as the house cools off throughout the day. We'll see how his plan works.

We got an email recently from an old high school friend who lives in Australia. He was really nervous to get up in front of 800 Aussies at church to pray for Bart but he did it anyway. His last line was "1 Weavervillian and 800 Aussies". They boosted Bart's prayer network over the top. It worked.

Bart turns 60 on Friday. What a joyous birthday present. Thank you. Your love and your prayers are all powerful.

Houston, we have shrinkage. Let's party.

January 12

Bart stoked the heat at 6 AM in preparation for the all-day power outage. Power went off promptly at 8 AM. Bart got cozy on the couch and went to sleep for several hours.

I looked around and saw so many things I needed to do that I felt paralyzed. I didn't know what to do first so I took a nap.

Power came back online early at 12:30.

At 3:00 Dallas came home from school with a headache. No doubt he's pocketing his lunch money instead of eating. Matty did that, too. All the boys in this family refuse to ever pack a lunch, Matthew, Dallas and Bart as well. I think Dallas once carried around a petrified backpack sandwich for a month.

Wednesdays Dallas has drum and piano lessons. When he gets home I start dinner and attempt conversation with the young lad. Here's the extent of our discussion on what went down at school today. Dallas: "My friend Kelsey is a vegetarian. Kaden was eating pizza and dropped a pepperoni on the ground. Kelsey picked it up off the ground and ate it."

That was it. Then HE had to go lie down. It was a big nap day for all of us apparently.

Bart's doing really well, still weak, not a lot of energy to walk much but the embolism isn't bothering him and his appetite is good. Pain management is also decent and the nurses removed his PICC line. He gets one weekly dose of Gemzar on Mondays which can be done intravenously since it's infrequent. Removing the PICC means lower risk of infection and Bart can take a shower without Saran wrap.

We did have quite the go around today trying to figure out which pharmacies carried the blood thinner, syringes, Lovenox and which ones would fill the oral chemo drug Xeloda. I was on the phone with an insurance company associate at one point who tried connecting me to other departments while I was on the line. Every number she tried went to voicemail, not a human, which got her increasingly frustrated. It struck me so funny when she exclaimed and sighed with annoyance at her own company! I told her that I fully appreciated this reaction. Why is it that voicemail menus can have 20 options, none of which have anything to do with the problem you are calling about? With help from our Hills case manager all the pharmaceutical issues got resolved.

The lights of joy are still shining brightly at our house. I'm debating whether or not they should stay up. I don't relish putting myself through that debacle again next year.

Twenty years ago a repair guy drove me home from the shop and commented on how ridiculous it was that the folks in the pink house left their lights up until March! He used the term redneck or something. I didn't respond. I liked those people and had no problem with Christmas lights in March.

Who's to say lights of joy shouldn't be up all year round? That guy's comment stuck with me though. What would the neighbors think? I feel social pressure to take them down before Valentine's Day.

I was happy to see that one family in our 'hood (you know who you are) still has their lights up too. Ours will remain lit, at least until after Bart's birthday celebration. So if you're coming over Saturday, our house is easy to find, just follow the light!

January 13

Bart was quiet today. I asked how he felt but he didn't feel like talking. I prepared shepherd's pie early in the day so the boys could pop it in the oven if I wasn't home when they got hungry. Thursday is trash night. Dallas cleared the poop deck and got the trash can up to the curb thankfully.

I had intended to attend TKD but Bart had selected a movie and it's always better to watch with someone. Plus, our impromptu late afternoon meeting at Sandi's to talk about Bart's birthday menu included wine. Not conducive to optimum athletic performance.

It was interesting that Bart is choosing movies lately that could be categorized as "chick flicks". He has this weird sense though; a sort of innate ability to know what has redeeming viewer value. Tonight, we enjoyed "Leap Year" a movie that had spectacular Ireland cinematography. It's fun to watch scenes in the land of one's ancestry.

All is well. Martin, our Bel Air pharmacist, called to say he had the Lovenox syringes, so life is good.

January 14

It is Bart's birthday today! I prepared a favorite breakfast, French toast with sourdough bread then pre-made enchiladas for dinner. Bart said he felt pretty good on his birthing day.

Lori and Sandi came over to help me clean the house. It was really nice to get everything so orderly. I couldn't have done it without them. They'll agree.

I had a twinge of concern thinking Dallas would have to come home. I wanted the cleanliness to last longer and he can be quite the whirling dervish.

Last week Bart reprimanded Dal for wastefulness. I too reminded Dallas that he doesn't need a small cereal bowl full of ketchup for two corn dogs! I'd already saved his last ketchup helping in a Tupperware and asked him to use that first. Dallas said of course he would, NEXT time. It's always next time. He also said he'd save what he didn't consume this time. What he really meant was that he'd cram crumpled paper towels into the ketchup so he couldn't possibly put it back.

I told Dallas if we let him live to adulthood he would have to buy his own condiments.

Tomorrow the Steelers play at 1:30 PM, and folks will be stopping by at their leisure for an open house of sorts. There will be football and good cheer. We celebrate the beginning of the end for those beastly tumors and of course Bart's 60th year on the planet.

We haven't seen some of our neighbors since the great garbage capers of the 90's! In some sort of weird self-amusement ritual, teenaged vandals would drive-by kidnapping trashcans, drag them down the road and dump the contents on someone else's driveway. We fondly remember one night when Doug and Donna came traipsing up the road at 11 PM, Doug in his pajamas and Donna in her robe. Bart and I were already out on the driveway dressed in similar attire surveying the filthy spread with brooms in hand. As our neighbors emerged from the fog in their nighties, we all laughed and said, "we really must stop meeting like this." It was definitely an impromptu and entertaining social encounter, except for the mess.

But that was a small price to pay for a most memorable visit with our good neighbors. So often we go about our lives on autopilot and don't fully enjoy and appreciate the wonderfully fun folks who live so close. It's like not taking advantage of the tourist attractions in your own town!

I think Bart is really looking forward to seeing people tomorrow. He also has slight trepidation that his level of energy may not be up for entertaining but I assured him, everyone understands. No expectations.

Bart took his anti-nausea meds tonight which make him drowsy and combined with other meds can even make him dizzy. So, he's off to bed just after 11 PM. Bart must rest up for the big fun. Steeler fans and friends, gird your loins, there will be plenty of hooting and hollering around here tomorrow.

Happy Birthing Day, Barton!

January 16

Bart had a wonderful time Saturday. Many terrific friends and neighbors made for a perfect lively and engaging day. Bart even stayed awake until 12:30 at night. It was extra special in so many ways. Plus, the Steelers won.

I had written all this last night and a short synopsis of the soiree but evidently did not hit the "post" button. I must have been falling asleep in my chair and dreamt I posted it all. Instead it disappeared.

And no, I wasn't even in the bag! Much too busy having fun talking to everyone. Plus I kept misplacing my adult beverage all night long. Lots of laughs to be had and can't miss a single one.

Bart wishes to relay his heartfelt thanks to each and every one of you, including all of you who weren't able to stop by. He was truly touched by the constant flow of well wishes, smiling guests and even gifts.

January 18

Monday morning. Bart usually wakes with some stomach upset but taking his morning medications and breakfast helps alleviate the discomfort. Lori drove me to the train station for my one and only annual business trip to the Western Fairs Convention. I left Dallas in charge of helping Dad. God help us. Bart told Dallas they would talk about important life stuff.

Dallas rolled his eyes. I wonder where he got that familiar gesture. All day Sunday we relived all the fun we had at the big 60 party. Even Phaddy hit the lottery. The Donlans bestowed a bag of dog treats to delight even the most sedentary of canines.

We all got a kick out of watching Phaddy marvel at the bag and try to sneak a peek inside. The dog is continuously mesmerized by the big mysterious source of joy. Bart thoroughly enjoyed his prizes too. I went to put my phone in the charger and Bart barked "don't touch my gnome"! His Steelers gnome courtesy of D. Kick has a permanent home on the TV altar.

J-Dizz made him a super cozy Steeler blanket which he wasted no time napping with. Bethy topped Bart with Steeler Super Bowl ball caps and Pringles, the perfect chemo snack. Bart was also moved by a monogrammed Gist silver belt buckle. We also re-read all his cards just for repetitive laughs.

A Note from Bart:

Hi all, I want to say a special thanks to all of you who attended my birthday bash. It was quite spectacular. I had a really good time. I paid for it the next day, really tired, but it was worth it. I'm sorry that those of you who had cold or flu symptoms couldn't make it but being immune-compromised it was best I didn't chance it. Next time.

Went to Chemo today and found out that three of my largest liver tumors had shrunk about 10 percent and the main pancreatic tumor shrunk from 4 cm to about 3.4 cm. That all seems good so we are staying on this course of Chemo.

Sorry I'm not as eloquent as my bride but she has a gift. I write like I'm writing a technical manual. Just the facts! ;-)

I'll let you know if any further news crops up.

Love y'all Bart

January 20

Bart's been doing really well this week. Dallas on the other hand got the flu Tuesday, the day after I left, and he missed two days of school. Monday morning (MLK holiday) I woke Dallas to say goodbye. Phaddy had slept on Dally's bed that night. Apparently the dog marks his territory with vomit. He'd consumed some green grass somewhere and left a small deposit at the foot of Dallas' bed. I superficially cleaned it, said good bye and left. What he didn't know wouldn't hurt him. Besides Bart told me Dallas lost his lunch a time or two later that day. Remarkably Bart did not catch Dally's flu bug. We are still feeling so good about the news that Bart's chemotherapy is working. It must be like a vaccine.

Tuesday morning my laptop crapped out and was down for the count. I had no computer for the remainder of my conference in Reno.

How is it that a machine works fine for months; you take it on one little trip and that's when it goes belly up? It is most inconvenient.

My friend Lori picked me up at the train station and we stopped at the pharmacy to pick up Bart's five prescription refills. When I got home, Dal's sheets were in the washer. He'd evidently been sleeping on the mattress pad. Bart said he felt a bit tired today, cat napping most of the day. Dallas was feeling good, catching up on his homework and Phaddy was anxious to go for a walk.

Tonight we're all in our places and the lights of joy have been switched on.

January 22

Bart said he was very tired today. He had pain this morning when he got up. He is maintaining his regular med schedule though and the painkillers usually kick in after breakfast. It was French toast today. We understand why God made teenagers so wildly irritating. When they leave parting is not sweet sorrow but rather cause for celebration. God is just trying to make it easier on all of us. After all, God knows we've been through an interactional meat grinder since freshman year. At least we all agree on check-out time.

Dallas chose to sleep on top of the clean, wadded fitted sheet and mattress pad. Heaven forbid he should take one minute to stretch them over the bed. It is just too much effort for him, like flossing. That would certainly kill him.

Dallas couldn't even finish making mashed potatoes from a box. His toilet time conveniently lasted right through dinner preparation. Bart is not often up to coming to the dinner table anymore so we've not had as many of our sit down family meals like we used to. Even though Dallas may only grunt a time or two during mealtime, I still miss those table talks.

We did get Dallas to sit with us for an hour tonight. He likes to watch House. I suspect both the Reagan boys admire the sarcastic and insulting nature of the main character. They certainly seem to emulate it whenever possible.

Tomorrow's another day, another chance to get this kid to see the wonders of dental floss. Let us pray. Love to all.

January 23

Bart woke up this morning before I did which isn't unusual on weekends. If I don't get out there soon though, he will only eat cereal.

Okay, today he had cereal but I was really excited about dinner. I'd been marinating flank steak per Diane D's recipe. It had been soaking since Friday night.

Today felt time-compressed. I'd already slept in too long so getting everything done today was not in the cards.

First thing, take Phaddy on a walk. It was a beautiful day. Sunshine put an extra spring in my step. Phaddy typically sniffs more than he hikes so I try to keep him moving without too many unnecessary pit stops.

As we walked along Sudbury Road I spontaneously chose to cut off the road and get on the trail. The familiar street was getting a bit routine. My neighbor Matt said that the trail wasn't too muddy either.

The path is a rocky creek bed on the way up the mountain and also down with red clay in between. I flashed concern that Phaddy's belly might scrape on the rocks but quickly dismissed that worry. He would need to buck up and deal with it. No time like the present to step up his weight loss program. Those short little legs would just have to maneuver his girth around any obstacles. I needed it so he'd have to adjust.

The short-bodied dog is slow but he made the three-mile loop just fine, no belly scrapes, and no hang-ups except for that manzanita bush that ripped the ear buds out of my head. The dog was somewhat tired when we returned. He didn't even follow me into the kitchen!

Bart needed a Lidoderm patch put on his back and a heating pad. He wasn't feeling good enough to do the mailbox walk. Come to think of it, Bart never participated when the family initiated a mailbox run in more than 15 years.

We used to have family meetings every week on Sunday nights after dinner. At those meetings we assigned a secretary who took the minutes and a meeting master who pounded the gavel. We started with reading minutes of the last meeting, old business (follow up on previous problems), then new business, where we would often adjust or augment our meeting rules of conduct. Next was announcements, where we'd plan out the whole week of family activities and finally end with finances. Our family bank paid for food, essential school supplies and clothing. Other things like fancy pens, sunglasses and accessories the kids would have to budget for themselves.

At times our discussions would get elevated and tempers flared. We all wanted to be heard, so the family negotiated a scheme for handling tense moments when madness reigned and voices got loud. We voted unanimously on a solution. We amended the rules to say; *whenever yelling occurs or family members are getting too angry to engage in productive talks then anyone of can holler* "mailbox".

Once "mailbox" was invoked, everybody in the family had to run as fast as possible down to the mailbox. It was a rule. First one to touch it won and got unlimited bragging rights. But the rule stated that "all" of us had to race for it.

One summer when a patio chair went flying and Bart started raising his voice, Megan yelled "mailbox". We all clamored from the table and scurried with the utmost urgency around the deck, down the stairs speeding to the mailbox. All but one of us made it, tagging the box looking at each other, breathing heavily, smiling and giggling. The race seemed so ridiculous that the previous argument did not matter. It always struck me funny. It worked so well.

But where was Bart? He was still on the back deck in his deck chair. His excuse was that because he had a bad knee he'd be the last one to get there so why bother? He never got out of his chair! Mailbox was a technique we used for probably a decade or more and yet none of us remember Bart ever tagging the box even once. I guess he was a conscientious objector.

One thing for sure, nobody was upset by the time we got to the mailbox. That ship had sailed. The concept of running away to the street seemed crazy and unrelated to the problems at hand. Yet tempers always diffused there. Racing the kids and seeing them seriously try to win completely obliterated contentious issues that caused us to be aggravated with one another in the first place. Except for Bart, perhaps, who never bolted to the mailbox himself.

The same seems true today. I will gently suggest from time to time that Bart venture to the post box. The sunshine would do him good, I say. Plus he might get a glimpse of the squirrel and narrow down the coordinates. One thing I've always loved about Bart, is there is no uncertainty. No. That's it, no explanation, just that he's not doing that @#!*. Bart did vote years ago however, in favor of the "mailbox" concept but that apparently didn't mean he would do it. I think he secretly liked to see the rest of us run like idiots for no reason. I can support that justification.

It was fun. If only Bart would have tried it. The mailbox was also our family meeting place in case of fire. It was a pillar, a veritable monument to our clan, except when it got smashed to death by rogue teens. Word of caution, don't get a cow mailbox or some other really cute one. They're magnets for vandals but I digress.

No mailbox today for Bart.

I rushed back from my errands to get dinner started. The flank steak would be a real treat after marinating in the magic solution. I grilled the meat, baked potatoes, broccoli, garlic bread and fruit. I was thinking this would be one of my best offerings.

It was hot off the grill, thinly sliced, the steak seemed just right. I presented an aesthetic plate to Bart with anticipation.

Bart tasted it and reported that he did not like it. He didn't care for the garlic in the marinade or on the bread. Chemo alters his taste buds. Bart was the king of doubling the garlic before. I did not even use as much as the recipe called for yet it was still too much for Bart's constitution these days.

Dallas and his buddy Austin went next door to babysit the kids. It was poker night at our other neighbor's house. Caryn stopped by on her way so I went along too. I had to pay neighborly respects and see who was winning. Neighbor Matt (our resident police officer) was cleaning house. It looked like he had almost every chip. He ended up winning about $100. That's huge in these parts.

I enjoyed hanging with neighbors for a short while. Bart wasn't up for the trek. I returned from the party only to be asked to relieve Dallas from his babysitting charges so he could make it to the end of a poker night at his friend's home. At least Dal did his chores before leaving this time.

Hallelujah. Bart's in bed and I must turn the lights out and retire myself. I need to get up before Bart to get a jump on breakfast. At least the coffee is set up to brew automatically via timer. One of life's little pleasures... coffee and timers. That and mailboxes.

January 24

Devices are only as good as their programmers. Imagine my perplexed disappointment at no freshly brewed coffee this morning. I thought I was so careful but it was set for PM. Bart didn't mind as he was already fast asleep in his chair. He needs a good night's sleep so he can rest up. After all, it would be a big game day Steelers vs. Jets.

Bart was extremely fatigued this morning.

After breakfast and a few loads of laundry, Bart said I'd better go before football starts.

Off we went, the dog and I. I intended to bring training treats but of course I forgot. Once off the street I decided that if we were ever going to get a workout together then he would have to speed up or catch up. I took a chance. Let the dog off leash and ran as fast as I could to lose him and see if he would follow.

Turns out that curious little canine was holding out on me. He was running as fast as I've ever seen him fly to catch up with me. I ran even faster and still he was gaining. Looking over my shoulder and seeing his ears flop at top speed was a funny sight. The dog busted quite the move. I didn't need the leash again until we reached the road. Nice to know the dog found me worthy of chasing.

Bart was awake and moving about when we returned. I took advantage of the sunshine doing some trimming and planting. Winter vegetables were beginning to sprout.

Bart enjoyed chicken pot pie for lunch and was feeling up for the game. He was finally regaining a little energy. Bart saw me outside with shovel in hand planting the Christmas tree given to us by our dentist. If it lives, and it will, we plan to extend lights to it next year. We decided that forever more, this tree shall be called "The Chan-Tree" for our family dentist. It's a gift that keeps on giving to be sure and a reminder for Dallas that he should floss. He rolled his eyes and walked away.

My first attempt at stuffed manicotti was the big plan for tonight's football dinner. I was thrilled that the stuffing-to-shell ratio came out even, which I believed was an omen that Bart would like this meal. Dallas and his friend Adam along with Bill and Lori liked it. But would Bart? He did. Score!

I thought it needed Tabasco and garlic myself but a win is a win. Steelers did too. If was great to see Bart totally relish the victory. I certainly did. He liked his dinner. Touchdown!

January 25

Chemotherapy was tough on Bart today. Sandi drove him to Creekside Lounge this afternoon and Dallas picked him up this evening. I rode the bus home from work and we all converged on the homestead about the same time. Bart was napping when I got home. Phaddy was excited and raced around the house jumping up on sleeping Bart every loop through the family room. That was painful. Dallas was off on miscellaneous errands for Dad. Thank goodness it was leftovers night.

I answered phone messages, re-heated dinner, did laundry, school prep etc. and before you know it, it was 9 PM, time to sit and relax. Bart told Dallas and I not to talk to him or ask him any questions as he was on the cusp of nausea and not feeling well enough to converse. Bart did throw a wadded-up sock for the dog twice. That was the extent of his exertion this evening.

Bart chose to watch a little television, rest his eyes and let the pain meds kick in. We were both amused at one line on *CSI: Las Vegas* when the coroner arrived at a crime scene, looked over the embankment, stared a moment and said "Why can't they die closer to the road?" Bart looked over at me. I was laughing heartily, so Bart smiled himself. We are really all so similar. We don't ask much, just for life to be more convenient.

Speaking of convenience, I promised I would once again try to set the coffee timer for AM instead of PM.

January 26

It was a better day than yesterday for Bart. When asked if he would be posting today while I was at work he simply replied "no."

It was a big day though, Bart went to the mailbox. Evidently he's been withholding key accomplishments like that. Tonight he bragged that he's done it a few times. His sugar numbers have also been good so we've had silence on that front too. No news is definitely good news.

Bart did report that Phaddeus the wonder dog had another play date. Lauryn and her little brother Chase came by to see if Phaddy could come out and play at their house. The dog's got more engagements on his social calendar than we do. Last week young Bridgette and her mom came all the way from Greenstone to take Phaddy out.

Bart thinks the dog needs more food because he's always ravenous. It's possible, because this morning at 5:30 the dog jumped off the bed making the all too familiar horking sound. This time he urped on the carpet near the bedroom door. I opened it and he galloped down the hall hacking all the way. He was on the hardwood (easy cleaning surface) by the front door, but gacked precisely right next to it on the carpet. The object spewed forth was some unidentifiable chunk of hard blue vinyl that I could not place. It didn't look like any of his toys or anything else that we own for that matter. It's a mystery that remains to be solved but Bart thinks he's just not getting enough food or he wouldn't eat random stuff. But if the animal is always hungry I don't get the distinction? He'd likely eat himself to death if left to his own devices.

On my way home from work the boys were hungry. Bart sent me a request to pick up a very specific order at KFC. I guess I haven't bought fast food in a while; an 8-piece meal was $25!

Dallas, his friend, and Bart served themselves but Bart pointed out that the mac-n-cheese was missing. I checked the receipt and sure enough, I'd paid for it. I really didn't want to go out again.

I tried to call the place but the only listing was an 888 number, which kept disconnecting. I sent the boys back with the receipt.

Bart wanted what he ordered. Soon, the phone rang. Dallas said that the manager didn't believe him. He gave me a number to call back. That poor young manager recounted some nasty situations with hoodlums. Here she had two respectful young men but her attitude had already been tainted. They accomplished the mission but told us tales of unwarranted rudeness. Bart threatened to write a letter. It pleased the boys to hear Dad's validation.

I took off for black belt class at Cameron Park TKD. Bart felt pretty good this evening. So good, he's got to sleep it off.

January 27

So I asked Bart about having a Super Bowl soiree this year in honor of his beloved Steelers. His response was "I haven't recovered from my birthday party yet." If you know Bart, then you can hear the tone of voice just reading that line.

I've been asked to shed a little light on the England connection. Both Bart and I worked for Ford Aerospace in the early 80s and did a tour of duty in England. That tidbit might explain some of the entertaining guestbook postings from our friends, Dennis Clan-of-the-Cave "Blair", Fred, "Stubby" Tonsing, et al. Anyone making reference to Crew 4, or

England, is likely one of these lifelong connections where crews worked 12-hour shifts and after would meet at the bar and *spoof* to see who paid. Often one of our crew members would end up paying for other crew members' adult beverages if they didn't watch their wallet. We were a close but brutal group where there was a tacit understanding never to show weakness. The unspoken rule was to tease the weak unmercifully. If they broke, immediate dismissal from Crew 4 occurred. Ah, such warm, fond memories.

Bart has been really tired this evening. Not bad, just not up for any exertion beyond heading to the bathroom or bed. He says it's definitely bedtime now because David Letterman is on. It's no secret Bart dislikes Letterman. He won't even tolerate the top ten list. I guess that's my cue.

January 28

Bart said he had a crappy day and didn't feel much like talking about it. He said his guts were on fire when he got up this morning. As the day wore on Bart took over-the-counter remedies which helped a little.

Bart was feeling like tuna casserole for dinner. He warned me to make it as bland as possible.

I obliged but he still did not care for it. Dallas and I on the other hand liked it. Although it really was bland and tasted much better with ample Tabasco. Bart ended up making himself pierogies. Dallas and his chemistry buddy spent four hours this evening on their hot air balloon project. It's quite the floater. About three feet of varied shades of tissue paper glued together.

Phaddy sported a new "do" this week thanks to Classy Clips, the dog beauty salon. Soft and fluffy gradually became comfortably dirty. Phaddy thoroughly enjoys his long trail walks. Dallas has been insisting that the dog sleep with him now. He has to trap him in his room, where eventually Phaddy succumbs for the night. But the moment that bedroom door opens a slit, Phaddy hops to with the agility of a cat speeding through the opening and out to the kitchen where he proceeds to scour the hardwood for anything remotely edible. The news is over now and Bart says it's Bedtime for Bonzos. That would be us, definitely Bonzos.

January 30

Bart awoke Saturday morning with difficult abdominal cramping. I got breakfast in him but he nursed an upset stomach continuously throughout the day and his back hurt. The heating pad was working overtime.

After breakfast Phaddy and I set out for the trail. The dog is taking a few more liberties "off leash" these days, sniffing longer and marking bushes but always catching up in due time. Bart and I were thinking this 3-mile daily loop might wear him down enough to lounge instead of trolling around the house in the evenings. Now we fear that these longer runs are serving to energize him. He seems to want to constantly play. All evening long he is tossing toys in our laps to throw for him. I find these games very hard to resist but Bart will simply steal the object of Phaddy's attention and that's it. Game over.

We appreciate good advice from friends and the book "Dogs for Dummies" that Tracey gave us in the giant dog treat birthday bag. From both sources we learn tricks to teach an old dog anything. For instance, I keep treats now near the door so when the dog wanders off I yell "treat" and in theory he's supposed to come running. Instead he stands there. Eventually I have to sit down on the driveway with the treat and when he's darn good and ready he comes back. Friday evening we forgot to put the dog out. (Having imbibed a bit much) I realize that accident is on me but geez he's not that big, you'd think he could hold it longer or at least tell us.

Yesterday Bart craved Chinese food all day long. After work I picked up our friend Lori on my way home. Bart's favorite dishes would be ordered and delivered by dinner time about 6:30 PM.

We bought a few good bottles from local wineries to enjoy with dinner. After all it was Friday night. On the Friday fun menu, a movie "The Jones" on DVD.

I've learned that one does not post when you're somewhat lit. Bart said we were definitely happy.

Dallas decided that it would be fun to go low tech. He installed Matty's old Nintendo system then no less than 4 boys came over for the experience. I wish they'd retreat to even lower tech entertainment like board games. We still have a whole wardrobe cabinet filled with them.

The Christmas lights of joy came down a lot easier than they went up. It was cold. My left little finger took more hours than I care to admit to regain feeling.

I left red strings up around the door for Valentine's Day. There's something about those lights I like.

Bart just shook his head but didn't disagree out loud. I don't think he believes in the concept of Valentine's lights but at least he's willing to let the light shine for a while longer.

Bart said he had a better day than yesterday but still not good enough to sit up at the dinner table tonight.

We had a visit from a long lost friend and former Sudbury neighbor, Cindy, who even attempted a little Phaddy dog training while she was here. Phaddy may be only mildly dense. There is hope although marking laundry baskets is completely unacceptable and will not be tolerated. Even Dogs for Dummies has no chapter on that.

Since Dallas got Matthew's original Nintendo to work, he and his friends have been nonstop on the low tech kick. They played all night long trying all the old games. I was glad to see him come up for air long enough to do homework and a load of laundry. Folding still seems to be a foreign concept to that child.

Things were going fairly well this evening until Dallas backed out of the driveway and sheared the driver's side mirror clean off the car. The worst part is that I had just been talking to him through the open car window about being careful and driving slowly to avoid accidents. Of course he knew all that. Then milli-seconds later the crunch-o-rama.

I was hollering at him from the porch that he was too close to the tree but Mr. know-it-all heard and saw nothing but fog apparently.

Even as I heard the crunching, instead of stopping he just kept right on moving backwards until the whole mirror apparatus was hanging by a wire. Just to make sure we add a little insult to injury here, Dallas also ran over the clay plant pot that Matty didn't smash at Christmas time. Now of course I will need to get up at o'dark thirty and play chauffeur for Dallas again. I just can't believe this kid.

Sandi will be escorting Bart to Creekside Lounge tomorrow. Dallas is obviously no longer available to pick his dad up until he fixes the car. Oh and he has to repair the driver's door too. The door won't open. Appears the lock mechanism fell inside the door. Dallas has to crawl in & out of the passenger side. Bart didn't react much. He wanted to watch a movie and wasn't too interested in allowing me a forum to vent. This has certainly dampened my evening mood. I sure hope the kid learns faster than the dog. Otherwise, he could be riding the little bus to and from school from now on.

No joy this morning as Bart had that nasty perpetual cramping, pain and feelings of nausea. Today marks the first day of a week off. No chemo this week, just blood tests and doctor appointments. It's his week to rest up for the next round.

Bart passed his blood test with flying colors; all the numbers were in the ideal range.

Too bad Bart didn't feel as good as his blood looked. He asked to see the doctor because he felt so bad. He'd removed his Fentanyl patch in the morning and did not replace it before leaving the house. Considering that he still had severe cramping, nausea and bad back pain it was decided he would stay at Creekside Lounge for treatment. He would receive fluids, pain meds, nausea relief and Pepcid AC via IV.

By 5:30 PM when I collected Bart from Creekside Lounge he was 100 percent better. What a change. He was more talkative. So much so Bart had no qualms commenting on my driving. I happen to think that using your blinker when you're in a dedicated left turn lane with a left turn signal light is redundant. Bart on the other hand, does not. He says a turn is a turn. He maintains that blinker indicators are required by law no matter what. If I used my blinker that much it would malfunction from overuse I say. Bart completely disagrees. Blinkers are meant to blink says he. So now I use my blinkers to a ridiculous degree. What's the harm? They can only go on the "blink".

Bart and I stopped at the credit union ATM then onto the Bel-Air Pharmacy to refill Bart's Fentanyl pain patches. Bart told me to deliver the prescription while he entered the store from the other side because that's where the motor carts are.

I do believe that since our previous rather destructive visits, they have disabled the acceleration feature of the grocery carts. Even Bart thought the cart was slower than usual. No matter, we still tangled it up, but it wasn't Bart's fault this time.

Rounding an end aisle display corner we screech to a halt facing a young man with a three-foot wide push mop. Startled that he almost ran into us, I scuttled around Bart's cart to get out of the way only to get slapped in the face by Bart's big red bumper flag. At first I didn't know what hit me so I stepped aside again. The mop guy was still trying to get around us but Bart moved the cart so I got wrapped around the flag so to speak. I was a bit embarrassed to be so clumsy. After all, I didn't have a cart or a mop to contend with and yet I got all tripped up just moving aside. I took a picture of Bart at check out laughing at me this time. You can clearly see how that flag might slap you silly if you get too close or maybe Bart just knows all too well how to fling it around.

Back at the ranch, we summoned Dallas to help us unload the groceries. After a very chaotic unloading Dallas revealed some problems he was having with two teachers apparently not recording his work, resulting in missing assignments on the books. Dallas assured us he would take care of it tomorrow and that it was the teacher's mistake.

He said he had done the work. We shall see, but on the heels of last night's mirror accident, this was not good news and I could feel the rise of stress within me. Dallas' laundry was still strewn about and the dishwasher not yet unloaded. Then the sight of the explosion that obviously occurred in his room didn't please me either. Then there was the bath towel soaked with some spilled beverage sitting on top of a borrowed sofa seat cushion. I just had to close the door. We will surely have to replace any household carpet that interacted with Dallas for any length of time.

Ultimately we all had to settle on cheese and crackers, apples and grapes for dinner. I tried warming up Dal's corn dog and Brie but ended up burning it beyond recognition. There are too many tasks so little time. After all the random action no one had the patience to wait for anything that took longer to prepare than uncooked "snacks".

Bart felt really good tonight (despite the absence of a real dinner) after the regenerative session at Creekside. Phaddy sat with him in his chair for a spell; the dog even did his loving little nibbling behavior on Bart's knee. We have noticed that when Phaddy really likes something he delicately nibbles at it: tennis balls, people, bedspreads, you name it. If it's something he likes then he's tickled it with dog nibbles. At Christmas time, Matty was especially amused whenever the dog would do that. It oddly makes sense to us.

Bart and I exchanged more than a few laughs and some knowing smiles tonight from between our two chairs.

All's well that ends well for a Monday.

Chapter Ten

Making Lemonade

February 2

A Note from Bart:

Today was a relatively pain free day. Not much going on. Just hanging out at home wondering when I will feel good enough to golf again. Good news is I get to watch the really good golfers on TV starting tomorrow. Then Super Bowl Sunday. Go Steelers!!! I think it will have to coincide with not wearing this opiate patch and taking tons of pain meds. Anything earlier may cause an issue with my "driving" if y'all know what I mean. ;-)

I love reading the stories and replies to Mel's postings. They crack me up. You guys are the best.

Have to tell the doctor that the "cocktail" they mixed up on Monday when I was feeling bad was great. I felt better than I have in a long time. Maybe he can set me up for the same combo at home.

More later, Bart

February 3

Bart's doing pretty darn good tonight. Especially fun to have our little nephew Kirky Alexander Polka and his parents (my brother Michael and his wife Stephanie) here for a few days. Sandi cooked a great meal. It was wonderful to see her hard at work in my kitchen when I got home from work. Besides, everyone likes her cooking better (me too). Bart enjoyed it and ate well, cherry glazed pork tenderloin (emphasis on the tender), asparagus and pumpkin pie spiced yams. Sandi truly has creative culinary skills.

Our little nephew is quite the articulate conversationalist. He sat with Uncle Bart tonight and asked him what was on television. Bart answered "a commercial". Kirky said "I think it's an ad. There are lots of those on TV but they are just like commercials".

Dogs and little boys are quite entertaining. Kirky chased Jasper, (Sandi's Beagle) and the dog ran like crazy in figure eights. Jasper hid behind a couch then bolted out to get chased some more. Kirk also got a kick out of throwing toys that Phaddy happily fetched over and over again. Then there was a game of hide-n-seek, always exciting, especially when "the hidden" betrays their position with giggles. There was much ado and great fun. Dallas got into the act too. He loves his Uncle Mike's sense of humor as we all do and has the cutest talks with Kirky.

It was a very enjoyable evening. We wish they didn't have to go back to Florida. After a couple days with us however, they might relish the departure. Oh sure, we're fun, but you might not want to live near us. Bart enjoyed reading the latest CB posts this evening and has favorable comments about the book "The Girl with the Dragon Tattoo". I told him to give us a book report when he's done.

Dallas took the Red Dragon (car) to our neighbor Dalton's house. They're going to investigate why the driver's door no longer opens. Dallas is buying a new eye for the dragon (mirror assembly) at Pick-n-Pull after school tomorrow provided an aunt or uncle is willing to drive him there. TGIF tomorrow, it's my favorite day of the week. You have full anticipation of the weekend ahead without having spent much of it yet. And it's Super bowl weekend too! May the commercials, uh "ads" as our nephew would say, be almost as good as the game.

February 6

A Note from Bart:

Well I just watched a very good Super Bowl game, in spite of the fact my team lost. The Packers played a good game; the Steelers had one too many turnovers. I start my next round of Chemo tomorrow and I'm going to try and get the same cocktail they gave me last Monday. It really seemed to help. I am doing fairly well, just some pain in my back. I can't tell if it's my cancer or my arthritis. It doesn't really make any difference to my body. If I take my pain meds I'm usually in pretty good shape.

Tomorrow we are giving my Oncology lab a gift. It's a sign handcrafted by our friends Lisa and Lee: www.jdizzigns.com. It says Creekside Lounge, a name my family coined to describe all us chemotherapy patrons sitting in lounge chairs getting cocktails. Not the good kind either. ;-)

Bart

February 7

Bart wasn't too broken up about the Steeler's loss. Not being from Pittsburgh myself (although my dad was), I was somewhat ambivalent. My dad used to tell me I had legs like a Green Bay Packer so I assumed because he loved football so much that it was a good thing.

They must be a deserving team since they evidently all had Polka legs.

It's Monday and that means Bart's weekly appointment at Creekside Lounge. We were anxious this time because Bart would be delivering the special sign dedicated to the chemo lab. We were called in from the waiting area. After being weighed, Bart awarded the beautifully handcrafted wooden moniker creation to the chemo cocktail waitresses and staff. They posed for a photo under the entrance to the lounge.

Bart's come to depend on these lovely ladies to deliver welcome relief with a smile. The oncologist even grinned when he saw the sign. I told him, it's appropriate considering all the patrons receive their cocktails intravenously in a lounge chair. He added that they don't get intoxicated either. I respectfully begged to differ reminding the oncologist that some "loungers" puked their guts out like there was no tomorrow.

We hope the next time we venture to Creekside, a picture of the Lounge entrance will be graced by the sign dedicated to Bart. Lisa even created the unique lettering and called it "Bart Font". Sounds French but never mind, it's an honor Bart loves.

It was sister Sandi's birthday tonight. Bart felt pretty good too. Dallas became Sandi's chauffeur for the evening. He drove to pick Aunt Sandi up and deliver her to our house for the evening natal day festivities. We had a really nice dinner. When it came to gift time I thought oh boy, I was so ahead of the curve because I'd purchased her gift way back on January 2nd. It was safe, ready to be wrapped, just sitting on my closet shelf. It had been on that shelf since January yet suddenly on her birthday eve, I can't find it anywhere. What in the name of our Lord happened to it in such short order?

This was so ultimately frustrating. So much so that our friend Lori had to take up reins at the BBQ grill so I could frantically run about the house supposedly tracing my steps whatever they might have been? I recall thinking that I needed to wrap it. I must have taken the gift to the wrapping area only it wasn't there! What could I have been doing and why was this so hard and why at this very crucial birthday moment?

I jolted out of my chair and spontaneously scouted any nook or cranny that popped into my head. Eventually I had to give up the futile search and join the party. I had to try to put out of my mind how ridiculous I felt for losing her present on her birthday.

Dallas drove Aunt Sandi home with only mild assurance that her birthday gift might soon turn up.

Although my mind cannot fathom what I might have done with her gift, Lori's mom Bev reminded me that often if you sleep on it, the mind will solve your mystery. Dallas was very kind and reassuring which was quite splendid. He sincerely told me that it happens to the best of us (sarcasm not withstanding) and that he was sure I'd find it. I even got the half hug with a pat on the head. What a sweet boy to calm his frantic mother. Bart on the other hand held up a pound of butter I'd left out on the counter and announced "this is why you lose things". I see now that he was referring to me forgetting to put the butter back in the refrigerator but at the time I thought maybe it could be in the frdge! I'd better check.

Bart says he felt pretty good this evening despite his frustration over my losing Sandi's present. Creekside IV nourishment did him proud and he was able to join us at the dinner table for a full evening meal. Bart's voice is still strong and the oncologist says we will stay the course. Ya don't mess with what's working.

I'll be working on solving Sandi's missing birthday present in my sleep.

February 8

Bart had a decent enough day. His lower back hurt which he says could be the sudden colder temperatures and his arthritis piling on. We gently slapped a Lidoderm patch on his back this evening. Earlier he decided to stretch out on the floor. Phaddy took that gesture as a signal for playtime. The dog zipped around stealing Bart's ball cap and tossing his eviscerated toys poised to fetch. Even Dallas had to get in on this action.

Fortunately it was leftover night. I got home from work with just enough time to re-heat dinner and transfer laundry before Taekwondo. As I picked up a folded stack of clothes on top of the dryer there it was, Sandi's birthday present in a mesh drawstring bag. Woo hoo! And only a day late. I put this discovery in the category of small miracles.

Bart's got one last injection before bedtime. It's my 30 minute warning. Bart keeps me on a reasonable bedtime schedule otherwise I'm in danger of getting my usual second wind after TKD and staying up too late.

At least I can rest easy knowing Sandi will get her birthday present, that is if I can keep track of it until tomorrow.

February 9

Not a good day for Bart. Things had been going so well. I rode the bus to work and was at the mercy of the PM schedule which does not accommodate an early return home. Bart got a ride to Creekside Lounge where he spent the afternoon. By the time I got home at 6PM Bart was home but sleeping peacefully with his Steelers blanket. He had no interest in dinner but later said waffles sounded palatable. Both Bart and Dallas ate waffles. Neither one had a bite of the primarily vegetable dinner I had prepared.

By about 9:15 PM Bart felt mildly human again enough to sit up, yet not good enough to stay awake. Bart was soon napping in his chair then off to bed. I have to go to work again tomorrow but we are blessed with friends and family who are at the ready to deliver Bart to Creekside should treatment be necessary.

February 12

Thursday Bart felt sketchy so he got a ride to Creekside for treatment. Dallas picked him up late afternoon. I rode the bus home from work, stopped at the market then home to begin preparing dinner.

I knew Bart must be feeling so much better because he was highly vocal with the dinner complaints. It was a sure sign he was much improved. Bart said the asparagus was overcooked, salmon too salty and whatever I had done to the potatoes he didn't like it one bit. His sour notes didn't bother me though. Dallas and I liked it. Bart attributed his distaste for this meal to chemo-tongue. His final comment before handing me his full plate "what are you trying to do, make me lose weight"? Bart then asked me, "What can I eat"? Well, he got a four minute Banquet microwave beef potpie. He ate all of it too. I was sure all his finicky grousing was a good sign. Still I knew black belt class was just what the doctor ordered for me.

Friday I went to work and Bart got one last dose of fluids etc. to top him off for the weekend. More errands after work yet I was home before Bart and Dallas. Bart was craving Chinese food so he and Dal were out picking it up from the local Shanghai restaurant.

Bart was doing pretty well until after dinner when he experienced some post Chinese food discomfort and had to stay close to the loo. Couldn't help but think that my cooking has a much better track record.

February 13

Despite Friday's top off at Creekside, Saturday morning didn't start well. Bart had intestinal distress, cramping and a lot of pain. It was so very disappointing and so hard for me to see him hurting. After breakfast Bart said he was heading downstairs to the computer room and asked me to check on him in case he passed out from the exertion.

Bart did make it back upstairs in a few hours.

He was still feeling poorly so we took his blood pressure, 185/110 so I had him take it again. It soon began trending down but I still called the help nurse just in case. She said that Bart's pain likely had something to do with the blood pressure spike, that and the hike up the 18 stairs.

Later his blood pressure returned to normal levels. After taking supplemental pain pills, Bart napped.

I thought I'd better check Dallas for bedsores. Carefully I made my way into the booby-trapped war zone that is Dal's bedroom. As I opened the window blind a box of colored candies the size of peppercorns, Wonka Rainbow Nerds tipped and spilled onto the kids' head, trailing around his pillow and all over the sheet. Of Course he didn't wake up until I pulled the blanket off. Dallas wasn't bothered in the least to sleep with a sheet full of candy pebbles. I only scooped them up so the dog wouldn't eat them.

Now, stepping back to the door would be like avoiding alarmed laser beams. His drum set, piano, dishes, cola cans, water bottles, juice boxes and a wardrobe of dirty laundry littered the floor. I hit the wastebasket and Phaddy was there at light speed snatching a half-eaten egg roll, inhaling it before I could intervene. The dog was giving that famished quick check look, to gauge how much time he had to eat it before I could stop him.

At that point I figured I'd let the dog clean bits off the floor. Exiting the room I noticed yet another dirty plate behind the television and lo and behold I see 2 crumpled pillow cases there! Is he using the pillowcases for napkins I wondered? It always puzzled me how all of his pillows ended up sans covers. I've never worked over a pillow so hard that it completely lost its case by morning. He apparently does so, on a nightly basis. That's why Dallas gets the cheap pillows.

I made a healthy vegetable beef stew for dinner but Bart wasn't keen on the concept. Instead he opted for a turkey pot pie, trusty frozen food to the rescue. By bedtime more analgesics to keep his pain at bay. Dallas is said to be still working on cleaning his room. I haven't seen much concerted effort in there, other than a pile of laundry outside the door. Another tidbit to gripe about was seeing perfectly clean folded clothing piled in among the dirty stuff. Just wait until he has to use his own quarters to wash this stuff.

Both laundry and the dog got washed today. Bart said Phaddy was starting to acquire the scent of homelessness. Because he had another little accident in the house, we're going to open the Christmas box tomorrow to look for a bell to hang on the door lever. A friend told us it might be a helpful training tool. Theory is the dog will ring the bell to indicate he has to go out. That's the theory. I'm only worried about how to actually train him to do that. I'll have to read up on Pavlov's techniques.

Another critter alert: I was beginning to think the squirrel might be gone. Reason being I saw one dead on upper Sudbury, road kill. I felt a mild evil satisfaction too. Then this afternoon I heard him on the roof while I was standing at the bathroom sink. That's a new spot for the squirrel, southwest corner. I ran out back, grabbed the hose and squirted indiscriminately up there suddenly realizing I was wetting the solar panels in the sunlight, a big no-no. That clever devil escaped again. Tomorrow I set the trap with attractive peanuts in the shell. Watch, I'll probably catch a Blue Jay or Phaddy dog!

It was mostly a bad day for Bart. He finally felt better about 2:00 PM but that didn't last long. He got really tired of the ever present internal cramping and pain but kept up with his meds, watched a little golf and a rather frightening show called "When Vacations Attack" the horror stories of holidays gone terribly wrong. He also cat napped quite a bit. I would have thought those aggressive fish, erupting volcanoes and 70 mph hail storms might have given him nightmares but not even. Bart dozed easily on and off throughout the day.

Cheryl, Phaddy and I ran on the trail this morning. It was a beautiful day. We could see Cameron Park and Folsom Lakes plus the idle towers of Rancho Seco from the high point. Back at the house we put our heads together to figure out how to set the squirrel trap. Deed completed, Cheryl wished us luck. Luck indeed.

A few hours later I had the rare chance to "take out" a spry grey squirrel that errantly froze in the middle of the street. I was driving straight at him. He didn't move a muscle even as I approached at 25 mph. I knew I could get him. I was so close and he was not moving. In the last tenth of a second I thought, I'll just run over his tail, but that tail might flip him up into my wheel well. I just couldn't do it. Besides I had no real evidence that he was the actual squirrel squatter. He was very lucky I let him live.

Our sons Matty and Dallas might be disappointed in me considering they did not hesitate given a similar scenario. They ate squirrel on their "man versus wild" weekend adventure last summer. The boys were determined to live off the land. They were going to hunt and fish for their food, no groceries. The first day, on the way to their campsite they killed a squirrel with the truck. The initial plan was to stay for more than a week, then later it was reduced to just a weekend. After the squirrel dinner, the adventure turned into just an overnight. They got home at 3 PM the next day and were all devouring Subway foot long sandwiches in front of the television. So much for man versus the wild. Chalk one up for the wild.

On a mission to get donuts for Dad, Dallas told us that he rolled all the windows down and blasted the volume on the car stereo as loud as it would go, bumping and moving with the music especially at stoplights. Dal said his head was bopping as he waited at a red light when an elderly gentleman in the lane next to him looked over. But his look wasn't a disapproving stare, for the music blaring was Beethoven! The guy gave a congenial nod, which Dallas returned in kind. Dal said he had Mozart, Bach, Strauss and Tchaikovsky in the queue. Bart and I agreed that if you're going to pump up the volume obnoxiously loud then it may as well be classical music.

While we were talking, I was able to inquire about why I found pillowcases among the dishes in his room. Dallas admitted that he and his friends experienced a wee "soda spill" and rather than expend the effort to exit the room in order to get a towel, pillow cases were handy rags. There is evidently no limit to their laziness.

Bart wants me to have a talk with Dallas tomorrow. Bart thinks Dallas' laundry situation needs to be elevated to Def Con four. Bart strongly suggested that I schedule the talk during chemotherapy so Dad won't be around (???). I get that Bart doesn't need the added stress. He'd likely lose patience and go for the drill sergeant solution, which has not proven effective with this kid.

I could use the "girls might not like boys who dress like wrinkled street urchins" argument but then again I might just use the meeting time more wisely and call it Dallas' basic large appliance training and make him demonstrate his domestic acumen while reviewing the guide to carefree laundering.

Sandi cooked dinner tonight, a delicious roasted chicken with my Meyer lemon and her homegrown thyme. We all loved it but Bart couldn't eat very much. After dinner he took his injections. Sugar levels have been great lately. Blood pressure is normal. Some things are going right. Bart's got to rest up for a big chemo day tomorrow. Sandi's taking him to Creekside and Dallas has the return trip covered.

Bart typically feels better after Gemzar chemo Mondays. He gets vitamins/minerals and supplemental nausea, pain and stomach remedies in addition to the Gemzar that seem to make him feel more human for a while.

Thanks again for your guest book postings. Bart checks it often and sincerely enjoys reading every word from everyone all the time. We often get a lot of laughs out of your comments.

Remember you don't ever have to have anything to say either.

We don't and we still post!

February 14

Happy Valentine's Day.

Three out of four of our clan woke up ill this morning. The dog jumped off the bed just before 6 AM and threw up on the bedroom carpet in two places. I suppose I should be thankful he spared the bedspread but geez?

Dallas was already in the bathroom feeling sick.

Bart wasn't feeling so hot either but at least he didn't upchuck. Great start to the week.

Monday is Bart's Creekside Chemo day. I was hopeful that today's chemo regimen might actually help Bart to feel better since they usually pump him full of other stuff to relieve his symptoms.

Late afternoon Dallas was feeling better, so much so that he was motivated to clean his room. We did have our little laundry chat. I doubt that it was talk that motivated him though. Dallas said when he hates himself then it's time to clean. At one point I even heard the vacuum. He was rewarded with homemade chicken noodle soup.

There was no critter in the humane squirrel trap. Although we did receive squirrel underpants in today's mail from Gene and Jeanne! A portion of the proceeds from the pants are donated to the "Small Animal Decency Fund" which seeks to rid our neighborhoods of any potentially offensive naturally occurring indecent exposures. The poor things don't even know that they are naked. In keeping with the squirrel theme, Bart gave me a squirrel card but I hesitate to repeat the lovely sentiment.

I picked Bart up after 5 PM from Creekside and indeed he felt a bit better than he had all weekend. I took him home then returned to the pharmacy to fill his prescriptions. The doctor upped the dose for his Fentynl patches since Bart had such a rough weekend.

Dallas announced that one of our kitchen cabinet doors fell off again. It was likely due to the extra heavy use of that snack cupboard by Mr. Hammer Hands. I'd fixed it three or four times myself. Tonight Bart decided he would have a go. Clearly we needed screws with a slightly larger heads to secure the bracket. Of course we couldn't find the right size screwdriver bit for the power drill so Bart opted for a regular screwdriver. After he twisted it into the wood the head fell off and of course so did the cabinet door. I laughed. Bart wasn't laughing. He simply said this is a job for your cousin Bob "the builder". Meanwhile Dallas has easier access to the snack shelf.

Bart's watching the news and giving the 10 minute warning for bedtime. It's great to see him awake and feeling better on this Valentine's Day. And tomorrow, the day after V-Day, it's legal to eat chocolate for breakfast.

February 16

A Note from Bart:

Hi all,

Well after several days of treatments I think maybe I'm getting a little relief. Today and tonight has been relatively pain free. Hopefully I can stay ahead of this and keep the momentum going. So in honor of my pain free day God put on a little wild weather show for us. We had heavy rain, followed by a hail storm then some thunder and lightning. It was crazy.

We still haven't caught Mel's squirrel. I'm thinking he doesn't want to get caught. Nuts, huh?

I love all the posts and interactions on this site. It keeps me smiling when I have a little pain.

We are trying to figure out what holiday Mel can use the lights for next, since they obviously are never coming down. Next big holiday is my brides birthday. We could use them for that. :-)

I'm working on when I can get out to the golf course next. It's tough when I take so many drugs for pain I can hardly walk let alone swing a club like I mean it. I'm still working on it. Not giving up.

My Creekside Lounge folks should have the sign up soon. I'll post a picture of me under it. Not much more to report except my lack of pain. It's been a really good day.

love ya'll Bart

February 18

Frick, this just blows. Bart felt crappy today, bad back pain, cramping, upset stomach and nausea. I knew he must be feeling badly because he didn't send many emails to me at work today.

We were both concerned about Dallas who had a meltdown last night. Dallas complained that he hated his life and besides family he felt he had no one to talk to. He was weepy and sad. Dallas did tell me that he really liked the last therapist so I drove him to Folsom tonight for another appointment after work. We had just enough time afterwards to get to the music school for his jazz band practice and piano lesson. The boys requested McDonalds for dinner. I cringed and Bart said he choked back the quarter pounder. Both boys weren't too keen on vegetables. I made a vegetable stir fry but neither one of them ate it. I admit it was prepared late due to TKD black belt class. The instructors were snowed in so Lisa and I (fourth degree instructors) taught the class. It was fun.

Bart dozed off and on this evening. He was not much for conversation and barely stayed awake for his nightly television. He went to bed at 11 PM which is when I first hit "post" and due to some weird glitch, lost the whole thing. I'm not happy about losing what I had composed tonight over several hours.

I hate computers.

February 19

Bart felt ok. He told me to go ahead and go to the Pacific Five Star Taekwondo Tournament this morning since Dallas would be home if he needed anything.

I checked in with Bart via text during the afternoon competition. He said he felt crappy but it wouldn't help any for me to be at home. At one point Bart instructed me to stop texting him and go compete so he could get some rest. I took the dog for a walk this evening while Bart was napping and reheated leftovers upon my return. Bart chose my chicken noodle soup only.

This time I was the one who fell asleep snoring while Bart stayed awake watching television. Dallas considered joining us but relayed that he was in good with the slave traders and had acquired an Ibot to train which was too crucial to his mission to even consider leaving his post.

Bart woke me up so I could finish this message so thank him. By the way, I won. Gold in forms and sparring today surprised me more than anybody. Chalk one up for old broads. Bart wasn't feeling too social tonight but hopes that some combination of his meds will soon provide some relief. I was so tired and frustrated for him today. He amazes me with his strong constitution, never gives up. May you all have a stellar holiday weekend. We will. I'm going to search new recipes from the cancer cookbook tomorrow. Food is good.

February 21

Sunday was not the best day for Bart. Back pain persisted with continued stomach churning. Nonetheless it was a full day, so much so, I was thankful to have Monday to complete many of the usual weekend maintenance chores.

Bart did not sleep well Sunday night. He was up all hours. He finally gave up and went out to his chair, took his pain meds and added the heating pad, which allowed him to sleep some in his recliner.

It was particularly tough to see him hurting for so long today. Dallas hung with Dad while I ran about town. Bart requested Sheppard's pie for dinner and his wish was my command.

Our cousins Bob and Sue stopped by in the early evening to diagnose the cabinet door problem. It's such a blessing to have handy friends/family.

Bart, Dallas and I watched a post dinner movie tonight that was unexpectedly moving, at least for me. I don't think Dallas even paid attention. He donned his headphones the whole time. Oddly enough I thought the Disney movie Secretariat was poignant or perhaps it was because I was already in a somewhat melancholy mood. Still there were lots of life lessons if you chose to see them.

Tomorrow we hope he'll get a feel better cocktail with his chemotherapy at Creekside Lounge. Bart wants to have his picture taken under the new sign. We hope they've had a chance to hang it during the long weekend.

Again, thank you for the guestbook notes. Your comments always give Bart something to look forward to. That and lovely sunsets from our back deck. Let's hope they give way for a brighter day tomorrow.

February 24

A Note from Bart:
Hi all,

Sorry for not posting for a couple of days but I don't want to complain all the time, especially when there is nothing to be done. I had a couple of good days and some bad ones.

There is no way of telling why or when. So rest assured I think of you guys every day whether I write or not. On the bad days (today) I mostly can't write. On the good days I have no excuses except I don't. I start my third round of Chemo of this cycle on Monday. After that round I think I get another CT scan to see what progress we are making. I just need to make some progress on the pain. :-)

Mel has been so busy working and taking care of me that she often can't write. Understand that she wants to, every day.

Thanks for all your support. Bart

February 26

Bart had a few rough days, with short intermittent periods of feeling ok. He said when he was doing mildly better he didn't want to brag and when he was feeling jagged he didn't want to complain. The fact that it's a very busy time at work left precious few moments to share with you.

Praise be! Since we last talked, Dallas cleaned his room. That's the good news. Dallas also currently enjoys restricted driving privileges and a stark social calendar due to some less than stellar choices. He's attending regular counseling appointments as well to help him develop healthy coping skills. As he is want to do, Dallas tried an academic tactic to avoid consequences for those less than stellar choices by attempting to educate me about the fact that teenagers haven't yet developed a part of their brain that controls good judgment. Really? Nice try but it didn't help his case any.

As our family is sometimes wont to do, Dallas is at times compelled to share weird stuff with us at the oddest moments that he finds irresistibly intriguing.

I was walking down the hallway the other day as I heard him asking me from behind the closed bathroom door to peek in to where he had his laptop set up next to the sink. It was a video of Christmas lights set to music by the Trans-Siberian Orchestra! The performance just couldn't wait until he got out of the bathroom, no...I had to see it right then. Nip instant gratification in the bud, I thought and demanded that he forego multitasking while on the toilet. I assured him we would still be sufficiently awestruck in the family room later after his afternoon ritual.

It was truly a very cool display I must say. You can find it on YouTube; it is best viewed outside of the loo, however

Sandi said Bart was a chatterbox after chemo last week. That's always a sure sign he feels next to normal. But when he's hurting there's nary a word. It has been quiet of late.

Bart does seem to enjoy watching golf on television. I only hope he can someday play it himself once again. Meantime at least he's got fantasy golf to manage.

Cheryl's coming in the morning for our standing Sunday morning jogging date. We've pretty much settled on the trail route so that Phaddy can get his daily constitutional with us. I think Phaddy is becoming somewhat infamous in the neighborhood. If I'm out front with him, sometimes he bolts to race after a dog and its human companion. The last jogger commented that she thought Phaddy was losing weight! Her observation was appreciated yet I had no idea who she was. Either I'm getting senile or Phaddy gets around visiting more neighbors than I do.

The recent cold snap, wind and hailstorms have certainly not been encouraging to my lemon crop.

Sadly the string of lights on the Meyer lemon tree suddenly went dark. I awoke at 3 AM worrying about one stupid remaining cluster of lemon buds. I had to get up, couldn't sleep. Found a woefully short string of rope lights in the garage. It was 32 degrees out there. I put them up, but someone had evidently unplugged the extension cord and the plug was packed with mud! 3 AM is not the time one wishes to dig mud out of an extension plug with a toothpick just to save five stinkin' baby lemons but of course that was what I did while the rest of the world slept. Sadly it appeared to me that all the other potential fetal lemons had aborted their mission. There was just one small cluster of five remaining. The rope string lit up finally but didn't seem to emit much warmth through the thick clear plastic vinyl. I wrapped it around the cluster as best I could. The stiff strand didn't bend easily.

I hung up my coat quietly and went back to bed but Bart woke up asking "What the hell is going on?" I had to admit that it was not an intruder, (that would have been legit). I was just staving off frost, I explained and he sternly told me "3 AM was not the time to be doing stupid crap like that." Back in bed, I was still wide awake and now worrying about Parsley and Lantana that I forgot to cover in the front yard! I just couldn't get up again. Bart would surely scold me mercilessly. I must go back to sleep and resist the urge to rescue any other plants. After all, it was close to 4 AM. Herbs and lemons aren't that important anyway so why was I so obsessed? My conclusion was that I just didn't want anything on this property to die. Not on my watch. Saturday night all the little and large plants got a proper tucking in, all safely cloaked for the night.

I'll sleep better tonight. Bart will too, knowing that I won't be "gardening" at 3AM.

February 27

I wish I could report better, but it was a touch and go day for Bart. We teetered on the verge of calling the on-call oncologist. I prepared myself for a trip to the emergency room. There was no fever but Bart didn't register a fever when he went into septic shock either. His medications did not seem to quell severe cramping and hardcore pain. Bart tried to nap on the couch with his Steelers blanket. He was trying to outlast the bad spell but was eager for his next pain dose. The meds finally took the edge off after dinner. Bart said he could probably wait until his Monday Creekside appointment now.

Phaddy got a bath tonight. Cheryl and I took the dog on the trail today and he had obviously delighted himself by getting caked in red clay mud enjoying every moment to its fullest. He's just so close to the ground that he's like a pot belly pig.

Everybody here is clean and ready for bed finally. Sleep well. Until tomorrow.

February 28

No pain no gain. That phrase rings so true tonight.

Bart had his oncology/lab appointment this afternoon prior to his chemotherapy. I was at work. Mr. D, (one of my premiere TKD senior instructors) drove Bart to Creekside Lounge.

Dallas picked him up after school. He'd had such a bad weekend I was concerned, even more so when I received a call from Bart while on the bus home tonight. Bart rarely calls me, prefers email or text to talking. He requested I stop by to pick up a new nausea prescription at the pharmacy. The oncologist thought that the Zofran anti-nausea drug might be causing Bart's extreme gastrointestinal anguish (understatement).

The good news involves Bart's lab results. According to the specific pancreatic cancer marker scale, any number above 37 is considered abnormal. Bart's markers reached 61,000. After six to nine weeks on a Gemzar/Xeloda chemo combination protocol Bart's markers were down to 37,000.

Today, after a most uncomfortable couple of weeks, Bart's pancreatic cancer markers scored 7,000! That's an amazing reduction of 54-thousand! The oncologist says the plan is to continue with what's working.

When I got home I threw dinner in the oven, took the dog for a walk and when I returned I thought how lucky are we? Bart said "Looks like you'll have to put up with me a bit longer" and I said well I think I could handle that. I even thought about buying champagne to celebrate this auspicious moment but sparkling cider would do. We'll reserve that champagne pleasure for a Friday. The perpetual best holiday of the work week.

Dallas rallied too, even working double hard on a math analysis extra credit problem. He called his sister to double check his answer. Dallas seemed really proud of himself because the task was worth 100 points and his sister verified his conclusion. He even showed me his work which teachers have often complained they haven't seen enough of lately.

At our brief evening family meeting it was decided that Dallas would stay home instead of attending his brother's Army Ranger School graduation April 1st in Columbus, Georgia. Dal couldn't miss school and he thought it better to be home with Megan and Bart for his birthday April 3rd. His grades determine whether he's eligible to miss two days of school. Having a doctor daughter at home relieves my worry about leaving the state for a few days.

Bart feels so much better tonight and a big part of that is the news that his cancer markers are so dramatically down. Tomorrow our pharmacist should have sorted out the new nausea prescription. We pray that will reduce the incidences of sheer pain.

Again, thank you all for every word posted. You are a tonic that ensures his continued success at this cancer fighting business. After the last two scans, Bart 2 Cancer 0. Let's keep it that way.

Road Kill

I ran over a squirrel tonight. It was a bit of a minor trauma. I didn't want to do it. When I spotted him along the road, he seemed to panic. I hoped squirrely wouldn't dart into the street; the creature seemed so undecided. Perhaps to protect the big acorn nut in his mouth, he jutted to then fro, and I prayed. Suddenly a quick thud-plunk and it was done. I was quickly yards past the scene of the crime. Phaddy was sitting up, alert on the passenger seat. I wondered, doesn't he have some kind of animal empathy or extra sensory canine perception to help me out here? Evidently not.

Later that night, Dallas heard me on the phone telling Sandi about the squirrel squashing. He bolted up from the couch holding a book he had been engrossed in, and exclaimed, "that was YOU who killed that squirrel?" Dallas said he had to swerve to miss the carcass on his way to music class, and commented to his bros about the belly-up bushy-tail. After Dallas drove off for his jazz combo class this evening, I received the following text from him: "hit that squirrel Mom, just making sure you got it."

Oh dear.

Chapter Eleven

Happy Hour Cocktails at Creekside Lounge

March 2

A new day dawns and Bart still doesn't feel good but it must be due to the painful death of many a cancer cell. Bit of a snafu with insurance and the new nausea drug. It is not available until March 15. In the meantime Bart's trying a patch in conjunction with his other prescribed remedies. It's always a dance to get the right combination of stuff that alleviates his ever-present pain and discomfort.

No complaints however. We're good. Monday's lab news definitely elevated everyone's attitude around here. Dallas even took Phaddy for a walk. Returning from the pharmacy tonight, I parked in the driveway and heard Dallas singing at the top of his lungs while walking down the road with the dog, his headphones obviously blurring any vocal inhibitions. I think he should stick to playing instruments perhaps confining his singing to the shower, but I'll never tell him that.

Tomorrow evening Dallas has his counseling appointment followed by jazz band combo practice and it's also a Taekwondo night. I've been doing a bit better at dinner planning so if I can do it right again tomorrow, I could have my cake and eat it too (so to speak).

I noticed tonight that the squirrel trap peanuts remain untouched and well-soaked, obviously unappealing or the squirrel's too cagey for that ruse. I seem to be sleeping better now that it's raining instead of freezing. I Still have hope my small cluster of citrus might plump, but maybe not until next year. I'm lucky that my work colleague shared his bumper crop so I can still feel lemon rich regardless.

Bart's asleep in his recliner. It's past Bedtime for Bonzos. Later gators.

March 4

A Note from Bart:

Hi all,

Today was hydration day at the Creekside Lounge and consensus seems to be that the pain is the dying tumors. If that is so then I know there is end in sight and I can whip the bast**ds!

I felt a little better today as I had "slightly" more substantial food. I lost five lbs. the past week so that had to be contributing to my overall malaise. I am going to try and get some one person meals that appeal to me and my warped taste buds. Salisbury steak, chicken fried steak, etc. That coupled with pain meds every four-five hours should keep me going until I can wipe these friggin' tumors out. I feel better tonight than I have in two weeks. So things should be looking up.

Our weather has turned spring like which means hot then cold, sunny then cloudy, calm then windy. It's time to break out my allergy meds.

I'll keep you informed of any changes, good or bad, although I'm looking for good myself.

Love y'all Bart

March 5

What a day! Bart slept in thankfully. He slept better than he had in weeks. Bart had volunteered me to take Dallas shopping for new clothes and shoes Saturday. We hadn't taken Dallas shopping in several years for reasons that will soon be obvious.

I told Dallas that until he can take care of the clothes he already has then I'm not inclined to add more "new" to the floor. At 9AM I warned him that the shopping bus leaves no later than 11 and before that trip could happen his clothes must be neatly put away and the bathroom disaster picked up. It was clear and understood.

At 10:50 AM Dallas' friend said, "Dallas is working on it" through his closed door. I gave the 10 minute warning. At 10:57 I knocked and entered for inspection. Shoving piles of folded laundry behind closet doors was just not acceptable, so we had words. Bart woke up and wasn't exactly pleased at hearing such a contentious exchange. Not having been privy to our previous morning agreement, Bart chimed in, which was like throwing gasoline on a fire. It was uncertain whether the shopping trip would even fly at this point, but with seconds to spare, order was delicately, albeit tenuously, restored. Dallas' friend kept him from succumbing to his righteous indignation or it could have been worse.

In the car, we realized we were not yet complete with the truce. I asked Dallas again, no matter whether I'm in the car or not, that he drive at or below the posted speed limit. Dallas argued that he was driving safely. Nonetheless, that was NOT the request and clearly a non-compliance with my request not to mention breaking the law. Still he argued and I was ready to pound him.

This nearly resulted in an aborted mission. It was touch and go there for a few moments, but eventually we made it to the store and completed our shopping goals on schedule. It ended up being a pleasant enough experience after all. En route home we drove through In & Out Burger to get lunch for Bart. We made it home in time for me to dress and drive to our tri-school Black Belt pre-test panel.

Afterwards, I had quite a list of items to procure from the grocery list Bart composed Friday night.

Bart and I discussed having pre-cooked packaged meals on hand so that he can maintain high calories while I'm at work. Bart lost five precious pounds last week which he hopes to find again thanks to the varied frozen meals and processed foods I bought for him today. I was acutely aware that most of the items I placed on the check-out belt were NOT indicative of a "healthy" diet but when you have to ensure your husband puts on weight then you do what you have to do.

I resisted the urge to explain the plethora of pre-packaged frozen processed meals and high calorie snacks in my grocery purchase. I did have token bananas but so meager by comparison to the rest of my selections. Bart napped off and on throughout the day. He said he felt marginal with moments of OK but he also acknowledged that the pain is likely the result of those nasty cancer cells dying off in great numbers. We believe that. It doesn't make Bart feel physically much better but keeps our mental outlook optimistic.

Several items on my list didn't get done but Bart invited me to watch a movie with him this evening. Always an offer I cannot refuse. However, I do hope I can fit in all the stuff I missed today and get them done tomorrow.

If I don't work out and run tomorrow I'm sure I'll start twitching or worse. As Bart observes, my temperament could take a turn for the worse.

I feel fortunate for ADHD tendencies. I actually want to get up and get more stuff done. I recognize that it can be irritating but I love checking stuff off my list.

Dallas and Phaddy got invited to the Meyer's for an overnight. Phaddy was most excited and flew right into their car. As much as the little beast annoyed me with his "leak" in the hallway last night, I kind of miss him. Perish the thought.

Bart is resting up to get ready for bed. He wants to watch the video of Charlie Sheen night at a hockey game where some player went crazy. Leave it to some Hollywood types to make the rest of us feel somewhat normal.

You're all rock stars in our book. Good night!

March 7

It wasn't the most stellar of weekends for Bart. He said he felt like crap. It's not fun. This afternoon, we will visit Creekside Lounge. The oncologist changed up Bart's pain plan. He wrote a new Morphine prescription to be used in conjunction with the usual Fentanyl patch and oral Vicodin regimen. He believes this new triad might alleviate the intensity of Bart's constant pain. Bart felt a little better tonight after several hours at the lounge. We drove straight to Bel Air Market to submit the new prescriptions. Bart made me park near the entrance with the motor carts. Again after delivering the prescriptions I had a hell of a time finding him. When I did, he seemed pretty annoyed that I seemed always in the way whenever he lurched forward. Every cart has its idiosyncrasies apparently. He almost mowed me down right in front of the pharmacist.

Still it was good to be at the market together. At least Bart got exactly what he desired, instead of a second hand interpretation.

Dallas actually said thank you for his new jeans and shirts! We discussed closet organization and his laundry routine to keep his stuff in semi-reasonable order. We'll see. While I picked up Dad from Creekside, Dallas took Phaddy for a walk and later watched Phaddy with the doggy IQ puzzle. (It's another treasure from the magic Donlan dog gift bag.)

Dal's take was that Phaddy is kind of stupid. We had to fudge a little just to give him a clue that the discs moved to expose the treats. Still, all three of us were entertained just watching him continuously fail even though we all wished for a win.

We hope your weekly goals are easily attainable. IQ test or no, Phaddy seems happy. Wait a minute; perhaps he tricked us into helping him since we're the ones with opposable thumbs? Hmmm?

March 9

Sandi drove Bart to Creekside Lounge this afternoon for his midweek constitutional. After Dallas' drum/piano lessons he drove to Folsom to pick up his dad. Bart must have been feeling somewhat more human tonight because I got a text with a list of items to pick up when I got home from work. Fortunately the hour bus ride gives me a chance to nap and contemplate the evening dinner plan. Lately Bart's cravings are pretty simple yet notably high in fat. Good for him, not so palatable for me but I'll partake for the team if necessary. Dallas is of course good with the "all boy" foods. After dinner Bart reminded me that I forgot one essential item, his Pepcid AC. Back to the store again for that and a few other staples. I cajoled Dallas into taking the dog for a walk while I was gone.

Bart told me he felt "fair". That's better than usual so we'll take it. He goes back to Creekside again Friday and we hope they'll give him a good shot of the good stuff to last through the weekend. We also hope they'll have the sign up by then, geez.

March 11

A Note from Bart:

Wow! What a day. There was a major earthquake that hit Japan, followed by a tsunami. I was so enthralled I stayed up much later than I normally do. I was woken up at 10 AM by a phone call announcing that on Monday I have a CT scan scheduled for 8 AM. I must report in at 7:30 AM. I don't know if it's the excitement of the earthquake, my lack of sleep or the cocktail and hydration at the Creekside Lounge, no matter, I feel pretty good today. Here's hoping for more good news with the CT scan on Monday and continued pain free days.

We just got word that our son Matt finished the Mountain phase of his ranger training with very high marks. I am so proud of him.

I just wanted to keep y'all informed of the events of the day. If things continue to progress I may be able to make it back to the golf course (albeit briefly) this summer. Other than the pain the thing holding me back are the pain med's. I can't drive. There are too many opiates and pain-killers.

My thoughts and prayers are with y'all and I ask that you join me in praying for the folks in Japan and those in the path of the Tsunamis.

Love, Bart

March 13

Bart said he had a good morning but he was feeling some pain by early evening. Thank goodness for Martin, our Pharmacist who saved the day. Bart crossed tracks with the pain train when he went six hours between meds instead of the usual four.

Sometimes he just has to test the waters.

I'll relay a few events of last week since I'd already made notes but then Bart pleasantly surprised me by sharing his thoughts with you.

On Thursday I found Bart in the kitchen when I got home from work. He'd begun cooking the ground beef for a wildly anticipated evening meal. Bart was quick to express that he preferred I get home much earlier to cook. I begged exception reminding him that Dallas was more than capable. Besides it appeared that Bart himself was doing a great job although he didn't relish standing at the stove that long. The boys said they were both really hungry and couldn't wait for the night's dinner, Asian hamburger helper. I know, I know high sodium, fat etc. and I cringed, but B and D liked it. Again, I'm all about what Bart will eat and he gets any damn thing he chooses. Palatability and weight gain is all we want here. Dallas of course is quite pleased with the chemo friendly menu, suits him just fine.

We were blessed with a pre-dinner show from little Lauryn, our talented young neighbor who wanted to perform the song she would be singing at her El Dorado Theatre recital later this month. All of us, even Phaddy enjoyed the recital and gave Lauryn a rousing ovation. After the live evening entertainment the boys finished their "helper" meal. I walked Lauryn home then took Phaddy for a much needed walk. It was my hope that Bart and Dallas would have eaten the whole pan by the time Phaddy and I got back. I didn't want to take that stuff for the team.

We did get an exciting phone call from Afghanistan this evening. Matty's girlfriend Jen is an Army intelligence officer serving a tour of duty. She told us to expect a call from Matty soon. It was good to hear that Jen would finally be coming home herself on April 11th, only her home is in Florida. Matty did call Friday night as Jen predicted, announcing the completion of Army Ranger School mountain phase. He will be moving on to Florida for the final swamp phase. He said his peer evaluations were 95 percent thus far. When you consider that these guys are so sleep-deprived, starved and stressed that they often hallucinate, it's really something that Matty's comrades still saw clearly enough to name Matty as their squad's top performer.

Friday, after I collected Bart from Creekside, he was feeling pretty good. I felt so happy that night because he was engaged and talkative. The whole evening I kept thinking "this is great" he's Bart again. It was one of the best nights we've had. Life is good. Then we watched horrific news of the earthquake and tsunami in Japan. Bart lived in Japan for a time while he was in the Air Force. He acquired a heartfelt and deep affection for the Japanese people. In these moments of human tragedy, all of us have heavy hearts and connection to people affected.

A postscript of a lighter note: one of my dear colleagues at work delivered a treasured gift. It was a Squirrel mug. She knows of course how we are not necessarily huge fans of said beast yet the gesture brought genuine amusement to the Reagan household. The trap still remains empty and the peanuts untouched. We do believe that our resident squatter just may have met his demise on the pavement of upper Sudbury Road. Not by any of us mind you, but since then all has been quiet on the roof front. We can now relive the reign of the squirrel over morning coffee.

I hope you remembered to set your clocks ahead. Sleep fast.

March 15

It was an unusually early morning for Bart. He had to eat breakfast by 6:00 AM per instructions. Dallas drove himself to school at 6:30 AM. Bart and I drove off to Folsom for the big CT Scan at 7:00 AM. We filled out the obligatory forms and he was called in due time. Bart only had to shake me twice to wake me up afterwards.

Watching those fish in the waiting area is like hypnotism, puts me right to sleep, that and the Sacramento Bee, all sufficiently sleep-inducing. After my nap, I was good to go for work. Bart would rest up before his afternoon meeting with the oncologist.

My black belt buddy Lisa arrived to transport Bart to his oncology appointment at Creekside. The lounge nurses promised that somebody's boyfriend would actually hang the sign someday soon (Lisa and Lee handcrafted the sign and we all awaited its elevation to the point of entry at Creekside Lounge) this week. I sure hope they can figure out how to hang a sign?

Maybe it's like that old joke, how many people does it take to replace a light bulb? We think the sign will be a welcome lift for chemo patrons crossing the threshold into that space each and every day. Maybe they ought to have a "happy hour" too? It couldn't hurt.

We were pleasantly surprised that the oncologist called for Bart's AM scan results during his appointment this afternoon. We have commonly waited two or three days for results in the past.

Report was, quote "stable". What does that mean?

Stable is good. It means that first you must arrest development of the cancer before you begin shrinking it. That may be a simplistic interpretation but sums it up nonetheless. No growth is a huge win! Now we tackle the existing tumors, and those bastards are going down. Bart got his new chemo schedule today from the Lounge babes. It lists Gemzar treatments for the next two Mondays with a follow-up on April 4th. Keep doing what's working and that appears to be the Gemzar/Xeloda combo.

Bart was super tired this evening. The early morning thing really tuckered him out.

He was however awake about 9:30 PM when I discovered a strange new occupant in the squirrel trap!

The creature was squeaking and Phaddy was going crazy. It was no squirrel, no. We captured a well fed rat. He didn't appear rabid or nasty in any way. Even though I had had a pet rat in elementary school, not for a moment did I consider making this guy into a pet, but there was no way I was going to eradicate him either. Dallas offered to target shoot. No. My decree was final. The plan is relocation and there's no discussion. It makes you wonder. Would the squirrel have squared off against the rat for those peanuts? Or, was the squirrel flattened in the hit and run on the road? Do squirrels live alone? Certainly they don't share much with rats!

I told Bart and Dallas that I would drive the rat away tomorrow night and release him. Our daughter, Megan, suggested I release him close to the freeway. Phaddy meantime is proud he has a job, to bark at and protest this caged rat. Milk Bone treats trumped rats though and Phaddy gave up barking at the rat for a morsel. It's good to have priorities. Bart agreed with the Tuesday rat relocation plan.

Bart also relayed to me the newest pain instructions from the oncologist. Bart is now allowed to take a different pain killer after two hours instead of four to quell the severe pain. Bart thinks the shorter interval between different pain meds might work better than suffering for four hours because once the pain takes hold its relentless and harder to put down than if you squelch it to begin with

The juggling act is to medicate for pain but not to the degree that the meds sedate him. It's no fun for Bart or the rest of us for him to be out of it. I think it's going to be a work in progress. What works now may not work later but at least the oncologist is getting Bart to agree that pain is not acceptable.

Even though Bart was really tired tonight, he ate well. I fixed the Betty Crocker cancer cookbook recipe: baked Tilapia with red potatoes and green beans.

Both boys wanted Moose Tracks ice cream for dessert. We then watched a recorded episode of House. The medical mysteries are certainly interesting even though Doctor House is a real jerk sometimes. Megan called tonight with her own stories of "different" teaching doctors. Her real life anecdotes are every bit as interesting as House.

Good night rat and squirrel.

March 16

Bart had a fairly good day. I felt extremely grateful today. Bart was so thoughtful that I couldn't help but feel appreciation. Relocating the rat was not something I looked forward to. Like I needed another task added to my list. Where would I take him and how much gas would I be willing to expend to ensure the rat's safe release far enough from our house?

Unbeknownst to me, Bart called Clark Pest Control requesting humane disposal of our captured rat. Bart got a Clark guy to come out, pick up the rat, release it somewhere and then he came back to return the cage. It was a superb plan because it didn't involve me.

I have no idea if he released the little feller near the freeway or not. Dallas and I agreed that the rat was kind of cute. Nonetheless, we recognized that he was a wild creature and looks can be deceiving. Phaddy seemed disappointed to see that the trap was empty. Dallas insisted that tonight Phaddy dog would be spending the night in his room. So, off they went. Dallas had a little smoky sausage on a stick to ensure that the dog was motivated.

Bart says it was a fine day, relatively low pain. It was definitely a normal day because Bart and I had an exchange about Dallas where we disagreed.

Even that was good. Everybody here had a comfortable evening. Frozen pizza can be most delicious.

March 17

A Note from Bart:

Thanks all for the words of encouragement. I have been feeling somewhat better as long as I remember to take my pain meds on schedule. Things on the CT scan/marker front are looking up.

As for the rat, Dallas offered to take him out (with his BB gun) but Mom wouldn't have it. And we don't have any friends with snakes we could have passed him along to. :-)

Well the rat is gone to other lands and the squirrel has been absent, recently, too.

Hope things find you and yours doing well and you are safe from the path of any future tsunami.

Take care Love y'all Bart

March 19

Bart had a fairly good Friday. He was home alone most of the day until Dallas got back from school. Dal didn't stay long. He purportedly did his chores and then was off to a friend's house. I got home from work just before 7PM. Sandi and Jasper the Beagle were there when I got home. It's always fun to have peeps over on a Friday night if only for a short spell.

Thanks to dear friends, home cooked dinner was only micro-minutes away. Luxury!

The new Squirrel mug (thanks Emily) is in use and the trap is empty again. My radio buddy Marilyn shared a story with us that we must share with you. An Illinois man set his townhouse on fire. He was trying to get rid of squirrels. He said they "went awry", so a smoke bomb in the gutter seemed like a good idea at the time since the squirrels resided somewhere in his roof.

The smoke however set the home on fire. The family was able to get out uninjured and the squirrels apparently did so too.

This story made us feel a whole lot better about the squirrel measures we've taken thus far. We've managed to avoid setting the place on fire at least. There's been no fires and no squirrels lately either.

Even though the weather is expected to be cold, windy and severe, it will be a wonderful weekend for us. Bart and I believe he is getting better and that is a boost in itself. It's a dose of contentment. Plus we are anticipating a girls (over 50) slumber party at the end of the month. Many Trinity High School pals will be here. There is to be fun on the menu. How could Bart resist a bunch of doting women?

My indulgence tonight is staying up to watch a little crap TV. Disappointing because I don't even know who some of these Hollywood people are? I end up switching to news, Discovery or the food channel. You'd think with more than 500 satellite channels you could find something appealing. Bed sounds most appealing among the viewing choices at this hour.

March 20

Bart slept in today. The other day he told me he never wanted to sleep later than 11 because of his shots and meds schedule. So when the clock rolled just past 11 I went in to check on him. He knows how I hate to wake him when he's sleeping so comfortably.

Gently, I whispered that it was 11AM. Bart rolled his eyes open and turned his head toward me accusingly "Why did you wake me up?" Oh man, I should have left well enough alone. Just when I thought it was safe to interrupt his slumber! Dang.

Buttery French toast with maple syrup, a hot cup of coffee, one syringe and insulin was waiting for Bart. Since he couldn't go back to sleep, he showered and sauntered out to switch on the television. Saturday morning it's always the golf channel. I was at the kitchen sink looking out at the rain coming down when I heard it loud and clear. Son of a %@!&#! I didn't care that I had no jacket and only my slippers on. I flew outside onto the wet windy driveway and looked up. There he was that bastard, huge ass squirrel sitting up there on the roof chewing. I picked up a rock but he was already gone. I didn't know whether to swear or cry.

That critter lulled us into complacency by laying low for so long and fooling us with that rat. Why won't he just leave? It's so very disappointing. Bart and I discussed it and decided to place the trap on the other side of the house. In addition I will brave the elements and trim trees that may give him an easy bridge to the roof. Although, Bart thinks he scampers right up the side of our stucco house. There's still no red carpet for him.

Tree trimming wasn't one of the tasks on today's list and frankly I resent having to do it but my annoyance with his invasion of our home is motive enough to face those trees that will likely slap me in the face with all this wind and rain.

Time is a wasting.

March 21

I was just watching Bart inject his final Lovenox dose of the evening. It takes about 10 seconds for him to depress the plunger all the way into his skin. It looked as though he had to press it hard and steadily, like pumping air into a basketball, there's a lot of resistance. I asked Bart if those shots hurt? He said "sometimes". Four times a day, two Lovenox injections and two Humalin insulin injections every single day.

Occasionally I see his dinner napkin spotted with blood. It worries me to see that since he's injecting blood thinners so I wonder how long it takes to stop the blood. Bart says it won't be long. If he's not concerned about it then I'm not as on edge either. That tiny little needle puncture can't possibly cause him to bleed to death so I've really got to lighten up.

Good news on the numbers front of late. Bart's sugar levels are settling into a constant acceptable range without the irregular spikes he used to see. Tonight while walking the dog, inhaling the cold crisp air and watching the beautiful sunset I felt very happy. Bart had a good weekend. He seems to be inching along better and better. Sure Bart's tired and sleeps a lot, but narcotics and being the valiant cancer slayer takes a whole hell of a lot out of our superhero.

It was a busy weekend in our household despite the fact that Bart didn't go anywhere. Saturday there was squirrel anxiety. Sunday we slept in embarrassingly late then took a nap. It was double speed after that trying to get a whole day's work done in a half day.

We had a knock down drag out negotiation with Dallas which ultimately ended in a productive solution. He is to be more proactive, grade conscious and responsible in exchange for more rope. I'll spare you the details but so far so good.

Dallas has been great as far as picking up his father from Creekside Lounge and being on time. These small spells when life works, inspires hope that we may survive his senior year relatively unscathed. Although Dallas managed to avoid changing Aunt Sandi's fluorescents he has been punctual and pleasant.

Today in fact Dallas and I had a laugh at Dad's expense. Dal wanted to shoot baskets with his friend at our house after school so he texted me and asked if I could pick Dad up after work so he could play basketball. I was on the road anyway so I agreed. Next thing I hear is a sound indicating I got a text message, but I'm driving so I ignore it.

At a stoplight I see the message from Bart. I can hear the clear sarcasm in his typing "I'm so glad you and Dallas stay in touch with me. It's not like I have a life-threatening illness or anything..... oh wait. I do"!!!!!! Back at the ranch, I bring up said text (which I had copied and sent to Dallas previously). Dallas' response "nice".

At home we bring it up with Dad, hmmm, Mr. Reagan, don't you think you're milking this thing a bit? It gave us all a few laughs. Bart happily reported that the Creekside Lounge babes had finally hung the revered sign!

As promised, Bart had his picture taken standing underneath it as did nurses Tegan and Mindy. The Creekside nurses said many patients asked if that sign had been there all along.

I think that's a sign (pardon the pun) that it was meant to be. Thanks again to Lisa and Lee for creating the "Bart font" and dedicating the placard to Bart. It will forever grace the entrance to Sierra Hematology and Oncology Chemo Lab, or Creekside Lounge for short.

Long live the patrons of that lounge, for they are served cocktails in a very special way, with TLC.

March 23

Tuesday was a blur. I went to work in an off-white suit, clutching my West Point commuter coffee mug (the one Bart gave me for Christmas). Bart said he felt ok in the morning and wanted to sleep in as long as possible. The day after chemo is always taxing.

I bid my farewell, grabbed my coat and bags and took off. My suit sleeve caught perfectly on the door handle as I was rushing out to the car. It jerked me up short to a sudden and disconcerting stop. Miraculously my sleeve didn't rip off completely but I did spill coffee and dropped the purse. What are the odds you wreck yourself on your own doorknob?

Driving to the bus stop I noticed my slacks were wet, not only wet, but stained with French roast coffee! The damn new commuter mug was leaking. The one day I wore an off-white pants suit of course. There was no time to turn around. I'm already perilously late, cutting it too close for comfort to get to the bus by departure time. If I make every light and no other cars are on the road then I could get there as fast as 7 minutes but I need 12-13 minutes to have enough time to park, gather my stuff and lock the car.

A consistent dribble, coupled with getting jerked by a door handle can begin to dampen one's mood. Of course, Bart had just tossed the receipt for this faulty mug that very day so there was no possibility I might exchange this traitorous coffee conveyance.

At the office I realized that a newly purchased book of bus tickets was missing. Losing things is something that causes great feelings of inadequacy already (without outside encouragement). Bart is much more logical and organized, thus has little tolerance for "Dory" brain (Finding Nemo).

That $100 is my financial pain threshold, so losing a ticket booklet valued at exactly $100 was definitely not acceptable. I knew it was in my checkbook. Well, it wasn't. Panic first. I called home that afternoon and forced Dallas to search while I turned my office inside out. The more I tense up about something lost the more its discovery evades me. It felt like I was going crazy not remembering just where I had tucked away such a valuable commodity. I did recall however; that I had indeed tucked it away someplace safe.

I'd planned ahead for once and thawed salmon for dinner. Allrecipes.com is my newest best friend. I prepared broccoli, corn and fresh mashed red potatoes to accompany the salmon. I used my garden parsley, fresh lime, California olive oil and spices on the fish. It pained me to omit the garlic but the goal was for Bart to actually like it. Both boys had no complaints. Had they not, my delicate sensibilities might have snapped. Tonight's barometer was a low negativity tolerance. I could have lost it had there been complaining.

Dallas took Phaddy for a walk and dinner was prepared upon their return. Bart ate pretty well and said he slept most of the day adjusting the new medication, plus he's always tired a few days after Monday Gemzar chemotherapy. Cancer slaying is not a journey for wimps. Yet Bart rarely complains. He might complain about my memory, or my judgment, or his taste in food, but he doesn't fuss about his condition. Sometimes I think it hurts me more than him.

He's been a trooper with me going to work all week. Bart's had to fend for himself. I think he's noted that it's important to eat more often rather than let enough time lapse for cramps to set in. It was a good evening.

The dishes are done and the dog's asleep. That signals Bedtime for Bonzos.

Good night dear friends and remember, post freely, frequently and often (yes redundancy intended).

March 24

A Note from Bart:

Hi all,

I sometimes fail to read Mel's postings thoroughly. I voraciously read the guestbook. She had a very bad day yesterday, I was remiss in seeing this, and she doesn't want to burden me by telling me things. A phrase from my military days (way back) is; "When you are up to your ass in alligators; it's hard to remember your main objective was to drain the swamp."

We get caught up in what's right in front of us and can't see the forest for the trees.

Okay enough metaphors. This week has been fairly good. If I maintain my medicines at the right times I can keep the nausea and pain at bay. Now I have to convince my bride that we are in this together and I need her to share things with me so I can help (or tease her if I feel that's right).

Bart ;-)

March 27

A Note from Bart:

Hi all,

So far this Sunday morning I'm feeling pretty good. Hopefully it will last as my bride needs me today. She had a jewelry/clothing/drinking party last night with the girls. Today she isn't feeling so good. Hopefully she will recover soon. Dallas and I will be taking care of her today. It only seems fair.

As for me, as I mentioned I feel better than I have in a while. I woke up at 10 to a houseful of women. They took care of me for breakfast and I took my meds. I don't have any cramps (knock on wood) or any pain to speak of.

Maybe we will post more this evening if there is any further news. If all goes well Mel will sleep and when she awakens she will be better. I don't need her to be ill (hung-over I can handle). We are running out of drivers. Sandi, Cheryl and Mel are leaving on Thursday for Matt's Ranger graduation. I wish I could see it I'm sure it will be awesome and, at least for me, emotional.

Sunday, the 3rd, is Dallas's 17th birthday. It will be a big party of 3 (Meg, Dallas and me). I hope I'm up for it. ;-o

I'm sure it will be fine. Since Mel is feeling poorly, I will try and take over the posting duties. Y'all just need to understand my posts are succinct compared to Mel's. So you may not get all the funny side play that she gives. I'll keep you informed with who feels good, who doesn't, any amusing events that transpired along with any un-amusing events. My doc isn't big on giving prognosis. He merely states the facts. My markers are down, tumors have shrunk and were stable last time, etc. We are left to our own devices (and brains) to determine what that means.

I choose to think this means Chemo is doing what it's supposed to and the pain I feel is an indication that the tumors are fighting as they die. If this is the case I can tolerate more pain knowing it's for a good cause and not just causing pain for pain's sake.

And that there should be a light at the end of tunnel, that isn't an oncoming freight train. This gives me reason to believe. I can't use the word Hope as it has been usurped to mean things I disagree with. I trust that God is apolitical and that is good.

Now before my overly medicated brain causes me to say something that will irritate my liberal friends I will leave off for now.

God loves all sides Democrats, Liberals, Republicans and Conservatives. So do I.

Love y'all Bart

March 30

It was such fun to receive Trinity High School friends Friday night at the house. Bart enjoyed talking to someone other than me for a change. I could tell it was a nice time for him.

The girls were hoping Bart would call his buddy Marty, who posted a threat that he didn’t care if gas was five dollars a gallon not to misplace his number that he’d willingly drive over the canyon and through the foothills in an instant should Bart need added testosterone at this Estrofest. I guess Bart felt he could go it alone. Sandi threw a great party Saturday night.

JL Doodles Jewelry, designed and handcrafted by Jeanne Gravette (aka, Clean Jeanne) was a hit and a good time was had by all. I was concerned though about slight raspy respiratory symptoms. We shall see and yes, I took Emergen-C. Over indulgence was definitely not the problem. I was a good student and did my training well.

Thanks to the girls, Bart was able to heat stuff up and fend for himself for the most part. Poor guy, I know he was tired as well but I just couldn't stay upright long enough and no sense spreading any germs either.

I was paranoid that Bart could catch it so I sterilized all the doorknobs, light switches, appliance handles, faucets, phones, keyboards, car radio buttons and even the toilet handles.

Thank goodness my Estro-sisters left the refrigerator stocked. Jan had prepared chicken noodle soup Saturday. It was a perfect dinner for the infirmed.

Monday I still felt bad but not completely bed-ridden like Sunday.

Bart felt tired and is running low on several pain pills.

I took Bart to his chemotherapy appointment at Creekside Lounge. We left the house at 1:30 PM. Dropped him in front of the building at about 1:45-1:50 PM then slept in the car until he was ready to go at 5:30 PM! I had a surprise visit at my window from Cheryl and Steve who were driving their dogs to the dog park. In my dream, I envisioned someone who looked like Cheryl calling "Mel, Mel" but it turned out to be real and there she was at the car window.

They graciously stopped by knowing I was waiting in the car for Bart. I still felt rotten by the time Bart got into the car but thought about the fact that he goes through worse than this every single day so I had nothing to complain about.

I heated leftovers, (thanks to my cookin' Estro-sisters) then proceeded to sterilize anything I may have touched in the house and even slept in the guest room so as not to contaminate Bart.

I was still under the weather Tuesday, but there was much running around that had yet to be done. The oncologist made an error on Bart's prescriptions which meant I had to go back in the afternoon and get new scripts, then on to Roseville to deliver all the tax stuff, then on to grocery shopping, pick up Bart's UPS mail, carwash, and back to the pharmacy.

Let this be a lesson to others, if the doctor tells you take these as needed and if "needed" could be up to four pills per day, then make damn sure that the prescription is rewritten for the Pharmacist as four per day because if it says two then you're screwed. The insurance won't authorize a refill until after the date determined by two per day. The pharmacy was swamped tonight so I got home later than expected. I cooked one of Bart's favorite comfort foods, Sheppard's pie for dinner.

Bart wasn't too hungry by this late hour and didn't feel very good either which made him understandably a bit grumpy. I relate to this state quite well.

The gyrations with the doctor and pharmacy scripts added to his stress. Bart said he felt like he had the precursor headache to getting a cold! Oh man that thought was making me pretty damn grumpy myself. I had been so careful too.

Bart said his sugar level wasn't so good last night and his blood pressure was a bit elevated today, but we figured that was due to all the jacking around with his prescriptions, lots of phone ringing, and a later than usual dinner. Bart's so good at trying to maintain a decent schedule, but distractions abound for his care giver - me.

I've always thought that he keeps me on a normal human schedule; otherwise I might spin off into psycho-schedule doing random stuff at inappropriate times. Feeling so crappy these past couple days has given me even more appreciation for what Bart continues to handle with equanimity, fortitude and determination.

He is working on getting the lifestyle back that he most enjoys (golf) and he'll keep doing what it takes to get there. It still sucks to have this cough and cold but I am grateful for it because as miserable as I think I feel, it's only temporary.

I must carry Phaddy to bed to be with his master. By the way, Phaddy dog is still the same size, he hasn't lost a pound, same huge girth. This dog somehow must be a closet eater. I think he finds food in Dallas' room and/or on the street. I thought for sure he'd be a tad smaller by now but not at all. Sandi and I decided that plump is his natural state and to just go with it.

I will retire with my box of tissues to the guest room but not before one more go round with the anti-viral wipes. Safety is first.

March 31

Mr. Reagan was feeling a bit stressed today. I had to go to work. Sandi was able to drive Bart back to Creekside in Folsom yet again to attain another corrected prescription then it was back to the Cameron Park Pharmacy.

Bart got a call that Dallas had run out of gas. Apparently the gas money Bart gave him for transporting Dad to Creekside wasn't going into the tank. Again Aunt Sandi came to the rescue. She drove Bart to Dallas' car after school with gas can in hand. I'll spare you the details but suffice it to say there was a myriad of assorted tasks, errands and follow ups today.

It was also a hectic day for me at work. Why is it that sometimes it's a lot of work just to take two days vacation? Tomorrow daughter Megan flies into Sac International about the time Sandi, Cheryl and I arrive. The brilliant crossover plan is to intercept her at Southwest about 10:30, and transfer the car keys before we take off at 11:30 for Atlanta, Georgia. (Destination Army Ranger School graduation in Columbus, GA Fort Benning) Because our arrangement sounded too easy, we decided to have a backup plan.

Matty finally called after completion of the final leg of Ranger training. He said the swamp phase was most horrifying and he couldn't wait to gross us out with the horrid details. He also told me that over the last month they only got an hour of sleep per night. He said last night was the first time that he would get eight hours of sleep. Matty said it was such deep sleep and so confusing that he wet the bed. He laughed as we all did. I think many Rangers likely had similar experiences. I especially appreciated that story because when Matty was little he was mortified when it happened. He would hide any evidence of such mishaps under his mattress or attempt a sheet change on his own. Tonight we were laughing heartily, Matty due to his relief that it was over and mine for such fond sweet memories of that little red-headed boy. I promised Bart to attempt video of the grad proceedings and will send pictures for posting.

Packing is such a dreaded chore. I ridiculously think I must have every shred of laundry done so I can select from everything I own. I am also paranoid I'll forget something essential like my glasses. Packing does seem to cause me some anxiety. I believe I need two of everything so that I don't have to wait until morning to zip up the suitcase. Intellectually I know that nothing short of my jacket, glasses and my wallet are true necessities so you'd think I could relax about it. I think I haven't gotten enough experience travelling so that's why it's a challenge to pack.

I think Bart is looking forward to a weekend with the almost doctor and Dallas. He's been rolling his eyes a lot of late so a respite from his ADHD wife might be just what the doctor ordered.

Go Army. (And Air Force) Ok, and maybe a little Go Navy for Lori's cadet. It's all American either way. USA!

U.S. ARMY

Chapter Twelve

Drip Side Manor

April 1

A Note from Bart:

Well we have a new Army Ranger. I couldn't be more proud. I'm sad I wasn't able to go to the graduation but I'm glad I was able to hang around to witness (from afar) the completion.

My soon to be doctor daughter Meg (who also makes me very proud) is here making sure I behave and follow doctors' orders.

It's also Dallas's birthday weekend (Sunday he will be 17) so Meg is helping plan a mini-party for him.

I am planning to stay out of the way.

All is going fairly well today. Just my typical everyday cramping until my drugs kick in.

I will keep y'all updated a much as I can about the new Ranger.

Love, Bart

April 2

A Note from Bart:

Today was a fairly good day. Weather was sunny and mild (about 65) unlike yesterday where it was 80 and waaaay too early for that heat. By August we will be begging for "only" 80 degrees. I can't wait for my bride to get home tomorrow. My whole routine seems off when she isn't around. It was fun with Meggie today, we watched cheesy Science Fiction movies and I watched golf. In a few minutes we will be invaded by teenagers for a birthday party for Dallas. Megan has lots of stuff planned. I think it's mostly food related. :-)

My pain has been tolerable and not too bad on the cramping. Still extremely tired but I think that's pain meds. Megan goes home tomorrow. Her visit was too short. And for a brief period (several hours) it will just be Dallas and me tomorrow. I suspect it won't be too exciting, not that I can handle too much excitement. But it is fun sometimes.

All in all things are going good today. Spring has sprung. And now my allergies will add to my other ailments. yay! :-(

Bart

April 5

A Note from Bart:

Hi all,

Well it's been 3 days in a row of feeling pretty good. I'm on my way to feeling great. Until I can feel this way without the pain patches and pain meds I won't be driving (either a car or a golf ball) but it's a start.

Anyone living near me knows I will need folks to help/check up on me April 17th to the 20th. Mel is leaving for Weaverville for a combination business/pleasure trip and Dallas is going to check on a couple of colleges he may want to attend. I probably will be ok. Sandi signed up to drive me to Chemo that day. Hopefully she can drive me home as well. If not I'll seek another.

Here's to more pain free days.

Bart

April 7

A Note from Bart:

Hi everyone, I must say you people overwhelmed me with your outpouring of support.

If I could, I'd show you the tears you brought to my eyes. Thanks for all the offers of help and I think I have it covered. Several of you left phone numbers that I will be sure to call if needed.

Yesterday and today were a little rocky but all in all I think I'm getting better (at least from the pain and cramping).

I'll let y'all know how I'm doing when my peeps are gone. Take care,

Love Bart

April 9

Bart has been doing well. Friday he got topped off at Creekside Lounge for the weekend.

He felt so good after that he announced that if he felt this good over the weekend we'd be headed for the driving range. No driving range sojourn yet but still a gradual and marked improvement in Bart's condition since last month.

The different over the counter remedies combined with a dynamic pain control plan seems to be more effective than the same pharmaceutical regimen day after day. It's a little trial and error, and a lot of perseverance.

Having been gone four days to Georgia there was much for me to catch up on.

On the home front, however, Megan did a great job holding down the fort. She even orchestrated a crazy hat poker party for Dallas' birthday.

Dal reported a fun and satisfying natal day despite missing his brother's graduation, which was exactly like his video game "Call of Duty Black Ops."

Watching the graduation demonstration of what Army Rangers endure was awe-inspiring.

I attempted a video recording for Bart but found myself looking away from the viewfinder for the real time scene. I think the result was a little choppy for the viewer.

The audience got to see exploding buildings, Rangers dropping from helicopters into the Chattahoochee River and being extracted, then flying away all clinging to a rope dangling from the chopper.

The Rangers ran across beams high above the water jumping over obstacles then upon command flinging themselves into the muddy water of the river below outfitted with full gear. Rangers emerged from a high-rise wall running downward at perpendicular angles, weapons ready to fire.

They demonstrated hand-to-hand combat, demolitions, weaponry, speed, agility and never hesitation even at great heights. They are the toughest of the tough. They are individuals who operate as a lethal family. They simply do not quit no matter what the odds.

After the ceremony, Matty declared that Iraq was going to be so much easier than Ranger School.

His other combat buddies agreed, they said serving in a war zone didn't compare to the extreme conditions they endured at Ranger School.

There seemed a consensus that the Florida swamp phase was the worst. Neck deep dark water, poisonous snakes, alligators, quick sand, hallucinations from no sleep and wet, nasty conditions led to low resistance and illness. Most were feverish, infected, hungry, sleep-deprived, exhausted and sick yet they put one foot in front of the other, dragging their buddies if necessary all with a 100 pound ruck-sack on their backs and trekked miles through impossible terrain to complete their missions.

Voluntarily, these American soldiers put themselves through training that would likely be considered illegal in any other human context.

There were 400 who started out January 2nd and 161 who graduated in Matty's class April 1st. No fooling, it was an emotional and gratifying moment for all in attendance. It was also touching how the Army welcomed an honorary Ranger, a young Make-a-Wish recipient who longed to be among the military elite, the highly regarded Army Rangers.

This young man was authorized to take command of the Rangers throughout the training demonstrations.

At one point, he even directed the loser of the unarmed combat match to be tossed into the drink. The winner carried the loser over his shoulder requesting permission to dispatch said opponent into the cold river.

What a thrill for the young man to be included in the ranks of these elite warriors let alone command them for a day. I can't say my video taping ability created a feeling of being there, but Bart got the gist of it.

Bart was familiar with Eglin Air Force Base where he had been stationed for a time during his 11-year stint in the Air Force. Rangers endured the dreaded swamp phase near Eglin AFB in Florida.

They saved the worst for last apparently. Out of the swamp, infected cuts will begin to heal, the Rangers will get more than one hour of sleep, and a real meal. These young men don't take anything for granted.

We got to taste a meal ready to eat (MRE) ourselves. The Rangers had only five minutes to eat.

We were barely done reading the instructions in five. Matty exclaimed that the Ranger MRE's were most delicious. Good only if you're starving to death we guessed. A sense of humor sustains these young men and their sense of brotherhood unites them.

Sandi, Cheryl and I took a group of Rangers out for a celebratory graduation dinner that evening. You have never seen young men enjoy a meal more than these guys.

Bart got a vicarious thrill out of Matty's Ranger stories and of course he had my amateur video to complain about. Bart certainly has the Ranger mentality when it comes to cancer. When the going gets tough you simply have to "Ranger Up."

Thank you all for posting messages. It's a tonic like no other, even better than a Ranger MRE for feeding his spirit.

April 10

It was a low key yet a great Sunday. Bart felt fairly good all day. I got a lot of laundry done. Kitchen cleaned and even prepared an extra casserole for the freezer.

I took Phaddy for a trail adventure in the afternoon and may have overdone a bit. I double looped the trail because it was such a beautiful day and I needed it.

Phaddy appeared to be slowing down but when I stopped to wait for him he'd duck into the bushes. I assumed he was just dilly-dallying and enjoying the off leash freedom. Upon our return, Bart informed me that Phaddy dog was in fact limping. The dog seemed to be having a good time, but in the back of my mind I did wonder if the rocky trek was too much for the little guy. I crushed some of former Kenai dog's Ascriptin (aspirin/Maalox) to add to Phaddy's dinner. Secretly I had hoped Phaddy would be lethargic (finally) and would choose to sleep instead of playing with toys to the point of annoying. Once the aspirin kicked in sure enough, no more limping; he wanted to play. Perhaps we should have cut his dose? When you want to relax and the dog keeps shoving a tennis ball in your lap, it tends to make you anxious.

Bart doesn't succumb but I always cave. Lori came by and suggested perhaps a burr in the paw. We used a magnifying glass but couldn't see anything unusual in his paw. Tonight the dog seems fine. Maybe he just needs to "Ranger up."

Bart and Lori shared golf stories then we all watched a fish show about river monsters. Huge ass man-eating fish!

We have a big week ahead. Bart has chemo tomorrow. He and I agreed that we believe he's beating the beast into submission. Another few weeks and we'll get another progress report.

Bart was happy to report that his mom in Pennsylvania is doing well. Thanks to his sisters.

Bart said he had a pretty good weekend and the week is starting out ok too. He tells me he never has a really mild or pain free day but by comparison these are good times.

Sandi chauffeured Bart to and from his late afternoon chemo appointment. When the bus dropped me off in the evening it was straight to the pharmacy.

With all the diabetic supplies, lancets, strips, over the counter stuff and other prescriptions, the co-pay was well over $100.

Bart and I always joke about how my threshold for pain is $100. Spending $98 or under is more palatable and I feel like I won a prize if I keep any spending under that number. No wonder Bart makes the house payments.

Dallas left some rather questionable stuff up on my laptop so we had a family meeting about it when he got home from his friend's house. In the whole scheme of things, we decided not to make a federal case out of it.

Evidently his computer has faulty keys and mine is faster. *Cyber Police* doesn't catch everything apparently.

That night I had a wonderful dream and that made for a happy Tuesday morning. Bart was laughing, active and milling about in the dream and I told him how good he looked and that I believed he had cured himself. He said he thought so too. I think the dream was a reflection of how well Bart has been doing the last few days. Not great mind you, but he seems to be managing his discomfort and beating the hard pain into submission.

Bart was still sleeping when I left for the morning bus. En route I realized that I had used my last bus ticket. I made a quick detour to the market to buy another book of passes. I hoped for no delays because I only had a total of 9 minutes to complete this transaction and make it to the last bus pick up point of the morning.

The closed sign at the customer service window indicated that it didn't open until 10. That was news to me because many times before I had gone early and purchased bus tickets. This just wasn't going to work for me and now I had only 7 minutes. I stood at the counter and wrote out my check until somebody walked by. I told him what I urgently needed.

He tossed a book of tickets my way and seemed mildly put off that I had the audacity to request a receipt too. I was most grateful and did thank him profusely.

Running to my car I replayed the exchange in my mind and noted that the clerk never said a single word. At least I got what I wanted but it was odd that he never even uttered a grunt or anything?

I made it to the stop with two whole minutes to spare. It was a busy workday but I did receive a few emails from Bart.

He was doing fine, eating leftovers and resting.

Later that day on my way home, I didn't get a text from Bart while on the bus so I decided to forego the nightly trip to the pharmacy since it was a karate night and I needed to prepare something for dinner. The prescription would wait until Wednesday. Bart wanted pork & beans with his salmon burgers but we only had baked beans. I prepared the salmon burgers and heated the sub-par baked beans. Dallas showed up with two cans of pork & beans but it was too late. Dinner was ready.

I put on my TKD uniform and went to transfer Bart's laundry to the dryer. The inside of my dryer was like a tie-dyed tee shirt, splattered completely with blue ink. Dallas didn't say a word. I tried using various cleaning agents but nothing removed the ink. White board cleaner had the best result but woefully short of effective.

I would have been living in the dryer for days using more elbow grease than I cared to and only removing a fraction of the blue stuff in there. Easier just to throw wet jeans in and hope for the best. The good news is that the blue seems permanently affixed to the dryer walls and hasn't rubbed off on anything else other than when the initial pen explosion occurred. Of course Dallas said it ruined the brand new shirts I'd just purchased for him.

Bart was doing well so I drove off to karate school. I returned about an hour and a half later.

When I walked into the house, I asked Bart if he was cooking something, 'cause it sure smelled like something was. Oh yes, something was cooking all right. I never turned off the heat to the baked beans!

They were baked all right for about two hours on the stovetop. I wonder how much that cost us in propane! It better be under $100 or it adds insult to injury.

Our house still smells like baked beans and burnt brown sugar.

April 14

Wednesday was an eventful day. Dallas said goodbye to Dad and I drove him to school at 6:30 AM with his backpack, sleeping bag and overnight case. It was the first day of the Every Fifteen Minutes program at Ponderosa High. I could not miss work this day so I caught the bus to Sac. Bart slept in until about 10 AM. At about that time, I got a call on my cell while working at my desk. It was the El Dorado County Sheriff's Department chaplain. I expected this as part of the program and yet hearing the words "your son Dallas has been killed in a car crash" was most sobering. At the high school, a total of 34 students were removed from classes every fifteen minutes symbolizing the loss of a teenager in a car crash every fifteen minutes across the United States.

The Chaplain said she was standing on my porch. She said she rang the doorbell and called the house phone and then my cell.

We concluded our call and hung up. Unbeknownst to me Bart saw her on the porch and answered the door. He told me later that the chaplain came in and delivered the same shocking message.

I was most concerned about Bart's heart dropping into his already stressed and hurting stomach. Not a good thing but we both agreed months ago that this program would be worth it for Dallas. Still, I'd hoped to shield Bart from the face to face. Turns out that Bart and the chaplain had a very good visit. She ended up staying and praying with Bart. They talked a while. It was a good thing.

I got off the bus about 5:30 PM, made my usual swing to the pharmacy for Lovenox syringes and whatever else was ready.

I got home and Bart suggested I take the dog for a walk, which I did since he'd been cooped up all day. I prepared a quick dinner then rushed to the school for the parents' retreat.

At the retreat, we were told what the kids were doing and we listened to a courageous mom who lost her teenage son 11 years ago.

It was so very sad but important to hear. Our task was to write a letter to our teen. The kids would be doing the same thing at their overnight retreat. At home with Bart's input I composed our letter.

Afterward we had a quiet evening without the boy.

Thursday morning parents were to be back at the high school promptly at 8:30 am. The whole student body (2,000 plus) and parents watched a video presentation of what occurred on campus the day before. We watched a simulated fatal crash, life flight, CHP, Fire Department, jaws of life, El Dorado County Sheriffs, and living dead students on film. It was intense and heart-stopping. We heard from a dynamic speaker still suffering from his decision to drive under the influence 21 years later.

Some of the living dead shared their letters to their parents and the parent's shared theirs in front of each the assembly.

Afterwards Dallas actually hugged me, which was a first.

He then assertively shook the hand of CHP Officer Stark and said "thank you sir" twice!

Dallas told me he was glad for the experience and wanted to share it with his friends. At the retreat the students only slept two hours. Because he was so tired, Dallas insisted we postpone our letter exchange until tomorrow.

Bart had a fairly rough pain day and was pretty fatigued but he perked up when his living dead son walked through the front door very much alive. Dallas kept saying "I love you Dad" and before he drove away to run an errand for Dad he promised me that he would be safe and said, "I love you" through the open driver's window.

He seemed happy and that made us glad. Bart's feeling a bit better tonight at bedtime. Dallas went to sleep early and knowing he's safe in his bed is very comforting after the pretense of his death.

Having your teen agree to text or call you every day he drives somewhere is definitely a win-win.

It was a worthy program indeed.

Bart announced the news is over so it's once again Bedtime for Bonzos.

April 15

It's finally Friday. Lori drove Bart to Creekside Lounge this afternoon for a fluid "top off."

It makes for a more comfortable weekend. Bart says he's feeling pretty good right now, a big improvement over yesterday. I'm trying to take note of what he does hours before a "feeling pretty good" report.

To that end Bart found some brain game challenge software. He says the program is designed to improve your memory function. I can't for the life of me remember the actual name of it.

Bart won't tell me again either. (I think he may have forgotten too.)

He asked me to send him an email reminding him to install it on my computer tomorrow.

Dallas picked up his dad from Creekside this evening and they thankfully ordered Chinese food for dinner before making the nightly pharmacy run. It was a mildly hectic and steady workday for me.

First I had a meeting at Cal Expo then a rush to get all my hearing prep done before spring break.

At the end of the day, I ran across the street to the Capitol office but it was all locked up. I guess they went home?

I eventually got myself out of there just by 6 pm. It was just enough time to drive home, feed the dog and then dress for TKD.

Tonight the two of us testing for fifth degrees would get to experiment with our selected board breaking techniques. Good thing the test isn't until July.

Bart was still feeling right when I got home.

He put on a recorded program NCIS. Our surround sound is really good. It must be because it fools the dog. Doorbell rings on the TV and the dog barks. A horn honked on the TV and the dog barks. The dog barks on the TV and the dog barks. But the real kicker was when Bart tooted and the dog barked. We both laughed heartily at that one.

Dallas came home right on time tonight. I told him we appreciated his punctuality.

It prevents undue parental anxiety that can manifest into fewer privileges. Dallas would often push the envelope but no argument tonight. Perhaps his experience being dead for two days has changed his perspective a bit. It worked for us.

April 19

Time has gotten away from me and my good intentions never hit "post." A compilation of notes from the past few days follows:

Saturday was a rough day for Bart.

The French toast wasn't as magic as it had been Friday morning. It didn't sit well in his stomach. I was so disappointed to see him hurting again after such a good Friday night.

I retrieved Bart's pain meds from the safe. (We decided such an array of medications warranted safekeeping.)

It was not fun to see Bart so uncomfortable. It's frustrating not being able to do anything about his discomfort. I get a little tense and angry sometimes. Once he'd eaten breakfast, taken his shots and morning meds, I thought it was a good time to take the dog for a hike. Running up and down those rocky creek beds always eases my mind when it's wrapped too tight.

Phaddy has to be on the leash until we reach the trail head. Off Sudbury we turn on Este Vista to access the trail. There at the corner lives a cute little Lhasa female named Nikki.

Phaddy was electrified at the sight of her. Walt the homeowner was out mowing. We started chatting while Phaddy wagged, barked and shuddered. I let him off leash and Phaddy took off across the grass to play with Nikki. Next thing I know Mary was coming out of the house carrying Nikki in her arms. She said Phaddy barged right in and helped himself to snacks and a drink. I believe he devoured Nikki's bowl of food. What a way to meet your neighbors!

My runs are forever ruined due to a girl. I thought that would only be a problem with children not dogs.

Before Nikki, Phaddy would run to beat hell to catch up with me. I would take him off leash at the creek which is the big barrier where there's no looking back. He always follows me up the hill rather than brave crossing back over the water. I called for him and waited longer than usual.

Sure enough he'd gone back to the girl's house. I had to backtrack and recapture Phaddy in their back yard. I tried to avoid being seen.

I didn't want to have to explain why I didn't have my dog under control let alone on a leash a full 20 minutes after I left the first time.

While I was gone Bart installed "Brain Workshop" on my computer (that's the simple name I couldn't remember). It does not build your confidence when you can't even figure out how to decrease the difficulty level back to one. Apparently the game starts at two and F1-12 keys operate differently on a Mac. I kept dimming the screen until Bart told me how to properly use the functions. Of course, my first score was zero, learning the process. Second attempt 75 percent and third 100 percent. It's remedial but I'm going to stay at level one until I'm more than sure I can safely move on without psychological damage.

Dallas, Bart and I finally exchanged the Every Fifteen Minutes letters. That's the final task (closure) in the program where Dallas was dead for two days. He wrote a letter to us and we wrote one to him.

Dallas had been stalling this exchange because he didn't want to discuss anything out loud. We made a deal that we wouldn't talk about it. He could read our letter and we would read his. I will share with you the gist of Dal's letter. "A parents biggest fear is to outlive a child" said Barton D. Reagan.

Dallas wrote that he thought a lot about that statement by his dad. He said reality set in for him during this experience.

He went on to say that although he disagreed with us most of the time he loved us and realized how devastating it would be for us if something happened to him. He closed with "If you promise to stay strong Dad, I promise to stay safe." Dallas did tell us at dinner that our letter was real and he liked it (thumbs up). That was it and we didn't push for further comment.

Our Ranger son Matty called with exciting news. He was in Miami with his lovely girlfriend Jen who just returned from Afghanistan for a brief home leave. Matty told us he popped the question and Jen said "yes." We are gaining another beautiful daughter in the family. We're all very happy and Bart is definitely on track to attend the ceremony sometime next year.

It's spring break this week for Dallas and for the state Senate. My boss, Senator Doug LaMalfa embarks on a District tour and his first stop is Weaverville. Being the only staffer with roots there, I insisted on coordinating the stop. Thanks to my lifelong friend Jeanne and my sister Sandi I was able to head north and actually be there for the event. Bart would never have protested but we were all much more at ease knowing Jeanne and Sandi would be keeping Bart company. Today Jeanne gave him a much-needed haircut.

Bart called tonight and he sounded wonderful. It was great to hear that he was having such fun with the girls. His voice was strong and confident, just like it was in my dream a week ago.

Sandi drove Bart to Chemotherapy today where he got the results of the latest scan. Bart's cancer markers were down again, down 700 to be exact. In addition, the oncologist said the tumors in his liver had actually shrunk for the first time!

It's the power of prayer, friendship and family. Thank you, thank you, thank you.

My mom and I really should go to bed but it's hard to sleep when you're this happy. The news is even better than French toast and that's pretty damn good.

April 21

A Note from Bart:

Lately I've had 3-4 days in a row free of cramping. I had mentioned to the oncologist that every morning I was having severe cramping in my upper abdomen. He asked if I was taking Pepcid AC and I assured him I was every morning.

He suggested I try taking it at night and, lo and behold, the very first night I take it, next morning I am pain free. Then I read the bottle and notice it says I can take it twice a day and so that's what I do now. So far 4 straight days cramp free. Couple that with staying on top of my pain meds, which I now take a pain pill (different one) every two hours. But it's making me feel better than at any point since all of this started.

So with that in mind I am really thinking I may be able to, at the very least, ride the golf course with friends, as soon as our weather co-operates. We are still getting rain, here in Northern California, at the end of April. Those of you familiar with this know that is very unusual.

Since my immune system has been compromised due to the Chemo I'm not taking any chances on getting an illness.

I'll keep y'all informed about how things transpire. I'm not sure when my next CT Scan is but I'll let you know about that too.

I wanted to write this for my bride so she can relax and not stress.

Bart

April 22

Bart thinks he may have jinxed himself with his last note. He reports that tonight is not good. The less he talks or moves the better he feels. Good thing he's not ADHD or he'd be in a multiplied world of hurt. He is still and asked me to be still near him enlisting my company to watch TV to take his mind off any discomfort. I hope it's easing.

Bart was able to consume one of my protein blender concoctions late this evening. It takes the edge off and helps fill him up.

It's been fun to hear about the last few days with our buddy Clean Jeanne. Bart said he was about to compliment Jeanne on how she straightened the rug and couch without a compulsion to vacuum like I do, but then she pulled out the vacuum and said "oh no, we have to do that." I felt so vindicated! Isn't it a rule that when you move rugs or furniture you must vacuum before putting it all back? Bart said Jeanne told him in no uncertain terms that it's a requirement and there's no use resisting. A change of company really does him good.

He's not only seen the light about every woman's power tool (the vacuum cleaner) but he's been sharing many anecdotes also, which has been fun. We all know that familiarity can breed contempt so it makes sense that breaks from the usual must be healthy.

May you break bread with friends and eggs with kids this Easter weekend. Enjoy and God bless.

April 23

A Note from Bart:

Today was a mixed bag. I felt mostly good with some spots of cramps that quickly went away. Reading of all my friends' aches and pains makes me feel that I'm not alone and we are all getting older.

So at the hospital they always ask, "How's your pain on a scale of 1-10?"

"I'd give today a 2-3."

Some days that is almost being pain free so I'm good.

I hope all you "old" folks recover soon from your various aches and pains and no one has to suffer any further.

I spent the day watching golf on TV (it's a start) and getting a quote for some fence work. Had to get my toolbox out. My toolbox these days consists of my checkbook. It's a lot easier on me physically and stuff gets done right the first time (usually).

Take care and love y'all, Bart

April 25

If it's Monday it must be Chemo, a regularly scheduled date for Sandi to take Bart to Creekside Lounge. Bart texted me this evening to say he felt pretty good.

He gets the good cocktails at the Lounge and tends to do well afterwards. He is better than yesterday. Bart wasn't up to going outside on the back deck or even to the front porch to watch Dallas search for the traditional hidden Easter basket. I was the only witness this year but Bart did suggest that I videotape the auspicious event. It was entertaining to observe our 17 year old in a velvet King's crown hunting through the bushes, trees and garden plants ultimately having to beg for hints! Mom wins again. For Dallas it's an obligatory annual sport he partakes in willingly for the spoils.

The Reagan laundry bins were expanding like peeps in a microwave oven on Easter Sunday so Dad was recruited to assist. My wish was to find a mate for every stray sock so I washed every single sock I could find anywhere. After which I noted the same age-old perplexing disparity between Bart and I.

What Bart thinks are pairs and what I know to be, never match up. He thinks just because one is stretched out that it isn't a mate. There was no convincing Bart on this point so I just matched up the stretched ones later and off those socks went to their respective drawers. After that "soulful" effort, I still had a tub full of singles which was disheartening. Do socks really try to escape or what? Another mom of a teen and I have taken to exchanging our single sock bins occasionally and guess what? Yes, we have solved a pair or two, it's most satisfying indeed.

Bart's Easter gift to me was finding a cleaning service. He invited Johnny Sparkles to the house for an estimate while I was out with Dallas at a doctor appointment. Sparkles left a folder of information and I read every word of it. I highlighted one particular sentence of interest. Sparkles requested that clients prep for cleaning by picking up, putting away and clearing surfaces and floors. Ahah!

Johnny Sparkles had it in writing. Right there on his brochure "please pick up and put away items including dishes" so they can focus on cleaning. I've been trying to explain that concept to Bart for more than 20 years! He has always accused me of "cleaning" for the cleaning people. Bart would roll his eyes and comment on how ludicrous it was for me to clean up first.

He doesn't seem to get the distinction between tidying and cleaning. It's so they don't have to spend extra time moving your crap. Bart was still reluctant to acknowledge this lesson even though Johnny Sparkles had it there in black and white. Although I did notice that Bart didn't say a word as I went room to room putting stuff away all evening.

Changing bed sheets costs extra and I definitely know why. Changing sheets is a very dangerous job. I can break boards without so much as a hangnail but tugging a fitted sheet snuggly around a mattress, now that's a very different story. I not only broke the nail off on my middle finger but right down to the bloody quick.

It took me two days before I got the top sheet, blankets and comforter on that guest bed. Bart suggests next time I pay the extra bed fee and let Sparkles slay that mattress beast. I'll stick to breaking boards. It's far less dangerous.

April 27

Bart visited Creekside Lounge today for hydration. He said he felt ok just very tired and slept quite a bit all day. I leave for work just after Dallas, before 7AM and return in the evening just before 7PM.

Tonight as usual, I made my usual swing by the pharmacy. I think they have an obsession with staples there. We try to salvage receipts for our insurance but the staples cause them to get ripped to bits.

One day I picked up a large order in a paper grocery bag. The bag was stapled together at the top. Maybe staples represent super security? To peer into your bag, it would take extra superhuman x-ray vision to ever see the small print and discover what medicine you've got in there.

Is that the concern? Maybe there's a state HIPAA staple regulation? I'm too embarrassed to ask because every clerk seems so intent on stapling that I think it must be a directive. Receipts can be completely mutilated so maybe the instructions will leap out of the bag if they're not affixed with seven staples.

I digress. I asked Bart why he hadn't reported to me his sugar levels lately. He said because they're boring. I say that's for the listener to decide. He tells me his sugar levels fluctuate 70-230. Normal functioning people are under 100. A good reading for Bart is 110-130. The Humalin seems to be doing the job. He's staying in that range.

Bart explained to Dallas that he will have to get screened regularly for signs of pancreatic cancer.

It's hereditary. Dallas disregards his dad's warnings on the outside but it could be just because he doesn't want to acknowledge grave concerns for his dad on the inside.

Dallas has been quite happy lately because of a lovely 17-year-old young lady, he likes.

We are particularly pleased about his discerning taste because we've known this young girl since fourth grade and she is exceptional. She has great parents so this is good. We moms though are still inclined to be careful, tread lightly, and try to get as much information about this relationship as possible.

Bart was feeling pretty good about himself because he prepared hot dogs with Pillsbury crescent rolls and American cheese. He and Dallas loved those when I made them last month and can't seem to get enough. Dal made the mistake of setting his plate down on the living room coffee table for a moment while skipping to the loo. I wasn't paying attention either but when I turned around Phaddy had consumed both of his dogs ever so ravenously and in less than five seconds.

Dallas was incensed. He put Phaddy out and said there had better be two more "dogs in a blanket" with cheese or he was going to have somebody's head on a platter!

Thankfully there were extras tonight. Phaddy had to serve his sentence of an extra hour outside as penance for his misbehavior. He hasn't gotten the "leave it alone" command yet.

Bart announced that we are all turning in early tonight so I bid adieu. It might already be too late to be early!

One step forward and another step back

I wish I could report better news. Bart said his day was rough.

I had to leave early again this morning for work. We had a big Fairs Committee hearing scheduled at the Capitol. That meant another long day for me. Bart fought increased pain and cramping despite his regular pain pill schedule. Tonight, he says he has major pain around his chest and back and it hurts to breathe deeply.

Dallas came home after school today but he had a counselimg appointment in Folsom at 5PM followed by jazz combo class.

I didn't get home until about 6:30 PM. I had a mini freak out when the music school called because Dallas wasn't there yet and I couldn't reach him on his cell. Dallas drove up just when I was really getting frothed into a lather. He simply had to come home to get his drum cymbals and music. Whew. After that experience where Dallas was "dead" for two days, I was quick to panic about not being able to reach him right away.

Due to sleeping on the bus, I didn't see Bart's text about wanting Subway for dinner. I prepared tortellini instead, but it didn't sit too well with Bart. Strawberry shortcake did better. Because Dal was at Jazz Band practice, I was going to stay home instead of going to black belt class. Bart told me to go to Taekwondo though so he could watch the NFL draft in peace.

I was back in an hour. Bart and Dal were setting up a desktop computer in Dallas' room. It was a great normal sight to see, the two of them in there doing computer stuff. Dal was all excited about getting such a fast system and I was having something akin to buyer's remorse by agreeing to let Dallas have my desktop computer in the first place.

I was secretly afraid he would mess it up. Well, at least Dallas won't be using my laptop anymore (I hope).

Phaddy didn't steal anyone's dinner tonight but he did scour Dallas' room for morsels. Then he ran about chasing and tossing his eviscerated toys throughout the house leaving their guts (stuffing) on the floor.

Bart took another pain dose, an electrolyte drink and other remedies then headed to bed early.

I'm a bit worried tonight because he looked so incredibly uncomfortable but hopefully a good night's rest will do him good. I'm thinking the same is true for me.

April 30

Bart woke up hurting. I was concerned about going to work. When I scooped up that dollop of toothpaste I thought fell off my toothbrush, I should have known the day might not go well.

It was shaving cream. There are two sinks in our bathroom. I say those who shave their faces should use the boy sink. Dallas has taken to popping into our bathroom in the mornings and now I know why. Evidently Dad has better grooming products.

Dallas gets home earlier on Fridays but he's still a teenager and doesn't want to hang with his dad on a Friday. Bart said he felt horrible and asked if I would call Creekside to find out what we should do. I knew it must be bad if Bart wanted me to call someone.

Bart hates to talk when he's hurting so he gave me short cursory answers and I immediately felt anxious before the call. I asked if I dialed, would he talk, but he said no. Even though I'm with Bart day in and day out, I just can't know precisely how it feels and what to say to the doctors. All I know is that when he tells me to make the call it must be really awful for him.

Bart seemed to expect that I would know exactly what to say about how he has been doing and what over the counter stuff he took and when. They ask so many questions that I cannot confidently answer.

The nurse queries, "Exactly how long has he had this, how many times has he taken this/that and when, what was the duration of this symptom and that?"

I feel so incredibly inadequate, stupid and confused that I end up giving them my impression of what's going on. Then I just want to cry and say, just do something to fix him, please.

Bart was able to tell me afterwards that I got it all wrong. He wasn't enthused by any of their suggestions either. I get so mad at myself in these situations. I don't do a good job of describing what Bart is feeling and I don't have a chart of exactly what he took and when either.

Listening to today's phone conversation probably left Bart frustrated too. Doctors and nurses never seem to have a magic course of action that results in Bart feeling better now. Everything takes time, precious time. It's definitely not an exact science.

I worried that Bart didn't consume enough calories today. I prepared noodles with broth and later a blender drink but Bart did not finish either one. I suggested a hot pad for his stomach hoping it would give some relief if food didn't.

I tried to ask Bart what he thought might make him feel better and he said, "Not talking, so quit asking me questions."

I get how having to answer questions is taxing in and of itself. Just ask anyone who is not a morning person how they like questions before they're ready? However, not getting answers also leads to guesswork on my part. I question whether I'm feeding him the right stuff or giving him the right kind of care and support.

Tonight Bart told me to go ahead and go to Taekwondo testing (higher rank instructors are needed on the judging panel). Bart said he wasn't going to eat anything else and seemed to want to rest on the couch... alone. He was still on the couch in that position when I returned. Bart finally got up and ambled to his chair late evening. We watched the news. Bart took his evening medications and went to bed. I waited up for Dallas who came home at curfew with a couple of friends. I heated up Tortellini and they all ate a very late dinner. I suspect it was the second dinner they'd had tonight but better home than elsewhere.

Everybody is tucked in safely including the Phaddy dog. I sure hope Bart gets a good night's rest and wakes up without pain as I know you all do too.

Chapter Thirteen

Crossing the Threshold

May 1

Bart said he had a better night's sleep but not a good night's sleep. No, he would not expound on what that means. Bart arose to take his morning pain dosage then went back to bed. When he finally did get up around 10:00 AM, he looked better than yesterday. I was hopeful.

Blueberry scones fresh out of the oven but Dallas and his pal Gus had already made a Sunday morning donut run. They came back with Bart's favorite blueberry donuts. Then they messed up the room, destroyed the bathroom and went on about their day leaving random stuff in their wake. I suspect they are doing similar destructive activities at Gus' house this afternoon. I note that this does not rankle me anymore; in part due to the "Every Fifteen Minutes" experience where Dallas was dead for two days. It puts everything in perspective.

Cheryl arrived for our Sunday morning constitutional (trail run) and the boys were to hang with Dad until we returned. Bart was feeling ok.

Bart tells me I have a remarkable capacity to hurt myself without even trying. During our last Estrofest, I cracked my forehead open just bending over to clean something. There's a nice tiny mark to remember it by. I also have to be very careful about opening anything hermetically sealed in plastic. Why in the world do innocuous products require such a fortress of packaging? They're almost impossible to open safely. It becomes necessary to pull out small power tools just to open a toilet brush!

I've been moved to expletives trying to extract a zip drive from its impenetrable Fort Knox frame. Opening protective plastic can cause a wound if you're not especially careful. I've tried carpet scissors, channel lock pliers and wire cutters on that crap. Take it from me and beware of buying anything sealed in plastic encasement. I have the scars to prove it, but I digress.

When Cheryl and I returned, all Bart could say was "What in the hell happened to you" knees, right elbow and palm bloody and scraped. When you run in new shoes, don't take them out too fast unless you know what they can do. I was testing out a new method of rock running to try and spare my knees. It wasn't the rocks that were perilous it was a little loose dirt on a slope that did it and I fell downhill into the rocks.

Had I not been trying this new knee-saving method I would have returned unscathed. Nonetheless, I "Rangered up" and finished the run like normal. So much for the stupid knee-saving method.

Bart ate well today. Even though he snacked on Top Ramen soup, at least it goes down well despite the sodium. He also had sausage biscuits, turkey potpie, protein shakes, sandwiches and various other substantial foods. I was pleased compared to his calorie intake yesterday.

Dallas reported a good day and he was home right on time. It was nice to see the car still clean. I required that he and his friends wash, wax, vacuum and detail the Red Dragon yesterday or their parents would have to pick them up. They obliged nicely I must say.

We have both work and school tomorrow. Our friend Tracey will be testing her ability to be on time tomorrow. She agreed to drive Bart to his chemotherapy at Creekside. Former Air Force conditioning stays with you, if you're not 15 minutes early, you're late according to Bart. No stress Tracey, they're always late calling him in on a busy Monday anyway! Good luck.

Our eldest son Matty called tonight saying all the soldiers at Fort Bragg were going out for a beer to celebrate May Day, the day the U.S. military announced the death of Osama Bin Laden. He also announced that he would be joining the 82nd Airborne. God Bless our U.S. military forces in every branch. May they stay safe and conquer.

We hope you all have a comfortable evening. The Reagan's bid you a safe and celebratory Sunday evening, with love.

May 2

Monday is chemo day.

A friend signed up for Creekside taxi duty. She was sweating bullets to shed her tendency to run late because of Bart's 15 minutes early or you're late thing. Bart said she passed with flying colors. They were early.

Before chemo Bart met with the oncologist about his consistent pain and cramping problems. With all the heavy duty analgesics Bart is taking, the doctor saw no reason why Bart should have such intense and constant discomfort.

It's amazing Bart can even keep his pill taking schedule straight. He alternates between Dilaudid and Norco every two hours. The Fentanyl pain patch is always on. He changes it every three days. On top of that Bart takes morphine pills twice daily plus three separate nausea prescriptions every day: Compazine, Lorazepam and one more I can't remember but I do remember that it costs our insurance $1900! That seems ridiculously excessive for a pill, but what do I know? Plus Bart has a whole cabinet filled with over the counter symptom management remedies he consumes daily.

Bart thinks side effects of the pain meds could be contributing to his cramping. As for the cold hard pain, the oncologist wants Bart to chart his every dose and all his symptoms through Friday. At that time, the oncologist may refer Bart to a pain management specialist if necessary.

Dallas retrieved Bart from Creekside this evening and they decided to drive through KFC for dinner (boy food).

I love chemo Mondays because Bart always seems to feel better Monday evening. He's more talkative. He even laughs and life is so comfortably normal. The nurses must really juice him up with lots of extra good stuff along with the Gemzar. The super fluid cocktail meds just seem more effective through an IV.

Tonight is one of those great evenings. Bart is more active than I've seen him in a long time. He fed Phaddy, composed his med/symptom chart on the laptop, changed landline phone batteries and unpacked some computer gadget he ordered online. Bart got up later and fixed himself strawberry shortcake then he harassed his sister (and others) on email (you know who you are) and told me all about one of his new favorite shows "Mounted in Alaska." Who knew taxidermy could be so fascinating?

Dallas is asleep. Bart skipped to the loo. When he returns we will finish watching a recorded program before it's Bedtime for Bonzos. Hope your evening was as good as ours.

May 4

The day after chemo Bart is generally very tired. It's nice that we usually get to enjoy one stellar evening but beyond that the oral chemo drugs are added to the mix and that causes bone numbing exhaustion. Bart said he slept most of day today. He also had nagging pain rear its ugly head. We hope that by the end of the week, Bart's logs will help zero in on a solution to the ever-present pain train.

The antics of Phaddeus, Phaddy, the wonder dog, had us all amused. He's a precious little funny creature which means he desperately needs training. We're saving that privilege for when Dallas can fit training into his schedule.

Megan sent two small fun packages for our family enjoyment. We opened a cute stuffed white blood cell and silly sanitizer for Bart, some crazy monster covers for Mom's tiny IPod shuffle, and a book of hilarious test answers for Dallas. Here's a sample test question: What are the small tributary streams running into the Nile River called? Juveniles.

It all made for a fun evening. Dallas read nearly the whole book to us. Every time Bart tried to start the TV recording of "House" Phaddy would run and squeak his three tiered squeaky snake. Bart would roll his eyes and pause the show. Then Phaddy dared to steal the stuffed white blood cell and Bart had to step in. That's what we call exercise friends. Phaddy wasn't going to get Bart's stuffed cell from Dr. Meg. I've got to close before this session times out. There are many household chores to accomplish before bed. May all your stuff get done.

May 5

Bart said he felt terrible early this morning when he awoke. He could not get comfortable even after he administered his pain dosages. He paced, sat on the edge of the bed and then lay down under the covers. At one point, I thought Bart was trying to stand on his head but he was just repositioning to see if it would help alleviate the pain. When I left the house, he had finally dozed off.

Dallas warned us that he would be getting a detention today. In order to make the Jazz Band try-outs he would have to miss the first 15 minutes of third period. Apparently some teachers don't think it's worthy to authorize 15 minutes for music auditions. Bart, Dallas and I all agreed that in Dal's case it most certainly is worth it and he would take the hit. Sure enough we got a call from the school. Instead of excusing the absence we opted for Saturday school. Students must do homework on Saturdays which is preferable to after-school detentions where they do not force kids to work. Dallas is not exactly self-motivated to complete homework so he was good with serving even two Saturday detentions if necessary.

Bart assured me that he would manage just fine if I attended Coach Clark's funeral service in Lincoln. It was an honor to be there and to visit with his family and guests. It was almost like a Trinity High School reunion of sorts. Former THS students in attendance spanned more than a decade of graduating classes. Coach Clark will be remembered fondly for his passionate outbursts from the bench and tirades along the sidelines. He was such a good influence that I'm thinking kids today just need to be yelled at a lot more like he did.

Dal told us tonight that his audition went smoothly and that he made Jazz band. He also announced that because he did so well he would not be unloading the dishwasher tonight. Apparently that's some kind of reward. Ok then the task would wait for Dallas to bask in his glory. I also announced that because I drove to work and fed a parking meter that I would not be brewing coffee Friday morning either. It seems fair, especially since Dallas hoards all the commuter mugs.

Bart said he felt better as the day wore on. He's keeping a diary of meds. Bart still won't tell me if he's also noting his symptoms but I do know when I should just let it go. He'll do what he wants to do anyway. (The Clark kids said their dad told them the same thing. You'll do what you want anyway so it doesn't matter what I say.) Truer words were never spoken.

Sandi and her Beagle, Jasper, dropped by after I got home from work. While she was here, our son Matthew called from Fort Bragg to update us on his new command etc. We were chatting away when all of a sudden Bart called my attention to the time. His stomach isn't patient and dinner was overdue. Fortunately there were two of us. Sandi took control of the stove. I boiled pasta, clipped greens and she sautéed. Bart had his meal in no time. He was doing pretty well and even better after he ate.

It’s Taekwondo night and I had missed a day due to my running injuries. I can't afford to miss classes if I'm to test for fifth degree in July. I also can't afford to hurt myself anymore.

Tomorrow Bart goes to Creekside where he will discuss his medication/pain chart with the oncologist. Bart should come home with a referral to a pain specialist. We hope that doctors can find the right combination of treatments that will keep Bart free of the debilitating cramps and pain. That's just the worst, watching Bart suffer in needless pain and I can't do anything about it. I guess I could make dinner on time at least. That would help.

We will let you know the results of the pain diary inquest tomorrow and what the next step will be on the road to “pain free.” Thanks again for every word posted in the guestbook. Bart checks it multiple times a day. Whale away!

May 8

Bart submitted his medication chart for evaluation at Creekside Lounge. It's likely that a pain specialist is in Bart's future but the oncologist wants Bart to chart through Monday. The oncologist will either have other suggestions or we will be scheduling an appointment with someone new.

I got home just before 6:00 PM in a bad mood. Bart wasn’t feeling his best either. I had hoped to find my calendar notebook at the office. I kept all passwords, logins and account settings for anything and everything in that book. I lost it once before and found it so I learned my lesson. NOT. I promised Bart I would transfer all the data to a computer safeguard program he installed for me to save him from the aggravation of seeing me frantic, crazed and searching for it again and again. It’s the ultimate aggravation to lose that damn book again. Precisely the time when I needed key information I'd been collecting for two years the stupid thing disappears.

I've checked all the cars, suitcases, cabinets, drawers, couch cushions, closets and paper piles to no avail.

I was mad at myself ergo the bad mood. Bart was right to be chastising me. It was so frustrating for him since he did warn me before. I prepared a pizza for dinner then decided I needed to take Phaddy for a drive.

A change of scene was necessary and Phaddy likes Jasper’s toys. Sandi was entertaining a couple friends by the pool. The visit with the girls was great and diffused my negative mood. When I got home Bart had a program cued up. After his nightly shots and pills we watched a show together and called it a night.

Saturday morning I went to the giant warehouse store with my big list. I whipped around tossing stuff in my basket fast. Saturdays it's so busy and there's no cart traffic control. As I was wheeling toward the exit, I saw a woman returning the very $30 dollar pillows I just bought. Not a reassuring sight. Just in case I'll file the receipt and keep the box. The bank was next on my schedule then on to the pharmacy and market.

We would be celebrating Bart's close friend and golfing buddy Bill's birthday Saturday night. Bill and his lovely wife would be bringing dinner from Papa G's and I was to prepare the epic salad. Lori and Sandi filled in the dining blanks. Although Bart still wasn't feeling good at all, having friends/family over was nice. Good friends are better than over the counter meds.

Bart even ventured to the mailbox. He announced his mail journey just in case he didn't come back we could send a search party. Later Bart even came to the dinner table and sat with us for a long while.

Bart must have had a good time Saturday night because his sugar level was 302 Sunday morning. It's high but nothing a little insulin can't handle. It was not a stellar morning for the Bart man. He was concerned and told me he felt something happening and to stay close.

Dallas brought white roses and blueberry donuts for Dad. He also offered to wash and wax my car but he asked that I not take it to the bus stop so he could do it after school. I told him the story about Megan almost washing my car once for Mother's day. Meg "accidently" took out a small portion of the house trim backing the car out of the garage to clean it for me. In reality, she used a crow bar to create the damage to the house as cover for the fact that she actually went for a joy ride and hit a big rock. I think she did a lot of homework assignments for Matty in exchange for his silence.

We took calls from the twins and finally got sheets changed and laundry done. Bart and I watched a very exciting movie with lots of explosions. Phaddy's antics with a new shark toy stuffed with squeaky eggs, were most amusing.

It was a warm and comforting day having connected with our moms and our children.

About 8:00 PM Bart said "nothing like feeling like crap all day only to feel better when the day is over." Operative phrase: "he feels better." I'll take that. It's a great day finally.

May 9

A Note from Bart:

Well saw the doc today before my Chemo. He is still a little puzzled about why I'm in pain (unless according to him it's the tumors dying). He wants me to try steroid shots a couple of days a week to see if that helps with the pain. I will start with M-W-F and see how that goes. He mentioned me taking prednisone but said he wanted to try Decodron shots first. My CA-19 markers were down again.

The numbers are down another 1200 to 5300 from 6500. That is more good news that tumors are shrinking. Now if we can manage the pain life would be good.

I like the good news but I guess we must be tempered by some reality too.

Will keep y'all informed as to how the steroids work.

Love, Bart

May 11

Bart told me that he sat around and suffered Tuesday. It's very distressful. We had high hopes that the oncologist could prescribe something else to fix this. Bart is obviously very tough and doesn't want to push until the doctor exhausts other options. I don't get it because I do want to push. I hate seeing him hurt as much as you hate hearing about it.

Tuesday night I got home late from work. Bart had already prepared Top Ramen and didn't want any more substantial fare. He couldn't stomach anything else so he said I should just go to TKD which I did. Wednesday was another packed, busy day.... doctors, prescription pick up, grocery shopping and miscellaneous errands.

Tonight we were graced with a visit from our Las Vegas friends Bob and Sue who are traveling the country in their RV. It's always a vicarious thrill to hear of their adventures. Visits with friends buoys the spirit. Bart certainly seems to rally although not too far from his throne. No trip to the mailbox today. I did not find my lost calendar notebook either. We'll sleep on it again. We will wish for good luck and good fortune again tomorrow. Sleep tight.

May 12

A Note from Bart:

Thanks to all my peeps for the support from these pages. I'm undeserving. I just do what I do. Survive day to day. I think most people would do the same. At least it's what I like to believe. Nothing special here. ;-)

Today marks the day I started taking Decadron to see if it handles the pain. Today after my hydration and cocktail treatment I have felt 100 percent better. Tomorrow if the pain returns I use the Decadron then we will see what happens. Pray for good news. The prayers are working I'm sure.

They are worried about giving me 'roids cause I can get addicted. If it takes away the pain until I beat this thing then I can get un-addicted. At least that's my theory.

Thanks again for all the love and support and I will keep fighting, especially if I think it helps even one of you out there, I will fight for you.

Love y'all, Bart

May 14

A Note from Bart:

Well it's been a couple of days since we posted so here we go. After my cocktail Thursday I had 18 hours almost totally pain free so something in that mix (or combination) is helping. Now I have to find a way to get similar results without going in there every day (M-F) and have a home remedy. I have a home prescription for Decadron (a steroid), which is one of the cocktail drugs. Anyway I took one at 9:00 AM Friday after I started experiencing pain. Nothing seemed to happen for a while until 6 ish when I took a second one for the day.

The pain seemed to subside after taking my pain meds and I got some decent sleep. So far today by staying on top of my meds and taking a Decadron I seemed to be fairly good. It's 6:45 and I'm feeling a bit cramped but we are having dinner in a few then if needed I will try the second Decadron. I'll keep y'all informed but basically I've informed the doc that if this doesn't provide me pain relief on a consistent basis I want to see a pain management specialist.. So far it's 50/50 whether the new drugs are the answer or not.

My pain levels were definitely down but still at the fringes. So enough whining. All in all my day was pretty good. I see the doctor again on

Monday and will let everyone know how it goes. I have several more steps I can take on my pain med levels before I change to more powerful drugs. They don't like to take you to the more powerful drugs right away because if they fail for whatever reason there isn't any place else to go.

So keep the stories and good wishes coming I feel the payers are helping. Since my markers are down (don't know when my next CT scan is maybe next week) the doc thinks it still could be the tumors dying causing the pain, since they don't know all the places where it's connected. If that's the case then it's a light at the end of the tunnel for me and I can hang in there.

Thanks for all the well wishes.

Love y'all Bart

May 15

Bart was extremely fatigued today. He said he drifted in and out of consciousness throughout the day. He ate pretty well though despite not feeling very hungry. When he wasn't eating he sat hugging a sofa pillow to support his midsection.

The midday hailstorm was exciting. I was trying to get the place reasonably cleaned up, organize our papers, misc. stuff and plan for dinner. Hail was a nice break.

Dallas had ALL of his laundry to do. I am quite sure there was not one single solitary item of clean clothing in the whole of his kingdom. Of course Dallas completely underestimated the time it takes to do such a vast geographic expanse of dirty clothes.

He was fast asleep before 10:00 PM and yet his laundry lives on tumbling in the dryer since about 10 this morning and fanning out elsewhere too. We're waiting in the clean clothes cue, a few baskets of his wet laundry eager for dryer time and a couple of dry baskets setting their wrinkles while waiting to be folded. Bart was even texting Dallas dryer reminders every few hours from his throne. We didn't want the marathon process to stall or no one else would get anything laundered today.

The washer and dryer definitely worked significant overtime. Fortunately Dallas' lovely friend Anna was here to show him just how laundry should be done. She helped him separate it into piles, folded stuff and helped him put it away. Anna even told Dallas to clean up his room! I love her.

Bart thought pierogies sounded good for dinner. I actually made my own gravy, something I'd never have suspected of myself. Bart ate well despite the insidious cramping that so tests his daily constitution. He's doing mildly better late this evening but it's not a stellar day by any stretch. Bart is insisting that I check in with my doctor tomorrow before leaving for work. I too had a painful night after practicing double board breaks in black belt class. I was sent to x-ray to see if anything was broken. The doctor's office closed early Friday so no one was there to receive results. I was told to buy a splint for the weekend and immobilize.

Bart agreed to report on his progress if he has any. I encourage him to do so but he's his own man. It's really hard to type with this big fat splint. Have a stimulating workweek but don't hurt yourself. Be safe out there.

May 16

Our Friend Mr. D took Bart to and from chemo. It's just like my former TKD instructor to donate his time to our cause on his birthday. Bart returned with scripts which I filled, and Sandi stopped by the pharmacy a few minutes later with yet another script she was filling per Bart's request. The Pharmacist was surprised to see such concierge service.

On the home front we fret no more about spilled stuff on the floor. Phaddy apparently likes berries too. Serving Bart his strawberry shortcake there was a hitch in my get-along and I dropped the bowl all over the hardwood floor. Phaddy set his controls to "vacuum."

We are all trying to teach him to be better about food stuff around people by taking his bone away and reward him by giving it back if he does not snarl.

Phaddy may soon be going to college to learn how to be the best dog he can be at least according to "Super Dog" school. I think it's a good project for Dallas this summer if he doesn't find a job first.

Daughter Meg called to tell us about her first 30 hour shift at the hospital. She said it was grueling except for the major trauma accidents that definitely got her adrenaline pumping.

At one point, she had a motorcyclist's heart in her bare hands resuscitating him manually. He lived, but because he was not wearing a helmet the traumatic brain injury seemed so great that she was not sure about long range recovery. Hers is an intense and fascinating career.

My doc says my wrist may not be broken but I need to return in a week. So much for the palm heel break technique.

May 18

A Note from Bart:

Hi everyone. Today was one of those sleepy days. Not too much pain (between 2-4 on the scale) but extremely tired. Just read some emails and slept a lot. Tomorrow is my CT scan to see what the tumors look like. I'm praying for big changes in size and quantity of tumors. I'll let everyone know when I do.

Looks like the Motrin may help keep the pain down, even though it's not completely gone it seems to be abated. I don't mind sleeping if it's helping with the cancer. I just would like some moments of lucidity once in a while. :-) So all in all it's a better week so far let's just see how long it lasts.

If I could convince my bride that when it's bed time she should come to bed and get some rest instead of trying to post when she barely keeps her eyes open. Then we can all share in whatever fantasy she is writing about. :-o

She is too funny because she feels obligated to post every day no matter her physical state. I'm working to convince her that as much as we want to post every day it isn't absolutely necessary. Just frequent postings when we have news to report.

You guys write some funny stuff. It keeps me laughing and keeps this whole thing in perspective. I feel strongly about your letters, prayers and support I will beat this. Then we will need to have a celebration of life when I have won (with your help).

Thanks to all, love y'all, Bart

May 19

A Note from Bart:

Well today was a mixed bag. I felt pretty good most of the day. I had a couple of hiccups and am still waiting for word from the pain management specialist. Doc says it can take a couple of weeks to get in. After my CT scan the preliminary findings are that the numbers of my liver tumors have fallen (less tumors) which is good news. We should get the full report on Monday. Still have the blood clot on my right lung, which is why I take the blood thinner. According to the doctor, there's no reason for major concern. When I get the full results I will report but I expect the main tumor to have shrunk or at least stayed stable.

It's a short report but mostly good news.

Love y'all, Bart

May 22

A Note from Bart:

This weekend was fairly slow. Not much pain but very tired. Watched a little golf, dozed off several times, read a little and slept some more. I have a referral to a pain management clinic on the June 14th to see if we can control the pain without making me comatose. ;-)

Things seem to be looking up. Tomorrow we get the complete results of my latest CT scan and will share those. Preliminary results are good.

With that being said, I'm back to baseball on TV. Good luck to whoever on the Club Championship. We will need a ruling on my "steroid" use when I get back.

Love y'all, Bart

May 23

Here's the latest from Bart's doctor appointment. I had hoped for a bit more detail but Bart says this is all he said. I doubted that Bart asked any in depth questions so I inquired. Well, my doubt was not well-received and I got the sinister eye roll plus the "tone " loud and clear so......

Here's the lowdown such as it is quoting Bart: "The cancer markers are down and the number of liver tumors were fewer. The oncologist wants to get something called a celiac block. It's supposed to serve as a pain barrier. Trouble is the pain management guys said they haven't done one in 8 years. If they don't feel comfortable performing the block then they will refer me to a doc in Citrus Heights and if he can't do it they will send me to UCSF."

Bart was busy researching the celiac block on the Internet tonight. I asked him how he felt and the answer was "so so" with a horizontal tilting hand wave. Phaddy went to bed with Dallas (only because he spills food and leaves morsel coated plates in there). Even despite the fact that today was our once per month cleaning day with "Johnny Sparkles," Dallas' room looked like nobody dared enter to clean a thing! I believe he messed it up before I got home. Why can't I just enjoy the clean for a day?

Bart went to the loo after his nightly medication routine. Then he'll return to admonish me about "Bedtime for Bonzos". Here he comes.

May 26

Bart had hydration at Creekside so he's feeling decent this evening. He scheduled an appointment with the pain management doctor June 14th, the earliest slot available. Bart's been keeping a chart of all the medications he ingests throughout the day including all over the counter remedies. We hope the specialist can evaluate the myriad of stuff Bart is taking and see some clear reason for his constant discomfort and correct it.

It's finals week for Dallas. I get somewhat concerned because I do not see him study very much. While I'm on the bus ride home each evening, I check in with Dal over the phone. He tells me that's when he's studying. When I get home, he's always done so I can't say that I've actually witnessed any real studying. All week Dallas has indicated that he's done well on all his tests.

Today he “destroyed” his math analysis test. Yesterday he “phoned” (a new term for aced) his math final.

We got a call today from Dal's English teacher. Dallas forgot to turn in his final project worth 52 percent of his grade. He insists that it's completed but he just didn't print it out or turn it in and gave no reason! I would have died a thousand deaths before I would have forgotten to turn in a project worth more than half my grade. This boy is a very different animal. He doesn't even seem worried about it. I talked to his teacher tonight. She gave Dallas the benefit of the doubt and talked to him over the phone while I was at Taekwondo this evening.

I was anxious to hear what the story was when I got home. Dallas said he was simply going to print it out and turn it in tomorrow and no further comment necessary. I wanted answers, why, why, why? Dallas just kept saying he didn't know, just that he would do it tomorrow and didn't seem all that stressed about it.

I know Dal is smart because we've seen A's on tests, but based on the overall performance of homework, projects, and turning stuff in, his grades seem to vacillate dramatically. He's currently grounded.

I always enjoy that time. Grounding gives us more of a chance to get Dallas to talk to us since he has to be around here anyway. Fortunately for intelligence sake, one of Dal's music instructors is also a dedicated student (third degree black belt) at Cameron Park Taekwondo.

He tells me that Dallas is doing really well which is reassuring. Dallas is in Jazz band and summer drum line camp so we will look forward to a performance at the El Dorado County Fair next month. Bart and I laughed this evening because I said I think Dallas will someday be very successful. I clarified my statement and said "well, maybe not at high school but beyond" in life most assuredly. Bart almost did a spit take laughing and agreeing that perhaps high school isn't Dal's thing.

We can only hope he'll hit his stride in college.

May 28

A Note from Bart:

Today was a crap day for me but it's my bride's birthday so I'm making the best of it. Things are calming down some as the day wears on. So I have a pain management appointment on Friday to see what they can do for me and in the, when it rains it pours category, I have a second pain management referral with a different doc. Not sure when that is but I'm thinking I should maybe do one at a time. ;-) I will let y'all know when I have news to report.

Love to all, Bart

May 30

Our anniversary.

It was wonderful to sleep in. Dallas, however, was up early. He fell asleep at 6:00 PM Friday, which resulted in an unusual early rise the rest of the weekend. Bart was up and down and up taking his pills then back in bed. Dallas had already cooked bacon, eggs and heart shaped waffles but because Dad slumbered on, he and his friend ate every bit aside from the odd waffle heart Cheryl and I may have consumed.

Cheryl and I delayed our jogging ritual waiting for Bart to emerge from the bedroom. I checked on him and didn't have the heart to wake him, breakfast or no breakfast. I finally woke him because if we didn't shuffle off soon it would be too late. Dallas agreed to avail his breakfast skills should Dad require them. We were all hopeful that Bart would wake up feeling better than yesterday.

He really sucked it up on my birthday (Saturday night) and I could tell that he was not feeling it. Still it was fun to enjoy someone else's cooking. Dallas was large and in charge with the steak/chicken barbecuing adventure. Bart ate pretty well but he wasn't feeling as sociable as he'd hope. Bart was still grateful to have two guys who talked man stuff. It was good to counteract the estrogen (or lack thereof in some of us older broads) because women outnumber guys around here most days.

Sunday was a day of laundry, pharmacy duties and general household tasks. I got a few things planted and welcomed little visitors from next door and a few bigger ones too. Bart's social calendar is full.

We were thankful to have the Memorial holiday to catch up with ourselves as well as honor the flag and veterans who gave their lives for our freedoms. This is their day. It's also a commercial retail bonus day.

Bart needed new jeans and Dallas needed shoes and shorts for summer. I took Anna and Dallas and off we went to a number of outlets and stores. It was fun for me to spend time with the kids and we accomplished our mission.

Dallas did have a mini-meltdown complaining about Dad not unblocking his phone. These learning moments can be most challenging. I worry Dallas needs to learn more tolerance, patience and understanding. All in due time I suppose.

This afternoon we enjoyed little visitors from next door who seem to enjoy the different environment at Aunt Mel and Uncle Bart's house. Phaddy likes it too. I enjoyed a fun visit from friends tonight. All is right with the world for the moment.

Sheets are changed, beds are made and dinner is done. Bart and I are watching a few reruns before bed. He's reading a Tom Clancy novel on his iPad. Not sure how to spell Clancy but I do know how to spell a very good Memorial Day weekend. We also had a very nice anniversary today . Bart and I exchanged a few rather humorous anecdotes from the last couple decades like our vows. We promised never to call each other anything that ends in hole or head.

Life is good.

May 31

A Note from Bart:

Today was a relatively easy day. Not too much pain, a little tired and a decent appetite. Can't wait to see what the pain management folks have in store or me on Friday.

If I can lose the pain I can venture out to the odd event here and there without too much fear. It will stretch my world. I will be sure to keep all informed.

Love, Bart

Chapter Fourteen

Go With the Flow

June 2

Bart and I head off to the big pain management appointment at 8:00 tomorrow morning. We're looking forward to it and will let you all know what transpires.

Bart had hydration later at Creekside so he fared better this evening. He's off to bed. Dallas is out of school and in Jazz Combo Camp this week. I'm thinking tonight how life flows on and stuff just happens.

June 3

Well, that's one morning Bart and I will never get back. What a waste of time. They even refunded our co-pay. This doctor does not perform celiac blocks. Bart believed that the oncologist really wants a celiac block and he was afraid that if we continued with this guy and got started with a program that it would ultimately complicate the situation should the oncologist still insist on the celiac.

From what Bart says I think the oncologist may have been thinking out loud and intended on having his office schedule an appointment for Bart with the celiac guy but Bart secured an appointment first. Perhaps if I had been privy to their doctor patient exchange I could have added my two cents. I did anyway suggesting that Bart go ahead with the consult since we were already there. How could it hurt? Bart thought better of it and decided no, stick with the oncologist's intention and pursue the celiac.

We did have a nice drive and even made a trip to the market together. Bart was in his red-flagged bumper car and me running around making returns and delivering the dry cleaning next door. We got out just at my pain threshold of $100.40.

Dallas helped us unload the groceries before preparing to leave for his Jazz class. He announced that he was chewing one of the special Chiclets Megan sent in my birthday box. They were called "Having a wonderful time with my Mother," magical gum that makes you really want to enjoy time with mom. I said to him "See how beautifully that gum is working." It was a true 1950's Mother knows best moment.

I may have to get more of that. I also got a box of "Get Along with your Co-Workers" Tea! This special hot beverage makes you say things like, "Awesome photocopy Steve" and, "I love that ketchup stain on your tie Stan, it makes you look so beatnik and edgy." It's quite a blend.

Bart requested chicken pot pie for lunch. We determined Swanson sucks, he likes Banquet.

Phaddy must have thought Dallas' room was a toxic dump and therefore, he could relieve himself in there on Dal's throw rug.

As the laundry churns, the dishwasher hums.

I've got updates to the medical binder and work email to check. Then again, maybe it's tea time!

A Note from Bart:

Okay today's pain management meeting was "much ado about nothing." The oncologist, referred me to two different pain specialists. I was under the impression he was going to talk to both of them and refer me to the one who would do what he wants. But that didn't happen and the first pain folks who got back in touch don't perform the procedure he wants done. So after going there and wasting over an hour I am now waiting to see the second pain specialist. Current appointment date is now June 21st. They will call me if they get an earlier opening.

The procedure is called a Celiac Block and there seems to be some debate over whether this procedure works (on the Internet). So I'll keep y'all informed when and if I hear more.

Dang!

Bart

June 4

Bart said today was so-so. He's still keeping a log of his medications and admitted that sometimes it's difficult to remember all of them. Tomorrow is the last day of the oral chemotherapy drugs then he has a week off. This morning I made my "melt in your mouth" pancakes for the boys. Dallas and his friend got up before Bart so they got the first of the griddle cakes. Bart did consume quite the healthy stack with butter and sugar free syrup. I preferred mine with yogurt and fresh strawberries and blueberries. That concept was not at all appealing to Bart and the teenage boys.

After Phaddy had his early meal, I took him for a walk. He's so much better now and steps out briskly versus stopping every few feet to mark everything. We were all wondering if all this walking and food discipline was working for the tubby little canine. We first adopted him in September so it was time to "weigh in." Back in September the Vet said his ideal weight should be about 17 pounds. Phaddy weighed 24.9 back then.

Today he weighed 24. That's almost a whole pound down in more than eight months. Bart suggested perhaps he's acquired muscle mass from all the walking. Dallas commented that Phaddy knows he has to stay fat to live up to his name. Regardless of the reason, we all agreed that we like him this way. His girth is obviously not for lack of exercise or over feeding. He gets a half cup in the morning and a half cup of food in the evening. Paddy's food-centric nature though does cause him to root out anything remotely edible and that includes whatever occupies the bird feeder.

Whenever he escapes, he comes back with a burger. We fully expect he'll sniff out truffles soon enough. Bart does get a kick out of the little Phaddy dog. It's funny when he shoves his pet shark onto our chairs with the big wide teeth, looks like he's trying to scare us with his land shark but he always wants the same thing. He waits for us to throw it so he can chase it and bring it back. What is so fun about doing that over and over again? It must be a dog thing. It's Bedtime for Bonzos and tubby dogs.

Bart's Report Card

June 7

Bart hasn't felt too good lately but we got good news nonetheless.

The oncologist reported that Bart's latest blood test showed his cancer markers down again!

His report card: 4,600, that's down about 1,000! When we started this whole affair last August his markers were around 61,000. That's progress my friends. Progress indeed. We just wish Bart felt as good as his report card shows. Cancer killing is certainly painful business but the good numbers were music to our ears. Speaking of music, Dallas starts his summer drum line tomorrow morning at Ponderosa High School. He's also performing with the Jazz Band at Cameron Park Community Day this weekend and next week at the El Dorado County Fair.

His dance card is certainly full this summer. Hopefully it will feel like summer soon enough. I was getting confused about when to plant my garden because the weather has been more like February. Bart's doing ok this evening. He's reading a book on his iPad. News is over now and you guessed it Bedtime for Bonzos.

Day of Rest

June 8

Bart said he slept most of the day. He was very tired. Bart slept a bit better last night but not I. The dog had some strange problem where he was twitching, flipping over, rubbing his face on the carpet and after every hour or so of whipping himself around as though he was hurting he began momentary episodes of whining. As long as I rubbed his back he quieted but the moment I stopped he continued his turning and twitching as though he was having some sort of convulsion. It was quite a mystery to figure out what was wrong with him.

When Dallas got home from drum line, he and his girlfriend assessed the dog situation and called me at work. They thought Phaddy had some allergic reaction to the flea and tick stuff and had developed hives! When I got home tonight after work, Phaddy appeared a lot less tortured.

After preparing Bart's pierogies, I took Phaddy for a walk. He seemed much better. Just so we could sleep tonight I gave Phaddy a Benadryl to counteract any allergic hive reaction he may exhibit. Animals can be just like babies at night keeping you awake with their every discomfort.

Dallas is home with his friend Tim. They are proceeding to eat us out of house and home. He has amazing capacity for food and noise. I'm ok with that as long as they're home safe and sound.

I'm super sleepy so good night all.

June 9

Bart said today that if doctors can just get his pain under control then he might be able to see the light at the end of the tunnel. Mr. D transported Bart to and from Creekside for hydration etc. He thought Bart looked better than he's seen him in months.

I tend to agree. If only Bart could feel better. All in due time. We have not exhausted all the options to be sure. June 21st: pain management and the celiac block. We're looking forward to that.

I'm fortunate to have a friend who's an inspirational advocate. She and her hubby both had cancer. She survived and lives strong reminding us not to tolerate pain. We push until something works. I'm grateful for her counsel.

Tuesday/Thursday nights (for life) I have Taekwondo so I am trying to condition myself to pre-plan dinner on those days. Tonight, of all things, the boys both wanted pierogies again! Lucky for me they're super easy but really? I'm going to have to learn how to make these things because we're depleting the market's frozen supply. It's crazy.

The dryer is calling.

June 12

It was a busy weekend but not such a good one for Bart. I can always tell when Bart is feeling rough because he doesn't want to talk much if at all. We were all set to go to Dallas' jazz band performance at the Cameron Park Community Day Saturday morning. Just when I said let's go, get in the car, Bart said he couldn't; he didn't feel up to it. At first I wasn't having it and said "get in the car Mister" but Bart insisted and then broke out that darn video camera. That's when I thought hey buddy; you're milking this now because you know how much I hate using video equipment. I do not get along well with recording devices. Remember the three minutes of Matty's Ranger School graduation I managed to tape? I artfully maneuvered the thing for over an hour and a half yet somehow failed to record the event. I didn't even get to enjoy it live due to keeping my watchful eye on the darn viewfinder.

The Community Day jazz band performance was a couple of hours late but only because Dallas didn't give us the actual time for his group and instead offered a conservative estimate. I did enjoy wandering among the various booths and running into other Ponderosa parents. After the live performances, Dal whisked the camera home in the late afternoon to show Dad while I headed to the market, pharmacy etc. I found out later that the audio wasn't very good but at least I actually recorded something this time.

Sunday Bart wasn't much better. He was tired and went from his throne to the couch most of the day. Bart just needed to rest. I got a lot of outdoor stuff done and Dallas got the Dragon washed and waxed. (Matty had dubbed his car the "Red Dragon" and when Dallas inherited the vehicle he chose to shorten its name to "the Dragon".) That way when he was authorized to take passengers he could say "Enter the Dragon."

Poor Phaddy isn't allowed to "enter the dragon" or most rooms in the house either these days. Suddenly he's taken to marking some of the interior territory. We thought we were done with that but no! Phaddy relieves himself constantly on our daily walks so we had false confidence that he was learning not to do that in the house. I can't be having any such action so Phaddy now has his most comfortable bed and a spacious back yard to mark to his heart's content. It does break our hearts a little to have to banish him to the back more often but his indiscretions have created way too much work for me. Before long I'll be replacing the carpeting if he keeps up.

His little stains do not come out easily if at all. Bart is also disappointed but he can't constantly watch the sneaky little devil. Dallas weighed in heavily on the decision too because he discovered markings on his bed and pillow! This may be a job for dog trainer, Uncle Matty. We've already consulted with Super Dog but they were as pricey as all the fencing we had built in the backyard. We sure hope you can "teach an old dog new tricks."

Bart had an Epsom salt foot bath this evening. His toes have been giving him trouble. Bart's feeling like things in his guts might be calming down slightly. After the news, it's bedtime. Dallas and I have to get up early tomorrow so Bart generously sets him an alarm.

Dallas has summer drum line and I'll be catching the bus to Sacramento. Monday afternoon Bart has chemotherapy. Bart is good about posting rides on lotsahelpinghands.org whenever he needs transportation. Friends and neighbors have been indispensable in getting Bart to and fro. We're most grateful. It's a blessing.

June 13

A Note from Bart:

Well today certainly is the 13th. Dallas had a small run in with the CHP. He rolled thru a red-light then couldn't find his license. The cop thought Dallas was playing him when he had him get out of the car and empty his pockets and his license fell out. Dallas was just nervous.

In anticipation of the State suspending his license until he is 18, since it's a probationary, we went to the garage to look for my bike for him to ride. It's gone missing. Sooooo, luckily I've felt pretty good today. That offset some of the bad stuff. It's one more week until the pain management appointment. Then we will see what is what.

Stay tuned love y'all, Bart

June 18

Friday wasn't stellar but Bart managed to get through the day as usual although he was downing the Tums early evening.

Sis and I leave tomorrow for a cooking class at the Culinary Academy where we will learn the fine points of pairing food and wine. It ought to be fun. One of my high school buddies will join us for the big fun. Dallas, his dad, and Phaddy will be doing their favorite boy stuff while we're away. I think they'll have a relaxing time with the semi-peace and quiet. Tuesday is the greatly anticipated pain management appointment so Bart's plan is to stay out of pain until then.

Have a fun Father's Day weekend and don't set the BBQ on fire.

June 21

A Note from Bart:

Well we finally saw the pain guy and he feels certain he can eliminate most of my pain and get me back to driving. Maybe even the golf course.

We have a tentative date of the 27th to have a pain pump installed. If all goes well, I should be on my way to being pain free on that date. It fits under my skin and connects into my spinal cord around T-10 where most of my pain is. I'm praying for big results. We will, as always, keep everyone informed.

Pray for us, Bart

June 22

Monday was such a great day. Dr. Payne is my new favorite medical professional (next to my daughter) and I did not miss the opportunity to tease him about his popularity. His first question for us was "How did you get here?"

Bart and I both answered at the same time. Bart said "my oncologist" and I said "We drove." Dr. Payne said our answers demonstrated our polar opposite dispositions.

We listened to him carefully and quickly understood that this new procedure could be life-changing for Bart. Because the pain medication is injected directly into the spinal fluid of the corresponding nerve center, Bart would not be as impaired as with the multitude of analgesics and narcotics that he takes right now.

Dr. Payne said that means he could likely drive again! Of course Bart may need the occasional narcotic supplement but by and large the spinal dose will manage his pain with a lot less medication that he currently takes orally and through the skin. It was such an uplifting appointment. I felt so happy and inspired that Bart could soon be back on the golf course.

In no uncertain terms, I communicated these quality of life issues to Dr. Payne. Clearly he understood that being back on the green would be a HUGE life extender and boost Bart's happiness quotient to an all-time high. The possibilities that arose out of that relatively short meeting with Dr. Payne was just the tonic we needed.

It was like I was in second grade again. Later in the day I wondered why I was so happy.

Then I remembered. It was either that Bart would get a huge lease on life or I would be riding a school bus for the first time to East Weaver for my first overnight play date with Jeanne. That's how I felt Monday; the pure definition of anticipation and excitement. Tuesday after work there was still much laundry to run through despite Dallas' practice of "laundry surprise." We had several stinky weeks. Unpleasant yet the silver lining here is that Dallas is still alive. It is always a point to be celebrated.

Bart will have to stop injecting the blood thinning drugs for a few days before he can undergo the surgery. The pump will be installed in his abdomen; it's about the size of a heavy tape measure. The tubing is inserted under the skin and around his waist up into his spinal column. The computer program in the "tape measure" dispenses a conservative dose (certainly appropriate considering Bart's political persuasion) but if

Bart needs more he can use an overlay device that would tell the computer to administer a bolus (bonus round).

Of course, it might take a few weeks to adjust the doses so that Bart will feel "no" pain. This plan is "a dream come true." Dr. Payne accommodated our request to move up the procedure as soon as possible. The only real consideration was suspending the blood thinning injections and making sure CT scans and other tests showed no other complications. Monday Bart will go under the knife to get the tape measure (pump) and tubing implanted in his abdomen.

It may not sound like your idea of fun but to us it's truly exciting. This could mean that Bart will be comfortable enough to travel to Weaverville for the Fourth of July celebration. Bart hasn't ventured away from home for almost a year now and we are anticipating a comforting sojourn to our happy place at long last. That means you dear neighbors will be asked to keep our garden and flowers from dying a terrible death. (Yes, neighbors beware).

Monday when I got home, Johnny Sparkles cleaning crew was at the house. I had errands to run and kids to deliver (Dallas, Gus and Anna) to the Bridle Wood community pool. Alas, I had hoped to see a more detailed cleaning of his room before departure and a better effort with the other chores but alas. At least he can be somewhat entertaining at times. Thank goodness because he'd be six feet under by now if he weren't kind of funny.

Tuesday it seemed to me like Bart should feel better because we had such an uplifting experience Monday at the pain management clinic. Not so, but he still held up until after 11:30 PM.

There are so many pills and so little real improvement. Monday could be our turning point. We are confident this procedure will be superior to the pain regimen Bart's currently on which isn't working.

June 27

There have been sparse postings this week due to an always overactive calendar this time of year. Some long days for me, but Bart and Dallas managed pretty well. I had to take the last bus home almost every night, which got me back to Cameron Park circa 7:30PM.

Then the usual pharmacy/grocery runs, among other myriad errands made for very compressed weekday evenings.

Bart did not complain but he didn't experience any respite from his arduous stomach pain either. We're looking forward to tomorrow's procedure though, as a positive. Dr. Payne gave us a DVD about the pain pump system, which we watched dutifully.

Thursday night Dallas was busy at the stove preparing breakfast for dinner when I got home. The smell of bacon was savory, I thought "sweet." Dinner done, it allowed me to attend my TKD class that night. Dallas said Dad's only comment was that the "over easy" eggs were "over hard" but otherwise he liked the meal.

Dallas made me laugh recounting the events of the evening. He said after all his slaving away at the stove, Dad's initial negative comment made him roll his eyes. "Hmmm," I said, "doesn't feel good not to be appreciated for your efforts does it?" We shared a knowing chuckle and acknowledged that Dad has little energy for nuance.

Bart is amazingly stoic and does not complain even though I know it's got to be difficult for him to maintain his calorie intake as well as traipse to the safe to retrieve all the medications he needs every two hours when I'm away at work. Bart's been pretty tired, not very talkative, and naps often, it's a sure indication that he doesn't feel good enough to even talk about it. He doesn't have a great appetite either. Nothing sounds good to him so I try to prepare stuff he won't find too offensive. We also have emergency 90-second meals in the cupboard just in case hunger strikes.

The next day was another long one and those kinds of days always seem to bring the unexpected. Bart was napping when I got home so I went outside to play with Phaddy and do a little bit of his much-needed training. It's been so gratifying to see the little doggie's progress after only about five or ten minutes a day. He's not completely consistent yet, but progress is progress. Bart never seems to be as impressed with Paddy's elementary obedience as I am.

While I was out on the grass with Phaddy, I noticed three bubbling founts of water pulsing out of the ground between the house and the grass area. There was also a river of water running along the lower cement edge of the lawn. Quite the river of red clay mud was forming below. I tried turning off the automatic sprinkler system and still the water flowed. I hoped it wasn't the water pipes to the house. After searching high and low for the main shut off around the perimeter of the house it slowed.

Then I discovered the wet erosion occurring on the south side where we had the draining of the flotation waterbed watershed experience of last year. I found several drip hoses freely whipping around like loose electrical cables. I also discovered one of our maple trees... it's dead. Our redwood tree also on that drip line had signs of severe dehydration. I'm really adverse to anything at all dying around here and I was getting really worked up.

Fortunately it looked like only the drip pipeline was affected, likely by the very roots of the trees it was feeding. I was able to fix a few of the whipping hoses and shut down the backyard watering system. It was after 9:00 PM when I finally went inside. Bart arranged for our garden fellow to check it out Friday afternoon.

Bart had an appointment Friday with our primary care doctor for his pre-surgery EKG. Once the receptionist was able to figure out how to tape and attach all the connections the EKG itself was quick. She did have trouble getting Bart's blood pressure so the doctor did have to come in to get his pressure 120/70. All systems go and we're set for surgery Monday morning.

Saturday Bart slept mostly, watched a little golf, read books on his iPad and kept up his pain med schedule despite not looking like he felt any better as a result.

Dallas kept emerging from his cave that night to talk to his dad. He'd saunter out with his head hanging complaining that his X-Box was automatically turning off and this was his summer vacation. It wasn't fair he protested. Dad was having some trouble fixing this. Dallas meantime commented with quite the exaggerated and curious tone how Dad's stuff seems to be working just fine. It's pretty funny. Dad, unfortunately, wasn't feeling good enough to figure out how to change the shutdown hour so the boy has to deal.

Dallas elected to wait at home, translated "sleep in" while we head to Mercy San Juan for Dr. Payne to install the much anticipated pain pump.

June 28

The tape measure pain device is installed. Now we wait to see if this pain solution measures up. Here's how the day unfolded ... The alarm went off at 5:00 AM. I got up at 5:15 AM, closed all the windows and gathered our paraphernalia. Bart got up about 5:30 AM obviously in pain. We drove away at 5:45 AM and got to the surgery center just before 6:30AM. Bart was hurting and after signing in he gave me the look every time someone else got called in before us. By 7:00 AM Bart was in a gown and on a gurney in pre-op. He was clearly not happy. His pain was about 7-8 on a scale of 10.

Come to find out, doctors don't like their patients to be under the influence of any narcotic before they ask them what procedure they're expecting. All a result of the guy who got the wrong leg amputated. He must have blamed it on the pain killers that his doctors cut off the wrong appendage. So, Bart suffered through 5 hours of excruciating pain because some moron couldn't remember which leg was bad.

I asked him what his pain was like (1-10 scale) he said “don't ask me any questions, I don't feel good.” Then he proceeded to politely answer all the same constant and repetitive questions without the "don't annoy me" tone. One nurse asked Bart if he had any removable dental work. Bart's response was "not that I know of" which elicited more than a few laughs from the doctor and the other needle nurse present.

I was dismissed before Bart was wheeled into surgery. I waited in the car and got a call about 11:00 AM that he was in recovery. Dr. Payne told us everything went really well and that Bart would need a few days to recover from the incisions in his abdomen and the one in his back. Bart doesn't remember, but when they woke him up post-surgery his first question was "When can I golf?"

I sat with Bart for a while. He drank water and dozed off and on. Then we got word that the doctor wanted him to stay there most of the day to make sure everything was copasetic. After Bart went to sleep I drove to the nearest supermarket. I took my time leisurely strolling about the store getting all the stuff on the list I forgot yesterday.

Bart was released about 4:00 PM, sore and tired. We got home both exhausted. Bart insisted on cheap canned chicken noodle soup and of course that was the only kind of soup we didn’t have. I hated the thought of going back to the store yet again, but off I went while Bart napped on the couch. It wasn't good that he barely touched that darn soup, but anesthesia will do that to you.

The pump is set to the very lowest dose of morphine. Bart did have to supplement with Dilaudid and Norco plus more anti-nausea medications since he's been home. Dr. Payne will adjust the dosage Thursday. At that time, we will ask if Bart's able to travel to Trinity County for the fourth of July holiday weekend.

Bart certainly felt better than he did when we walked in this morning and time will tell. Phaddy got a walk tonight and we even got a load of laundry cycled through. Dishes got done but not without mishap. It's bad enough that I retain bruises from board/brick breaking but the worst injuries always happen at home! Rounding the corner to the trash I hit my own hip on the corner of our granite kitchen counter.

That's definitely leaving a mark. Apparently I just don't watch where I'm going.

Bart's doing ok, he's just really tired. The incision sites are quite sore. We're still thinking this procedure will work out best to manage Bart's ever-present discomfort.

I'm really tired but happy that this pain installation is complete. Every day is a gift and we look forward to more cool prizes tomorrow after a good night's rest.

One step forward another step back

June 29

Bart did not feel at all well when he arose late this morning. He couldn't stomach his usual small bowl of cereal and instead opted for a little chicken noodle soup. Even that didn't sit well. I was concerned because he hadn't eaten anything since Sunday night. He tried to drink as many fluids as possible.

Bart said he didn't have much pain, which was new, but he totally felt like crap. He took some nausea medication and about an hour later he was clutching his favorite vomitorium (one of my finest garage sale finds) and heaving his guts out.

There was just no way Bart could eat or drink enough to ward off dehydration. I was also concerned about layering malnutrition on top of this mix. Bart said he'd lost two pounds since the night before. After several hours, and many calls to the doctor's office, we were on our way to the Emergency Room.

Bart checked into Mercy Folsom Hospital about 9:00 PM this evening. His white blood cell count was high and his appetite low. In the hospital, he will get the hydration and nourishment he needs to finally recover from yesterday's surgery. Recuperation for patients like you and I might be a lot easier but for Bart, you have to add in complications from chemo, stress from constant pain, his diabetes and a weakened immune system. It would make sense that he needs a little help here. At 9:00 PM the announcement was made that visitors needed to depart. Bart turned to me and said "ok dear, get the hell out." He was feeling better already.

I walked in the house to witness Dallas and Sandi watching a really horrible horror movie involving man-eating alien eels. It was so nice to hear that Dallas and Aunt Sandi had enjoyed such a nice evening together. They were able to salvage Dal's rain-soaked letter "from out of the side pocket of the Red Dragon (car). I left the windows down. Bart did ask Dallas to roll them up as we backed out of the driveway but I had hidden the keys to prevent any driving temptation while we were away. My bad. Still, it was nice to know that he valued that letter from his parents enough to blow dry it.

They raved about dinner at Jim Boys Tacos and boasted that Dallas had completed all of his home chores (with a little help from Auntie no doubt). He unloaded the dishwasher alright but then realized that all those dishes were dirty! Dal said he did retrieve most of them and ran them through again. In Dal's room, you could actually see the floor too. It was nice to have good news to report when Bart called just after 11:00 PM with his room number.

I also told Bart about Aunt Sandi discovering a huge puddle of water on the passenger side of her car which was likely due to a very large uncapped water bottle. When she came into the kitchen for towels, she said calmly, "well you've got your own problems, your dishwasher is overflowing."

Indeed the floor was soaked, and the sight of massive foam figures emerging from the appliance like whipped cream crawling onto the cabinets and hardwood floor immediately reminded me of the old Dick Van Dyke Show. In one episode the whole kitchen was filled with suds that resembled whiteout conditions in a snowstorm. I quickly asked Dallas, "What kind of dishwashing soap did you use in there anyway?"

Yes, he filled the reservoir with dishwashing liquid, not dishwasher soap. I could see how that might be confusing to a young lad. So, Dallas mopped as I scooped suds and told him all about old sit coms.

Bart listened to all this over the phone then told me that he had to go. The nurse was there. His voice sounded really good for a change. It was so much stronger than it had been just a few hours prior. We expect Bart will be released tomorrow afternoon after he's proven that he can keep a meal down for a few hours.

The good news is the pump is definitely suppressing much of the hard pain and when the pump is calibrated properly to his pain level then the use of supplemental oral pain meds will be drastically reduced.

We believe the pump installation was still a big step forward today and any unpleasantness associated with its installment just a speed bump to recovery. Tomorrow is a new day and Bart should feel like a new man.

June 30

It's Thursday and Bart's doctors now say that it could be Friday before he will be released from the hospital. He cannot keep food down and barely tolerates a clear liquid and Jell-O diet. After two bites of breakfast he tossed it all. Lunch, same deal, by 1:00 PM he vomited that. Bart felt like hell most of the day. There are a number of possible causes. It's been since Monday that Bart had anesthesia so that's unlikely. It could be compacted or obstructed bowels, a side effect of pain meds or it could be that introducing morphine into pristine spinal fluid didn't agree with Bart's system causing nausea and vomiting. Everyone's tolerance is different and even though Bart tolerated oral morphine, the interaction with the central nervous system could affect him adversely. Hopefully by morning a few more causes can be eliminated and we'll get more definitive answers.

It seems like he traded one form of discomfort for another. Needless to say, we all are determined to make Bart feel well again.

After work Sandi, Dallas and I visited and Bart said at the moment he was feeling mildly better. He'd held down two Jell-O cups and some juice. Later we took Dal and two friends to Buffalo Wild Wings for dinner. Sandi and I definitely understood why they love it. Boy food and 72 televisions all tuned to sports.

Back at home the dishwasher finally settled down and actually ran its cycle without flooding. Dallas fell asleep on the couch and I have dozed off a few times in this chair already.

Chapter Fifteen

When it Rains, it's Weather

July 1

Looks like Bart may celebrate our country's birth from his hospital bed. It's likely he won't be released now until Sunday. Tonight the doctor put Bart on a full liquid diet. I asked if that meant he had been on a half liquid diet. Apparently Jell-O is not on the full liquid regime. Bart was not able to ingest any solid food at all today and it took him several hours of very slow ingestion to keep the liquids down.

Bart's hard pain has lessened but this nagging nausea is almost as bad. Per our request, Dr. Payne did confer over the phone with the hospital doctor. Dr. Payne suggested weaning Bart from any supplemental pain medication (Fentanyl, Norco, Dilaudid) for the breakthrough pain he was having in favor of increasing the pump dose. (Bart reported his pain level reduced by more than half since the pump was installed at its lowest dose). If Bart's nausea continues and there are no other intestinal causes for it then switching the pump from Morphine to another drug might be the next step.

Bart told me that his oncologist paid him a visit this afternoon. I left a message with the oncologist's office in the morning explaining what was transpiring with Bart's case. Bart said the oncologist expressed disappointment that Bart received the pump surgery instead of his recommended celiac block! Mind you, it was the oncologist who sent us to Dr. Payne and after consulting with Pain we three concluded that the pump was the superior choice.

Apparently it was terribly wrong of us to assume that the oncologist might have had a conversation with Dr. Payne before he sent us there. It might have been helpful for him to explain his celiac preference.

Bart said the oncologist went so far as to say he thought we should have gone to San Francisco to have the celiac block and still thinks we should. If he felt so strongly about it then perhaps he should have talked to the pain management doctor himself before he sent us to him in the first place! It gripes me to no end that specialists refer patients to other specialists to perform some procedure they don't do and yet they don't think having a brief chat with them first might be a good idea?

Touching base to make sure they understand each other sounds like a reasonable step to me.

The oncologist has been the doc "running the show" since this ordeal began. Our understanding from Dr. Payne was that celiac blocks are not as effective as pumps. We went to Payne for pain management after all so once we had discussed all the options, the procedure which promised the greatest chance of success was the one we chose. The oncologist has yet to explain to us why in the hell he's so married to that celiac procedure when clearly pain management specialists aren't doing it anymore! Ok, enough venting.

The one thing Bart was most disappointed about this evening was missing the deadline for his fantasy golf sign ups online. Per Bart's request, Dallas called Dad's room last night about 9:00 PM ready to follow instructions to get this fantasy golf thing set up. Bart didn't want to lose all his good players this round so it had to be done Wednesday night. Unfortunately, Bart had just tossed his Jell-O when Dallas rang and wasn't feeling at all up to giving direction. Today it's too late to register and Bart was none too pleased.

When the nurse appeared in Bart's room with the "Fleet" and began snapping her rubber gloves it was time for me to go.

When I got home, teenage boys had rearranged my living room. There they were sitting like the three see, hear and speak no evil monkeys all in a row on the couch, barely two feet from the television. The coffee table was in close proximity littered with drinks, papers and pizza.

Great! No cooking required. The boys were happy and had just put in a movie so I changed into my TKD uniform, told them to have fun with their horror flick and waved goodbye.

I was back from black belt class in an hour. We watched an episode of "I Shouldn't Be Alive" about a young woman ultra-runner who fell in the mountain canyons of Utah, breaking her back. Her dog actually saved her from freezing to death after 53 hours flat on her back. After that show, Dallas and I tried to coax Phaddy over to tell him he must aspire to be a great dog like that. We may need him one day. Dallas seems to think Phaddy might just eat us alive instead to save his own skin.

Phaddy is pretty darn food-centric to be sure. Be safe out there this holiday weekend and don't get eaten alive.

July 2

Bart held some food down today for about four hours. Hoorah! He still has some intestinal issues which have to be dealt with before doctors can divert attention to the pharmaceuticals. Apparently his doctors did confer today. I don't know which ones and with whom but I'll take that as progress. All we know is that Bart has to keep solid food down for a day concurrent with a working digestive tract before they will consider his release. In addition, Dr. Payne has to send someone over to check the pump and adjust the dosage.

Happy Fourth of July weekend to all. Fly those flags with pride.

July 3

Bart is home.

I arrived at the hospital at 12:30 PM and Bart was eating his lunch, spaghetti with meat sauce and green beans. Eating has become a slow process for Bart. He takes a few bites, washes it down with Glucerna (diabetic Ensure) then waits five minutes to make sure it settles before repeating. At one point, I was getting sleepy waiting so I stretched out on the edge of his hospital bed. Despite Bart's protests, I reclined there until the nurse came in to give Bart his insulin and pneumonia vaccine shots. That's when he got me to move to the chair.

We must be getting good at this discharge thing, because even before the nurse dispatched a wheelchair, I took off for the parking lot. Bart was out in front waiting before I even got the car around. That's motivation.

On the ride home Bart said he felt about as good as he did when he went in only hydrated. He wasn't losing his lunch though so that's an improvement.

We have a busy week ahead with the first visit to the pain doc. Dr. Payne needs to adjust the pump to dispense larger doses of painkiller.

Next, we make an appointment with the oncologist and get him to confer with Dr. Payne, so there are no more surprises. We are scheduled to see our primary care doctor to fill him in on all the excitement so he's fully briefed just in case he has to be "in the know."

Tonight I grilled chicken for dinner and Bart ate pretty well. He's happy to be home and thrilled to have his LCD TV screen back. That hospital television just wasn't cutting it. News is on and Bart says that's about all the thrills he can handle for his first night home in four days.

Just when you think it is safe...there I was sitting at the kitchen table checking email on my laptop when suddenly I heard it. There was no mistaking that sound. I knew what was going on out there. And just when I thought we were rid of that freeloader. It enraged me. I haven't been home on weekdays so he must simply have been laying low on the weekends when he knows I'm there.

I scrambled out of my chair so fast that it fell over but I was already out the back door. There wasn't a tenth of a second to waste. There he was that bastard, clinging to the side of my house right next to the kitchen window. The nerve. I grabbed the hose, relieved that I'd left the spigot on, aimed the nozzle and squeezed the trigger. Normally I have the thing set to jet or full, but what came out was mist! I never put the stupid thing on mist. What the??? Squirrel and I were only about three feet apart. I dialed up the jet setting and let him have it. What he did next, I did not expect. That dastardly rodent jumped from the side of the house to our back deck, even closer to me! Are you kidding me? Really? You want to play squirrel?

I blasted him with the hose and that's when he jumped off and into the thick of our maple trees. I kept squirting and hollering and have no idea which way he escaped. Well, he won't be using that tree for access anymore.

Later my TKD friend came by with her "Sawzall." I held the tree as she powered through. It's a bit harder to saw through green wood than the dry stuff so it vibrated the two of us so much and so violently I think we experienced several G's. Our loud racket woke Dallas and his friend who were sleeping in the downstairs room next to our job site. They wanted to know what was so funny.

We brought that giant maple appendage right down to the ground. We were lucky we got through it too because we were both laughing so hard we could easily have cut off our own limbs! It was just so funny to see each other wobbling at warp speed like that. Not very flattering either which is probably why we couldn't stop laughing.

July 4

At least I had a story to tell Bart at the hospital that afternoon. We hope Bart's story will be one of no pain and no discomfort soon enough. Tomorrow works for us. Today would be better.

Happy Fourth of July! Here's to freedom and the birth of our country! Please drink to that (responsibly of course). Be careful out there.

July 5

Bart had a pretty good Independence Day despite not sleeping well. He took anti-nausea and other meds at regular intervals but the morphine pump definitely takes the edge off.

Tomorrow we hope to see Dr. Payne to begin the dance to adjust Bart's morphine with the goal of eliminating the use of supplemental drugs for the breakthrough pain. We don't want any breakthrough pain.

Bart was mighty ambitious after breakfast, announcing he might take a walk up the driveway but the day proved too hot for him. It was a good day to be poolside however so I drove the teenagers over to Aunt Sandi's for some water play. Phaddy even endured swimming lessons courtesy of Dallas and friend. It was entertaining to watch Phaddy's continuous dog paddle. He kept up the piston motion even when lifted up out of the water. He wasn't taking any chances evidently as to when they might dunk him back in.

July 6

Tuesday our much anticipated pain doc appointment was scheduled for 3:00 PM. I knew Dr. Payne was a popular guy but that place was crazy with people. Some were sleeping in the hallway, others parked on courtesy benches near the elevators and spilling out into the public areas waiting for their turn.

It was more like try outs for Barnum and Bailey's traveling circus than a doctor's waiting room. It was quite the cast of colorful characters milling about. I was curious just who among us had real chronic pain but it was impossible to tell. And there was drama. I overheard one patient telling the receptionist that her tires had been slashed. She was filling out a police report alongside her pain questionnaire. Another patient was talking to herself. There were wheel chairs, walkers, canes and companions holding people with various maladies upright. It felt more like a group of actors auditioning for some bent reality show than a bunch of people in severe pain.

We had an hour to people watch before it was our turn in the doctors' studio.

Dr. Payne is a great guy and such a personable doctor. He even promised to call the oncologist and explain why celiac blocks are virtually obsolete and Bart expressed his desire to be taken out of the middle on the issue. I underscored the sentiment that the two doctors needed to talk. It jacks with our piece of mind to think that Bart just went through major surgery only to hear the oncologist complain that it wasn't right.

Dr. Payne upped Bart's morphine and programmed the pump so that Bart could give himself a bonus morphine round three times per day at two hour intervals. If Bart does, in fact, use three in a day then we will have Dr. Payne program another increase. Three boluses per day equates to another milligram of morphine which could easily be administered automatically. Bart would still have the option to augment his pump dose with a bolus as well.

When the programming was complete Bart had one excellent question, "How do I give myself the bolus?" Dr. Payne said "Oh yeah, I forgot that, yes very important." He went to get the patient device which is basically a relay type thing that syncs with the pump when you hold it over the implant site. You push a button and voilà, the pump processes the command to release the juice.

While the doctor was out of the exam room, I was playing with a plastic model of the spinal column. The different sections showed healthy and herniated spinal maladies. Well, I dropped one of the pieces and it tumbled across the floor under the exam table Bart was sitting on. Bart snapped "Quit playing with that stuff" then the doctor half stepped back in the room and chided, "Please control your child."

When he came back with the bolus device, I was fumbling to put the spine back together.

Bart said to the doctor, "I can only take her places twice; the second time is to apologize, so you may never see her again."

To figure out how the damn bolus thing worked, Dr. Payne called in one of the "adolescent" nurse's assistants. She showed Bart in less than two seconds, while the doctor laughed at himself and his own ineptitude. He just installs them, he explained, which doesn't seem to mean he has to know how they work. The doctor sent us home with a mini-manual and instructions to come back in a week for a tweak.

We left right on time for the peak of rush hour. My passenger and "driving coach" would tell me to slow down whenever he spied brake lights a mile in the distance. I said "hey thanks *Eagle Eye*, I might not have thought to apply brakes had you not warned me a mile in advance."

I share this because the Bart warning system can sometimes be dangerous. Traveling through a green light intersection on Howe Avenue he blurted "don't go, stop." His urgent tone freaked me out momentarily because I didn't understand. The shock and confusion caused me to whack my open water bottle tossing it onto the center console spilling all over the car and Bart too.

The light was green and although I could see traffic slowing in my lane ahead I knew I could clear the intersection but Mr. Safety did not. So what was the panic? Sure enough, there was a stalled bus up ahead. I tossed Bart my spill towel, standard equipment I keep at the ready just for spastic maneuvers like this one.

I told Bart how happy I was that he could be driving again soon. He might need me to fluster him as he so expertly does to me.

This evening went pretty well. I grilled chicken that looked really good but might have experienced a little climate burn while hiding in the recesses of our freezer. The rest of it was good except for the part where Bart started to feel an allergic reaction coming on from the rice. He used to get shortness of breath from Basmati rice. This was plain brown rice but definitely not worth testing his resistance.

Bart did administer two bolus doses of morphine tonight about three hours apart. He said he could feel it take effect immediately. We believe that as he adjusts, Bart will be able to minimize his cramping and control the back pain with just this one device. Ridding his system of the constipating narcotics would be a huge blessing. The simplification is terrific and giving Bart instant control is even better. No more waiting a half hour for the drugs to kick in. The pump is like being the conductor of your own pain train, you're always out in front. (Just be sure to duct tape the mouth of the back seat driver.)

Good night all. Sleep fast. Morning comes early.

A Note from Bart:

Hi y'all,

I wanted to try and post tonight so my bride didn't have to. She has done so much for me the last week. I know Dennis, it's not the Crew four way to say something nice about a fellow team member. I must be getting soft in my old age. ☺ Well as you know by now I was treated to another really fun five days (and nights) in the hospital. It's sort of an all-inclusive vacation. It's unclear whether the surgery itself or the new pump and morphine in my system were the factors contributing to my overall weakness but whatever it was, it sucked.

I am home now and the pain pump had its dose upped. I have been given the ability to give myself a bolus. It's an extra hit of the pain med to take the edge off breakthrough pain. So far it seems to be working. After giving myself a bolus at bedtime I was able to sleep five hours straight (with the aid of a sleeping pill). That's a really long night for me these days. And I woke up relatively pain free. As pain free as a man can at my age with the condition of my body, plus years of abuse playing sports in the Air Force, and abuse just for fun.

Anyway, things on the pain front are looking up. My doctor will up the dose if I take enough bolus doses. I'm still at a minimal level of morphine. It goes directly into my central nervous system. It's an interesting feeling. When I had morphine before for past injuries it made me loose, giddy, and I didn't care very much. This time I don't react that way. Occasionally I feel light headed but that's about it. I make sure I take my anti-nausea meds before I take a bolus. Don't want to risk a repeat of what landed me in the hospital.

Looking forward to when I may finally see light on the horizon and the pain relief battle could be the beginning of the end for pain. I'm hoping I restart my chemo next week (Sunday) that's the big test of the pain and nausea.

Stay tuned, love y'all, Bart

July 7

Bart didn't feel very good today. He was very tired and generally felt ill despite the anti-nausea pills. He got a call from Creekside this afternoon asking that he come in right away for a potassium test. I was gone delivering Dallas to his Thursday medical appointments so Bart told the nurse no can do.

Bart resumes chemotherapy Monday so they agreed to do the potassium test then, but in the meantime he was instructed to stop eating any foods with high potassium. Coincidentally high potassium symptoms include fatigue, nausea and weakness. That could explain a few things. The sudden dietary restriction changed dinner plans and, unfortunately, reduced the number of calories Bart consumed this evening.

Bart administered two bolus rounds and attempted to do the third and final one before bedtime, but the device refused. Evidently Dr. Payne was right about his lack of technical programming expertise because Bart got locked out every time he tried for the third bolus. In fact the pump responded with, "you have to wait another four hours now buddy." Really? That would be well past midnight, it's not going to happen, so Bart was back on the Norco to supplement the morphine. We now know that the device must be reprogrammed with another increase, good information to have.

Bart insisted that I stop at Home Depot on the way home from Dallas' doctor appointment this evening to buy two plug-in carbon monoxide detectors. There's a new law requiring them on each floor of your home. Why? Because nationwide, tens of thousands of people met their demise and those folks were likely burning charcoal indoors but legislators in their infinite wisdom think everyone should be forced to spend money because somebody else was stupid. I call this $50 purchase a tax and certainly a bonus for the makers of these devices. Of course, the expensive models Bart wanted didn't even fit in our outlets. They fell right out, screeching that piercing beeping noise all the while. As of this evening, those detector things are barely hanging in the wall. If you walk by too heavily they fall out and scream. I feel like screaming too. These nanny laws are inconvenient.

I'm thinking lawmakers ought to just cut to the chase and impose a stupid tax. Ever hear of the Darwin awards? It is an "honor" awarded to people who kill themselves doing incredibly stupid stuff and in the process cleanse the gene pool. It's natural selection in perhaps its purest form, but again, I digress.

Poor Phaddy didn't get his walk tonight. Dallas was too busy with his friends. When we got home at 5:45 PM his two pals were still there, a full three hours later! Apparently they are all hooked on a show called "Sons of Anarchy." I fired up the grill and cooked Buffalo burgers for all. The boys ate two a piece, plus beans, rice and watermelon. Bart barely finished half a burger with no bun. Sadly, only two beans were left in the bowl but

Bart didn't feel much like eating anyway. Hopefully he will make up for lost calories tomorrow. I have a long day at work so Bart is stocked with microwavable meals and snacks.

Good night all. TGIF.

July 10

Bart said he had a good day until he didn't. His words were "mostly ok with a few hours here and there where I felt terrible." Bart's still mighty fatigued but overall he seems a lot more alert than he was before the pump. I believe that things might be looking up.

We were happy to welcome Dallas' girlfriend for the day. It's fun to have her around and enjoyable to interact with the kids and hear all about what they're interested in. The kids accompanied me to the market too. They had lunch there while I shopped and later followed me around the place, unbeknownst to me, sending random texts watching my silly reactions. I'm sure it was most amusing.

I worried about this potassium thing hoping Creekside staff would sort it out. It's messing with my dinner menus. Tonight I grilled a tri-tip that had marinated for 24 hours. Tri-tip is Dallas' favorite and Bart also seems to enjoy it but he had to avoid the potatoes and a few of the vegetables because of their potassium content.

Bart gave himself a bolus round after dinner. I don't think it was because of my cooking.

He was trying to save the second bolus for bedtime but couldn't wait. Bart's been attempting to get comfortable all day. Moving positions on the couch didn't do it so it was over to the chair then back again. The Phaddy dog seemed to emulate Dad's movements going from napping on the sheepskin rug, to hardwood floor, to carpet.

After dinner Phaddy and I took a walk. We ran into one of our wonderful neighbors along the way. They'd been planting backyard trees and the back forty looked great. Their Pug dogs Yogi and Coco thought Phaddy was an exciting guest. They had to get to know each other real quick so it was a short but intense sniff fest. Phaddy's tail was spinning like a Kitchen Aid whisk attachment. I find it somewhat odd that a dog not motivated at all by affection just loves other dogs so much. He tenses up and the tail starts spinning, straining on the leash to get to any dog.

Phaddy's down for the count now. Bart's hanging in there too waiting for the news to come on and getting his supplemental pain meds to see him through the night. Dallas meantime, is heating up pizza!

Tomorrow is Dallas's Jazz Band recital at Church. We hope Bart will feel good enough to go. Tonight he just can't get comfortable so he's off on a comfort quest to Sterns & Foster.

July 11

A Note from Bart:

Hi all, 'tis I and it's Monday evening after Chemo. I'm feeling fairly well. My pain level is about a 2 which I can usually mange to tolerate. Tomorrow is an update from the pain management doc. He most likely will up my dose and alter my bolus (extra pain shot for breakthrough pain) rate. Today overall was a good day I'm praying it's a trend.

So mostly we hung out and visited with Mel's nephew, his wife and baby. It was fun. Our weather here in Nor Cal was spectacular. It was sunny and clear with a high of 77. That for us in July is wild. As those of you who live here or visited we can and normally do experience triple digit degree heat this time of year. Looks like it might be a cool summer. It must be global warming. ;-)

There was one little irritation today (although it was mostly irritating for my incredible bride and our youngest son Dallas). They got up dutifully at 6:30 AM to be at the Juvenile court by 8:30 AM. When they arrived, the bailiff checking them in told them they didn't have court today. Seems the arresting officer hasn't turned his paperwork in. Even though he has had over three weeks to do so. So the court says we will get a notice in the mail of when we need to go back. Any bets it happens after he starts school? It would be par for the course. Oh well. Such is life.

I'm shooting for pain free relief soon, maybe this week, then getting good sleep, gaining back some weight, and knocking this cancer down. My markers were down slightly from 4600 to 4500. It's still down so I'll take it. I will let y'all know how it goes tomorrow.

Take care and love y'all, Bart

July 12

Today Dr. Payne increased the daily dose of morphine on Bart's tape measure thing. I worked from home until we left for our appointment in the afternoon. Sandi invited the kids over to swim so Bart and I dropped them off at her house on the way. It took us about an hour to get to the bad part of town. The doctor must get cheap rent in that building because the neighborhood is definitely not desirable. I found it especially funny that he advertised on the building's digital sign. He is a really nice guy but how much business could he get from high tech billboard advertising in this area and was it worth it? Marketing minds want to know.

We waited 20 minutes for a five-minute appointment but that was just fine with us. Dr. Payne got right down to it. He hiked the regular interval dosages over a 24-hour period and gave Bart the ability to administer three bonus rounds (morphine boosts) per day. He removed the Velcro body belt that was supporting the device and told Bart he was cleared to shower again. Dr. Payne asked about Bart's specific pain complaints and we both answered. I thought Bart was sandbagging so I repeated complaints Bart had expressed and that I had witnessed. Dr. Payne said he would direct his questions to me. Ok then, but just in case he was being facetious, I explained to the doctor that Bart always seems to feel better in his presence. Doc said that's not what his wife says. I responded with "evidently that's how Bart feels too" because his pain is worse around me!

I believe that Bart wants to be a cooperative patient and does not want to make a federal case out of anything. He has always had a very high tolerance for pain so it's hard for Bart to accept that we don't want him to tolerate ANY pain. I'm not sure Bart accepts the concept that no pain is a realistic goal. I'm the one who sees how miserable Bart is and I'm not willing to tolerate his continued discomfort and neither should he. I'm fortunate to have friends in the know, who have encouraged and backed me up on this notion.

Riding in the car with Dallas tonight, Bart brought up the unspoken topic. He said, "Dallas, should something happen to me, I want to be cremated. How would that be to have an urn with Dad's ashes on the mantle?" Bart went on about how silly it was to spend so much money for a burial plot. Even though urns might be expensive it's a much more pragmatic option.

Dallas thought about it for a minute and responded with "Can't we just put you in an Ovaltine jar?" Dallas liked the uniqueness of "Ovaltine-dad, Oval-dad etc. plus he really likes Ovaltine.

We all laughed and quipped about that for a minute or two.

Bart questioned us out loud, asking if we were "hinky" about keeping an ash urn around. I reminded him that we were all good with Bootsie's.

Ordering our beloved kitty, Bootsie's, cremated remains was a big family decision. Matty still drags the kitty (box) out sometimes to rub heads and say "who's a kitty" just like old times. Little Dallas and Bootsie had "kitty time" every morning before school. The kids lovingly complained that the cat was affectionate to the point of annoying but again I digress.

We couldn't forget the East to West, back to East coast, juggling of Bart's Dad's ash urn either. After a year or two shipping him back and forth across the country, the family finally arranged a burial of Bob Reagan's ashes next to Reagan ancestors in Masontown, Pennsylvania. Bart got the point. His wish is our command. Nobody was "hinky."

We had a pretty good day and a very good (albeit somewhat short and humorous) talk in the car.

I thought it was wise and wonderful for Bart to engage his youngest son in that way even though we don't expect to have to buy Ovaltine anytime soon. Bart's phenomenal progress has already been duly noted.

Bart gave himself a bolus after dinner. He also took a supplemental oral painkiller within the two-hour window of the bolus. (He can only administer three total bolus doses each day, two hours apart.) The day after chemotherapy Bart used to crash for most of the day so we can still see progress regardless.

We will give the pump a day or two for the new dose to level out but we won't hesitate to call Dr. Payne again if we have to. He promised to slip us into his schedule should Bart need another adjustment. Bart told us that his oncologist conceded that Dr. Payne will handle Bart's pain issues and the oncologist will handle the cancer. Case closed; everybody's cool.

Bart and I kept after Dallas to get packing tonight. I drive him to the airport tomorrow morning so he can spend a week in Tucson with his sister Megan and brother-in-law Ben. His bag is finally zipped up by the door, complete with the crazy hat collection and a bag of rawhide bones for Abby dog.

Bart and I are looking forward to the respite. I'm thinking fewer messes, fewer carpet stains, fewer closet doors off their hinges, and perhaps a little less excitement but it's all good. Megan and Ben meantime are gearing up for a week with the whirling dervish.

Good luck, good times and always a good night.

July 13

This morning Dallas and I said goodbye to Dad and drove off for the airport. I was mildly apprehensive with no one left at home, but Bart shooed us out the door.

The package (Dallas) arrived in Tucson by the close of business. Dal sent text messages first from Phoenix complaining about the 2.5 hour layover. He sent another text to Dad saying that he would miss him. That was nice but unusual and certainly appreciated. Dallas is rising to occasions.

On the road home, I called and Bart didn't sound good. He said he wasn't feeling well.

He'd felt nauseated all day and wanted me to stop for Chinese food. I got home with the food at about 7:00 PM. Bart tried it but the taste didn't set well and Bart asked me to boil Top Ramen instead. He had given himself one bolus and a Norco. I had hoped for a better day thanks to the increased morphine and hoped that supplemental analgesics would not be necessary but everything in due time apparently.

Bart braved to watch another serial drama tonight but he's sleeping on the couch instead. Bart reported fatigue and discomfort today with slight improvement by late evening. He didn't eat much. I'm not happy with this report but it's only been a few days since chemo and patience is a virtue. It is nice not to have to worry about Dallas. Instead I'll have to wake Bart to go to bed. I hope it doesn't awaken any pain in him.

We haven't heard a word from Dallas or Megan since Dally arrived in Tucson. We know it's because they are busy having fun and can't be bothered by checking in. The first few summers we sent Dallas to Megan's house we called every day and asked lots of questions. Finally they said "you can't be calling us every day, we have stuff planned and it just takes up our time to have to relay everything to you." They told us we could hear all about it later. We got the message. They must have their fun, uninterrupted by constant parental inquiry. Plus we get more time to enjoy the quiet here at home.

Bart's off to bed and I'm close behind. We hope to learn something new from tomorrow's primary care doc appointment. Likely it will be just a waste of a co-pay. We will try to come up with some questions to make the visit educational at the very least.

Here's to health and TGIF.

July 14

Bart apologized for not feeling good enough to post himself today. He's extremely tired. He also had nausea but no vomiting, thank goodness. Bart's sugar levels were better. He said he took measurements at the wrong times which skewed the results.

Bart administered two bolus doses today and may take a third before bedtime. That means we will need another adjustment of the daily releases soon.

Bart has his primary care doctor appointment in the morning. Between the two of us, we can't come up with a valid reason why we even have this appointment. The hospital doctor made the appointment for us. Perhaps he should have told us what he thought we were seeing the primary doc for?

We are even considering canceling the appointment because there's nothing Dr. D is handling that we need help with at this time. The insulin injections are going fine. Bart says he's still really tired and his back is sore. I doubt there's much Dr. D can do that our pain management doctor cannot, but we will try anything and you never know where the best ideas may come from.

We are rationalizing after the trauma of surgery, the hospitalization followed shortly by chemotherapy, that just one of those things could knock you out. I suggested perhaps he delay chemo until he was stronger but in true Bart fashion he said "no rest for the cancer, no."
I like that attitude. It gives us renewed hope.

Bart has been most entertained by Phaddy since Dallas has been gone. Phaddy wants to play with all his squeaky toys, laying them right in our laps and waiting patiently for the big throw. Then he chases like mad and repeats. Throw, fetch, repeat.

Once in a while he'll throw in a tug of war and a cute little growl to seem tough. By 11:00 PM though, Phaddy's done. He lies down waiting to be lifted off to bed like some prince.

Bart's off to bed.

Here's to health. TGIF.

July 15

We kept the primary care doctor appointment because it got too late to cancel. I filled the doc in on Bart's current condition and asked a lot of questions but nothing new. He acknowledged that the oncologist manages Bart's cancer treatment and Dr. Payne handles all the pain issues. That leaves only the diabetes for Dr. D. He did explain how Bart might adjust his insulin should his numbers ever get too low. Bart knew that.

July 17

We both slept in way too late. Bart ate well though. He started with cereal while I prepared a heartier breakfast of potatoes and eggs. He ate every bit. Bart reported a little nausea and at times endured pain about five on the one-ten pain scale.

He gave himself two bolus morphine doses today and the third before bedtime. I will need to call Dr. Payne Monday to see if we can schedule another adjustment for Tuesday. It's frustrating that Bart's still feeling poorly and having significant pain but I guess it's a process to achieve the right formula.

It was such a busy day and yet we never left home. Laundry piles shrunk and even all the filing got done today but I'm definitely as drip-system challenged as I am challenged with computers. The underground pipes were repaired again yesterday. It looks dry so far. They'd been steadily leaking. Not good. I messed around with the automatic timer system for hours and still couldn't figure out if I left the configuration such that it would actually work. Too damn many gizmos.

We finally heard from the kids in Tucson. A couple of pictures showed up. From the photos, it appears they are having real redneck fun there in Tucson.

July 19

Bart hasn't felt good at all for the last few days. We have an appointment with Dr. Payne in the morning to up the morphine again. Bart's taken three bolus doses per day and tried to give himself one this morning (after 12 hours) but the contraption locked him out, said he had to wait two more hours even though he is supposed to be able to dose himself every two hours! Computers! They're only as good as their programmers. Mr. D arrived this afternoon to escort Bart to his standard Monday chemotherapy. I took a brief break from painting Dallas' bedroom to greet Mr. D. and see them off. I was a little concerned because Bart seemed so very tired today but he always gets a lab report card before getting hooked up to a lounge chair. The oncologist would determine if all systems were a go.

When they returned this evening my friend and I were still diligently painting Dallas's room.

Bart reported that no chemotherapy happened today, only hydration and feel good juices. He was simply too weak to endure the normal regimen. The oncologist decided that Bart needed more time to recuperate in between chemo weeks because of his extreme fatigue. Bart will take a break from chemo for a while and when the doctor deems appropriate, Bart will resume a one week on and one week off schedule.

While Bart was at Creekside, the central outdoor watering system I thought was fixed flooded again. It seemed the only method to ensure no flood was to turn everything off. The gardener showed up while I was out buying spackle and running errands. I saw PVC pipe in the trash and evidence he did something but I didn't really have a clue what or whether he left the automatic watering timer thing on. Evidently not because nothing got watered today but then again nothing leaked or flooded either.

As for painting Dallas' bedroom, one gallon wasn't enough so we had to trek down to Sherwin Williams in Folsom. I've never been to that store before and never ever expected to see someone I knew, especially not my college dorm pal of 30+ years ago! That was serendipity.

I certainly am grateful to have friends and a sister who can paint. I find the exercise terribly maddening. At one point in the project, I painted the curtain, yet my friend was able to fix it while I panicked. (My motto is, always, always panic first to get it out of the way.) Then I backed into a wall and somehow gouged a chunk out of the freshly painted wall. I couldn't seem to keep my brush or roller from painting over the protective tape and onto forbidden surfaces either, nor could I prevent paint dripping on the one microscopic sliver of carpet not covered by sheets. Like I said, good thing I have friends with good manual dexterity because I would never have taken on this project without help. It would be just too frustrating and wrought with horrible accidents. Fifth degree testing is Saturday and yet I couldn't manage to refrain from hurting myself during this supposedly innocuous painting ritual. Who would suspect one could move fast enough in two steps to do damage? Those corners on metal bed frames are dangerous! I can't fit the instep of my right foot comfortably into shoes right now. At least I only need the heel for board breaks.

After my painting companion left, Bart wandered by, stuck his head in the room and told me not to do anything further without adult supervision.

I'm to wait for back up before even taking the lid off the paint can. Ok, fine. Instead I cooked dinner for Bart even though he wasn't enamored much with eating but he did say mushroom chicken and rice sounded good. Bart ate a good portion of it.

I went to my short TKD practice tonight and afterwards collected Phaddy from his play date at Sandi's. She and her gal pals were obviously having a marvelous time discussing some hated bachelor. Back at the Reagan Ranch, Bart said he was feeling a bit more alert. He actually wanted to watch a recorded program at 11:00 PM. Bart said he was more awake than he had been all day which was music to my ears. He'd slept most of the day so keeping his eyes open for the hour program wasn't a problem (for him).

I was dead tired but not about to throw in the towel. Bart said he would rest his eyes while waiting for me to finish this post. He's fast asleep with a ball cap over his eyes. It's time to wake sleeping beauty and get him to bed. I have lots of questions for Dr. Payne tomorrow so I'd better sleep fast and get there early.

A Note from Bart:

This process of getting the pain meds adjusted is something else. We are trying to wean me off all oral and patch narcotics so when I stop taking one or more of those the pain dose needs to be adjusted up. To go along with that when I started my latest round of chemo my oral med's made me overwhelmingly tired. It was all I could do to stand up and go to the bathroom. I slept all the time. Because of that we are changing my regimen from two weeks with one week off to one week on and one week off. I didn't take my oral chemo drugs today and feel slightly less tired, even though I had my pain pump dosage increased. I'm sure this will work out in the end.

So other than being in pain and being tired, I'm doing as well as can be expected. I can sleep most days (sometimes even without sleeping pills). So that is a plus. Sleep = no pain!

Tomorrow I see the chemo doc for a blood test and to see when I resume chemo. I'll keep y'all informed.

Take care and God bless Bart

July 20

A Note from Bart:

Well I don't know what to say about this. "When it rains it pours" ... "No good deed goes unpunished." Last night Mel tweaked her shoulder at Tae Kwon Do (TKD). She didn't think too much about it until this morning when she was in very bad pain. She went to the doc and she has a torn rotator cuff, right arm of course. So now, luckily, Dallas is back from visiting his sister as I can't pick up anything over five lbs. for another few weeks and Mel is out of commission for about six weeks (minimum). If she doesn't heal from rest she will need surgery. Great, eh?

My blood test results were good and my potassium levels were normal. So that's good news. We will find out Monday when I'm going to resume chemo. It may be Monday.

I just wanted to post something so that my bride doesn't feel the need to post and can rest her arm. She is mightily upset as you can well imagine. She has been working four years to test for her fifth degree black belt and testing is this Saturday. Needless to say she will be watching from the sidelines. We will keep y'all informed on her and my progress.

Take care, God bless, Bart

July 22

Bart walked down the hall Tuesday morning and hollered into the "green" room "Put down the brushes we have to go now." My friend had to come over early because Bart didn't trust me alone in there and with good reason. It takes about an hour to get to the pain management clinic from Cameron Park. Tuesday Bart and I met with Dr. K. I was thinking because Dr. K was so much younger than Dr. Payne he might be a lot more proficient at programming the pump. Dr. K ordered a bolus for Bart while we were sitting in his office annex (a tiny office outside the main clinic near the elevators, sort of a dog house but with faster service).

Dr. K answered all our questions. He increased Bart's automatic daily morphine dose and gave Bart the ability to administer four small supplemental hits throughout the day. Bart said he noticed a very slight improvement from the office bolus. Four per day was absolutely necessary so we don't have to turn around and drive back in 36 hours. We do have to come back in a week just because. Unfortunately, there is no office any closer.

When we got home Tuesday, I fixed lunch then Bart was ready for a long nap. I changed back into my painting garb and touched up all four walls, alone! I got away with it because Bart was sleeping. Carol returned to help me with the furniture Feng Shui and remove all the trim tape etc. That's when it happened. I knocked over the entire gallon can of paint. It spilled so quickly spreading out in a semi-circle over the cracked plastic chair runner filtering through to the rug below. The expanding paint was perilously close to running off the plastic and onto the beige wall-to-wall carpet. I panicked first, got that out of the way, then sought out Carol to orchestrate a proper clean up. So, we sacrificed a desk runner, a sheet, and a lot of paint. Bart just shook his head knowingly. He didn't really want to know what happened.

Bart felt better Tuesday night. He was tired and sleepy during the afternoon but had a bit more energy in the evening. I fixed shepherd's pie. Bart usually likes it a lot but my attempt to make the dish tastier was met with righteous complaints that it was too salty. I tried to squeeze all the salty stuff out hoping he'd find it more palatable, which rarely ever happens. Phaddy certainly enjoyed the savory runoff.

Bart said Tuesday night was better but indicated that his current automatic morphine dose was still too light. Really? I get that it has to be a somewhat gradual increase but I'm about at rock bottom patience when it comes to tolerating one more day of this intense pain for Bart. Anything over a one on the pain scale is too high. He reported a level five and although he has displaced many of the usual narcotic analgesics with intrathecal pump morphine, the constant level of pain is still the same as before the pump! That said I remain encouraged because the more Bart is weaned off the prescription pain drugs the better his intestines may function.

Wednesday Dal's girlfriend, Phaddy and I retrieved Dallas from the airport and surprised him with his new green room. Bart thought he would hate it. We had a friendly five dollar bet. Either way, I didn't really care if he liked it or not because Dallas would be leaving for college so that room will become guest space or in other words, ours to do with what we please. On the way back from the airport, I stopped at our primary care doctor's office barely making my 4:30 PM appointment. He said I tore my rotator cuff. I'm very mad at myself. Why didn't I just *not* practice full speed? If I'd had those four cement things to break, there would have been no damage whatsoever to my shoulder. This really sucks. Bart was most understanding having had shoulder surgery himself.

Bart is doing better. He's used the extra bolus rounds a few times during the day but all in all he's doing a bit better. We even think we might have some new weight gain strategies. Speaking of eating, while I was en route to collect the kid, Sandi drove Bart to Creekside for lab tests and hydration. We got back and I noticed he left a portion of shepherd's pie in the pan on the drain board. Since it had been sitting out for Lord knows how long, I thought it wasn't a good idea for him to eat it so I did. Bart of course said, "what happened to my food?"

The one-time he said something finally tasted good and he was looking forward to eating that solitary portion, it's gone. What we have here is "failure to communicate." I prepared another pie but Bart said, "too late" he was on to other culinary thoughts.

Sandi brought dinner. It was tough for Sandi to refrain from spicing it up, but she did great and he ate it. Bart was happy with the huge carbo load, homemade Mac-n-Cheese, scalloped potatoes and vegetables from her garden.

It's been fun listening to the fun filled antics from Dallas' Tucson vacation. Megan had a theme for each day of the week. The first day was Redneck day where they woke Dallas up with mullet wigs, teeth and bad grammar. They had the big fun doing redneck stuff all day like shooting guns in the desert. It ended in a trip to Waffle House. Military Day they woke Dallas with whistles, yelling at him "What do you think this is, a nursery school?"

They had him doing pushups, and then went to the Air and Space Museum. On Cool-Day/Pool-Day, they sprayed Dallas with a squeeze breeze while dressed in floaties and Megan in a blow up duck pool toy. They had to drive out just to look at a pool though, but because of lightning the pool was closed. On English Day, they went out to lunch with an elderly British woman then later had a tea party. There's more and it's all in great fun (which they certainly had) but could border on tasteless humor lest I continue.

Both Bart and I took naps today, so we were rested up and able to stay awake after midnight watching a fantastic movie, "Lincoln Lawyer" and a couple other things. Bart seemed to do very well this evening. When he's doing well I'm happy.

July 23

I am so glad we have an appointment with Dr. Payne, for I cannot take one more day of Bart suffering. He used his several bolus and oral supplements for breakthrough pain and nausea. Bart may not complain, but I certainly will. He's not had a good day. He noted every supplement and at what time he dosed. I expect that logging those specifics over the last couple days will help Dr. Payne to determine what Bart needs and fix it.

Bart's tenacity, courage, and ability to deal with each day as though things were still normal amazes me. I am so frustrated with just an arm injury. Having one limb incapacitated is maddening, yet it pales in comparison to what Bart's dealing with. Bart endures much worse on a daily basis. I definitely have even more sensitivity and appreciation for how he is handling this crappy disease.

Bart has always been the self-appointed keeper of the family calendar. First thing this morning I tried to squint and see what time it was. (The clock is on Bart's side of the bed.) Bart woke up and asked what time I needed to be at the TKD testing. Then he reminded me later when it was time to leave. It's the little things like that. When I got back from testing and told him all about it he asked me to convey congratulations to the successful testers he knew. I knew he didn't feel at all well because he didn't want to watch my amateur video. Well, on second thought, my filming skill might have made him dizzy.

Bart used the heating pad on his back today but hasn't reported much improvement this evening. We watched a little TV together but there was very little conversation. Tomorrow he may rally when two dear friends and sister will be grilling the Sunday meal.

Saturday Night Live is on. It's Bart's cue for bedtime. We don't know any of these actors and guests. Question is, are they funny? Not yet.

July 25

Bart had a terrible pain day Sunday. Not even ESPN helped. He did eat a good dinner thanks to our friends and family who put together a lovely BBQ dinner. It was not a stellar weekend for Bart. He warned me that it wasn't a good time to exchange pleasantries or any other small talk or even to sit on the couch too hard.

He didn't want to answer questions or explain so we didn't post yesterday. At Creekside the doctor determined he could resume chemotherapy but he also prescribed an appetite enhancer because Bart was down to 139. They juiced him up with all the good cocktails, Zofran, Decadron, Toradal, hydration etc. so when Bart got home about 6:00 PM he was feeling much better.

We had a really nice evening. We enjoyed home-cooked Cannelloni followed by peach pie ala-mode. Tomorrow we go to Dr. Payne's clinic for a morphine pump adjustment. Let the games begin. Bart says he's feeling awake and pretty good tonight and that your posts always improve his outlook. Thank you. Good night kids.

July 26

Bart gave his ten minute warning, telling everyone "get ready to go" for he knew somebody (me) would disappear or "jack around" as he put it just when he wanted to be backing out of the garage.

Did we have everything? What about the med log? I asked Bart if he had the notebook. His answer "I'll take care of it," that wasn't the question. This particular *Bart-ism* "I'll take care of it" means **no** he's not taking any stinking notebook. I wish he would just say that instead of using all these uniquely Bart code phrases. Now, I had to ask why?

I suggested perhaps we shouldn't always count on his computer brain to recall every detail. At our first appointment, I had to remind Bart about taking oral morphine prior and he admitted to forgetting about that. I certainly can't remember stuff (ok anything) unless I write it down. The notebook could just be backup. No.

Ok fine, then what about the four page pre-appointment symptom survey and a number two pencil? (You see unless you have extra survey sheets to fill out beforehand, the survey time can really delay your appointment). I grabbed a mechanical pencil and off we went piling into the car for this quasi-family outing.

Dallas and his girlfriend were in the back, Bart in his passenger "driver's" seat and I was at the wheel. Backing out Bart says "crappy pencil" the lead retreats with the slightest pressure. I put the parking brake on and jumped out much to Bart's protest. No pencil was going to stand in the way. This was a rare moment of us being prepared for a change. I hurried back to the car and Bart murmured "now this is a pencil."

En route, I tried to avoid bumps and potholes so Bart could color within the lines.

In Sacramento, we dropped the kids off at the Mall and made our way to the other side of the tracks.

We saw Dr. K again. He substantially increased the daily shipping and handling dose and also upped the four discretionary "bonus rounds" to a higher level. Bart can now remove the Fentanyl patch and discontinue Dialudid, two other strong supplemental pain killers. Bart will have only one supplemental oral pain medication, Norco, plus his three anti-nausea prescriptions along with various over the counter remedies. Dr. K said that for the pump to displace all those heavy-duty analgesics is progress in itself.

After his pump surgery, Bart was instructed not to lift anything over 5 pounds. I asked when that restriction could be lifted because I wanted to know if Bart could close the windows yet. With my one good arm, I have to hang on some of those suckers just to bring them down. At night we open all the windows and in the morning Bart reminds me to close them before I run to the bus stop. Of course, it's a three minute job closing windows when I only have one minute to spare. Dr. K said no windows for another month or so. Bart turned to me with a look that said, "did you hear that?"

On the way home, I mused over the fact that no matter how I tried to emulate Bart's driving choices, my brain will just never work like his. He'd calmly say, "I'd move over if I were you, or get over one more lane, do you see those cars, or this isn't the best lane, this one ends, speed up you're going too slow" etc. Coincidentally, Anna had a driving lesson with her dad, so we dropped her off and wished her luck with the manual transmission.

Next we stopped by the pharmacy and retrieved Bart's new appetite enhancing prescription. Our beloved pharmacist imparted these words of consult, "could cause drowsiness." Great, just what Bart did not want, more sleep but what the hell?

He promptly fell asleep for three plus hours. What good is the appetite enhancer if he sleeps through mealtime? It's another puzzle. There are so many variables in this pain equation that it becomes a process of elimination, addition, combination repeat.

Bart started to feel better about 8:00 PM and had a little strawberry shortcake and a nausea pill. We pray tomorrow yields better results.

July 29

Wednesday Creekside hydration. Bart felt slightly better afterwards, but tired. When I got home from work, Bart had already prepared dinner, a "gourmet" frozen pizza from a box. It was perfectly delicious perhaps because I didn't bake it. Dallas made his own pepperoni pizza and retreated downstairs to the game room, which has become a flophouse for teenage boys. I was pleasantly surprised to see a resurrection of old board games down there. They exchanged their electronic controllers for cards, dice, Battleship tokens and Monopoly money to name a few. As long as I keep the garage fridge stocked with drinks and have plenty of portable foods on hand, the boys seem content.

Thursday I expected Bart to feel significantly better. He had his pump boosted Tuesday then got all juiced up Wednesday at Creekside. It should have been a good day. Instead Bart was so exhausted he slept almost all day. We're thinking those three little words "could cause drowsiness" might be the problem. This appetite enhancer isn't helping his calorie intake at all. He's got to stay awake long enough to "consume mass quantities" like a good Cone head. (Dan Akroid SNL 1977)

The instructions say take two appetite pills per day but it doesn't say when. Thursday night Bart took the second one, ate a pudding cup and promptly fell asleep. We're going to have to figure out a better schedule so Bart might realize some actual benefit from this stuff. It works great as a sleeping pill. Friday he'll take it at bedtime.

Friday's fun menu was packed. I wanted to stay close to make sure Bart ate. He's been so pooped lately that he might not feel like exerting any effort in the kitchen. Working from home afforded me the luxury of monitoring him and putting in a few one-armed loads of laundry. Two-armed chores would have to wait.

Bart was doing fairly well but still complained of fatigue. He watched golf all morning switching to another marathon of a favorite program of his called the First 48. Bart really likes that show, me, not so much.

Real life police detectives try to find clues within the first 48 hours or the chances of solving a crime plummet to a "snowball"'s chance in hell.'

I went about my business. About 3:00 PM Bart told me he felt crappy. He asked me to retrieve a compliment of nausea meds from the safe. Remember I'd been listening to ambient audio from this crime program all afternoon and now there was no way I wasn't going to see what happened to the Iraqi family in Chicago, whose mom went missing. It was almost Mother's Day for God's sake so I had to know if they found her alive in time. Happy to see some grateful children when Chicago police detectives saved the day. I think Bart should wear headphones from now on to save me from these heart-wrenching stories. By 8:00 PM, Bart had some relief and invited me to watch something with him. It was either "Storage Wars" or a movie. I opted for the latter. The war on storage goes on all week.

No Appetite for Pain

July 31

The appetite enhancing sleeping pill doesn't work all that well over night. Bart was up several times and did not have much restful slumber. He had not taken his usual sleep aid Friday evening so we could see if the appetite sleeper pill did the trick. Evidently the appetite pills are not as long acting as they appear to be during the day. This morning I got up quietly (I didn't fall down or drop anything loud) hoping Bart could go back to sleep.

Phaddy was excited to get in an early walk buying me a little more time to prepare one of Bart's (and Dal's) favorite breakfasts, biscuits and country gravy. Turns out I had plenty of time. I did laundry, dishes, watering and even a little left-handed tree trimming before Bart got up. The Pest control guy evoked the tree trimming urgency. He confirmed my ugly suspicion that it wasn't just our squirrel wreaking havoc. We had rats also running amok, likely swinging from the trees closest to the house and onto the deck. More rodents!

I just couldn't wait until Sunday when Ms. Sawzall might be free to wield her fancy toy. The limb clipping was going quite well until I encountered one thick stubborn branch. I had to squeeze really, really hard. Sure enough, when the blades finally cut through the limb, the clipper handles snapped together like the Jaws of Life pinching my ring finger between them. Why does not one solitary tool in our household have any remnants of rubber hand grips left to soften the blows. I cracked my fingernail in two right smack across the center. If I were lucky, our superglue wouldn't be dried up and rock hard. I put the clippers away and marched back to the kitchen. A whisk, pan, and a toaster oven seemed somewhat safer tools for the moment.

Bart woke up about 9:30 AM and came out doubled over in pain. He had bad cramps and was uncharacteristically showing it, holding his midsection and maneuvering around to find any comfortable position in his chair.

I knew it was worse than usual because he said he couldn't handle the biscuits and gravy, just a bowl of cereal. Later I suggested a few snacks but Bart said only Top Ramen might suit his stomach. Holy Mary mother of God, I hoped the appetite pills weren't adding to gastrointestinal distress. He didn't finish the noodles and napped through lunchtime. Food just wasn't appealing with these stomach cramps. I sat next to him for several hours in case he wanted a morsel of anything. I used the time to attempt organizing pictures in my computer. I wanted to use the digital picture frame I got years ago. And after hours of endless filing Bart said I needed a storage device and proper attachment cable to ever complete the job. Nothing electronic is ever easy.

It was getting late and I had to get to the market. Bart needed electrolyte drinks and over the counter remedies and it was near time to get cracking at dinner. I'd planned a meal that Bart was looking forward to; grilled ball tip roast, mashed red potatoes, fresh zucchini, cauliflower, apple sauce and sweet corn.

Dallas and the horde of teens barely came up for air this weekend. Dallas usually helps put away groceries but he whined about it being the last vestige of summer vacation. Of course in all the debagging action, a pudding cup somehow split open and splattered all over my white shirt.

Phaddy was busy ripping the guts out of his large stuffed penguin and Bart had his head down listening to sports on TV.

Sandi came by but declined dinner. Politely reminding me that there were too many teenage boys in the house and there would never be enough food.

The grilled roast turned out exceptionally scrumptious, and perfectly done, thank goodness. I wish I could say the same for the vegetables. Bart ate a decent amount, although not enough to gain any weight. Tonight at bedtime Bart took a proper sleeping pill and the final (fourth) bolus of the day.

As he climbed into bed, Bart acquiesced that it was time to buy smaller jeans. A small defeat. That will go on tomorrow's shopping list right after my Sunday Sawzall tree trimming extravaganza. Rodents be damned.

Chapter Sixteen

Cramping Bart's Style

August 1

Officially, it was a tough weekend for Bart. Poor guy just couldn't get relief from the vice grip on his stomach. Nothing alleviated the pressure completely and that constant and nagging intestinal constriction squashed his enthusiasm for consuming much of anything despite the Marinol appetite enhancer. His sugar levels have been stable which isn't surprising; he's not eating enough to spike.

This morning wasn't quite as bad as Saturday but it wasn't good. I got up early in case the power tool crew showed up while it was still cool. When Bart got up he had cereal for breakfast then a morning bolus round followed by an attempt to ignore his discomfort by sleeping.

Sure enough friends arrived in all their glory with the Sawzall tool and on a mission. A young Digger pine went down. We cut back a thick of Maples, Redwoods, and Birch trees and shaped greenery that had run amok. I could not believe the small forest that we compressed into the bed of their pick-up. Seven years' worth of overgrowth was driven away. It was a cathartic moment.

Bart and I felt extreme gratitude for the generosity of friends. What a feeling of satisfaction and accomplishment thanks to friends with a willing attitude, a big truck, and a Sawzall. They even helped me interpret the mystery that was our drip system. All precious landscape is now secure thanks to a new nine volt battery. Had it not been for friends, our garden and peripheral landscaping would have croaked a dry choking death.

Thoroughly spent and basking in the post trimming glory, I sank into my chair to tell Bart all about it. He was dozing in and out of consciousness. Soon enough we were both in our respective chairs, fast asleep. When did we turn into our parents?

I woke up and tried plying Bart with delectable snacks but he wasn't having any of it. It's tough to adjust the larder when Bart's taste buds are so whacked because of prolonged chemotherapy.

My worry meter was pegged today. Bart had little interest in food and even less in any activity other than accommodating bodily functions and sleep.

Tonight I told Bart how concerned I was and he concurred. He said he was trying to figure this out too. Conversation was a chore however so I let him rest. I offered a little bit of everything but nothing tasted good to him. Returning one dish to the refrigerator ended up a cleaning nightmare or a dog's food frenzy depending on your perspective. The dish slipped out of my hands and I toppled a whole tuna casserole across the floor and throughout the refrigerator, in the hinges and beyond. Phaddy was so startled by my sudden expletive that he high tailed it out of there and never dared to sniff a crumb. He disappeared until it was safe to return. He definitely missed his chance.

I ended up driving to Papa Murphy's for a special Bart request for thin crust chicken and garlic pizza. Bart had one slice. Who does that? Who has just one slice of pizza? I didn't think that was possible. I'd eaten what I could rescue of the tuna casserole and still couldn't leave it at one slice of pizza. That explains why I'm the only one gaining weight around here.

Dallas played musical friends this afternoon with boys coming and going. They all got a lucrative offer to do yard work for gas money. Even though they mouthed yes, that was evidently code for "no, we'd rather stagnate here with our goldfish, saltines and Mr. Pibb all afternoon." I told Bart I'm counting down the days until check out time. Only then will Dallas begin to appreciate what it takes to maintain one's life.

Tomorrow it's Creekside. I plan to give Dr. Payne a call to see if Bart can come in for an adjustment. He's off to bed.

I pray for his uninterrupted sleep and a feel-good morning.

August 3

Bart's morning was decent but he reported degradation as the day wore on. We're wondering if the wild card here is the new appetite pill. No real improvement whatsoever on the appetite front and yet a measured worsening in the gut. We agree it might be prudent to give that stuff a pass. Surely there must be other options.

We were expecting a call back from the Pain Management Clinic but when we didn't get one, I rang them again. I made an appointment for tomorrow before Creekside. If we don't get to the bottom of this cramping business by Thursday, the oncologist will send Bart to a Gastroenterologist. Bart's not excited about having a tube thrust down his throat, but we want answers. There's got to be a way to alleviate his constant intestinal discomfort.

Speaking of discomfort, Dallas wasn't particularly comfortable talking about his launch from the nest. Dad and I filled out the student emergency card and signed the forms for Dallas' final year at Ponderosa. School starts Monday. I tried talking to Dallas about planning ahead for check out time. I was none too pleased that he didn't even want to discuss his future freedom in the least. Perhaps having his friends around made the discussion a non-starter.

It's been a revolving door of boys in and out, mostly in. I was getting concerned that some boys might have taken up residence here, spending three nights in a row. At least I know the parents well enough to feel at ease. As for me, I can't imagine three days without the kid at least coming home for clean clothes and a quick check in. Dallas is evidently sharing his clothes though. I recognize the shorts and shirts our teenaged "guests" are wearing. No wonder Dallas thinks I have to take him school shopping over the weekend. His friends have nothing to wear!

When Bart took a long nap early evening, I took off to run errands which included the usual UPS store, pharmacy, dry cleaners, Goodwill, grocery store, and Pet Smart. I was thrilled to find Grannick's citrus squirrel repellent and a half-priced squeak toy for Phaddeus, among other things.

I fixed tacos for dinner. Bart tried them but could not tolerate the flavors. He opted for corndogs instead. The boys, however, loved the tacos and made a clean sweep of two pounds of taco meat, refried beans and toppings.

Bart wanted strawberry shortcake for dessert, which I happily prepared. With his remote controls in hand Bart said he would be fine if I went to Taekwondo. Now that I'm not training I can teach until the shoulder fully heals. I had one student stop me after class asking if I would be teaching Thursday too. When I responded affirmatively, he then said perhaps he might have to take that night off. I get that it's a bit embarrassing not to know all your lower belt material but fear of getting caught not knowing it is a great motivator to practice.

Bart was awake when I got back from TKD. I asked him how he was doing and he said not very well but he still invited me to watch a recorded TV program with him. We talked a little about his pain appointment and what the next step would be then watched a little TV together. Bart took a couple of anti-nausea pills and headed to bed. Bart's medication notes showed four daily bolus doses and Norco supplements for pain. Same drill, because Bart still uses all four additional boosts and oral pain killers then the maintenance morphine may still be too low.

We shall see tomorrow.

August 4

Bart appeared mildly better Wednesday morning but he was never without some degree of that nagging constrictive gut ache. Even after a bolus he asked me to get him a Norco to take the edge off.

We tried to wake "The Dallas." He often refers to himself in the third person. We reminded him that he had guests downstairs, gave him instructions, then Bart and I took off for the pain clinic.

We met with Dr. Payne's other colleague this time. She increased the pump rate another whole step while leaving Bart's bonus doses at the same level. She agreed that the Marinol happy appetite stuff was suspect. Bart had already stopped using it. We didn't think it was a good idea to add anything new into the mix until his stomach pain is diagnosed. Thursday Bart would discuss it further with the oncologist.

On our way home, I thought we might stop and shop for Bart's Levi's. He'd been asking me to buy a smaller size for some time now but it was always either too late or too inconvenient to drive to the Folsom Factory Outlets.

Here we were driving right by but Bart wasn't feeling it. He really wanted those jeans though.

At home Bart got settled, ate a little something and then reclined to take a nap. I knew there would never be a convenient time so I took off for the Levi outlet. He'd finally get those darn jeans. I checked that off the list but I still had a significant number of grocery and drug store items plus bank, cleaners and a prescription waiting at the pharmacy.

Tilapia filets sounded good to Bart so I had them thawed and ready to cook. I was pleased with myself for remembering to take them out of the freezer in the first place. Good thing they're quick to prepare because I got home late.

I thought the recipe turned out rather tasty. Bart didn't. Dallas and his buddies weren't digging the fish thing either. They ran away to Buffalo Wild Wings. Bart's altered taste buds were repulsed by most everything on his plate. So there we were, this big dinner and I was the only one eating. Bart opted for a bowl of applesauce and a couple of frozen corndogs.

With all the angst lately, it is pure delight to see Bart chuckle once in a while. It's usually because of Phaddy and his puppy-like playful personality. Bart said Phaddy nosed through his toy basket last night, carefully selecting just the right thing. He delivered a tennis ball to the foot of Bart's throne and stared up at him intently. The little chunk of a dog trembled joyfully until Bart tossed the ball.

Then Phaddy repetitively skids across the hardwood floor, ruffling the entryway rug while rounding the corner and speeding down the hall for the kill.

We hope to kill Bart's latest bout of discomfort and forge ahead to better health post haste.

August 6

Bart had a rough couple of days. He didn't rest well and no position seemed comfortable. He was up and down, never really getting a good stretch of solid sleep. I was awake a lot too. Thursday morning came early and I had to get to work. Dallas got up and was primed and ready to care for his dad until I returned in the evening.

Our friend Bill transported Bart to Creekside in the afternoon for hydration. No matter how much water Bart drinks he just cannot seem to stay hydrated. Labs showed Bart's blood pressure was up, likely due to his elevated pain. The oncologist ordered a CT scan and a referral to a Gastroenterologist. He also brought up the celiac block thing again. The oncologist went so far as to say he would have UCSF call us to arrange it! Dr. Payne counseled us against it obviously the oncologist and Dr. Payne never talked. It's so frustrating. I left messages for Dr. Payne's office again requesting a joint consultation. Close follow up is obviously required. Bart wasn't in any shape to ask a lot of questions.

We were not pleased with the news from the lab that Bart's cancer markers were up for the first time. He went from an all-time low of 4500 up to 5000. After the pump surgery, he needed an extra week off chemo which evidently gave the cancer a little window.

Bart scheduled another hydration appointment for Friday afternoon. I had a big list of questions but the oncologist was not available. It wasn't a very busy day in the lounge so I sat in a chemo recliner next to Bart. While doing a wee bit of work I fell asleep and when I woke up Bart was fast asleep. After three plus hours on the drip Bart was done. He reported feeling somewhat better. It was good to have two consecutive days in the lounge.

Aunt Sandi took one for the team so I could accompany Bart to Creekside Friday. She accepted the challenge of driving Dallas and his friends school shopping at the Galleria in Roseville. Dallas had made the arrangements with her the night prior. Afterwards, he came out to the living room where Dad and I were and quizzically asked "Do you know what Aunt Sandi's biggest concern was about taking me? She wanted to know if she actually had to shop with me?" Evidently they worked out a satisfactory mall game plan. I was impressed that the kid made his modest budget stretch to cover all of his most urgent wardrobe needs.

As soon as Bart and I got back from Creekside, I launched into my latest dinner adventure. This would be my chicken and dumplings premiere. Bart liked the sound of that and his wish is mostly my command. It was a celebratory day when Bart said he really liked it! Bart ate the whole bowl of soup, dumplings and all, and so did Sandi. I finally have redemption.

I'm all packed for an overnight getaway with girlfriends from Trinity High. We're taking off for Weaverville tomorrow morning at the crack of dawn returning Sunday night. Some of the gals will float down the river while the rest of us hold down the fort at Camp Goodyear near Douglas City. I'm really looking forward to seeing my gal pals and my mom. Sandi and Dallas will take good care of Bart in the meantime. Have a great weekend dear friends and fam. Bart insists. He could get a vicarious thrill and that would be a good thing.

August 8

Bright and early Saturday morning I bid Bart adieu. The truck was packed and ready to go to the high country of Trinity County. I checked with Bart again to make sure he was ok and he shooed me off. I didn't make it very far because the truck had a dead battery. This was not a good start. But I had jumper cables and could hook up to my BMW for a jumpstart. Frustration set in when I couldn't find the battery on that car! I called my neighbor over and between the two of us we got nowhere except dirty. The manual indicated a sealed battery or some such thing that shouldn't be messed with by lowly owners. Eventually, I found our battery charger. With the engine finally started I said goodbye to Bart once again.

Shortly after arriving at camp some four-five hours later, I called Bart. He said he was hurting and not feeling well. I encouraged him to have Sandi just take him to the hospital if he couldn't get relief from that damn pain. Enough was enough. Sandi drove Bart to the Emergency Room that evening. Doctors ordered a battery of tests including a CT scan. The scan involved drinking a large volume of contrast liquid.

It took several hours for Bart to even get that down. Then he had to wait an hour before the imaging and another hour or more for results. He was finally admitted to the hospital after 1:00 AM. Sandi stayed with Bart the whole time.

This morning I checked in with Sandi as we packed up camp. She reported that Bart was finally getting a little sleep. The dichotomy of constant pain is that it causes intense stress such that it wears you out but yet prevents rest by keeping you awake. I can't imagine what it's like living daily with that kind of strain. At least Bart was finally comfortable enough to rest.

It was a long but familiar trek back from the mountains to Sacramento. I went straight to the hospital.

Sandi had given me the results of the CT scan over the phone but I read the report myself at the hospital. The liver masses showed some increase in size as did the pancreatic tumors.

Bart said he hadn't wanted to interrupt my overnight with the girls. Many have been my friends for more than 45 years. He knows that even a short time with these women is better than group therapy.

One of the doctors (described by Bart and Sandi as one with a bad bedside manner) discovered a major problem. During the course of the day, Bart had administered two boluses. Near the incision in his back appeared a spongy protrusion a bit larger than an egg. Nurses and doctors alike were puzzled as to why all that morphine wasn't making even a dent in the pain. They added Dilaudid injections every two hours just to bring Bart down from an eight (one-ten pain scale) to a six. The conclusion was that the line from the pump to the spinal column had somehow detached. It was likely that morphine was getting pumped into his tissues (subcutaneously) instead of into the main spinal nerve system.

Bart was prohibited from giving himself boluses. Just in the few hours I was there, after Bart stopped dosing, the swelling went down. The mad scramble was on to get in touch with Dr. Payne. He installed the pump so he would have to fix it. The problem was Dr. Payne doesn't have privileges at Mercy Folsom. No transport was allowed to a surgery center though, which is where Bart had the pump installed in the first place. Tomorrow morning we expect answers as to how it will all be sorted out.

It was almost dark when I got home. The Dallas and his three friends were gaming away downstairs so I took Phaddy for a walk.

Apparently the dog was excited to see me. I didn't discover the piddle puddle on my blonde hardwood kitchen floor until I had walked right through it in my bare feet extending puddle drips onto the kitchen rugs.

Dallas organized his room and got all of his supplies together for the first day of school tomorrow. I think he's looking forward to this, his final year of high school. If he's lucky he might keep a few of his good friends for as many decades as I have. Sandi is collecting son Matthew from the airport tomorrow morning while I meet with Bart and his doctors.

Can't We All Just Communicate?

August 10

Monday morning.

I Threw a few things Bart requested into a bag: shirt, socks etc. and drove to Mercy. I met with the hospital doctor. He reported that the spinal catheter was indeed out of place and not property positioned to deliver the goods. He said it needed to be fixed by he who had installed it.

The hospital would only treat Bart for the pain and the pump was a separate issue. That meant that Bart would have to resort to patches, pills and injections. All the things we had replaced with the pump. Our hospital doc was not familiar with a celiac block procedure either.

This show was breaking down and Bart was feeling the pain of it all. He was up to a seven-eight on the ten scale. When I heard that Bart would have to schedule repair surgery at a later date when he was released from the hospital I felt myself going ballistic.

It's logical that doctors want to take care of their respective specialty areas (of course) but there has to be a captain steering the ship. Somebody needs to take a little ownership of the case and share key information with all the part-time players. The whole context of Bart's medical situation must be clearly understood by all those involved and the only way to accomplish that is for the patient to do it.

I called the two pain docs and the oncologist multiple times insisting they consult together on the case immediately. I also requested confirmation and told them exactly what Bart and I wanted to happen. We wanted surgical repair of the pump and the celery (celiac) block done at the same time. We were not ok with going to San Francisco and requested it happen here in Sacramento.

Dr. K (pain clinic) indicated either he or Dr. Payne could in fact perform a celiac procedure they just don't do them very often because pumps outperform blocks in their opinion. The oncologist was adamant though. He wanted it so we wanted it.

Bart trusts the oncologist and even though I find him non-communicative and difficult to approach, Bart says that's the way he rolls. I offered that perhaps Bart likes the oncologist because he rolls that way too. One of Bart's favorite retorts to me is often, "Do I look like a friggin' people person?"

I finally asked Dr. K just what the hell is this celiac thing anyway? A celiac block is similar to getting Novocain at the dentist. A numbing agent is injected into a plexus of nerves situated in front of the aorta. That collection of nerves corresponds to several organs including the pancreas. It numbs affected areas for about ten months. That combined with a fully operational morphine pump could render Bart pain free for once, and that is the goal.

I kept calling offices until I got to talk to a doctor and relay some vital facts about Bart's condition. The pain was causing his blood pressure to rise 156/107 when it's normally low. His white blood cell count rose to 19 from 4 indicating a possible infection. It was unacceptable and unfair that Bart should suffer another day at seven-eight level pain. There was no time to waste.

Problem was that Bart got the pump at a surgery center and the pain guys wanted the repair done there. Not going to happen. Medical transport was not possible to a center, only hospital to hospital. I explained that I was not at all comfortable with that scenario. I emphasized that in Bart's weakened state, he absolutely must be in a hospital environment. Anything less would not work.

By 8:00 PM that evening, we got word that a hospital to hospital transfer was approved. The docs had finally talked. At 9:00 PM, three burly ambulance fellows showed up to whisk Bart away to Mercy San Juan Hospital in Citrus Heights. Once I figured out how to get out of the hospital post-closing time I drove away too. At home, I sat down to post but fell fast asleep in the chair.

By Tuesday morning, Bart was ensconced in room 4540 and he was "ready for go" as my dad used to say. I called the pain office early to ask about Bart's surgery, and to verify that both procedures would be done. Dr. K indicated that their surgical schedules were booked, but there was the OR calendar to consider so surgery might not happen today.

Later I got a frantic text from Bart saying that Dr. Payne had just returned from vacation and told Bart's nurses that he did not want to do the block. This wrinkle shot my last nerve right into orbit. I placed a call to Dr. K urgently advising him to talk to his boss right away because if there was some phantom reason or risk for not doing this procedure, he'd better spit it out at the oncologist and fast. Then the oncologist's office received a diplomatic scolding too. What we have here people is a "failure to communicate." These guys better get their acts together.

Later I was elated to get an actual phone call from Bart. He usually hates talking and still does.

He only called because I didn't answer his most recent message fast enough. Running around the house and yard with computer and cell phone strapped to my body is not happening. Bart would say yes it is, just get bigger pockets.

San Juan nurses notified Bart that his celiac/pump repair surgery was finally official: Thursday morning at 7:00 AM. This was great news.

Bart also reported that his blood pressure was normal again. His pain was a rough six but having these doctors on the same page was reassuring.

Matty, Dallas, and I thought Bart seemed a lot better tonight. He ate well and was talking freely. All that social activity tired him out though. Bedtime for Bonzos came before 9:00 PM tonight.

He'll have tomorrow to beef up and rest up for the big show on Thursday morning. We are looking forward to it.

August 11

Bart appreciated his buddy Bill coming by today and especially for setting up the Fantasy Golf thing. Bart was bummed about missing the fantasy golf deadline last round due to hospitalization.

Bart reports that he feels like he did before this whole pain conquering adventure began, back at square one. He says he's eating better though which makes me feel better. As you might expect, I've shared all this with our medical student daughter. I have to confess, however, that we do understand how it happens. I've unintentionally done it myself.

Coordinating one event, I covered every detail and double sent information and contact numbers then doubled back again, except that I forgot to cc someone back at the office. Sure as hell, she got thrown into the middle of a situation that she knew nothing about.

As a result, she experienced more than her fair share of frustration. A simple copied email would have made it so much easier for her. I violated a rule that I used to teach my own employees over the years. It's a concept called "over-communicate". Tell the whole department family what the hell you're doing, how, where, and why so we can cover for each other and won't waste time duplicating efforts. The same goes for medical care. Doctors are only human.

There's a point here. Megan sent us a copy of her personal statement which is significant part of the application process for medical residency. She asked me to read it to Bart at the hospital last night. As much as I wanted to, I couldn't do it. I used the excuse that Bart was sleepy but truth be told I knew I could not get through it.

I think it's more than appropriate to share it with you compliments of Bart and Meggie:

From our Dr. Meg:

My life adventure has been seasoned with many experiences that encouraged and strengthened my pursuit to become a family practice doctor, and medical school in particular has been colored with some distinctly poignant events. Just prior to medical school I was jumping out of airplanes, surviving in the woods, honing evasive strategies on enemy combatant territory, and sharpening my marksmanship in various firearms. I led combat camera units and spearheaded millions of dollars' worth of media and graphics initiatives for the Department of Defense as an Air Force communications officer. I enjoyed being in the throes of an exciting career that required leadership by example, discipline, effective teamwork, and attention to detail; characteristics that were constantly motivated by the sobering but stirring responsibility of the lives of other soldiers. But, my original aspiration had always been to utilize these same talents in a different form of service: in the lives of my patients. Subsequently, as the opportunity arose, I separated from the military to join my husband, a military pilot, in Tucson, AZ, where I began my next chapter of training as a medical student.

On the tails of this major transition, another developed in my personal life. Shortly after beginning medical school, it became apparent that my grandfather, a great rural family doctor and my most influential professional role model, was approaching the end of his time. My grandfather served as a small town doctor for over 50 years in a small community at the edge of a National forest in Northern California. When he first settled in 1951 he served as the dentist, veterinarian and family doctor all rolled into one. After working for over half a century in that community, he passed away at 94 in the very same hospital he served in so faithfully, down the street from the original home he built. As I mingled around during his memorial service and heard the stories of how my grandfather had delivered their kids...and their cows, sewn up their wounds, and in several cases even saved their lives, it was evident that Dr. Mike had earned a deep-rooted affection and respect from the entire county. The impact he had as a physician illustrated the importance of benevolent service to others. I was very grateful for my grandfather's example as a physician. As I mourned his loss, I reflected on my own development as a physician and I hope to follow in his caring footsteps.

Little did I know, another significant challenge was right around the corner. This one would probably create the greatest impact on my resolve to develop into a skilled and compassionate doctor. At 59 years old, my amazing dad was diagnosed with a terminal disease-stage four pancreatic cancer. I traveled home to California and traded one mode of training for another: delivering patient care to suddenly receiving patient care. As I went alongside my dad to his first rounds of chemo, and eventually accompanied him to the ICU while he was in septic shock, I experienced patient care from a different perspective.

After learning from the greatest doctor I know, I am privileged to learn from the greatest patient I know. He demonstrates great courage, strength, and poise as I watch him face the most difficult of circumstances. He even maintains his sense of humor during some times of intense suffering. My dad continues to make an indelible imprint on my outlook and my practice of medicine, and I hope to be a doctor that lives up to patients like him.

As I witness him receive both excellent and poor quality medical care, I secure my resolve to provide the same level of care to someone else's loved one that I desire for him.

I find that my desire for this benevolent, compassionate care that extends to the whole family from the beginning of life to the end is best suited for Family Practice medicine. This is the field that demands the teamwork, compassion, and care that all my life experiences have cemented into me.

From my military experience and my Grandfather's amazing example as a rural family doc, to fighting alongside my dad in his battle and my many experiences in volunteering, youth activities and outreach, and peer counseling programs, I know that family medicine is the best place for me to continue these diverse themes of service.

As I near the close of this chapter of medical school, some of my fondest memories in medicine are delivering a newborn baby to an anxious and excited mom, getting a hug from one of my pediatric patients as she skipped out of the hospital, balloons in hand, completely transformed and healed, seeing one of my geriatric patients wheel into clinic with all his flags proudly displayed from the back of his wheel chair, and attending clinic appointments that were really just meant for a social visit and a quick chat with their doc.

I have long anticipated enjoying experiences like these as I begin my next chapter of a lifelong, fulfilling career in the diverse field of family medicine.

Dr. Megan Moran

Morning of the Big Show

August 12

Talk about role reversal, Dallas got up early and then came in to wake me! I shuffled sleepily out to the kitchen with a hungry little morning dog at my heels. Dallas was pouring coffee into my West Point commuter mug. I put bouncing Phaddy and his breakfast outside. Dallas said "Mom, go get ready. I'll close the windows. You don't want to be late for Dad's surgery."

Wow, is this really my kid? I had less than a half hour to hit the road. Bart sent a text stating that everything was on schedule. I responded by querying if he would be having **both** procedures done. (Not having spoken with Dr. Payne myself, I was still apprehensive and unsure.) His answer was, "yes dear", which is Bart code for, "how many times do I have to tell you this?"

Mercy San Juan Medical Center is an immense metropolis especially when compared to our small-town Mercy Folsom Hospital. Quite by accident last night, I discovered a prime parking area behind Orthopedics. Score.

Graceful is not an adjective that remotely applies to the clumsy way I roll. Gathering up Bart's iPad, my computer bag, newspapers, and other hospital paraphernalia from the back seat of the car seems simple enough, but somehow it ends up with me crawling under the car grappling for my water bottle and chasing flying papers while stuff is dropping out of the bags. My white shirt now has pavement marks to compliment the giant coffee stains thanks to that bastard commuter mug.

That parking lot episode cost me. Bart had already been wheeled off to surgery by the time I got to his room. Oh well, his empty hospital bed looked most inviting. I could stretch out and read the paper in comfort. This was so much nicer than the square vinyl chair farm that posed as a waiting area.

I even got ice water. No one seemed to notice that I wasn't a patient. Bill stopped by and waited with me for an hour or so.

The statement "having your doctors on the same page is reassuring" was way too presumptive. At 10:00 AM Dr. Payne showed up to room 4540. He said he thought he'd find me here. Ok. Dr. Payne told me everything went well. Bart was in recovery all tightened up. He anchored the catheter securely and changed out morphine for a more powerful drug Dilaudid. Of course I asked about the celiac block.

No, he shook his head, seemingly tired of the question. Once he explained why he chose not to do it I understood. It just didn't make sense to add an unnecessary risk factor into the surgical equation. Let the pump do its job. Dr. Payne was uncomfortable injecting the alcohol numbing agent required for a block. Why add potential toxins?

Plus the invasion of another needle through the aorta to reach the plexus carries risk. Holy hell! No one ever mentioned jamming a needle through his heart before. Were there other routes? He said maybe but it was a useless notion unless the pump fails and he was quite sure it would not.

I wish he had warned us the first time around that bending over was ill advised.

When Bart is hurting, he hangs his head between his knees thus curving his spine and coaxing the catheter out. Dr. Payne said it's like a spaghetti noodle, once it recedes there's no going back, it just kind of coils up in there. He admitted that Bart not feeling the bolus administered in the office was a clue and the fact that we kept coming back for more, also clues. Still, it took severe pain and hospitalization to discover the major malfunction.

Bart is to lie flat for 24 hours then we'll see about going home. One more thing. I whipped out one of my business cards wrote the oncologist's name and number on it and scolded "You ARE going to call the oncologist and explain it to him yourself." My inside voice was saying, "my Army Ranger son will give you a celiac block where it counts if you don't."

Bart woke up about 1:00 PM. He had incision soreness but pain-wise he was better. I could tell because he started in with "get my nurse, move your stuff, plug in my charger, get my water, pull up my blankets, don't spill anything" etc. That's the bossy Bart I know. Last night he wanted to hold my hand, today he wanted snappy room service.

I told him nurses are here to save your ass, not kiss it.

Bart gets released

August 13

Bart is getting out today. I'm on my way to Mercy San Juan Hospital to spring him. Timing couldn't be better for we've planned a lovely engagement party for our son Matthew and his finance' Jen this evening. All the chicks are back in the nest and the house is full of life (chaos but in a good way).

August 14

A Note from Bart:

Wow as you all know by now I've just gotten out after having spent several days at the luxury hotel, better known as Mercy San Juan. Evidently at some point in the last five weeks the catheter in my spinal column sprung loose. What that caused in effect was all the pain killing meds were just going into the tissue in my back.

Not having the desired effect on the pain. So that explains why whenever we would reduce one of my external meds, pain would come back with a vengeance. The morning after the catheter was replaced I felt better. Not as much constant pain but a new side effect. I was dizzy light headed when standing up. Not good. The doctor came in and explained he had upped the dose and maybe we should lower it. I agreed.

So we lowered the dose from 4.5 to 4.0. So far most of the dizziness is gone and I am not having anywhere near the pain I was. I'm on Dilaudid in my pump now and I have external Dilaudid for breakthrough. We are tuning the dose to try and make for less breakthrough pain. That's our goal.

Sorry if this is a repeat but I felt I should take some of the duties from my blushing bride since she has done so much for me. This is the least I could do. The next few weeks should be the teller but after surgery this time I can feel a difference. I hope it's not psychosomatic. That would suck. I think it's real. I'm going to take a nap now. Just wanted to share a little as to what was going on with me.

Love y'all, Bart

August 15

Bart felt good this morning, not stellar but he was cautiously optimistic that his chronic pain might be subsiding. He appeared stronger, more upright and his stride stepping out.

Today we met with Gastroenterologist Dr. Piccolu. Bart calls him "Pikachu" of Pokémon fame. It was a wonderful uplifting consultation. Dr. Piccolu suggested that three out of four of the likeliest causes for Bart's terrible cramping might be rectified with new drug formulations. He said any one remedy could be a home run. In order to find out for sure Bart must get an endoscopy.

There was no time to waste and Piccolu agreed. He moved his schedule around so that Bart could get the procedure Wednesday morning. Also, Wednesday Bart had chemotherapy booked at Creekside but the oncologist said no chemo after an endoscopy procedure. Bart would be getting new and different chemo drugs this time so Bart's Creekside Lounge appointment was moved to Thursday.

We were eager to find out just what was causing Bart's severe cramping. Dr. Piccolu said it could be stomach acid, an ulcer, delayed stomach output due to chemo and other drugs, or worst case that the cancer had metastasized to the stomach. We believe, based on symptoms and the dramatic drop in cancer markers over the last nine months (aside from the last very minor rise) that it's likely one of the former causes. We will find out tomorrow.

Pikachu sent us with some of the stomach acid miracle samples and two new prescriptions, one of which won't be covered by insurance and can only be filled at a compound pharmacy.

We hope one of the other two remedies will do the trick first.

Bart's instructions were to take one of the sample pills per day to see if that alone might help. On the way home from Dr. Piccolu-choo in Placerville, we stopped at the market, pharmacy, dry cleaners and Subway in Cameron Park. Bart ordered the sandwich with the most calories. Then he ingested the pill sample. Shortly thereafter Bart complained of back pain and cramping. When it was time he administered a bolus (Dilaudid) but when I returned from TKD an hour later he had already taken a Norco as well.

I didn't like that his back hurt and that the miracle pill (referred to as Prilosec on steroids) wasn't working. Another bolus later Bart was still experiencing some degree of discomfort.

At least the oncologist had reported one good thing, he had actually spoken with Dr. Payne and they agreed that if the pump failed to address all of Bart's pain and the gastro doctor doesn't produce results then Dr. Payne agreed to perform a celiac block.

I Just woke up, still in my chair so I will hit "post" and bid you adieu.

August 17

All systems are go for the endoscopy. Bart said he felt ok this morning. Dallas woke him up at 5:50 AM so he could eat a bowl of cereal. That would be the last solid food until after the endoscopy. We drove to Creekside where Dr. Piccolu-choo performs his gastro-procedures across the parking lot from the Chemo Lounge.

It was a small waiting area. The endoscopy would take around two to three hours total. I had plenty of reading material but the library quiet was shattered when a rather brash lady and her elderly attaché exploded into the room. Why is it that some people use such loud voices for private conversations in close spaces? She had a hyena laugh and a smoker's wheeze and apparently a good sense of humor. This woman found most every line of each Inquirer celebrity article that she read aloud something to giggle and wheeze about. Since one of my personal mottos is "you can't get hurt by being too generous," I resisted the temptation to blurt "for crying out loud, shut the hell up for a moment."

Eventually the office door opened and Dr. Piccolu called "Reagan." I clamored to collect my stuff quickly. My purse dumped upside down next to my chair and the newspaper slid off my lap littering the floor.

After collecting myself and my scattered belongings, we were informed that Bart did have severe gastritis, reddening of the stomach lining causing nausea and cramping. The night before, Bart tried one of the sample acid-reducing pills Dr. Piccolu gave us.

My marching orders were to procure a drug I dubbed "Dom Perignon" and get Bart on it today.

Dr. Piccolu said Domperidone was originally formulated in Canada to help women lactate. In Bart's situation, it serves to empty the stomach contents into the intestines faster. Doctor Piccolu thinks Bart's stomach contents are lingering way too long, likely fermenting and causing extreme irritation to the stomach walls, an incredibly painful condition, not to mention what it does to mess up the bowel.

The one catch is that only a compounding pharmacy would be able to fill this prescription and insurance won't pay. A modest supply costs about $70. It's a small price to pay if this Dom Perignon pill spells relief. I called Grandpa's Pharmacy in Placerville but they said it would take 24 hours. I requested a call if they were able to do it faster and briefly explained the circumstances. Sure enough, I got a call about 5:00 PM and took off. I got home with the champagne pills by 6:00 PM.

I cooked a salmon dinner with fresh steamed veggies and homemade mashed potatoes. Bart opted for chicken noodle soup instead. He's got to take it slow after being knocked out for these procedures. Good news is that Bart weighed 136 which is up from last weigh in. Let's pray the trend continues.

As of bedtime, no change but Bart is to take the Domperidone capsules twice daily. Bart had to take two nausea pills this evening and a Norco before bedtime. That could mean there is still tweaking to do with the pump next week.

Tomorrow Bart begins a new chemotherapy regimen at Creekside Lounge. Both of us have already forgotten the names of the drugs the oncologist ordered. We will find out tomorrow. It's been quite the surgical adventure for Bart the last few weeks. Now we hope to settle down to some cancer killing chemo. At least he'll be in the comfort of a lounge chair.

August 18

A Note from Bart:

Today is the first day after the Endoscopy. I've been feeling very weak, dizzy and tired. My thought is too many surgeries (procedures) too close together. My body needs time to rest and recover. That being said, they found no cancer in the stomach (a big worry) and what they did find is treatable (we think). So now let's treat what we know and get back to fighting the BIG-C. Let's see if we can beat this thing. My body feels better, slightly, as far as pain goes. Now if we can get this stomach thing under control, I will feel better about the cancer fighting.

Wish me luck I think I see hope on the horizon. I will keep y'all informed as we go along.

In the last month and half I have had three surgeries/procedures, two stays in the hospital, and hopefully we can keep those to a small number going forward.

Bless you all, Bart

August 19

This week marks one year since Bart's pancreatic cancer diagnosis. It always seems to us that something poignant marks milestones. On the first anniversary of my dad's death April 15th, that very day Jen accepted Matty's proposal of marriage. Sandi pointed out what a sweet circle of life moment that was and we all agreed. It was a delightfully warm moment and a sweet and happy day. Then we held Matty and Jen's California engagement party this past weekend. It was more than a celebration of their upcoming wedding, it was also a toast to Bart's remarkable ability to get cancer to back down!

Bart and I think he might be turning the corner on this pain situation and will be fit to fight by Monday. Onward to Creekside Lounge early morning but no chemotherapy today just hydration. The oncologist said Monday Bart will take on a new and improved chemo cocktail. It appeared that his body might have become resistant to the Xeloda/Gemzar combo so a switch up seems reasonable.

Bart's pump is working but now that he's regaining his strength he might need to tweak the dose just a bit because he has been using the boluses and Norco at times.

The Domperidone (Dom Perignon as we like to call it) appears to be working and a bit too well. Bart had to forego the Colace and Senna Lax in favor of Imodium AD. Dr. Piccolu-Choo also asked Bart to try the sample acid reducing pill again. Bart said he didn't have such a violent reaction like last time so perhaps the intense stomach pain was a result of other factors.

Today Bart did well as he usually does post Creekside hydration cocktails. He takes fewer oral narcotics, which is awesome, and the stomach cramping may be fading. It's very positive.

Bart's smiling at Phaddy dog. Phaddy's really quite playful for an older overweight canine sprung from prison. Matty concluded "Phaddy is definitely a big dog in a little dog body busting to get out".

Bart hollers at him because every doorbell on the television sends the dog into orbit. Suddenly Phaddy prances defensively (clueless) but somehow with purpose. It's funny. Then he throws that tense energy into his toy box and tosses the contents until he finds just what he wants. Tonight that poor Penguin took it in the shorts.

Bart's feeling pretty good although he's pale but alert and awake, more so than I am.

TGIF.

August 20

Bart was up and down all night Friday. He didn't sleep well and I could hear him retrieving meds from the safe just about every few hours. Last night before bed he took another one of those turbo-acid reducing sample pills that Dr. Piccolu insisted he try one more time.

Bart's now sure that he's not going to do that again. For some reason Bart's system does not tolerate the Prilosec. Bart finishes his course of antibiotics tonight. That might help because it could be that the antibiotic is killing his good stomach bacteria thus exacerbating the pain and distress. There's always some wild variable which is why we have to eliminate pain culprits one at a time.

Bart just didn't feel well today. We think his pain booster device should be adjusted up a bit and possibly his shipping and handling dose as well.

Tomorrow we'll assess his condition (post antibiotics) and without complications from that pesky acid reduction pill. Bart swears that sample pill created more problems than it cured. We had a lovely visit from a dear friend tonight. She and her wonderful sister made a freezer full of dream meals and shared with us! What a terrific idea - let someone else do all the grocery shopping and clean up and you just show up to prepare your meals and take them home to your freezer. Dallas especially liked seeing the cooking instructions right on top of the package. (Me too). It's Bedtime for Bonzos.

August 21

Saturday was another restless night for Bart. This morning he was clearly uncomfortable. He dutifully administered his booster but needed supplemental Norco a while later. Breakfast sometimes helps. Life cereal is always a favorite. Bart says it seems to settle well on an empty stomach. I like the name.

First thing Dallas reported was that the bathroom toilet seat had finally given up, busted hinges so he took it off. I think he practiced his drumming in there which evidently shortens seat life. I added toilet seat shopping to my Sunday errand list. While cruising the plumbing aisle at Home Depot, I found there is a plethora of interesting seat options with a wide price variations. For example, the cost of the slam proof seat doubles if you get the "removable for cleaning" option. I'm pretty sure removing the whole seat is NOT something I am inclined to do when cleaning the bathroom. Based on the fact that Dallas would be "seated" for another year I opted for two slam proof, concealed hinge models. The spare was a must.

Tonight I was especially sympathetic to Bart's condition because I had a stomach ache myself. I didn't like it at all, it's very inconvenient to not feel good.

Bart's reluctance to describe what he's feeling on a daily basis is clear. Bart is just focused on getting past the feeling.

Talking is too much effort. I can't imagine having a chronic tummy ache. It would most certainly make me mad. This evening there was but sparse conversation, pass the Tums. We'd hoped Bart would feel almost good by now, but it hasn't worked out that way. It was necessary to review the current treatment arrangement so we could choose the next plan of attack.

Clearly, we think a pump adjustment is necessary. In the hospital, Bart was likely still recovering from anesthesia and that might explain why the higher dose made him so sleepy. Next, we will compare notes with Dr. Piccolu-choo on the gastritis remedies. If Bart has negative symptoms from taking supplemental pain pills, then there's another trick we can try. It's a shot that blocks the effects of narcotics on the colon. That would be four injections Bart would have to handle per day. I asked if he was beginning to feel like a pincushion. So far, however, Bart's not had the usual symptoms, almost opposite. Still it's a puzzle as to why we can't get him feeling better.

Tomorrow Bart has his first Creekside Chemo in about a month. He'll get a new lab report card beforehand. We expect straight A's. The oncologist has identified a new chemical cocktail combination and we're eager to get with the program.

August 22

A Note from Bart:

Today started off a little rough. Stomach cramps, etc. But after several of my meds I was able to power through it then went for my "new" chemo regimen, Gemzar/Abraxane. It may be wishful thinking, but I think I feel better tonight. A little tired but we will see. This is an every other week regime. In the meantime my doctor wants me to have my blood tested every Mon-Wed-Fri. until further notice. No reason why yet other than my white blood cell count was a bit high.

I was able to eat a plate of cannelloni tonight and my appetite seems "semi-normal." Maybe this concoction will allow me to eat and gain a little weight. Since today was the first day we will have to wait and see but there are signs of promise.

There's nothing much else going on. My weight was up? (down?) to 133.4 Nice, eh?

I weighed more in ninth grade and I wasn't this tall then. So either I need to shrink in height or gain some poundage. My doc said I can try a weight gain shake. I feel like a weight lifter who isn't lifting weights.

Tomorrow I shall convey any relevant news after seeing my pain doc to have my pump dose raised.

Take care and God bless y'all, Bart

August 25

A Note from Bart:

Today has been a fairly good day. Not much stomach cramping and most of my back pain is handled. Let's hope this is a step forward.

I Spent much of the day trying to get all the teams (the ones who said they would play) in our fantasy football league to actually sign up. The season starts in less than 2 weeks and we need to schedule or draft so that folks can make whatever changes or trades they want or can. I'm anxious to see what kind of league we will have and what kind of team I will have.

I'll post more as it goes but I'm praying for a turn around here.

Love y'all and God bless, Bart

August 28

You'd think we were slacking around here. It's as though every moment is so action packed that by late evening I sink into my chair and promptly fall asleep.

Mr. D even had Good-n-Plenty for the road. (That's Bart's favorite candy du jour.) You see Bart tries all the fun size sweets in Creekside's candy bowl all week long and when one strikes his fancy he puts it at the top of my grocery list. Friday he definitely had "plenty."

Bart's latest Creekside schedule is three days a week. Monday it's chemotherapy then hydration and labs Wednesday and Friday. Evidently Bart's new chemo combo of Abraxane and Gemzar can cause elevated white blood cells so the oncologist wants to keep a close eye on his lab work.

Tuesdays are reserved for Dr. Payne's, pain control. Last Tuesday Dr. K doubled the bolus rounds in Bart's PTM (personal therapeutic maintenance device). The double potency gives Bart more control over his pain. It seems to have helped somewhat. Bart still relies on the occasional Norco and Dilaudid but not quite as often. He still takes the full complement of daily nausea meds (Zofran, Compazine and Lorazepam) plus the special Dom Perignon compound (Domperadone) for gastritis.

Then there are the supplemental pancreatic enzymes, allergy pills and other prescribed over the counter intestinal aids he takes. As for injections, there are two insulin shots and a daily Lovenox (blood thinner). Bart dutifully writes it all down so we don't have to rely on either of our absent short term memories.

Something must be working because Bart's cramping has decreased just a little bit but he's been extremely fatigued. Overall I think the double bolus has helped. Bart at least felt good enough to engage in some fantasy football recruiting. Football is good.

Bart has good days and bad days. He says that good days are usually stretches of a few hours where he's awake, he has mild or no pain and modest "shipping and handling" discomfort and so is able to eat well.

Today was not one of his good days. Bart just didn't feel well and there was no talking about it either. He did ask for his trusty sick bucket just in case. Bart felt hot for a while then he was cold but no fever, chills nor high blood pressure. His sugar levels were also within an acceptable range and he was drinking fluids.

Bart weighed 135 which is actually up a tiny bit. I worry because he's lost so much muscle but then again he's got a huge muscle in his head and that one hasn't lost an ounce. He's got one hell of a determined constitution. It's remarkable indeed. I picked a great guy.

Before bedtime Bart shared that his system seemed to be functioning somewhat better. We hope the trends continues.

No Creekside Cocktails

August 29

Creekside called this morning to cancel Bart's Monday chemo. There are too many nurses out sick. Bart said he was looking forward to chemo because he usually feels better after an afternoon of cocktails. Until tomorrow then.

Bart said he endured some inconvenient bouts of urgent toilet runs today so perhaps the chemo delay was just as well.

Bart and I did have some terrific news late this afternoon; however, when the text came in which started with, "Your son Dal", my heart dropped fast into my stomach. What was it this time? A tardy, or unexcused absence? Worse, an accident? Or was it a delinquent behavioral problem, vandalism, or other criminal activity?

It turns out Dallas was just eager to tell Dad and I that he had scored so high on his AP statistics coursework thus far that he had a 100 percent average in the class. Mind you it's less than a month into the school year, but hey! This was a celebratory moment, a red letter day, and a communication that elevated our spirits! Sweet victory! I was suddenly glad I relented and purchased the two-pack of high tech commuter coffee mugs at Costco Saturday, Dripless Wonders and Dallas had just earned that prize.

It's definitely Bedtime for Bonzos.

August 30

Walking through the door with groceries in tow I could tell right away that Bart was the best he's been all week. Creekside hydration cocktails were just what the doctor ordered. I was suddenly happy.

Bart communicated a craving for ravioli this evening so his wish was my command. While water boiled I hauled his dry cleaning in from the car.

We've always had a larger than life dry cleaning bill. For more than 20 years, Bart has insisted that all his slacks and shirts be done by pros. On this he will not bend. Jeans, tee shirts, undies, and socks are the only items of Bart's that are laundered at home. I guess he's witnessed one too many loads of laundry emerge permanently pink. I may flinch but have never denied him this cleaning luxury.

Bart wanted his stuff back from the cleaners right away. Why the rush? He has quite an extensive shirt wardrobe that should be exercised first, but I said nothing. Over the years, I've come to believe that Bart simply wants the full and complete collection of everything he owns at all times before deciding what to wear.

When Mr. Clean presented a massive wad of heavy hangers before me, he said with an ever so slightly apologetic tone, that'll be $75. I almost choked. That was $75 dollars for shirts that could be laundered at home. I'm thinking maybe it's time to revisit this practice. Bart has consistently maintained that his shirts be laundered because otherwise they wrinkle and shrink. Excuse me? If I may be so bold as to point out that Bart himself has shrunk by about 65 pounds and yet he's still concerned about shirt shrinkage?

I'll give him credit that he plans on gaining weight, but really?

Yes, really, one has to look sharp at the Creekside Cocktail Lounge. The only shrinkage that will be tolerated is tumor shrinkage, not shirts.

So be it, you've got to dress for success, and I get it. Case closed. I wonder if we have a pre-tax cafeteria plan for dry cleaning expenses?

August 31

A Note from Bart:

Well pain has been on a small hold for a couple of days and with it came a slight return in appetite. Hopefully this is a sign of things to come. I see my chemo doc for hydration on Friday then Monday I go for round 2 of this latest regime of chemo. I'm hoping for the best. Our next round with the pain doc is Tuesday. He will most likely up my daily dose slightly at that time.

I want to take this time to wish a very Happy Birthday to all my friends who had birthdays in August I forgot to send cards/gifts to. Rest assured you were all on my mind.

Sorry such a short post maybe more later.

God bless and love y'all, Bart

Chapter Seventeen

Not the Best or the Worst of Times

September 1

Not the best of days but not the worst either.

Bart says stomach discomfort comes and goes. He gets very sleepy. I don't press by asking how he feels because that's just annoying.

I can pretty much figure it out when he scurries hurriedly to the loo every hour or so and asks for Imodium AD. It makes me watchful for signs of dehydration. Could be that Bart needs some kind of buffer to temper the Dom Perignon stomach flusher capsules. We will explore the question with Dr. Piccolu next week.

Bart is eating but not a lot, it's slow and steady. He's not fit for the Red Hawk buffet just yet but he's working on it. Bart feels ok this evening but not good. Creekside is tomorrow which should make it a good Friday night.

Meantime, Dallas has taken after his siblings. He's memorizing all the songs from the "Goofy Movie" in his spare time. (We literally wore that VHS out from overuse.) I admit I know all the lyrics myself. The "Goofy Movie" was a really good film.

It had a strong plot and lots of adventure plus the catchy tunes. I think it's become a sort of fad among Dal's circle of high school senior friends. It's Dal's favorite movie.

In fact, Dallas wrote a happy list. I'll share it with you. Happy List: finding Sunny D in the fridge, having exact change, being home alone, his Grandma, socks without holes, Batman boxers, writing music, shants, mechanical pencils with lead, fingerless gloves, drumming, piano, waking up to find your parents have not been murdered, winter drum line, jazz combo, Manchester game, kittens, Mountain Dew, poker, basketball, and when strangers are polite.

I think that pretty much sums it up. We especially like the, "not being murdered" item.

Happy Labor Day

September 4

A good friend delivered our patient to the Creekside Medical building Friday. Bart leisurely made his way to the second floor Lounge. There he sat on the floor in the hallway, until somebody finally unlocked the door. Eventually a Lab Technician beckoned him from the waiting area. She did her thing, then instructed Bart that he was free to go. What? No Lounge service, no juicy cocktails, no hydration?

The oncologist gave the waitresses an early holiday release. Ms. Nurse Practitioner advised Bart to try and hold out until Saturday, then go to the Emergency Room for hydration because Creekside would not open again until Tuesday. Bart had never needed to bring his pain meds before, but he wished he had this time.

Timing is everything. From his perch on the floor, Bart had sent me an urgent text to come and get him. Unfortunately, right at that moment, I was on my way to my boss' office but because I had put the phone on silent, I had not heard the text come in. After my meeting, I immediately went looking for my phone to check for Bart messages, but it was gone! So I retraced my steps throughout the Capitol searching for it. I knew it had to be in the Capitol office somewhere, and it was. It was in a trashcan on top of somebody's leftover Tex Mex combo meal. What the...?

Meanwhile, back in the Creekside hallway, Dr. Piccolu, Bart's gastroenterologist, happened to walk by. Dr. Piccolu brought Bart in to his office and instructed his nurse to start hydration using one of his corner exam rooms. I arrived just as Bart got hooked up to the first bag. Bart absorbed three liters of fluid. Dr. Piccolu was the only person left in the office by that time.

After detaching the last bag of liquid goodness, Dr. Piccolu poked around but couldn't find a Band-Aid. He said, "this is embarrassing" but we were so grateful we didn't care one bit. Dr. Piccolu answered all my questions and validated many of my suspicions. We got tips on how to prevent diarrhea by changing the way Bart ingests the "Dom" (stomach emptying capsules) and OTC stuff too. We felt good about the game plan.

When we got home, there was an energetic game of "base-ketball" going on in our driveway, bases and scores drawn with sidewalk chalk. At least a dozen kids milling around. I cooked an extra-large lasagna in case we had to feed the teen team. Bart got dinner, took his overdue bolus and other meds. Once the pump boost and meds kicked in, Bart was on the upswing. Dr. Piccolu really saved our whole holiday weekend. Hydration was the key. Dr. Piccolu said to forget drinking water because only electrolyte drinks and salty snacks will do the trick. Dr. Piccolu says water follows salt. It just works.

Bart and I watched the nightly news and were intrigued as well as grossed out by the last story.

Some nut ball bit a sizable chunk out of a snake! The Python had to get 15 stitches. The Vet said he never treated a reptile for a human bite before. The Vet's expression was priceless but not as good as the interview with the snake biter himself. Locked up in orange overalls Mr. Clueless said he doesn't remember anything about a snake. Then added "but I get drunk and I gets crazy."

I guess too much drink sometimes isn't enough for some people!

Saturday was a good day by comparison. I stocked up on more electrolyte drinks and the "Dom" pill timing adjustment was implemented. Bart was successful at staying in front of the pain by keeping up with his pump bolus rounds and supplementing when needed. He ate ok, (he has a lot of ground to make up for in that department). He was awake and interactive for hours.

Tonight we have about four-five boys overnight, which is why I'm not asleep yet. We received a funny and appropriate card from my neighbor that read "Here kids, fresh towels for you to leave rotting on the floor. Enjoy your 12 seconds of clean." No more truer words never spoken.

Labor Day Indeed

September 6

Sunday was a decent day. Bart ate pretty well. I barely salvaged two out of 20 biscuits & gravy from the teenage breakfast rampage. Three out of four boys ate everything. The fourth kid got up late so he had to settle for pop tarts and frozen fare. Bart amazed me by following the biscuits-n-gravy with a small bowl of cereal.

The dog got a long but fast walk because the temperature was rising. Air conditioning is good. Sure glad we got that solar!

Bart brought up the issue of meal planning so we chatted about it. He and I both knew improvement was necessary. I decided the first step was to inventory every single thing in the freezers. From that revelation, menu planning for the next week was a lot easier. I'm sure there's an app for that. Don't think I'm not looking.

Between driving Dallas to and from his social engagements plus all the random errands on our family to-do list, I didn't get back home until the dinner hour. Bart's back was hurting so we fired up the heating pad and retrieved appropriate drugs from the safe. He ate a bit of dinner and rested up for bed.

Happy to report only three supplemental Norco in a 12 hour period and that's a new record. Unfortunately, nausea and intestinal discomfort made for a rather laborious Labor Day. Bart didn't eat particularly well as a result.

Dallas and friends had a homework sit-in today. I was impressed when I discovered that Dallas had cleaned up the whole downstairs region plus his upstairs room! Hope springs eternal.

A Note from Bart:

I went to two different docs today, pain management and chemo. Had my pain pump dosage increased and bolus amount increased as well. Next week they are adding a numbing agent to my pump when they refill it. This is supposed to numb things which sounds a lot like the celiac block which the oncologist wanted to do way back when. I will let you know how it goes. So far tonight my appetite has returned a little, I had a Wendy's Double Cheeseburger on the way home and I had some peach pie with ice cream for dessert. So far so good. However, the caveat here is I had my chemo, hydration IV, and saline. The cocktail (Hydration IV) typically has this effect on me. I will know more later.

So not to look a gift horse in the mouth I'm going to enjoy the lack of pain as long as it lasts.

Ok short but to the point. Take care y'all and know you are in my thoughts and prayers and my heart.

Love, Bart

Bart is doing fairly well tonight. He's crediting the pump increase with some minor relief. Here's how it went down.

Tuesday morning we departed early for the pain clinic. Much to Bart's chagrin I had to stop for gas. He hates delays. While cruising down Highway 50 Bart said something like "good job" or "nice going." I responded with exasperation explaining the reason for my lane change.

But he said he wasn't being cheeky this time! Wow, I must have learned a thing from my passenger coach. Again, hope springs eternal.

We passed a car with a curious license plate cover "Don't drive faster than Tinker Bell can fly". What the hell does that mean? If you drive too "Tinker Bell" fast, you'll smash her like a bug on your windshield? Bart just shook his head not understanding in what circles my mind travels. He said it meant your guardian angel would not be able to keep up with you. Tinker Bell, a guardian angel? Really? I don't think so. Why would any driver think that anyway and why put that on your car? Please clue me in.

Even with the fuel stop we made it to the appointment in exactly one hour, right on time thanks to the carpool lane. We then had to endure the mandated 30-35 minutes in the waiting area before being invited to wait another 10-15 in the exam room.

It saves a lot of time to fill out the four page pre-appointment survey forms beforehand. The receptionist doesn't consider you present until she's fed your forms through the card reader. Bart ordered me to turn them in because he was embarrassed and absolutely sure they would not be accepted. To say the documents were folded, spindled, and mutilated might be an understatement. The coffee stains I blame on that dumbass commuter mug.

As for the mangled rips and folds, I guess it's the price of storage in my car. Ms. Perky, the receptionist, hardly flinched. She confirmed that the data had recorded just fine. Bart owes me a quarter.

Dr. K upped Bart's daily dose another full step for the bolus device. After explaining Bart's symptoms, stomach pain versus back pain, use of supplemental narcotics etc., Dr. K conferred with Dr. Payne. They concluded that a numbing agent would be added to the Dilaudid mix next week. We both asked how that differed from the originally proposed celiac block. Dr. K asserted that a numbing agent in the pump was superior to a celiac procedure. (I'd say that too if I were in their shoes.)

By the time we got home, there was just enough time for Bart to take a catnap before leaving again. We had an afternoon reservation at the Creekside Chemo Lounge.

Bart was finished about 5:45 PM and had the bandages to prove it. Many of his veins either collapsed or wouldn't cooperate so there was a lot of poking going on. No matter how they got the juice into Bart's system it did help.

Tuesday night I kept waking up hearing things. At first I rationalized the noises but eventually I knew better and had to go outside to check it out. I grabbed a flashlight but couldn't see anything through the thick of Maple trees. I sure heard it though. It Sounded like a herd of raccoons, squirrels or opossums rustling and roughing up tree branches or some damn thing. The backyard gate was unlocked and wide open. That was not how we left it. I was sure.

I set the nozzle to stun and squirted the hell out of the trees. That's when Phaddy, from the safety of our master bedroom, suddenly realized he was a watchdog. He barked and howled. Our "special" dog didn't register a thing while I was stomping about on the decks earlier. Now he was ready to defend. Alas it was too late. All intruders were in safe hiding once again. This is war.

Wednesday Bart sent me a message at work, he felt mildly better. He thought we might be closing in on the magic pain number. We're anxious to see effects of the numbing agent painkiller/mix next week. Our goal remains: no pain.

I got home from work too late to cook. Bart needed prescriptions so it was almost 8:00 PM when I crossed the threshold at home. Dallas had thankfully taken Phaddy for a walk and cooked a pizza for his dad. Spending long days at work while the Senate is in its final weeks of session are the norm, but the end draws near. Winter break here we come.

I'm equipped with a new squirrel trap and the old smaller version for back up. We're going to catch us some varmints!

Bart says goodnight. I hope to follow but sometimes I stay up way too late at night just because I want to be alone with myself. There's a gamut of emotions to experience anyway, so I may as well allow myself that luxury in solitude. Occasionally I enjoy mindless computer activities lacking in any sort of redeeming social value or I torture the dog with attention. That dog would much rather I left him alone. Phaddy is definitely not a dog motivated by affection but he endures it and I think he might even be learning to like it just a microscopic bit.

It's Bedtime for Bonzos and chubby dogs.

September 10

Bart's had a good day. It's amazing what a good haircut (head shave) can do. Thank goodness Jeanne came down because Bart would never let me go near him with a razor. The sudden hair loss is due to the chemo drug Abraxane. Today we noted the absence of eyebrows. Bart forbids any pictures of the process this time. I think he's waiting until he packs on a few more lbs.

I will fill you in on the latest excitement tomorrow when Bonzos are awake and alert.

Never Forget 9-11

September 11

With respect, reverence and patriotism we remember lives lost September 11th. We also thank and honor our heroes, too many of whom gave the ultimate sacrifice doing their duty.

We will never forget. Thank you.

We've been focused on getting Bart to feel good enough to keep up the calories. His Creekside weigh in Friday was 131 clothes on. Today Bart boasted 135.

By process of elimination, we eventually figured out that the Dom Pernignon (Domperidone) stomach emptying drug might be doing more harm than good. Dr. Piccolu ordered another experimental compound that blocks the effects of narcotics on the colon, but it's hard to get and is not covered by insurance like the Dom. We will try everything else first before plunking down $400 bucks for another drug that might not help.

It was a good weekend all in all. Our friend Tracey, who had Creekside duty Friday, found the elusive size 31-32 jeans. A perfect fit, just enough room in the waist to allow for the pump.

Bart may have been exhausted but he experienced a bit less pain and a more tolerable level of gut ache. By employing appropriate over the counter remedies, Bart was able to maintain bodily functions and eliminate the Dom. Although he still had intervals where he felt poorly, it was most assuredly better than last week.

Today Bart sat outside in the sun for 15 minutes. I was thrilled. He needs to get out more. Don't need a vitamin D deficiency too. Next I'm working on getting him to walk to the mailbox and back. Getting him moving might just help his system too.

Tomorrow is a big day.

First the pain doctor appointment where Bart gets the pump refilled with Dilaudid and a numbing agent followed closely by Bart's oncology appointment with the oncologist then chemotherapy. I hope to get answers to questions from Dr. Piccolu, Gastroenterologist, pharmacy queries, case manager tasks etc. We're on a roll. As long as the scale shows progress and the next lab test reveals lower cancer markers we prevail. At least Bart doesn't have to study for that test. He went to bed early in anticipation of the day ahead.

In a postscript on the Tinker tale, leave it to Dallas to settle the question. Dallas confidently said T. Bell is Peter Pan's guardian angel so Bart is right. There you have it.

Much love to you all, and may your guardian angel fly straight and keep up.

September 12

A Note from Bart:

This will be short but sweet, I hope. We went to the pain doctor and my chemo doc today. The pain doctor changed out my meds in the pump and added a numbing agent. Due to the use of the pump/catheter it will take 24 hours for the agent to begin working. As usual they are starting out slowly so I have to go back next week to adjust the dose but I'm hoping for big results.

From the chemo end, we are pretty much on hold. I'm taking Abraxane with Gemzar and doing testing, labs, CT scan and checking cancer markers soon. I can only say that if it's doing to the cancer what it's doing to my body, cancer must be getting it's butt kicked.

I'll let you guys know as soon as I figure out how the numbing agent works.

God bless y'all,

Love, Bart

September 13

Hallelujah! I am happy to report that Bart's had a few pretty good days.

Monday Dr. K refilled Bart's pump with Dilaudid and a numbing agent. It took 24 hours for the old medication to travel through the catheter before the new mix went into effect. That was clear but the fact that the bolus device wouldn't work for 24 hours was not. It would be back to the safe for pain pills during the daylong interim.

Bart went straight to Creekside Lounge for hydration Monday after his pump refueling. He weighed in on their scale at 131, to which I queried whether he was padding the home scale readings.

Bart has taken fewer oral narcotics over the last two days especially today because his bolus device is responding again. Stomach cramping and overall debilitating pain was less. I do believe we have turned a corner on this pain management. Bart even got outside for 15 minutes yesterday and walked to the mailbox. Tuesday Bart did not get sun kissed nor did he venture to the mailbox but easy does it. This is progress. Life is good.

The only frustration Bart may have had recently was perhaps witnessing my consistent inability to fold up sunshades. I battle with those wiry things like it's a badger attacking me in the face. Bart says "Way to go Slick Weeds, no wonder the shade thing is all bent up" adding "What is this, hire a *spaz* day?" (Bart actually used a less politically correct term for my perceived special ed challenges.) Several times Bart grabbed the sunshades from my hands and folded them up in a half second. He's got skills.

Tomorrow we welcome Bart's eldest daughter from North Carolina and her family. It's been at least a decade or so since we've seen her. Phaddy even went to the beauty salon for this auspicious occasion. And my new labeled freezer shelves and frozen inventory sheet made meal planning easier.

We should also know better if the numbing agent proves effective in controlling residual discomfort by tomorrow night. So far, so good and we are ever encouraged.

September 15

Bart's having a good week. He takes only a few oral narcotics per day and his gastritis is far better. He still must take an assortment of nausea meds but that's routine maintenance stuff now. It's a definite improvement on the pain front. Good times.

En route to pick up Bart's daughter and family from the airport hotel today we got a call from the school. Dallas was sick. He had to hang in there until after lunch. After our company got settled I took Dallas to the doctor. Sure enough, strep throat. Back at home it's a mad dash sterilizing everything Dallas may have touched. Quarantine again, alas. But, there's a silver lining here.

Dallas really did ask the doctor (heard it with my own ears) when he could go back to school? He said he didn't want to miss his stats test and he had an essay to turn in.

Did I hear that correctly? Yes, I heard it, and heard it correctly too. He didn't want to miss a test or turn in an essay late. There is a God.

Bart joined us all at the table tonight. Dallas didn't mind a bit having to miss our family dinner. He was free to play his strep tainted video game in solitude. We got to meet our 10 year old granddaughter, Cheyenne, for the first time today. She shyly talked to me about how she likes to kick.

Ok. I asked her to show me. To my amazement Cheyenne had a mighty good side kick for a young lady with no prior Taekwondo training. I showed her a few more techniques and next thing we knew, she's asking to go to a class. So Sandi turned down the flames on the pasta pot. With dinner on hold, I took her to my TKD school. My fifth degree pal Mrs. J. got Cheyenne a uniform and off she went to her first white belt class. The kid even earned her first stripe by reciting the tenets of TKD by memory. I think I've found a protégé'.

Needless to say, her family was very proud. Bart has enjoyed today's visit with daughter Melissa. She sat with her dad on the back deck (with the misters on) and even coaxed him to walk to the mailbox. Phaddy dog got into the act with a walkabout of his own and an exuberant game of fetch with our dog loving guests.

The after dinner conversation was good and then it was the usual Bedtime for Bonzos announcement. (I'm only up this late because those damn critters were squeaking and hollering, again the traps lie empty. More peanut butter I guess.) May you rest without rodents to rustle your slumber.

September 16

A Note from Bart:

Good evening y'all. Today was a much better day, overall, than many of the past. I had little if any pain that I couldn't manage with my bolus and the Norco. I feel like maybe, just maybe we could be turning the corner. I've been taking fewer Norco, I do however, use all my boluses. So a little more tweaking may be required there. Other than being down 65 pounds I feel almost like I did before all this started. Weaker, more tired, but all in all better. My pain level on a scale of zero-ten was about a 1 today. Oh other than the bowel issues. ;-)

Kathy, in response to your post, it depends what we catch. We might eat it. ;-p Thanks so much for writing on Caring Bridge. It makes me feel good and even laugh to read what you write.

As ever you know if I post it's going to be short and sweet so that's about it from me. I have my next round of chemo on Tuesday then I should get a CT scan shortly after to see what kind of progress we are making. I will let y'all know how things go.

Love to all and God bless, Bart

September 21

We will bid adieu to Melissa's family at the airport Wednesday morning. It has been a big week. It was wonderful for father and daughter to catch up and for us to get acquainted with Melissa's family. We hope Cheyenne can continue her Taekwondo training as a white belt back in North Carolina.

Bart has been reporting good days of late. He's been getting outside more and even trekking to the mailbox more often. Perhaps it was Melissa's encouragement combined with his lowered pain levels that did it. Either way, it's an excellent development. I hope to get time tomorrow to tell Bart all about the cancer seminar Jeanne and I attended over the weekend. It was such an educational event but also inspirational and ever encouraging that better days may come.

September 22

A Note from Bart:

Well, after a very hectic nine days of family visiting and a seemingly never ending stream of visitors we finally have some peace and quiet. It wears me out to have too much excitement going on around me. It's nice to have visitors but I need an equal amount of down time to recharge.

I had two doctor appointments today. Not much to report but my pain pump main dosage was increased just a tiny bit to try and get off too many boluses (extra doses). The 24 hour increase was equivalent to one and a half boluses. This should allow me to have less pain with fewer oral narcotics.

Not much to report beyond that. I'm feeling a little better the last few days just a little tired (chemo) and nauseous (also chemo). I should get another CT scan in a week or so to confirm if this latest chemo is working.

Everyone have a great day.

Love y'all and God bless, Bart

Super Saturday

September 25

What a good day! Bart had low pain levels, he only used a few of the available boluses on his pain pump and just one or two Norco. He took advantage of cooler temperatures too. We walked well beyond the mailbox and back. While I took the dog hiking on the trail, Bart soaked up some sunshine on our deck.

Bart even ate a heart balanced diet. After dinner, I prepared a lovely handcrafted fruit and yogurt parfait which he gladly consumed, yet later he requested Apple Hill pie for another dessert, a la mode. Food is fun again. Hope your weekend is as full of simple pleasures.

September 26

A Note from Bart:

I've had a pretty good day today. I had two, count 'em, two helpings of hamburger helper. Had some cereal and some "snacks" (real candy). I am running low on my Good & Plenty. I'll have to contact my dealer. :-). All in all I'm doing a little better. Never want to say "I'm doing great" because fate has a way of biting you in the ass. I walked to the mailbox and a little way down the street and sat in the sun for about 15 minutes. I think sitting in the sun helps.

If I can continue in this vein I have reason for optimism. CT scan is scheduled for October 10th. We should find out then if the tumor is shrinking. I think it is, because another side effect I've noticed is my blood sugar levels are down without using too much insulin. They are lower than they have been in a while and almost in the normal range. This gives me hope for some change, and those of you who know me know what I'm saying. ;-)

Keep all those thoughts and prayers coming. I'm sure they are working.

Love y'all Bart

September 29

A Note from Bart:

Sorry for the lag in posting. I have been fairly good. I've had more good days than bad. It's small steps. I've been sitting in the sun every day when it's not over 100 and taking small walks (just past the mailbox).

I'm eating more (slightly) and trying to not just maintain this weight but actually gain some. :-) I just found out my mom who is 5' nothing outweighs me. Dang! But I hope I'm turning a good corner. A lot of the calories I get are "empty" calories (candies, pies, etc.) but at least they are calories. I'm drinking an Ensure or Glucerna every day to try and gain more weight. I have to balance my intake of these calories with my diabetes but so far my blood sugars have been stable.

Dallas is doing well his senior year. He seems to have had an "aha" moment and decided to buckle down and do all his work. I'm glad.

Since this is more than I normally write I will sign off and hope to read your comments. They make me laugh and keep me going forward. As always my thoughts and prayers are with you.

God bless and love y'all, Bart

Chapter Eighteen

A Drop in the Bucket

October 1

Life in the Reagan household is pretty normal these days. Mr. Reagan has taken to expressing his cantankerous and opinionated sides with more regularity, very reassuring indeed. The last few days he's been eating like he means it too. The scale, according to Bart, read 137 this morning. No pain means weight gain in our situation. We like this trend.

Bart still administers a few daily pain pump boosts but rarely all four like he used to. The few Norco tablets are directed at the usual over 50 stuff, shoulder and joint pain, not cancer.

Bart got his tanning time on the deck today but no walk to the mailbox. There is the unpredictable digestive system that keeps him close to the facilities. We are working on the magic diet to settle the system.

Dallas has his usual gaggle of friends over this weekend. I identified eight tonight at last head count. I'm getting good at finding the best price for the largest quantity of frozen pizzas anywhere and certain off-brand drinks as well.

It's not only wayward teenagers we attract around here apparently. We now have rats as well! The teens spotted one boldly showing off at a downspout while they were out playing basketball.

Mr. Squirrel still remains elusive and now we think raccoons have joined in late night raucous shenanigans. Phaddy is on the case; nonetheless we are considering calling in the big guns.

Bart's doing pretty well, sleeping a lot better too. He has a down day now and then but is mostly up these days. October 10th is our report card date with the anticipated CT scan. We look forward to a good score, markers below 5000 and of course much shrinkage.

October 4

A Note from Bart:

Hi all,

Well we got the much anticipated markers and it wasn't good news. The CA 19-9 marker was over 10000 after being under 5000 from a high of >61000. First time it's gone back up like this. According to Dr.J we don't need to worry until we get the CT Scan (next Monday the 10th); he says that is the definitive answer). My bride is correct I seem to be having more good days than bad (slightly) and most of the Norco is directed at over 60 pain. I know she was being kind saying over 50 but that was a long time ago. ;-)

So I'm not going to fret until I see the results of the CT scan. If that is negative then they will reevaluate the regimen I'm on and possibly switch me up.

I've been enjoying a respite from the summer heat as our first fall storm of the season has arrived. It's cold-ish weather with some rain. I like it; I enjoy this type of weather.

I'm not going to stress about the CA marker until we get the results. Since I'm feeling better overall I can't help but think this is an aberration.

Y'all hang in there and keep those posts coming.

God bless and love y'all, Bart

October 5

Midweek Drips

Bart's been great. For the better part of a year, he has endured acute pain and severe discomfort. It's wonderful to see him human again. Even the small rise in cancer markers (up 5,000 to 10,000) does not worry us much. We began this journey at 67,000. We believe the uptick is like a sine wave on a path trending down. It's just a little beaver brush in the creek. It slows the flow but still runs to the sea.

Nowadays Bart is awake during the day, eating well and sleeping so much better at night. Life is good. It may not be quite as good for poor Dallas, however. Let me explain.

We have had a lot of teen boys over lately, and one day after school, two friends were cooking cheese pizza. I was mildly puzzled because these boys are all about the pepperoni. Normally cheese pizzas were reserved for our vegetarian girlfriend. Maybe they already ate the other four pies? The boys said Dallas instructed them to cook it. It was curious but ok, no big deal.

The following weekend, Dallas was being grumpy and quiet. He was so listless that I agreed to pick up friends and take as many as we could cram into the Red Dragon with us on our Sunday shopping excursion. We needed to find Jazz Band performance clothes, black shirt, slacks and a white tie. The company of his "bros" might cheer him up. It didn't. I finally cornered him in the Halloween shop behind some Styrofoam gravestones.

With his chin quivering Dallas told me that his girlfriend broke up with him. Well that explained the cheese pizza. It had been a week or two since we'd seen her. Dal would tell me she was on a field trip. I said "really long field trip" and left it at that. Alas, I suppose all good things must come to an end but it would have been great had it lasted a while longer. Dallas was doing so well. My sister would say that Dallas with her was like Dallas with adult supervision. Sunday was like a day of mourning. At one point that evening I think we were all crying.

Dal refused to do his homework and never wanted to go to school again. Both Bart and I stopped by his room at bedtime. Dallas' face was buried in pillows. I sat on the corner of his bed for a little while. He uttered "this really sucks". Agreed. I made some meager attempt to console him. He'll meet a lot of new friends in college, blah, blah, blah. It hurts, but in high school I think it's sort of a rite of passage.

Hearing the sobs of heartbreak late at night was sad. Such is life. We will most definitely miss that young lady's presence in our home. I could weep a little just writing that. I need to "Ranger up" here. Geez.

Wednesday was not such a good day. Maybe it's the sudden change in weather, but whatever the case, Bart was definitely under it. Not a good day for calorie consumption either, some hot soup and a warm blanket was about it. After preparing a quick dinner, I went to Dallas' jazz band/choir concert. He sounded great.

I could hear the drums but never saw the drummer. They're always in the back obscured by music stands and musicians.

Bart sent a text during the performance with news that Steve Jobs had passed away. I immediately thought how awful that must feel to know that

Jobs had the same disease and he died. I had to think about what to say when I got home.

Sure enough Bart was still thinking about Jobs when I came through the door. First thing he said was "That guy had the means to get the best medical treatment money can buy and he still died". I sat on the floor by his chair and said "Bart that may be so, but I don't know Steve Jobs, but I do know this, he's no Bart Reagan. Everybody's journey is different."

Then I had to jump up and get to the pharmacy. It was almost closing time. Tonight's order would fill up a paper grocery bag.

Bart looked mildly better when I got back but didn't feel much better. If only he would toss toys for the Phadmeister, I'm sure he'd perk up. Bart always grins at the senior pup's enthusiasm for play, but doesn't participate himself. The dog knows who the players are and there's only one, me. Phaddy plays fetch, tug of war, and even hides toys under my chair or the coffee table barking until somebody retrieves them, and the cycle repeats. He has assuredly trained me, not the other way around. Ok, that's the last retrieval of the night.

Phaddy has finally parked himself under Bart's legs and is curled up on the sheepskin. I guess it's bedtime.

Bart's Report Card

October 9

Tomorrow is the big test, Bart's CT scan. His instructions are to eat breakfast by 8:00 AM, and gulp 32 ounces of water prior to the 10:00 AM procedure.

The pictures reveal the effectiveness of Bart's current chemotherapy treatment more so than cancer markers. Results will help to determine the best course of treatment moving forward.

Bart had a pretty good weekend while I was in Weaverville. A dear friend surprised him with some fabulous food so he ate well and did not partake of many oral narcotics for breakthrough pain.

Dallas even had some encouraging news. He is going to the Ponderosa High Homecoming dance at the end of this month. A young lady (friend of a friend's girlfriend) accepted his invitation. Dad and I were rather surprised and pleased. This will be the first high school dance where Dallas will actually be escorting a date. I guess he's back in the game.

Monday Maniacs

October 11

So much for that weather girl's confident prediction last night: 50 percent chance of spotty showers, more like 100% heavy and constant rain all day. A semi-dry Bart dutifully checked in at the radiology counter while I parked the car. In the waiting room, I read the old fashioned newspaper while Bart surfed high tech news online via his fancy phone. Interesting how we gravitate to opposite ends of the technical spectrum. Bart says that he prefers to read books on an iPad now too. No need for a lamp or night light, font is adjustable, easy scroll versus book holding/page turning and it goes to sleep when you do. I do see the benefits.

The scan took a couple of hours. It was a long wait and then technicians shot extra pictures. Bart wondered why but did not ask. The nurse thought to leave Bart's IV in place to make it easier on him and the Creekside nurses but no one answered their phone so she plucked it out. If there's no harm and it saves the patient from being stuck umpteen times hunting for a vein already found, why not? Probably some litigious reason. On the way home we talked about the next step: stay the course, change protocols, or return to what worked. It's not time to worry. Bart felt relatively decent despite getting dosed with contrast fluid. He wanted a slice of leftover pizza for lunch. I caught up on my work, Bart with his fantasy football and before long we were off again to Folsom Creekside.

While he got hooked up to his IV cocktail, I checked in on a new prescription awaiting authorization. At his last visit to the clinic, Bart received an uptick in pain relief. He snoozed so frequently afterwards that I thought he might have narcolepsy. The latest script would counteract severe drowsiness caused by the other stuff he takes. That drug was denied, however, so the doc has Bart testing out a low dose of ADD meds (very familiar to us). So far so good.

Bart printed a dinner recipe he found appealing which I prepared thanks to my neighbors who happened to have the cancer fighting onion I needed. Froze two servings and tonight Bart ate a full helping of the vegetable chicken biscuit casserole.

I also heated up some leftover crescent dogs for the boys downstairs and chose to deliver them myself since they were all diligently doing their homework. That's when I happened to discover the disaster in the downstairs bathroom. When you have a lot of other things to do, very little time to do them, and then something horribly messy and unexpected occurs, that defines stress. I literally have no time for this sh*&@. Nobody said a word about the brutally clogged toilet. When I asked about it, all three of them blamed Alec, who conveniently wasn't there tonight. Alec is nonetheless on probation and the rest of them have been warned. No excessive TP consumption without corresponding courtesy flushes. Dallas and I both had a go at vigorous plunging but to no avail, too far gone. A plumber will have to be called, damn it.

Speaking of unexpected aggravation, teens, then dogs are the usual suspects. Phaddy suddenly appeared at the back door with a new dreadlock sort of look. I think he had been frenetically searching deep in the red clay mud for a dried bit of toast or biscuit. Days ago I'd thrown some out for the birds. This wasn't a pretty picture.

Phaddy had what appeared to be red clay turds hanging from his whiskers. This dog would first rub his dirty face and filthy body on the carpet. That means I must administer the emergency bath before irreversible stains set in. Sleepiness is setting in too so I'd better hurry.

October 12

It's a Red Letter day.

Bart used only one nausea pill (normal 3-4/day) zero Norco and no boluses either! He made two trips to the mailbox too. Hearing that is exciting. The halo from a Creekside "juicing" never lasted this long before. It's the simple pleasures.

Tuesday/Thursday are TKD nights (for life) so I try to prepare something quick for dinner or serve leftovers. Bart relayed that Dallas would be going to a college fair at Union Mine High School and because I had class he had a special request for dinner.

I got off the bus and drove to the market to fill Bart's order. At checkout I was so tempted to explain to the clerk that these boxes of bad food marching toward him on the conveyor belt were not really for me. It's embarrassing to admit that I fixed hamburger helper for Bart but he asked for it.

At least Dr. Piccolu assured us that extra salt in Bart's case is just fine. Thank goodness for small favors.

I got home from TKD at 9:00 PM ready to finally relax and find a bite to eat. Bart had other ideas. He insisted I execute an online bill pay first. I objected, bad timing but he aptly retorted "You need to know how to do this stuff right now in case I pull a "Jobs" on you". Point taken and humor appreciated.

Bart said he was too busy fixing my laptop today to call Creekside. Likewise, I didn't call either. It's a mystery when we might get the results of the Monday CT scan. Stay tuned.

Profuse thanks to those of you who looked in on Bart while I was in Weaverville over the weekend. The trip to see my mom and high school pals was such fun and would not have been possible without you. Bart is good about posting his needs online through our community of helping hands.

The social time Bart enjoys with each of you is invaluable and a big part of the healing process. The time with you is something he always looks forward to.

October 13

It's one good day and one bad. Today there were no mailbox journeys, no outdoor patio pauses, and definitely more pain and nausea pills than yesterday. It's curios how conditions change so quickly. Tonight Bart had additional discomfort around his abdominal pain pump protrusion. I applied a Lidoderm patch to the pump bump to see if that would alleviate some of the pain.

On the bus ride home from work, I happened to check my home email. I reread the message from my lovely daughter-in-law to be and discovered the deadline for fitting Dallas for a tuxedo was today, October 12th. So much for preparing the salmon filet I'd set out to thaw this morning. I asked Bart to check Men's Warehouse hours and he reported back that it's open until 9:00 PM. Dallas and I got to the store at about 7:00 PM. Coordinating pick up and drop off of a tux in a state you've never visited is much more complicated that you might think.

No CT results yet. Bart has a scheduled appointment next Monday. I hope we can reach the oncologist tomorrow to see what results we can get before then. Bedtime and I've got to step outside to cool off. Indoor thermometer says it's not 110 degrees in here, so it must just be me.

October 15

Bart said his day was ok. He thanks Mr. D and the waitresses at Creekside Lounge for the TGIF evening. Bart stayed awake past midnight. We enjoyed friends and sister Sandi for a fun impromptu evening. Those are always the best, no pre-planning just doing, and when your friends fix the toilet that's even better.

The four teenagers present for the reopening of downstairs teen facilities got the word that if they clog it they had better be able to fix it. I reiterated the rule: courtesy flush first. Teens and homeowners (us) are forever grateful.

One good turn deserves another. Toilet may be fixed but my reliable central vacuum stopped working properly. The brushes don't turn. I can't even figure out how to take the casing off to check for a busted belt. Why are these gadgets hermetically sealed and the instructions fail to address the very problem you are having? But I'm off on a tangent.

I'd best wake sleeping beauty for bedtime before he becomes a mouth breather.

A Note from Bart:

I'm filling in for my bride who had a very tough day. She went to a garage sale, shopped at Bel Air twice and spent three hours doing karate pre-testing. ;-)

So she asked me to fill in events of a fairly (okay) uneventful day.

I had some good moments and some not so good but all in all average. I watched a little college football, the American League Championship Series game six, which had the Texas Rangers advance to the World Series.

Mel made us an apple pie from Boa Vista in Apple Hill, I can't wait to have a slice with ice cream. Tomorrow we get the results from last week's CT scan. Keep your prayers coming.

Thanks and God bless all love y'all, Bart

Monday so it must be Creekside

October 17

Bart did fairly well over the weekend. He did minimal pill taking but he does think the numbing agent in the pump needs to be dialed down a tad. He's feeling tingly in all the wrong places.

Bart had general discomfort and stomach unrest. He was looking forward to getting hooked up right away so he could feel better. That's the usual routine on chemo Mondays, but not today. Bart weighed in at 133.6 pounds. Then we were seated in the oncologist's office and 35 minutes passed before the doctor joined us.

He plunked down a huge file about a foot thick, sat down and logged onto his computer. I asked, "Is that Bart's file? It's so huge." The oncologist responded in his soft-spoken accent "Yes it is. Bart does everything big. I've been here ten years and that is Bart."

The oncologist told us Bart's cancer markers went up. We bottomed out at 4500 but today they were up to 15,000. That meant the Abraxane chemotherapy drug wasn't working and a change is indicated.

He said the CT scan showed growth in all tumors, pancreas, liver, and even small lesions in Bart's lungs and on the outside of his stomach. We didn't even know about the lung tumors before! The oncologist said that the lung lesions were small but the fact that they grew was not good. The oncologist calmly explained that we had already been through most of the appropriate chemotherapy regimens.

He and his colleague at UCSF recommended a Genetic clinical trial. The oncologist handed me a blue sticky note with a number to call. I was positive we had handouts The oncologist gave us more than a year ago with chemo drug options we had not tried yet. He acknowledged that, barring any experimental clinical trial, we could try Tarceva. Bart has not been treated with that one yet.

What about going back to what worked best, Gemzar plus Tarceva? Bart thought the oncologist's expression and body language meant that he didn't think it would work. How do we know? We haven't tried it yet? Gemzar was certainly an old favorite. We had the most success with Gemzar-Xeloda.

Bart had to go. He excused himself because he couldn't wait a moment longer for the bathroom. I stayed behind to ask the oncologist a few more questions. What other trials are available, what about all the other drugs I read about that we haven't used yet? Had he talked to Bart about his prognosis? The oncologist said he didn't want to dampen the spirit of hope in his patients. The way he delivered that sentence I could read between the lines. I heard the oncologist clearly through his eyes.

The oncologist expressed that Bart is one of his most amazing patients, and that largely due to his stoic attitude and determined constitution, Bart is alive and kicking. He told me this news is not good, but we're not entirely out of tricks yet. I get the mission. We cannot let these cancer markers rise again. He nodded and said "call that number and we will confer Wednesday".

Bart was already settled into a lounge chair by this time. He looked up at me with an expression that said, not the news we were hoping for, was it? No, but we've got options. I told him "I'll be back."

I went outside to make calls. All four clinical trial studies were full, San Francisco, Arizona, Washington, and Massachusetts. I marched back into Creekside Lounge to intercept the oncologist between patients. I caught him, and explained. He said he would check with UC Davis and Stanford then we'd meet again Wednesday.

I asked about starting Bart on Tarceva/Gemzar today but he said no, we would wait until Wednesday to devise a plan. I reported to Bart that he couldn't start another treatment until we know for sure there is no other appropriate clinical trial for which he might qualify.

On the drive home, we talked a little about how far we've come and what we might do. He said he would make a list of things I needed to know. We acknowledged the seriousness of the situation, but also agreed that anything can happen and we are not done yet. Bart said he never ever fathomed something like this. Neither did I.

Dallas was doing his laundry when we got home. He responded to the look on my face and said, "yes, really." In the mailbox, we zeroed in on a familiar window envelope from Ponderosa High School - progress reports. In the past, these have generated much anxiety and stress. Tonight, two A's and the rest B's. Bart and I recognized two solid positive occurrences for the day. We thought two out of three isn't bad.

I cooked salmon cakes for dinner, a recipe I mixed and pattied this morning, because they sounded good to Bart. I still have the mess to clean up, but it will wait. Bart's making notes, checking email and life is good this evening. He will research clinical trials etc. tomorrow while I am at work. We will compare notes with the oncologist on Wednesday.

Bart is feeling ok tonight, just disappointed, which is understandable. Still, there's always football and he's invited me to watch recorded programs together when I'm done posting here. So that's a wrap. We will be in touch.

Love, Mel and Bart

October 18

Tonight's post includes Tuesday's entry too. It was lost on a cyber-clipboard. I woke up Tuesday night with my computer on my lap and a vague recollection that I had finished the Caring Bridge composition. Obviously, it wasn't there this morning and my document was blank. That stupid mouse failed to click paste (I have trouble with rodents of all sorts). Bart was still in bed Tuesday morning when I left for work. He whispered, "stay in touch via email." I left his insulin needle and a bowl full of cereal. That left seven minutes to get to the bus stop.

Later that morning when I hadn't received an email from Bart, I checked in. He was feeling down but ok otherwise.

He bravely declared, "I will call my mother today."

I could certainly understand Bart's mood, but there was more to it than his own disappointing news. Bart's best chemo buddies, Larry and Bill, had not been at the Lounge lately. He was afraid to ask. Nurse Mindy finally said it's not been a good year. Both Bill and Larry were no longer with us. Two new friends lost. The three Lounge lizards, Bart, Larry, and Bill had bonded over long conversation, a shared diagnosis of pancreatic cancer, and hours of IV cocktails. Their absence was a lot to process.

A dear friend gave me direction on regional research trials. As a result, we are prepared with our own list of available trials to share with the oncologist on Wednesday. Bart will also be sharing more President Reagan commemorative jelly belly packets, always a big hit with lounge patrons and staff.

October 19

Bart's Creekside weigh in today was 135. I credit the two course breakfast, cereal and Texas French toast. Bart was given the choice of getting hooked up before meeting with the doctor or after. He jumped at the chance to get the feel good juice first. I was reticent because once he's in the lounge chair, there's no privacy to talk to the doctor and ask questions. Bart said he could carry his IV to the office, but the doctor sometimes just talks to him in the lounge. That's exactly what happened. I handed him a printout, while dropping several other sheets of paper which flew like paper airplanes under two recliners. The oncologist said yes, that's the one. By the time I gathered up fly-away papers from under the chairs, he was gone. Again, why can't we discuss this in his office? He can't escape as easily there. Bart assured me it was fine and sent me away. I had errands to run and he said we would talk to the oncologist later.

When I returned to the Lounge hours later, Bart informed me that he didn't qualify for any of the available trials, not one. The new plan is to put Bart on a course of Gemzar and oral Tarceva. We had enjoyed success with Gemzar before, and yet that was precisely the reason why Bart did not qualify for the trials. No prior Gemzar treatments allowed.

Well, at least that's settled and we have a game plan.

On the drive home, Bart wondered aloud why the oncologist's first choice was a clinical trial before trying the Gemzar-Tarceva combo. See? That's why we need to meet in his office and not in front of a lounge chair. Bart says he'll ask him next time.

Driving up our road Bart asked me to take it extra slow and easy and keep it under 20 mph. There are too many bumps and divots that bounce and torture his poor bony body. Pain and discomfort inflicted from the damn road, and even in our nicest car. Suddenly, I was mad. Why is it that we get this crappy chip seal when El Dorado Hills gets nice smooth asphalt? Answer me that street people?

Bart can never ride in the Red Dragon.

At home, Bart told me he would begin writing a list of things I'd need to know and do. He said it would be hard for me to read. I responded affirmatively saying, "Yes your handwriting has always been very hard to read." That's when I got the look that said, "That's not what I meant." Oh, a different kind of hard to read. "Still, you'd better type it in the computer". I laughed, he smiled. It was a funny little moment.

Thursday is done, TGIF

October 20

Bart had an ok day. He said he got a lot done on the computer, but did not take in any sunshine or a mailbox run. I got home about 5:45 PM. There were four boys downstairs waiting for Dallas to return from his counseling appointment. I took reservations for dinner, and all elected to dine at the Reagan café.

I prepared spaghetti with meatballs, also pesto pasta, and crescent rolls. Bart ate a small bit of spaghetti, one meatball, and four crescent rolls! I cleared the outdoor table, lit the candles, and had the boys dine outside on the deck. They seemed to have a good time at their cool candlelight dinner outside. Their conversation, however crude, was very clever and creative. At one point, I apologized for momentarily joining them outside.

After dinner, the boys rinsed their dishes and I dressed for TKD. I got back about 8:45 PM. Bart was still awake and ready for us to watch a program together. I changed, then ran around opening windows. When in Dallas's room, I felt something moist on the bottom of my foot. Sure enough, that darn dog had "marked" the beanbag. Arrgh!

Dal got home right on time from driving his friend home. If we've said it once we've said it a thousand times, "keep the bedroom door closed." For Phaddy to confuse that room with a toxic dump might not be that much of a stretch, but geez when will he stop? A professional carpet cleaning is definitely in our future.

Bart rolled up a newspaper with rubber bands and called it the Phaddy-whacker. He said that slapping the floor with it would be enough to frighten the dog into submission. Meanwhile, Phaddy was trying to stuff his prized vinyl hamburger on and under my chair, which Bart said was dog-speak for trying to make up to me for his "accident" in Dal's room. When I ignored the canine long enough, however, Phaddy tensed up, stared at the thing and barked. Bart doesn't like the barking so he got the Phaddy-whacker out and whacked the floor with a stern "no."

We are not sure the dog really got the correlation of that, or anything else for that matter. Dogs just want to have fun.

It's trash night and to miss it is a cardinal sin. Dallas gathered up most, but there's still his "poop deck" job to add to the bin. Meantime Bart has announced it's Bedtime for Bonzos.

Tomorrow is hydration at Creekside, then TGIF.

Weekend Update with Bart Reagan

October 22

Friday at Creekside Bart got topped off for the weekend. He was also told that UCSF will call us to schedule a consultation with their pancreatic cancer specialist. Last attempt at a UCSF consultation we ended up two weeks in ICU. Hopefully the stars will align correctly this time.

Bart's doing fairly well. He taps at least two bolus supplements per day and an occasional pain pill with his nausea meds. Perhaps the frequency of football and baseball on TV plays into his better mood.

Saturday morning we awaited the arrival of the newest prescribed drug, Tarceva. It arrived on schedule at 9:22 AM. Tarceva is a targeted cancer treatment in pill form, not a chemo drug. It blocks the activity of a specific protein that cancer cells need in order to grow and divide.

The little wrinkle with this drug is that Bart can only take it on an empty stomach. That means he must stop snacking a couple hours before bedtime. It's not ideal to limit any calorie intake, but that's the deal. We cram calories into him earlier now. This morning Bart ate the usual cereal then I prepared his old favorite, biscuits and gravy. It was a bonus breakfast for the boys.

While Bart engaged in television sports, a friend and I ventured to Cielo Estate Winery and staffed the grill for their Grape Stomp event. The weather was beautiful. Bart couldn't believe they let me cook. To prove it, my pal made a house call, delivering Bart a burger hot off the grill. Wonders never cease.

This evening, Sandi brought over a delicious Spanish meal with green chilies from her garden. We supplemented this culinary delight with pizzas for the basketball boys who were playing outside on the driveway. I went out to see how many boys were staying for dinner. It was odd how the boys suddenly became motionless staring at each other like they were sharing some secret joke.

Dallas broke the silence, "look up at the garage Mom." One of the panes of glass in the garage door was completely busted out. Glass littered the hood and trunk of my car as well as the truck. Glass was speckled everywhere in the garage. What can you do? Give them another broom and a dustpan and go back in the house. They did clean it all up.

Dallas will have to find out how to replace the window and how much it will cost to do so. That task seemed to dim their enthusiasm for further driveway sports this evening. Bart says he's finally watched enough baseball for one day. He'd like to graduate to a recorded feature. That's my cue.

Tarceva Tuesday

October 25

We've been busier than one-armed paper-hangers around here. As promised on the label, Bart's new chemo drug Tarceva delivered on its listed side effects. Bart keeps the Imodium AD close and handy. He has also experienced nausea and dizziness. He says it's too soon to tell if he can tolerate this drug for the duration. We're managing the symptoms with oral meds. Hopefully, he will take the right pills at the right time to stave off ill effects.

No word from UCSF yet, but we are good with pursuing this current course (for now), as long as it does not significantly increase Bart's baseline discomfort. He's got to feel good enough to enjoy watching football and baseball.

Bart got a call from Creekside this morning. The oncologist wanted to know if Bart was experiencing any pain in his pelvis. He was not. The oncologist explained that the scan revealed a tumor on Bart's pelvic bone that could be troublesome. It was news to us. Bart is to report any pain in that area. Now we can add that to our list of "things to kill."

I did some major shopping tonight before Dallas' evening doctor appointment in Folsom. I stocked up on two of Bart's favorite desserts, apple pie and strawberry shortcake. Now if only he'll eat as much dinner as dessert.

Last night our friend (also Bart's Monday Creekside chauffeur) treated us to Applebee's car side to go. What a luxury to get home from work and have dinner already there. Tonight was efficient too.

I prepared chicken enchiladas and froze a whole pan so tonight is heat and eat.

The buzzer just went off for the apple pie so I'll be signing off. It's also TKD night.

Bart's dabbling on his computer and has one of his favorite reality crime shows on.

He sends his love to all and thanks each and every one of you for posting a word or two in the guestbook. He also wishes to express his appreciation for so generously signing up to provide his transportation on lotshelpinghands.com. We are blessed.

October 26

Wednesday morning just as I bid goodbye to Bart the electricity went off. Countdown was seven minutes to the bus and now I had to manually open and close the garage door. That meant climbing up on the truck tailgate to pull the thing back down. It slammed pretty hard jarring loose some of the broken glass. Backing out of the driveway I realized that my sunroof had been open when the original glass shattering event occurred landing a dozen or so shards into the car. Now there were only six minutes to get to the bus, but I made it, and without a bloody injury too. Wonders never cease.

Bart reported that the electricity came on about an hour after he got up. Thankfully I hadn't opened windows overnight so he didn't experience the big freeze when he awoke. Our friend Tracey was Bart's chauffeur du jour, escorting him to Creekside for another round of chemotherapy. She later delivered him back home safe and sound and with a beautiful homemade quiche plus apple turnovers. Bart loved it.

I had two stops after the restful hour long bus ride home: deliver payment to the music school and gas up the car for tomorrow's drive to Bart's pain management appointment.

At home Bart informed me that Creekside had arranged for him to get a bone scan November 3rd. He was not happy about the need for a bone scan, but the more information the better.

Bart said he wasn't feeling too bad tonight just very tired. Tossing toys for the dog was almost an over-exertion. Bart said he felt weak. Still, Bart walked to the mailbox while I was tending to dinner and Dallas. It's more important than ever for Bart to keep moving. The other night his ankle was mighty swollen. Thank goodness he gives himself daily blood thinning

Lovenox injections or I would have been really worried about blood clots. After some toe tapping and walking around the swelling went down considerably.

Tomorrow we'll see about fixing the "tingles" by adjusting the numbing agent in Bart's pump so he can use the pain boosts with confidence.

It's bedtime. The Bonzo snoring on the floor in front of me has been sawing logs for about an hour now.

October 28

Bart awoke with what appeared to be a sunburn. I asked if he fell asleep in the sun. No, this was simply another dirty little trick Tarceva likes to play on its victims, a nasty red rash. Compared to everything else, this condition didn't even seem to count. The Tarceva kit came complete with a sample skin soother and an online coupon for the full size. Bart has yet to even complain about the rash.

Our round trip to Dr. Payne's Pain Management Clinic was an eventful one. We gave ourselves an hour and a half to get there. Off we went. Bart had his number two pencil, a box of Good & Plenty, 32 ounces of PowerAde and a clipboard with his forms on it. En route I suggested we might give Business 80 a second chance since it wasn't rush hour. Bart said no, lunchtime traffic would be just as bad.

We arrived right on time (that's 15 minutes early if you know Bart). The small waiting area was full. Bart signed in and we waited in the overflow area by the elevator.

Again, the usual cast of colorful characters were there, some resting on benches with full body pillows, a few were sleeping, others pacing, talking on a cell phone, or chatting with one another. All walks of life have pain. I wondered what their stories were.

Through the window looking in to the waiting room, I saw and heard an agitated patient hollering at whoever was unlucky enough to be sitting at the reception window. She complained about waiting more than an hour for her appointment. I thought, oh dear, a backlog and these chairs are not comfortable.

The woman said her time was valuable too. Although I was embarrassed for the receptionist, part of me admired her assertiveness.

Our wait was about 50 minutes. Bart sternly warned me not to play with the spinal column or skeleton displays. Dr. Payne greeted us warmly then reprogrammed the pump to the prior setting. If Bart's numbness and tingling persists then Tarceva might be the culprit.

Dr. Payne complimented us for remaining quiet the whole time he was messing with the programming device. I know how distracting it is when someone asks a question while you're doing something tedious, besides I didn't want him to screw it up and have to come back again.

Dr. Payne gave Bart a CD with two recordings: one a pattern of rain sounds designed to help him focus and stay awake during the day. The other, a mix of chimes, bells and rain to help him sleep longer.

In the car, Bart strongly opposed my shortcut suggestion. His comment, "This area is bad enough and you want to take us deeper into the hood?" We backtracked the usual route but up ahead flashing lights, police cars, crowds of onlookers and an enclosed area of crime scene tape stretched liberally across all lanes, with no detour. We turned around and made our way to Business 80. I guess we would try it after all.

Traffic on the freeway was accordion-like but moving. Good thing I left a big gap. The truck directly in front of us braked suddenly then smacked into the car ahead of him who smashed into the next vehicle. Dragging broken bumpers the cars moved off to the side of the freeway.

We cruised past the scene ever so thankful we weren't sandwiched in that fender bender. Accidents are so very inconvenient.

Bart and I were talking on the drive home and we both forgot about exiting for our flu shot appointment.

"No turning around" is sort of our own road rule so we went straight home instead.

Walking in the door Bart said, "I hate those appointments, takes all friggin' day." Indeed, it was already time to start dinner.

My marinated roast cooked perfectly on the grill as did garden potatoes with onions and zucchini. It's one of Dallas favorite meals (without the green vegetables of course). Although it may have looked good to Bart, it didn't go down well at all. Leftover Sheppard's pie came to the rescue.

Friday Bart's buddy Bill had Creekside duty. I had work duty. It was such a pleasure to get home from work and see that my new housecleaning angel had blessed me with a visit.

Dallas asked if his friends could come over then added, "I've already invited them." Better here than elsewhere. I baked a couple pepperoni pizzas, lit the candles and served seven teenagers out on the deck. It was nice to hear them enjoying their candlelight dinner, such as it was.

Bart gave himself his nightly shots then savored Tracey's homemade quiche with bacon. Game seven was on TV and we were glad Bill stayed a while. I escorted Bart to the mailbox afterwards with Phaddy. That was the extent of the daily walk for both of them. Bart's tired tonight but he's not in pain.

He tells me there are days he feels good to go for a 61st birthday party but then other days not. We're planning that January birthday celebration to be sure.

October 30

Sunday wasn't the best day. Bart's stomach wasn't very cooperative. He had less than ample calorie consumption. He didn't do the mailbox walk either. Bart just wasn't feeling it today. One of the unfortunate warnings with Tarceva is "avoid the sun" so no excursions to the sun deck either.

UCSF finally called late Friday afternoon. Bart does not qualify for any clinical trials there. Unfortunately, pancreatic cancer is smarter than they are, by their own admission. The doctor said treatment protocols change to keep the cancer guessing. Those damn cells adapt and grow unless attacked in multiple ways. The UCSF pancreatic specialists weren't very encouraging about having Bart travel there for a consultation. They said he has already received the appropriate courses of treatment available.

Not the most encouraging news, however, I know Bart. He's no quitter. We will stay the course. Miracles happen every day and Bart has already surpassed every expectation a year ago.

Bart did ask me, partially in jest, if they make Pittsburgh Steeler urns? It is better than an Ovaltine jar we thought. I told him we would have to look into that.

Speaking of Dallas, (the originator of the Ovaltine jar concept) he had a good time on his double date. Before the homecoming festivities, we told him he had just enough freedom to hang himself. Bart delivered the responsible choices lecture etc. We touched base with the other parents too, just to be sure of the game plan. The kids went to dinner first then the dance.

No calls from law enforcement and all four got home safely so we declared the evening a success.

Dallas said he had a good time with his date. Still, today he asked if another girl (the first heartbreak of last year) could come over this afternoon? Ok, but Bart and I had the same impression of this girl as we did last year unfortunately. When kids cannot ever look you in the eye or converse with an adult, it's a problem for me. She was every bit as painfully sheepish as she was last year, not delighted but he seems to value her friendship so we will reserve judgment and give her the benefit of the doubt. (for now)

While Bart watched football, I recruited my adorable neighbor kids to decorate our driveways for Halloween. Afterwards, their mom, Caryn, and I sat on my porch to watch the kids have fun. They demonstrated their heels on wheels, scooter skills and basketball prowess. Sandi even came by to sit with us for a while and share a cold one. Only one football was lost on the roof. That's a good day. Bart felt mildly better by dinnertime although he didn't eat much. I'm constantly struck by Bart's ability to take feeling like crap all day in such stride. No complaint, just a drive to fight back this evil disease by following doctors' orders to a tee while diligently monitoring and adjusting his medications to feel better.

Last night we had a wonderful evening. It was such fun to see Bart laugh at this crazy movie called "Horrible Bosses." All is well when there's laughter .

It's interesting that even in adversity Bart remains forever true to himself. He's still watching and reading political stuff like before, checking email, doing his fantasy football etc., and enjoying football on TV. Bart still does stuff he likes to do except golf. That was his passion but now he's questioning whether he'll ever be able to swing those clubs again. As tempting as a ride in a golf cart might be, it's too risky for him to venture far from the comforts of home.

Saved by the bell. The laundry beckons so I must close.

Creekside Chemo is on the schedule for tomorrow.

Chapter Nineteen

Creekside Halloween

October 31

Hanging from the front door knob this morning, there were three boxes of Creekside comfort staples, Good & Plenty. Bart's chauffeur du jour left a Halloween prize. The funny thing is that one box was for him because his wife doesn't allow consumption of said treat due to the negative scented after effects. The trip to Creekside then, is like "man time" where men can be men and whale away with impunity. It is as it should be.

Last week as Bart was walking into the Creekside building his drawers were dragging'. I jovially commented how he was wearing his trousers like the kids do. Pants on the ground, I said. He turned around and gave me a serious evil stare. That's not funny.

As I feared, today's weigh in was down. It was not just a condemnation of my cooking either, 127 pounds. I won't have to bug Bart about eating now; he knows and is definitely motivated.

At the point when he fits into my clothes we're going to tussle.

Bart had a routine blood test today as well. It will take a few days for the cancer marker results. The oncologist also examined Bart's facial rash and said, "That's a good sign." My interpretation of that comment, based on the information manual Bart got with the drug is: patients responding to Tarceva do experience the most acute skin reactions. Thus far, Bart has had all of the common side effects listed: feeling tired, rash, nausea, loss of appetite, and diarrhea.

There has been a lot of skipping to the loo this evening, but we're hoping the Imodium kicks in to prevent any dehydration. Bart's been drinking fluid like mad but it's not enough if he can't keep it to himself so to speak.

Bart's special dinner request for shepherd's pie was granted obviously. Bart even asked for seconds and then a third small bowl! Hallelujah for repeat servings! For dessert I served a hot heaping helping of apple crisp alamode, which he also polished off handily.

Tonight was a very good night for calorie consumption, but just in case, the doctor ordered a script for Megace, an appetite enhancer. I will pick that one up tomorrow. Bart said he'd "gag it back" no matter what. I will try anything to help reverse this weight loss.

And as if he didn't have enough stuff going on with his body, Bart had quite the runny nose this evening. Vick's Vapo-rub and Allerclear pills were added to tonight's menu of multiple medications. He packed tissues in his nostrils until the antihistamine did its job.

After dinner we kept a lookout for trick-or-treaters. Our decorated porch was all lit up but sadly I think kids have either gotten smarter or lazier. Only the flat compact neighborhoods get the ghouls. It's all about maximum haul/minimum time I guess.

On our street, you have to work for it, lots of steep hills. In my day if you forged up long hilly driveways, it usually paid off. You got a full size candy bar or something great like homemade popcorn balls and stuff. It's all "fun" size candy now, meaning bite size bits.

Three little superheroes from next door finally did show up, followed by Dallas and friends sporting, in what they called blonde 70's wigs.

A total of six trick-or-treaters, that's it, and one of them was our own kid!

Oh well, Bart can at least indulge in a plethora of his favorite fun size candies this week.

The morning after Halloween is the only day of the year where it's legal to eat a bucket of candy for breakfast.

Halloween a Day After

November 1

A Note from Bart:

I see my bride posted another lovely entry. I just wanted to take a second, while I'm feeling fair to middlin', to let everyone know how my day was. All in all it was (and continues to be) pretty good. I didn't have too much nausea and the rash is subsiding some. I'm thinking the antibiotic helped with the rash and the Imodium helped with the other end.

Not too much more to report other than what Mel said but taking the Megace does seem to help my appetite. Keep your thoughts and prayers coming if you would and God bless all of you.

love y'all, Bart

Creekside Wednesday

November 2

Bart's rash seemed mildly better today. The antibiotics, creams, lotions and ointments are doing their thing. We're hopeful because as ugly as the rash may seem, it means the stuff is working.

We were at Creekside this afternoon. Bart was up one pound so roll out the barrels. Supplemental hydration cocktails really help. Hydration is not easy when you have cancer. There are so many other factors that cause the body to lose fluid that Bart has to drink constantly and often but it is not enough. His red blood cell count was down a bit but not enough to be too concerned.

Speaking of concerned, I got a little anxious when Bart texted me about Dallas' absence from school today. Oh dear, I thought. Déjà vu all over again, just like when Matty was a Senior (but he turned out more than ok so I needed to calm down). What didn't Dallas do?

When I got home I discovered one very studios child who was deeply involved in his Isaac Asimov required reading and had also completely cleaned and organized the whole teen lair downstairs and the same with his bedroom. I tend to be more of a hard "you know what" about absences but Bart convinced me that he and Dallas had talked about it and this was his one parental Mulligan. We also checked his grades and saw all A's, so no gut wrench there. Impressive.

Dallas explained his reasons. This was his one pass. He rose to the occasion, finished his books, got ahead of his homework and was in bed by 9:30.

Dallas was trying to maintain his streak of excellence so we elected to support that effort this time. No noise and all's well in the Reagan household tonight.

Good Time

November 7

Bart's doing alright. He is still sporting that nasty rash and despite the Megase, not necessarily a hearty appetite either. He often feels crummy but does have some stretches of feeling decent.

It's been a crazy week but we have been gifted with great friends who have helped pick up a bit of the meal slack the last few days. We are well fed and eternally grateful.

Thursday the movie "Horrible Bosses" showed up in the mail, of course after we had already rented it.

A TKD pal came over to prevent me from going to black belt class that night. She knew too well the risk that I might hurt myself the night before testing. We had trained four years for this.

Thursday was leftover night so she and I laid out the feast. Bart got served first then I went downstairs to call Dal's friends to the dinner table. It looked like a serious game of Monopoly but their dialog didn't sound like it. Dallas shouted "but dude you had an inappropriate blurt at a job interview". They were playing Public Assistance: The Welfare Game. Basically if you gain employment you lose. After dinner Dallas left for his counselor and Bart put that silly movie on again. Short-term memory loss can be a good thing because we all laughed as much as we did last week.

Friday Bart had hydration at Creekside. He downed about four 32-ounce bottles of PowerAde throughout the day and yet still absorbed hours of IV fluid. He seemed to be feeling somewhat better Friday evening.

I got home that night exhausted and looking like I'd been in a fight but with a big smile. Fifth degree testing was over but championships were the next morning.

At bedtime, Bart put in his ear buds with the sleep sounds prescribed by Dr. Payne. He read a while on his iPad and then fell asleep. We think the meditation sounds do help him relax and sleep more soundly. Bart snoozed right through the alarm Saturday morning. Since the clock resides on Bart's side I had to get out of bed and walk around to turn it off. I must have set something on instead of switching it off. A few moments later the thing spit out a loud ear-piercing screech compounded by bad AM radio static. Bart still slept.

He was asleep when I left for the TKD championships. Dallas scared the hell out of me in the driveway suddenly knocking on my driver's side window. He was in socking clad feet, freezing. I rolled down the window and he said "good luck Mom" then ran back into the house.

Bart was up and in his chair watching sports when I got home. On the hearth next to his throne we placed my sparring champion trophy. I told Bart, I'm in the fight as much as he is and we're both in it to win it.

Tarceva could prove effective at knocking out the progression of this cancer. That means we win an extension of Bart's lease on life and that's exactly what we're going to do.

We already got an extra hour just last night. Time is definitely the most precious commodity.

Now sleep fast.

Monday Creekside Chemo

November 8

Our neighbor Zoe escorted Bart to and from his chemo today. The oncologist visited Bart in his lounge chair to report the results of his bone scan. More spots found on his bones so the oncologist ordered a bone density drug called Zometa added to the IV during Bart's Creekside sessions. Bart explained this to me tonight matter of factly and didn't expound much. Bart said he couldn't distinguish whether or not he had bone pain, just that he did have pain which isn't unusual. Same remedies, bolus, Norco and nausea drugs.

I made a vat of beef stew in the slow cooker. Mom, Sandi and our friends Lori & Hazen came over tonight. They got the low down on the routine for the upcoming week.

Dallas, Sandi, my mom and I leave for Matty's wedding in Key West, Florida Wednesday morning. Our son and his lovely bride arranged for the wedding to be streamed live online so Bart can attend in the comforts of his own chair. He plans to connect his laptop to the big screen television so neighbors and friends can join Bart for the matrimonial festivities.

Thankfully our friends Lori and Hazen will be on duty at the homestead, helping Bart host a wedding, Saturday November 12, at 12:30 PM California time in our living room.

Dallas is the best man so Dad can witness first hand his youngest son's public speaking abilities. We will certainly try to post pictures but I encourage you to urge Bart to post while I'm away.

Many thanks to dear friends and neighbors. It is because of you that we are able to make this journey to Florida. Bart appreciates all the watchful eyes and so do I. Admittedly I'm nervous to be away for so long (almost six days) but I trust that Bart is in good hands.

November 8

Bart had a crappy day. He just didn't feel well. This did not settle my nervousness about leaving but there are many good people who will watch over Bart in my absence.

Tonight we were delighted by a special visit by a few of our favorite Gist Silversmith friends. They are like family to be sure and it was most enjoyable. Bart always seems to rally during these brief visits. It's always nice for him to have someone other than me to chat with.

There was much to do prior to Dallas and my departure Wednesday morning. All essentials are stocked and most errands done. Small decisions always seem to be the worst, which is probably why packing stresses me out. I don't know why it's so arduous but it just is. I tend to wait until the last minute so deadline pressure forces me to focus.

When I feel stressed or pressed for time I tend to do stupid mindless tasks at most inappropriate times. For instance, applying dog toothpaste on Phaddy's dryer ball because his dental hygiene was that important right then or eviscerated stuffing must be crammed into his toy penguin. I suddenly see the shredding basket is too full. It just has to be done. Once, I had to set out rat bait, immediately. Everyone else was getting in the car. Or, I'll see a rug that can't wait a moment longer to be shaken. And some of those potted plants might not live a minute more unless they're watered that instant.

Socks often scream out to be matched up during the departure process or tentacles of new growth Jasmine must be quickly threaded through the back deck railing, post haste. I realize that embarking on whatever activity is suddenly before my eyes may be completely inappropriate but sometimes I just can't help myself. It's a compulsion to get just one more thing done before it's too late. I'm sure that it's some kind of twisted moronic psychosis. I sure hope I can resist random acts before takeoff tomorrow. If I don't, I'm sure Sandi will have words for me. That's definitely incentive to get my act together.

Dallas and I are packed for the most part but I'm sure there are a number of things I've either neglected to do or forgotten to pack.

Remember y'all that son Matty's wedding should be on the big screen at 12:30 PM Saturday afternoon November 12. Bart would love to have company for the big event. Please see yourself in so Bart doesn't have to get up and answer the door.

I hope to see all of you on the big screen.

Coast to Coast

November 14

What a whirlwind exciting adventure we had in Key West, Florida. We hope to relay an online Web site with the wedding video. It was a most elegant and magical affair. Bart and guests didn't get to see all the festivities streaming live so we hope the video production can fill in the blanks.

Many thanks to friends and neighbors who shared the experience with Bart and to our extended family members who stayed with Bart and picked us up at the airport. Bart enjoyed all the company and the food. His weight report card was only one pound up, but that's at least one in the right direction.

November 15

I'm glad to be home but wished that Bart felt better. He slept in later than he wanted. Sleep time cuts into calorie consumption.

While I waited for Bart to stir, I heard Phaddy barking like crazy at the front door. I didn't see anyone out there but he was so serious about this guard dog thing that I obliged and opened the door. Phaddy leapt off the porch with his biggest bark on.

Then I saw the object of Phaddy's attention. That darn squirrel was perched atop our basketball hoop, flaunting! I bolted for the BB gun but Phaddy's ruckus scared the rodent away so I never even got a shot off. I did pull out the big trap though. We will see if that destructive little acorn eater takes the caged bait so we can find him a new address far, far away.

Bart had a rough day but it was interspersed with moments of conversation about events of the past week and stuff. He told me that he's slowing down a bit and is sometimes short of breath. Poor guy just felt like crap most of the day. He did crack a big smile though when my mother presented him with her little gift from the Houston Airport.

It was a shirt emblazoned with "HOUSTON, We have a problem".

That phrase always reminds her of Bart and never fails to evoke fond memories of the boys' cross-country adventures (Bart, Dallas and my dad).

On a trip to Pennsylvania a few years ago, Bart called me to report some amusing yet mildly disturbing side effects my dad had from a sleeping pill. Bart's first words to me were "Houston, we have a problem." Of course my dad told us not to make a "federal case out of it", which meant don't call Mom. Too late. It all got sorted out eventually but the episode as a whole, still makes us all chuckle.

Bart's fuel intake today was not optimum. Despite a lovely array of main dishes Bart didn't eat much. He did however try a piece of Patty's delicious chocolate celebration cake.

Tomorrow I hope to get the cancer marker report from Creekside to see if this Tarceva is helping. At some point we have to weigh what's more important, Bart's nutrition or that drug. It's a big concern of mine. Although the phrase "let them eat cake" does come to mind.

November 17

Bart had a painful day. Every time I woke him for breakfast he asked for more sleep time. The painkillers needed to take effect. Plus, Bart was just plain exhausted. Shower and shave plans thwarted in favor of rest. Fortunately it was a Creekside Wednesday.

The doctor ordered a CT scan for Thursday morning. The concern was that Bart's pump placement may have shifted because he was having more pain around that device. I asked Bart about the cancer marker test results. He told me yes, the markers were up but he did not say by how much. That may not be unusual. As I've explained before sine waves can trend down but they still go up at regular intervals. That said, Bart has not experienced marked improvement. Instead he's had increased discomfort and extreme fatigue.

There are so many causes that might be easily remedied so we must keep communicating directly with the oncologist. Sounds like a good idea but constant reporting is just not the way Bart rolls. He endures, powers through and accepts without complaint unless it becomes unbearable. I wish I could influence him to be more of a squeaky wheel but it just does not fit with Bart's style. I think he even edits his comments sometimes to prevent me from going berserk. Thoughtful of him, but berserk might be more productive sometimes.

I've received two Skype calls from Bart informing me that it's past Bedtime for Bonzos. Phaddy has already taken the liberty to jump on the leather couch which is certainly a sign it's after hours.

TGIF

November 18

Thursday was the big scan. We pulled up to the Radiology building. Bart requested I get a wheelchair. I thought, uh oh.

I have a phobia about wheelchair driving. I was once in charge of wheeling my late aunt.

Her oxygen lifeline got quickly tangled up so tight in the wheel I couldn't undo it. My uncle had to come to the rescue, cut the tubing and reconnect her to a much shorter lifeline while I stood back feeling like a complete idiot.

Maybe it runs in the family. Bart reminded me about his trip to the Air Force Academy football game with Dallas, Dr. Mike (dad) and brother Michael. There was an episode of a runaway wheelchair down a pretty steep slope. Then Dad almost tipped out of the chair when Michael hit a pothole or bump and another incident in the elevator. Dad seemed to enjoy the whole comedy of errors, laughing all the way despite being the one in peril.

I digress.

I got the wheelchair. I took a deep breath. I can do this. Bart gave me "how to" instructions which didn't help much. For heaven's sake, we were only traveling about seven feet. I felt good about not smashing into the swinging door so I continued up to the reception desk. Bart said, "you're a terrible wheelchair driver." A bit harsh, but probably accurate.

I ran his slipper shod feet into the desk. Bart gave me "the look." I didn't set the brake.

Of course they were running about 40 minutes behind and it was freezing in there. I tried to roll Bart to a less drafty spot and somehow dislodged the footrest. Bart said just park me and leave the chair alone.

All the other folks in there were mighty cold too. Much to Bart's chagrin, I climbed up on a chair to close the vent but couldn't reach it. Then I went out and got Bart's cane from the car but that didn't work either. Bart shook his head and told me to sit down and not to misplace his cane.

Another guy stepped up on the chair for a failed attempt at vent closure. The receptionist offered us all blankets. They were sorry they couldn't control the climate controls.

Soon it was our turn. I clumsily collected Bart's paraphernalia and safely wheeled him into the chamber. It took two guys to find a vein to inject scan dye. One technician commented that because chemotherapy is corrosive, Bart's veins had a lot of scar tissue. He warned us that we'd have to go to Roseville if they couldn't get it. Bart set them straight. He could just go across the street to Creekside Lounge and have one of the girls do it. Well those two men got it done and I got a catnap in the process.

Bart was told no Lovenox (blood thinner) or other injections for 48 hours to allow the dye to dissipate.

Bart was very tired this morning. He wanted to sleep. I brought him breakfast in bed (a bowl of his favorite cold cereal, Life).

I zipped off to drop Phaddy at the beauty salon and go to my own doctor's appointment while Mr. D collected Bart and transported him to his big blue lounge chair at Creekside.

I had a list of questions for the doctor and warned his office I was coming. After getting fluffy Phaddy home from the salon I drove to Creekside Lounge.

Bart was snoozing and halfway through the first IV bag. I filled the empty candy bowl with Jelly Bellies, delivered our Pittsburgh blankets to a few laps and then waited in the oncologist's office.

I could read his face as he stepped in. I asked how this treatment was helping Bart. The side effects were miserable. He explained to me that Bart's cancer had spread significantly and further treatment would not be enough. Then he told me that Bart was one of the nicest guys he's ever met.

He said the whole staff loves him and that they wish all their patients could be like Bart. The oncologist went further and expressed that Bart was his favorite patient.

I went into the lounge and sat in the chair next to Bart. The oncologist came over and talked to the both of us. The CT scan was bad news. Bart could come in anytime he wanted to for hydration but no more chemo. Bart said he knew and understood. The oncologist said they will forever be known as Creekside Lounge because of Bart. Someone from Snowline Hospice would be visiting us Saturday morning.

In typical Bart fashion he responded with "It had better not be during the football game."

We are now settled in for the evening. Bart ate really well; he had two helpings of my Sheppard's pie followed by apple pie a la mode.

Dallas knows what's going on and his friends seem to rally around him. There are six teenagers in the kitchen consuming mass quantities of food and freshly coiffed Phaddy is snoring. Moments ago Bart ordered all the boys to move their antics downstairs. He's ready to watch a program and waiting for me to finish this post. All is well for the night.

November 21

Bart's painful discomfort surrounding the pump wasn't the pump at all. He was told that the pancreatic tumor was now pressing on the device among other organs. Bart has experienced extreme fatigue and more shortness of breath lately and oddly so has the dog.

Since Phaddy got home from his salon experience he hacked and wheezed like there was a giant hairball or something stuck in his nasal passage. The dog seemed to be severely congested but there was no time for veterinary visits. We have a saying in our house, "Dads before Phads."

Phaddeus the underdog didn't pick up a single toy on Friday night. He must be sick not to play. At bedtime, he kept trying to suck air through his clogged pipes. I wondered why he didn't just breathe through his mouth.

Bart didn't seem disturbed by the late night intervals of sudden horking. He was breathing steadily but I had to listen closely sometimes to distinguish Phad from Dad. It was a restless night.

Rachael the Hospice lady arrived early Saturday morning.

We sat at the dining room table. She set up a laptop and pulled out a folder of paperwork. I signed form after form while she explained how this would all work. She handed me papers, booklets and said a lot of stuff. I felt heavy and out of place. It was time to check on Bart.

Nurse Rachael took his vitals, asked him some questions and told us to expect a delivery after lunch. Bart asked me to let him sleep another hour or so after that so Dallas took over Dad duty. Phaddy and I went to see the vet.

Diagnosis: a sinus infection, kennel cough or something else. Vet prescribed antibiotic pills and Benadryl twice daily for three weeks and stay away from other dogs.

About 12:45 PM a delivery truck pulled into our driveway. Those hospice folks are fast. A tall nice young man unloaded some equipment, did a quick assembly and was gone. I closed the door, turned around and there it was, a giant hospital bed sitting in the middle of my living room.

That bed initiated a full meltdown. We didn't need that yet. Why was it here? What now? I had to do something other than cry to clear a path.

Our neighbor friend Zoe picked up on the first ring. She dropped everything to come over and rearrange furniture with us all afternoon. Bart directed the action from his new wheelchair. He really has a knack for optimum room plans. I have to see it first. Dallas and friends carried the extra pieces downstairs.

After all that and just as I suspected Bart would not go near that bed. I was the one who ended up occupying it even though it made me cry. I configured it like a lazy chair. Bart did scold me for what he thought was abuse of the adjustment controls, but one must experiment to find the perfect position of comfort. He said he was sure he'd have his turn in it eventually but not this weekend.

Sunday Bart again requested a few more hours of rest so I thought why not join him? The boys went to Denny's for breakfast and it was cold out from under the covers. When I finally did get up, it was delightful to find Bart's buddy Bill with the game on, ready to watch some football with Bart.

By the time Bart awoke and was ready to be transported to the television I had been to the store and had all the groceries put away. Bart had a nice but short visit with Bill. Intestinal trouble wasn't fun today and Bart needed more break through pain relief than usual but he hung in there.

After lunch Dal's music pals started showing up with their instruments. There were a couple of guitar players, a trumpet guy, and Dal on drums. They played all afternoon and well into the evening. We have never been more impressed and so entertained by a group of young musicians since drum line competition two years ago. These kids were fantastic. Bart and I loved the music. I was moved to call their teacher on speaker phone to heap some high praise. The boys played their hearts out. Smooth jazz, upbeat instrumentals, or slow and soulful ballads they created beautiful music together. What a lift.

They took a short dinner break with two pizzas and some freshly baked cookies and then back to the music. By 9:30 PM the band was spent but they had great fun together. It was music to our ears.

Bart was spent by that time too and Phaddeus the wonder dog curled in quietly next to him.

November 22

It's been a rough Monday. Bart's pain intensity spiked and he felt worse than yesterday. He was rocking about seven on the one to ten scale. Snowline Nurse Cherie helped get shorter intervals between drug doses the doctor had approved. Bart can take certain drugs and pills every two hours instead of four and others every six hours versus eight. Even so it didn't help much. It's time for a pump adjustment.

That thing must be revved up to keep pace with the expansive abdominal horror Bart deals with now.

The problem is that Dr. Payne's clinic offers no option for patients who can no longer make the drive down to his office. Rolling over a hardwood floor threshold to the hallway carpet is bad enough on his damaged organs and our road is exponentially more gut wrenching. Crossing the tracks to Dr. Payne's part of town is out of the question. Something has to be worked out though because that device will run out of juice the first week of December.

What good is having a pain relief implant if they won't work with us on how to service it?

This afternoon I began to wonder if medications actually had calories. Bart was knocking back a whole lot of meds but perilously little food.

Sheppard's pie made him sick today but Friday he ate double helpings. It took about an hour for him to polish off a pudding cup. The hospice literature says this is often the hardest for caregivers to accept. It's normal for food to become less appealing.

Late afternoon the Snowline spiritual care provider paid us a visit. Then a good friend came over to help me update and retype Bart's medication spread sheet.

Bart sipped his PowerAde and we watched a little television in the evening.

He can't shake the nausea and still feels a world of hurt. In fact, as I type he walked out to request the sick bucket. If only I could suck the pain from him and into me I would do it in a heartbeat. His outlook, endurance and fortitude are unfathomable.

November 25

There's just no substitute for your own cozy mattress. The other night Bart looked comfortable in the hospital bed so I let him sleep and curled up on the couch. At 2:00AM he sat up and said, "I want to go to bed." Dang, just when Phaddy nestled in by my feet and we were all dozing off. I wheeled Bart to the bedroom, tucked him in and went back for Phaddy. The dog never moved a muscle as I laid him down. What did he do all day that was so exhausting anyway?

Almost every hour on the hour Bart sat up and sometimes switched positions, laying his head toward the foot of the bed and then back. Twice he pulled his shirt off. It reminded me of my dad, who clawed at his clothes in the final weeks. That gave me some cause for concern. I thought he must be freezing but he just sat. I was reluctant to dose Bart too often despite his obvious restlessness and discomfort. These were powerful drugs and I wanted desperately to alleviate his pain but how much was too much?

The hospice doctor reassured me that dispensing a full dose at more frequent intervals would not hurt. Whew. I learned the signs and now know the parameters. I am much more confident about administering his pain drugs. Between pain pump boosts, supplemental liquid Dilaudid and now Methadone, Bart's brow is not as furrowed. We've got a routine that seems to work better.

Wednesday was a scary one. Bart never got out of bed. He stayed there all day and all night.

He did not eat, drink or venture to the bathroom despite efforts to entice him to do anything.

Thanksgiving though was spectacular. When Bart has a decent day, I have a great one. To my surprise, Bart got up and walked (no wheelchair) to the bathroom on his own. He motioned me to stay put. This was a change. Yesterday he was not walking anywhere. Today he was scolding me to back off. Bart barked (a very soft bark) "put the game on and get out of my way." All righty then, he must be feeling better.

Our neighbors stopped by for a group hug and to offer a prayer of thanks. Bart had a small feast thanks to our extended neighborhood family. What a great sampling of holiday foods. Bart seemed to enjoy people who weren't "me." It's funny because no matter how dire the situation I always seem to manage somehow to annoy Bart. It's an odd comfort really, typical Dory as my friends would say, par for the course.

When it was time for Bart's pain meds I gently warned him and tickled his lips with the syringe. He quipped, "You really should wake me up first before you start shoving sh%# in my face."

Hey, I'm down with the program and when you're on a roll, the plan can't be blown for a cat nap, right?

Sandi cooked a magnificent top shelf Thanksgiving turkey meal with all the ornate fixings. It was a killer meal, viciously delicious.

Matty rang to tell us the package had landed. Dallas made it to North Carolina, via Houston and Charlotte. Megan arrived hours earlier (but without her husband Ben, Air Force EC-130 pilot deployed until January) so all the siblings except Ben: Matty, Jen, Meg, Dallas & Melissa (Bart's number one daughter) would be in North Carolina this Thanksgiving holiday without any parental units. Joy.

Football, family, friends and fun, plus a great day for Bart. Those are all the ingredients for a grandiose holiday.

We are indeed thankful. Bart indulged in a modest amount (miracle in and of itself). He rallied today and looked a world better than yesterday. I felt overwhelmingly grateful for having so many fun years with him and for his loyal friends.

Thank you all for your messages and postings. Bart appreciates every word, as do I.

Bedtime for this Bonzo.

The Big Cheese

November 27

Occasionally my late night posts are disjointed, I dare say incoherent so I'll try to write during waking hours if at all possible.

Friday was another good day for Bart ergo a super day for me.

Sleep schedule was better too. I got up for meds only, no retrieving shirts this time.

Phaddy evidently got a hold of some leftover turkey treats because he threw up all over the spread. Bart awoke and said "he's vomiting on you" but I was too tired to do anything about it. Whatever, it would be there in the morning and it was.

Bart got dressed the next morning and walked to the loo, a good sign. He ate a little cereal and later a repeat performance of Thanksgiving dinner for lunch.

Two hospice nurses came by, one for vitals and the other "home health" to make sure Bart was able to shower etc.

It was a bright beautiful crisp day. Bart was feeling well enough to say "take Phaddy for a walk."

I did a quick neighborhood figure eight, looping back to the house just in time. Bart was sitting up and ready to ride down the hall to the bathroom and back.

I hung up Phaddy's leash and told Bart that it was time for the annual lights of joy debacle, also known as our seasonal snafu, the big twinkled tango.

He was less than enthusiastic. Last year went so well, not. The postman interrupted our discussion of lights. He drove down the driveway and handed me a paper grocery bag taped up with our address on it. 'Twas a gift from Green Bay.

Somebody from Wisconsin knows who the head cheese is around here!

Houston, We Have a Problem

November 28

Bart's pain pump needs to be refilled and reprogrammed but he was not up to traveling to the Pain Management Clinic. I called hospice and let them try, but the result was the same, not an option to send a tech to us. We will see about tomorrow. Mr. D. (my TKD mentor) will carry Bart if necessary.

Sunday afternoon, Bart had a smile I hadn't seen in a while. Buddies Bill, Marty, Matt, Lori, and Hazen converged at our house to watch football and razz each other about their fantasy team prowess. It was entertaining. Bart dozed off, but was obviously engaged in the action during the time he was awake.

Bart's voice has changed. It's softer and more difficult to interpret, but his mind is as sharp as ever. He knows exactly how many doses and how many pills I give him and when. It's remarkable considering that he spends more time asleep than awake.

Bart goes to bed earlier and gets up later, sometimes spending 15-18 hours in bed. He is often restless and gets up during the night. At least much of his pain has diminished, thanks to more frequent treatments.

I knew that the Red Dragon should be moved back down on the driveway. It had been parked on the street for a few days, so I grabbed the keys to go move the beast myself. Someone had smeared cheap Taco Bell menu items all over the windows and crammed a whole chalupa under the door handle. Salsa bled into the window weather stripping and on the windshield wipers.

What a waste of a meal (or several)! Dallas would not be happy about this. I think I'll load the paintball gun just in case I see the vandals come by. Where was Phaddy's hyper sensitive sense of smell when food was being wasted?

Obviously he was sleeping on the job. Speaking of sleeping, it must be Bedtime for Bonzos.

Houston, We have Lift & Lights

November 29

Thankfully, Mr. Dallas was ready, willing, and able to help me transport Bart to the car for the hour-long ride to Dr. Payne's office. Even though Bart barely spoke or opened his eyes much today, he did manage to ask me what time we needed to leave.

I filled out Bart's pain forms as best I could, and we departed about noon. This time, no waiting. Dr. Payne increased the average pain pump dose by 40 percent and the bolus jolts 42 percent, adding another two for a total of six bonus rounds in a 24 hour period. Bart wasn't able to respond directly to the doctor, nor was he able to ascend to the exam table, so Dr. Payne made it happen in the wheelchair.

I had given Bart a bolus in the waiting area, and by the time we got him home, the new level seemed to have taken effect. What a lift. He was more relaxed. Bart napped a while in the living room before asking to be wheeled to bed at 6:30 PM.

Although he's been a bit restless, and still needs meds for breakthrough pain tonight, he has turned a corner on the pain train.

To celebrate Bart's progress toward pain level zero, our lights of joy are strung out on the driveway. Yesterday, my friends helped me test and replace about 60-plus tiny bulbs to get the whole string to completely light up. Tomorrow the hanging begins. Thankfully, I've got friends already enlisted to spot me and steady the ladder. All Bart has to do is assume the throne and let the light shine through.

Chapter Twenty

Guest Author Sums It All Up

December 1

Dear friends and family: Bart is resting comfortably tonight. I am pleased to honor Bart with our dear friend's recollection of our day, as she has more energy than I this evening and her musings are exact, certainly full of loving insight.

Clean Jeanne's guest post: Enjoy.

Wow – what can be said about such friends as those who join together to laugh, cry, and support this brave man who continues to hold his own against the raging beast called cancer. Love consumes this house as Bart calmly reclines on his special bed or on the couch, this gaggle of brilliant, strong and hilarious women congregate to share stories of everyday life and rush in to address monsieur's needs; whether that be help with a swig of PowerAde Zero, or an able bodied, three-woman assist in shifting his gluteus maximus (minimus?) to a new and better position. Bart clearly communicates his approval or disapproval using the most energy conserving, yet entirely effective, methods possible by giving a bold thumbs up in response to a comment, offering, or gesture, or the palm held at a stern 90 degree angle to indicate a very clear "knock it off." Whatever, the message is received and his harem obeys.

The day was mostly quiet, and a good portion spent figuring out the online bill pay process. Bart refrained from comment or criticism which probably created more anxiety on our part than if he actually said something. He has slowed down for certain, but do not question it. He is still there and I know that every word, action, or lack of perceived organization is not going unnoticed by him. Bart sees all and hears all, disturbing and yet reassuring at the same time.

Melanie and Phaddy are enjoying a little special time on Bart's living room bed because Bart has vacated it in favor of the main bed. What a cozy and delightful little treat it is for her on the motorized sleeping machine; however, it is time for slumber in the big bed and it is nigh time for that Bonzo to bid adieu for the night. Me too.

December 2

Overnight Bart slept calmly for the most part. It was a much more restful night. Early this morning Bart wanted to assume his perch atop the hospital bed so we wheeled away to the living room. Bart's pump is finally taking up more of the slack in the pain department. With six bonus rounds per day now, Bart consumes a bit less liquid Dilaudid yet maintains Methadone support and continues with nausea remedies.

He's not into food but watching him eat a single circus peanut and five Good & Plenty candies today was definitely in my current "thrill" category. It's the little things.

Today was challenging. December 1 and I had not done any bill paying in about 20 years! Bart did leave a list though, so it was time to face the paper. The top two items on the list: learn our online bill pay system and take it over. Fearful of penalties, late fees, and credit blemishes, I opened the three inch thick folder full of bills. I've always maintained that computers smell fear just like dogs. As a result I always seem to get bit.

My dearest friend Clean Jeanne would not let me flake on these important life tasks. She obviously took notes! Had it not been for her nudging, this mission might well have gone down in some expensive flames.

I offer Clean Jeanne's notes on events of this Thursday:

Of life's many challenges, online bill-pay has proven to be one that was nearly insurmountable today. After a couple hours of trying to figure out Bart's login, password, and username information, we finally got the great red-lettered warning that we were being blocked from any further pursuit online. So we called the customer service help desk and explained that the account is in Bart's name, with user name, password, etc. The gracious help-desk-lady was very friendly and after explaining the immediate difficulty we were experiencing, she asked to speak to the person whose name was on the account we were trying to access.

This, of course, was not possible, so we explained the complication and she advised that we would have to go to the actual bank location and present a power-of-attorney to change any login information.

Off to the bank we went after first securing the services of a lovely Hospice volunteer to come and stay with the Bart-man. At the bank we were greeted by a neatly suited young man who showed us the Wells Fargo way.

We explained the trials and tribulations of trying to sign on to the online account, the complication of Bart's condition, the dire need to pay bills, the fear that some may be overdue, and our utter frustration at the situation. After patiently listening to us, Mr. Banker kindly explained that a power-of-attorney was not necessary because Melanie is the spouse on the account anyway.

As Mr. Bankerl was busying himself on the computer, Melanie surreptitiously looked over at me with an expression of "zoiks!" and the message was instantly clear. We were not in the right bank. Well, you can imagine that a fair amount of mirth ensued as we doubled over snorting, gulping for air, and laughing our ever-loving heads off. Mr. Banker looked over at us and said coolly, "Wrong bank?" Yup.

All was not lost however, because changes needed to be made at that bank anyway and one more thing could be checked off Bart's to-do list! All's good on that score.

Bart was more communicative today, which made the inside of the house as sunny and lovely as it was outside. While he was obviously in pain, he still wanted to be part of the daily goings on by sitting up in the wheeled throne and issuing commentary here and there. Later in the day, he retreated to the hospital bed to take in an evening of football programming which was momentarily interrupted by a visit from the Hospice pastor, Tim. Pastor Tim shared some conversation and a special prayer for Bart, which touched us all deeply.

Our dear Bart is curled up and for the moment appears comfortable. May our hearts and prayers lift him on a cushion of love through a night of sweet sleep. Tomorrow's dawn brings another day that is made better by his presence. Be well.

December 3

Bart slept soundly Wednesday night. I had framed him in securely with pillows all around. Perhaps his slumber was more peaceful because he felt at some level that it would be his last night in this cozy bed. I tried to push that thought away, but knew it would be the last time we would share this room as husband and wife.

Never count Bart out though. He has continued to perplex hospice nurses. They tell me he is not following the usual progression. His case is atypical, a patient with an exceptional constitution and tremendous will.

His strength of spirit sustains him but his body betrays that will. The nurses were almost alarmed by Bart's late stage mobility. He was keeping on with nothing to go on.

Yet Bart still manages to call me "hammer hands" in the midst of all this. Warms my heart.

In the wee hours this morning, Bart was on the hospital bed and tried to sit up. He motioned me for help. I assisted, propping him with my arm around his bony shoulders. I really wanted to lie down, but sit we did. After a while, I succumbed to sleep and pulled Bart gently down with me on to the pillows. It occurred to me that Bart would never ever let me even <u>sit</u> on his hospital bed in any way shape or form before, ever! I felt lucky, like a dog on the good couch. Well not so fast, Bart later opened his eyes and gave me the shoo motion, shoo, get off the bed. That's Bart, true to form down to the very last drop. It was time to get up anyway. Those lights wouldn't string themselves.

I made a command decision this year that no ladder would be harmed in the twinkled tango. Joy would instead burst forth brilliantly from the various bushes lining our driveway.

Jeanne sat with Bart while he napped, and my industrious friend, Carol, and I spread joy from bush to bush until our fingers went numb from the cold. Thank goodness for Uncle Phil (dear friend Lee but Dallas insists he looks like a Phil, so it's been Uncle Phil ever since) who spent hours with me days before painstakingly replacing bad joy. One stupid tiny twinkle shuts off a whole damn string. Just as we readied the switch to light up our world, Jeanne informed me that Bart had inquired as to when the kids would arrive. Uh oh Houston, did we have a problem?

The kids called later that evening. It was their last night together in North Carolina. A bit of light chatter on the phone ensued, then Dallas uncharacteristically asked that the speaker phone be held to Dads ear. What I heard was tough for any parent. My heart broke as Dallas spoke through tears. He told Bart what a great dad he was and that he recognized and appreciated all the stuff he did for him and repeated, "I love you" several times. Bart managed to expel a breathy "I love you too buddy."

Dallas continued, but Bart raised his hand and pushed the phone away turning his head to the pillow.

I understood this gesture. Bart needs all his reserves if he is to finish the conversation in person. Any energy, stamina, and will power, must be summoned for survival right now. He would hold on for family to arrive. I know this.

Three kids are flying home tonight from across the country arriving at different hours. Tomorrow Bart's family will be here from Pennsylvania.

We can't change this. Bart could not have put up a more valiant fight against this disease and he's not done yet. He once said to me with pride "I've already outlived all expectations," and it's not over until the fat lady sings (and she could be tone deaf). One of the major components of Bart's inner courage is you. If you are reading this then **you** (yes, you read-only peeps too) are part of a community that has bolstered Bart's fighting spirit.

I read guestbook postings to Bart daily. He used to check CB first thing on his computer every morning. Of course, it occurs to me that quite possibly his early morning eagerness to read the postings was to reassure himself that his bride hadn't gone off her nut the night before and slapped some drunk post or other illiterate composition in there that was "typed while sleeping." It happens.

There is a rising sadness in me but it is tempered with tremendous gratitude for the many fun decades I've had with this man.

Bart sleeps most of the time now. My job is to stay ahead of the pain train for him. It's clear that he continues to wage this internal war yet communicates his love through osmosis. It's tough to talk (or write) with your heart in your throat but Jeanne nudges me to keep posting and generously offers her own notes as well.

It is with great pleasure that I share her thoughts with you tonight. Notes from Clean Jeanne:

Yesterday was such a full one that Melanie and I fell into our respective beds too exhausted to post last night, and tonight the kids are all coming. But here we sit now while Bart snoozes and decided to catch up.

Yesterday morning, as I was reading while sitting with Bart, I heard a peculiar sound coming from the side of the house and thought that someone was noisily walking around out there. I looked out the various windows to see who the offender might be, and saw nothing. Then the odd sound came again. Finally a slight movement up toward the roof caught my eye and the sound maker became apparent. It was The Squirrel mockingly clinging to the side of the house, head down and tail twitching. Since he was on the side of the house, and I on the upper floor inside the dining area, I knew I couldn't make it outside and around the corner fast enough to whack at him with a broom so I just opened the window and yelled at him. With a full body twitch he scampered down the side of the house where he got his comeuppance when two scrub jays came torpedoing down right at him as he landed on the ground! They dive-bombed him twice. He ran to a tree and leapt to safety, or so he thought, because the birds continued their argument with him by flying in and out of the tree where he clung. They eventually grew bored or the squirrel sneaked away, but soon all was quiet again and the woodland creatures were gone. I so wish I had been able to get a video of this because it would have given Melanie such a rush of satisfaction to see the Bastard Rodent being given "the bird."

Yesterday, a hospice nurse came by and the three of us formed Team Clean-Bart with a sponge bath, tooth brushing, a trimming of the facial hair (he has a fetching mustache and beard now), and a head shave. Since we knew the effort of being rolled from side to side, and being shifted about, would be so painfully draining to him, we sought to soften the impact of the activities by telling him we were three topless twenty year old nubile young women tending his every need. To this we got a very hearty thumbs-up. We can only hope that this visual suggestion helped even the slightest bit because any reprieve from the consuming battle is gratifying no matter how minuscule that may be. Now the Bart-babe is washed up, oiled down, and shined up for all the company to come this weekend (why is it, by the way, that we wash up, shine up, clean up, spiffy up, polish up, but oil down?).

Through all of this, I have to say again and again, Bart is the most incredible force of nature I have ever had the honor of knowing. This cruel disease torments its host with pain I am sure I cannot imagine, drains the body of its energy, taunts the spirit, and yet Bart bears it all with grace and dignity. His needs are pantomimed by a hand gesture indicating the need for water, a sweet treat, a position change, the need for pain meds, his glasses to be put on or taken off, or having his lips moistened. These small, every day physical efforts that we take for granted require a herculean effort on his part and render him utterly fatigued. But despite these tortures that ravage his frail body, we are even yet able to cajole the occasional smile from him over an act of silliness. I am awed.

While Bart stands with one foot in the physical world, and one foot in the spiritual world, I watch his journey unfold as Melanie cares for him and my heart is filled with such love and admiration for this extraordinary woman. She is tireless, intuitive, gentle, and tender with him while surrounding him with the comfort of her strength. There is nothing she would not do for this dear spirit. The sadness, frustration, hurt, fear, and fatigue of witnessing the love of her life suffering is certainly present, but through it all her fortitude, humor, energy, and largess of heart are the attributes which shine brightest.

Love and generosity fill this house in every gesture and extension of physical care. Friends call and stop by, acquaintances extend their support and concern, strangers come to pray and provide medical care. And through it all, even though the beast of cancer cannot be conquered, we take satisfaction in knowing that when Bart's body is at last defeated, the one thing that will rise to victory is his spirit. And his spirit will live forever within us all.

December 4

Bart was not up to using the remote control. With no football game on, I clicked around to see what else he might like. What Bart gave the nod to was a movie that surprised me. In retrospect, I believe he chose to amuse himself. In such a situation what could be more soothing than "Snakes on a Plane?" I find such reptiles most unnerving and Bart was fully cognizant of my aversion to all things that slither.

As the movie played, Bart watched a little then dosed off, but Clean Jeanne was laughing! This moment was so oddly amusing to me considering our dire situation.

Here we were witnessing violent and venomous attacks on unsuspecting airline passengers. Bart and the kids used to get such a big kick out of my primal reaction to snakes on TV. He may have gotten some element of pleasure in my repulsion while Clean Jeanne found the whole concept just hilarious. In retrospect it was a treasured moment. Snakes be damned.

I am also happy to relay, that at bedtime, this dog "got on the couch." There was no objection as I tucked myself in next to Bart on his hospital bed for what would be our last night together.

Sunday morning his breathing became painfully labored, but family updates as to the Reagan's ETA kept him pulsing along.

When they finally arrived, the rest of us retreated downstairs to give the family some privacy to say goodbye. After a respectful amount of time, the kids and I unanimously decided that I had to tell Bart it was okay to let go now, but first, I would need to include the Reagan women in this family discussion.

Climbing the stairs I started saying, "hey, we have to...."

But before I got the words out, I looked at Bart. Oh God, he was gone.

Heaven, We Have Lift Off

December 4

My groom did indeed power through some very rough hours as I knew he would. He held onto dear life just long enough to make sure every family member was okay and present. He passed away quietly.

Bart may have passed peacefully but that moment was anything but peaceful for me.

A boulder of panic hit me rock hard in the gut. I wrapped his frail body in my arms, lay next to him, and sobbed uncontrollably. It wouldn't stop. I wasn't sure that I would ever be able to let go of him. As much as this separation was anticipated, I didn't expect it.

I don't know how long it took exactly. My kids had to console me! When the youngest repeatedly assured me that it was going to be okay, I knew that he would be okay.

After perhaps a half hour or so, I consciously tried to slow these compulsive waves of tears and looked up at all those heartbroken teary-eyed faces.

What came to mind at that moment were the very words Bart uttered when it all began, "I'm sure glad we got that solar installed."

In keeping with my husband's final wishes, we welcome you to stop by our home this Friday, December 9th, for an informal wake or open house if you will.

In the wise words of little Sheridan (or maybe it was Lillian) Reagan, (Joanne's granddaughters) "Give hugs and you'll just feel better."

December 4

From Jeanne: "Sweet traveler now has release. We celebrate his life and boost him with our hearts on his journey. Love is greater than all else and he takes ours with him."

From Matthew: "This past day I witnessed the greatest feat of strength and bravery of my entire life. I am honored to call myself his son. It is a relief to see him at peace. Thank you for the continued support from our family and friends."

From Megan: "I definitely appreciate the privilege it was to learn from the greatest patient I know. But obviously he was much more to me than that. He was an amazing dad and just a great man. I miss him dearly. Thank you so much to all our friends who have rallied around us through all of this."

From Dallas: "I've never known nor met anyone stronger than my father. He fought until the very end and he waited until everybody was there before he let go. I love him, and I miss him already. He was the greatest father I could've ever asked for. Because of him, I am the way I am today. He's taught me some of the greatest principles of life and I'm never going to forget them. And I'm never going to forget him. Thank you, Dad, for always being there for me, for always believing in me, for putting up with me, and for loving me. I'm so happy to have been raised by such an incredible guy. I love you, Dad."

From Sandi: "I know you are being carried to your rest on wings of angels. RIP, our dear Bart. You will always be in our hearts and I am sure we will never be allowed to own computers without you!"

From Joanne: "I am so honored to have Bart as my brother and my friend; I doubt I could ever endure what he has gone through especially with all of his strength and determination. I love you so much and I am relieved that you are no longer in pain. RIP my dear, dear brother. All of my love....Joanne."

From Bobbie: "My brother will be sadly missed. He was my only brother. How can anyone express this? There are no words to fill this empty hole in our hearts. Love you more than anything."

From Bart's Mom, Patricia Kennedy Reagan: "I'm glad I made it on time but I knew my son would wait. Bart was a wonderful son."

(Bart's final wishes included throwing a "big ass party." Take that to mean the more asses there, the better.)

December 9

It's a rare treat to have all the kids at home. When our Chaplain Tim heard that Ben was deployed to Afghanistan, he made some very long distance calls. In less than two days, Ben was home. What a blessing and a great Christmas gift.

It would mean more troops to enlist in the "rid rodent" mission too.

Wednesday morning Joanne was having coffee in the living room and suddenly reported: "squirrel." Matty grabbed the gun and ran up the driveway in his skivvies. There was a lot of commotion. Matt scanned the roof from the top of the road. I scouted the perimeter. Matty did get a shot off but he didn't think the gun had enough range. It must have been quite a sight, me in my pjs and crazy bed hair and Matty sprinting barefoot up the street with a gun. No doubt a curious spectacle for the neighbors.

Later, Megan accompanied me to the appointment at Green Valley Mortuary. We sat in a carefully appointed room for a few long minutes before a young man in a white shirt and tie came in. I think they must go to school to learn to be slow talkers. I just wanted to get this over with, but his "sensitivity training" was really stalling the whole process. It was excruciating.

A false wall opened up and we walked through the opening to a display that looked more like the UPS box store. The young man explained that we had to buy a cremation casket. It wasn't clear at first that this was not an urn, but rather it was another receptacle used to burn. Paperwork had to be further edited and then he had to make more copies. It was hard to sit still. Waiting there I tipped my purse over, spilling the contents onto the floor.

Megan commented on how fast I said goodbye and flew out the door after Mr. Mortuary handed me those copies.

Back home Matthew had set up a stakeout for the squirrel.

There was much to do in the house but I didn't know what to do first. I expected a text from Bart. It was hard to imagine that I would not have that kind of communication with him anymore.

The whole family is looking forward to the influx of friends tomorrow. Bart had great friends and some we haven't even met yet.

Bobbi's inflatable bed is leaking so we'll be playing musical mattresses this evening.

Thank You

December 14

Thank you to those who graced us with your participation in last Friday's soiree. Serving trays, dishes, pans, baskets and pots are on my front porch bench. I couldn't keep up with who owns what, so it's almost a free for all out there. I offer free delivery by request, otherwise those wares will await pick up. The kids and I are madly flitting about with preparations for Saturday's memorial service and "big ass" party as Bart referred to it.

If you would be so kind as to post a note confirming your attendance it would be appreciated. I can best prepare the caterer that way. Bart would want to make sure all you party animals are fueled for the night since you are expected to dance your asses off.

Backing out of the garage today we almost had a disastrous mishap when my side mirror hooked a string of Christmas lights. Moving in reverse, the cord tightened and began to strangle one of the bushes near the house. Fortunately Jen observed this accident waiting to happen just in time. She stopped me before I most certainly would have ripped out much of our front yard landscaping.

Well, it's late and all is quiet, except for Phaddy's rhythmic snoring. Bedtime for Bonzo.

We Celebrate

December 16

This week I expected to get a text or email from Bart any minute. To keep his name in the top five of incoming calls/messages on my cell phone, as it's always been, I finally sent a text to his phone myself. I still wake up at 4:00 AM and 6:00 AM like clockwork, but there is no more pain to treat. These adjustments will happen eventually, I suppose. In the meantime, little things are my touchstones. Tomorrow is Bart's day.

Do not despair if you cannot make the festivities. Bart and I have friends with many talents and my friend Chandler is a most gifted videographer who does not actually do that stuff for a living. He graciously agreed to take video so a link will be posted at a later date.

I will keep this short because I must write a few notes for myself. I haven't written Bart's eulogy yet but I will have something to say. We will take time to toast and exchange stories after the service in the celebration hall.

Nosh a bit, enjoy a beer, soda or other libation with friends.

Be comfortable and wear your dancing shoes. Bart was no fan of dressing up.

December 21

Thank you all for following these posts for more than a year. Your interest and support certainly buoyed Bart. I sincerely believe it served to extend his quality of time with us. One day soon I must sign off for good in keeping with the intent and purpose of this caring online resource.

Tonight we had an abbreviated Christmas because of a different sort of sendoff.

Ben leaves in a few hours (5:00 AM) to return to duty, (Air Force command in Afghanistan). Our country is fortunate to have such solid, good, and qualified leaders among our ranks. In a few days son Matty and his bride Jen (my new daughter), will also resume their respective leadership posts within the U.S. Army infantry and intelligence.

Having expert militia in the house does have its benefits. Two mornings ago, our household nemesis was spotted in the digger pine outside the kitchen window. Captain Benjamin grabbed the BB gun and shot out the door to get him in the cross hairs. By the time I got up and smelled the coffee, it was mission accomplished! Ben took that vandal rodent with a single shot, but humanely double-tapped him to ensure the swiftest demise, no suffering. Just like that.

I realize there's a possibility of multiple vermin but hope that any squirrel witnessing the execution will tell their kind to opt for trees, not eaves.

Thankfully, the kids don't all leave the nest at once. I prefer sequential or staggered departures. It's gentler on my constitution.

Phaddy the Wonder Dog

Thursday, March 22

Bart was right.

Dogs do contribute something special. Our little Phad the pound puppy had developed quite a resume.

Phaddy dog, our always amusing, quirky and ever present kitchen catcher was also known as Phaddeus J. Hoover for his propensity to eat floor sweepings before I could grab the dustpan. During mini-training sessions he went by Phaddeus Thayer, after West Point's academic founder. Then there was the rowdy, rough and tumble moniker, Phaddemus Gordon from Gunsmoke fame. And of course for those moments of artful creativity, we called him Phaddeus (pronounced Fad-day-oous) Mozart.

When we played sniff out the treat in the back yard, you'd hear us call "Phaddy, Phaddy Phadson Free" and when he ran really fast, he was a Passing Phad.

Iterations like Phadmeister, Phaddenator etc. of course always fun too. Phaddy dog entertained.

No creature could possibly have had more fun and with random objects like a roll of first aid tape for instance. Once said roll hit the floor, first aid would not be happening ever again with that slobbery mass. Phaddy would toss it around and gallop in circles. In January, I had a big protective bandage on my finger. It fell off one day and Phaddy made a quick full turbo sweep, snatched it up and ate it before I could even react.

If he was lucky enough to dig up a tennis ball from his magic basket he'd tuck that ball next to you and keep nudging until you threw it. The chase game: toss, fetch, run, repeat, repeat over and over. If Phad could not engage a player to pitch then the little Mozart got creative.

He would use his snout to position a ball in a scrunched up blanket. Then he'd yank fast on that blanket until the ball popped up so he could chase it. Quite ingenious really.

Phaddy also invented snibbling, a verb I coined because it so aptly described ones behavior. If he really liked you or a thing (ball, toy, leather couch) he'd tickle nibble. Snibbling amounted to funny little quick gentle teethy mini-nibbles. This was Phaddy's way to show affection or extreme like.

Then there was the noun snibblers, referring to his favorite noisy toys. Bart would have to pause movies because Phaddeus McSqueaky voraciously attacked and surgically removed any squeak device post haste before snibbling it to death.

Phadantics were legendary. He was a good canine companion.

Late last night when my friend was leaving Phad launched himself through the front door at top speed. He loves to mark the rosemary near the mailbox. Lisa and I chatted on the porch a bit.

It was dark outside, no street lights., I saw a car stop on the road so I called out for Phaddy. He usually comes running at top speed because a treat always awaits a quick response. It worked almost every time. I called for him again.

The car on the road started to go again. We heard a thump followed by a squeal. Lisa and I ran. Phaddy was there on the side of the road. The car was gone.

I scooped him up not believing he had been run over. He might have a broken bone but I would have to see in the light. No blood, but he could not take a breath. Unbearable. He wasn't getting air. To emergency we sped, but with every attempted gasp, no sound. Phaddy was becoming weaker. Mouth to mouth yielded nothing. He was going. I felt life drain from his body right there in my arms. I was losing it. Sweet Phaddy went limp and still.

NO.

I could not breathe, writhing and sobbing they took him from me. For an hour or two, wracked with the deepest and most oppressive visceral pain I held that dog, stroked his face then collapsed on the floor of the clinic. I could not breathe. Pain was all consuming pierced with shock and sadness. I hurt. I cried and pleaded with God. Sobs, tears raw anguish continued through the night, the next day and the next. There is no salve for this wound. I do not function but for grief.

Dallas slept through the whole ordeal. I could not destroy his school day. We so loved that dog. Dallas and his posse even gave Phaddy his own day; Mondays were be nice to Phaddy day. Thankfully it was Tuesday. I broke the heart-wrenching news to Dal Wednesday as soon as he got home. Each word out of my mouth like a dagger seemed to rip open his heart that much more. I felt ill. We broke down together, crying and hugging.

Dal squeezed my hand. We were sick, infected with heartache.

Sometime later a friend made a curious and thought-provoking comment. Phaddy helped you really grieve for Bart. I pondered that thought for a long time. It was true. I dove deep into a pool of writhing wresting emotional hurt. Internal spontaneous combustion might be a relatively apt description. Phad's passing did indeed serve an important purpose. He was the catalyst for me to take that intimate plunge. For months it felt like an intense workout with sadness and guilt but just like going for a long jog in the hills I'm calmer now for having run it.

Rest Assured

April 15

Perhaps completion of audio/video from Bart's final celebration represents one too many endings that might close this once comfortable forum. It's a sort of reluctance to bring this exchange to a close. Bart's conversation should stay alive.

In that vein, I have a tidbit to share about Bart's mostly-happy place.

I like to return every so often to visit the Lounge. Every so often I deliver candy to the Lounge. It was on the last delivery that I learned of the newest moniker for the nurses there.

The Creekside Lounge sign still adorns the entrance to the chemotherapy suite, so I was curious as to what addendum there could possibly be. As I walked through the office door, and turned toward the chemo lounge, the oncologist appeared. He acknowledged my presence with a slight nod and professionally distant smile, but otherwise he seemed all business as usual.

I then turned my attention to the gals who grace the lounge with their lovely faces and warm personalities. Nurse Tegan told me about the new reference to the team. She said, "We're known as, ***The Oncologist. and the Drips"!*** I venture to assert there is not a more appropriate name for this group. ***The Oncologist and the Drips perform daily at Creekside Lounge*** and the cover charge is never more than a mere co-pay. Lounge lizards agree. A decent show, but Bart would have complained that their cocktail attire left a little something to be desired.

If the Drips wanted tips I'm sure my husband would have been the first on board *"to insure promptness"* (TIP) or whatever.

Creeks Fill Even if it's Just a Drip at a Time

Epilogue

It's been quite some time now since Bart joined Dad at that big Steeler Stadium in the heavens. I still cry, especially alone in the car but the intensity and duration might be waning a bit. Most of our accounts, bills, subscriptions etc. have been adjusted or consolidated. It's odd, though, what can trip you up. None of us in this Reagan family could for the life of us figure out the name of Bart's childhood best friend. That was one of the key security questions to access a relatively important account. My mother-in-law Pat Reagan would call me days later with another string of suggestions to no avail. It's possible Bart made one up but we will never know. He tried very hard to prepare me by composing a list of log-ins, passwords and codes but it was far from complete. I was often catapulted into a frenzied state of upset, tears and frustration over little things. Tiny details denied me access to his life, his stuff, him. Even online shopping (simple life business) could vitiate me into a puddle of paralyzing grief.

Looking back I recognize that it's never too soon for couples to set up a system for sharing access to the drawbridge, so to speak, and ensuring there are two sets of keys to the castle.

Reflections in the Creek

Sitting on the bridge by the creek one fall morning I thought about droplets of newfound wisdom. So often my epiphanies floated forth from a dream. I thought about sleeping in my chair. For months after Bart's death I would not go to bed. Somehow the act of purposely walking to our bedroom at night knowing that Bart would never be there again was not happening. The bed stayed made. One night, asleep in my chair, Bart woke me up. "It's time for you to go to bed." With outstretched arms he bent over to pick me up. "What are you doing? You are not strong enough to pick me up, Bart. You'll hurt yourself." That's all I remember but I woke up in our bed. I'm not so anxious about bedtime anymore.

There were periods I thought I would drown in sadness. I had little motivation to participate, preferring to isolate myself even more. One morning I awoke still dreaming, with images crystal clear and palpable.

I was in a place that didn't feel like home but knew I lived there. There were other people around and I could hear them conversing easily although I wasn't sure how I knew them ,or even if I did. The house was dark, outdated, cluttered, and dirty. The carpet was a matted dark green shag that in a former life had been a deep, plush, pile. I carried cleaning supplies with me from room to room to scrub every area before fully entering any of them. The filth was overwhelming, and I knew I had to clean it to make sure I did not inhale bad air or come in contact with some sort of contaminant. To feel remotely comfortable in this filthy space, I had to be stocked with sanitizing cleaners and armed with the energy to get it done no matter how overwhelming the project.

Peering into the bathroom was an exhausting sight. It was consumed by mold, so I scrubbed for hours to cleanse the shower and interior surfaces. There was so much work to do in every room. I felt bone numbingly tired.

There were a few respites and some quiet moments of welcome and satisfying rest. I became aware of an unseen visitor who called to me, but it wasn't clear who it was and it didn't seem to matter. It seemed to me though that at some ill-defined time this mystery person and I had passed sweet time together without a care.

Then I found myself falling asleep with my head on the visitor's lap and every time I woke, I asked to go with him. "May I please go home with you and live with you?"? I repeatedly told him it would be so much cleaner, safer, and happier. I begged that if he would only say yes, all would be perfect, but he never said that. Day after day, I pleaded but to no avail. Still the visitor returned. Since it was becoming obvious that no other answer would be forthcoming I continued to scrub, wipe, and sterilize, just in case there was no way out.

I thought about the dream metaphorically and a profound truth emerged. Could I have cleaned enough to survive in that house? It would surely have taken endless work and that's when I knew exactly what this dream meant.

Grief is a lot of work. Amidst seemingly endless drudgery there is life. It's moment to moment. Memories deliver restful getaways where soothing comfort washes over and sleep is easy.

Bart's message was gentle and clear. I'd have to keep going. Paddling upstream in a river where sadness is a mighty undertow. There would be no shortcut. It had to be. For interspersed in the journey are junctures to savor , where joy, light, and laughter still live.

Melanie Reagan

www.ADripintheCreek.com

Bart,

Thank you. I am grateful for every drip, every tear, every memory. Your love, life and musings will be for all time.

Your bride